I0886899

Research Data Access and Management in Modern Libraries

Raj Kumar Bhardwaj
University of Delhi, India

Paul Banks
The Royal Society of Medicine, UK

A volume in the Advances in Library and Information Science (ALIS) Book Series

Published in the United States of America by
IGI Global
Information Science Reference (an imprint of IGI Global)
701 E. Chocolate Avenue
Hershey PA, USA 17033
Tel: 717-533-8845
Fax: 717-533-8661
E-mail: cust@igi-global.com
Web site: http://www.igi-global.com

Library of Congress Cataloging-in-Publication Data

Names: Bhardwaj, Raj Kumar, 1980- editor. | Banks, Paul (Librarian), editor.
Title: Research data access and management in modern libraries / Raj Kumar Bhardwaj and Paul Banks, editors.
Description: Hershey, PA : Information Science Reference, [2020] | Includes index. | Includes bibliographical references.
Identifiers: LCCN 2018054446| ISBN 9781522584377 (hardcover) | ISBN 9781522584988 (softcover) | ISBN 9781522584384 (ebook)
Subjects: LCSH: Digital libraries--Management. | Database management in libraries. | Data curation in libraries. | Academic libraries--Information technology. | Research libraries--Information technology.
Classification: LCC ZA4080 .R47 2020 | DDC 025.1--dc23 LC record available at https://lccn.loc.gov/2018054446

This book is published in the IGI Global book series Advances in Library and Information Science (ALIS) (ISSN: 2326-4136; eISSN: 2326-4144)

British Cataloguing in Publication Data
A Cataloguing in Publication record for this book is available from the British Library.

All work contributed to this book is new, previously-unpublished material.
The views expressed in this book are those of the authors, but not necessarily of the publisher.

For electronic access to this publication, please contact: eresources@igi-global.com.

Advances in Library and Information Science (ALIS) Book Series

ISSN:2326-4136
EISSN:2326-4144

MISSION

The **Advances in Library and Information Science (ALIS) Book Series** is comprised of high quality, research-oriented publications on the continuing developments and trends affecting the public, school, and academic fields, as well as specialized libraries and librarians globally. These discussions on professional and organizational considerations in library and information resource development and management assist in showcasing the latest methodologies and tools in the field.

The **ALIS Book Series** aims to expand the body of library science literature by covering a wide range of topics affecting the profession and field at large. The series also seeks to provide readers with an essential resource for uncovering the latest research in library and information science management, development, and technologies.

COVERAGE

- Librarian Education
- Censorship
- Continuing Education for Library Professionals
- Knowledge Management Learning (Course) Management Software
- Human Resources Management
- Evidence-Based Librarianship
- University Libraries in Developing Countries
- Intellectual Freedom
- Library Performance and Service
- Archive Management

IGI Global is currently accepting manuscripts for publication within this series. To submit a proposal for a volume in this series, please contact our Acquisition Editors at Acquisitions@igi-global.com or visit: http://www.igi-global.com/publish/.

The Advances in Library and Information Science (ALIS) Book Series (ISSN 2326-4136) is published by IGI Global, 701 E. Chocolate Avenue, Hershey, PA 17033-1240, USA, www.igi-global.com. This series is composed of titles available for purchase individually; each title is edited to be contextually exclusive from any other title within the series. For pricing and ordering information please visit http://www.igi-global.com/book-series/advances-library-information-science/73002. Postmaster: Send all address changes to above address.

Titles in this Series

For a list of additional titles in this series, please visit:
https://www.igi-global.com/book-series/advances-library-information-science/73002

Handbook of Research on Transdisciplinary Knowledge Generation
Victor X. Wang (Liberty University, USA)
Information Science Reference • ©2019 • 475pp • H/C (ISBN: 9781522595311) • US $285.00

Social Media for Communication and Instruction in Academic Libraries
Jennifer Joe (University of Toledo, USA) and Elisabeth Knight (Western Kentucky University, USA)
Information Science Reference • ©2019 • 319pp • H/C (ISBN: 9781522580973) • US $195.00

Enhancing the Role of ICT in Doctoral Research Processes
Kwong Nui Sim (Victoria University of Wellington, New Zealand)
Information Science Reference • ©2019 • 278pp • H/C (ISBN: 9781522570653) • US $185.00

Social Research Methodology and New Techniques in Analysis, Interpretation, and Writing
M. Rezaul Islam (University of Dhaka, Bangladesh & University of Malaya, Malaysia)
Information Science Reference • ©2019 • 320pp • H/C (ISBN: 9781522578970) • US $195.00

Ethics in Research Practice and Innovation
Antonio Sandu (Stefan cel Mare University of Suceava, Romania) Ana Frunza (LUMEN Research Center in Social and Humanistic Sciences, Romania) and Elena Unguru (University of Oradea, Romania)
Information Science Reference • ©2019 • 373pp • H/C (ISBN: 9781522563105) • US $195.00

Marginalia in Modern Learning Contexts
Alan J. Reid (Coastal Carolina University, USA)
Information Science Reference • ©2019 • 250pp • H/C (ISBN: 9781522571834) • US $175.00

Scholarly Publishing and Research Methods Across Disciplines
Victor C.X. Wang (Grand Canyon University, USA)
Information Science Reference • ©2019 • 372pp • H/C (ISBN: 9781522577300) • US $195.00

For an entire list of titles in this series, please visit:
https://www.igi-global.com/book-series/advances-library-information-science/73002

IGI Global
DISSEMINATOR OF KNOWLEDGE

701 East Chocolate Avenue, Hershey, PA 17033, USA
Tel: 717-533-8845 x100 • Fax: 717-533-8661
E-Mail: cust@igi-global.com • www.igi-global.com

Editorial Advisory Board

Table of Contents

Detailed Table of Contents

National libraries have developed research data responsibilities for reasons of data ownership and cost-efficiency. Due to their multi-faceted and synergistic relationship with research data actors (publishers and researchers), their leadership in publication standards makes them a unique participant as advisors on research data archiving and citation, as much as for their discovery and licensing expertise. National libraries engage with the data community to raise awareness of the relevance of data management and so promote themselves as an essential place for data repositories and the researcher community. This chapter introduces a framework of five national libraries: the British Library, the Library of Congress, the National Library of Medicine, the German National Library of Science and Technology, and the German National Library of Medicine.

The chapter documents the proposed framework for the establishment of research data management services in research institutions in Zimbabwe. It has been indicated that there are no formal research data management services taking place in Zimbabwe as researchers are managing their own data. It is against such a background that a literature review was undertaken to understand how research institutions in other countries are engaging in research data services. E-mails were sent to the pioneers of research data services. It was discovered that there are challenges that are faced when establishing research data management services and it is important to consult all stakeholders at the planning stage. The framework consists of strategies, policies, guidelines, processes, technologies, and services.

Manu T. R., Central University of Gujarat, India & Adani Institute of Infrastructure Management, India
Minaxi Parmar, Central University of Gujarat, India
Shashikumara A. A., Dhirubhai Ambani Institute of Information and Communication Technology, India & Central University of Gujarat, India
Viral Asjola, Indian Institute of Technology Gandhinagar, India

Research information management systems (RIMS) are the emerging new service in academic and research libraries. RIMS support universities and libraries in managing their institute, faculty, and researcher information through a single interface. They also allow the researcher to deposit and share their research with the public and enable the reuse of that research. An implementation of RIMS in universities or libraries ensures the proper management of research information for future use. RIMS disseminates research information and publications and supports data, academic, and administrative work by faculty and researchers. Traditionally, an institutional repository, digital library, and research data management software were used to manage research information as part of an institutional repository, but these applications have failed to manage more specialist researcher information and more detailed faculty profiles, etc. Consequently, various specialist software companies have brought RIMS onto the market with applications and products that meet the requirements of individual researchers, libraries, and universities in the management of research information. This chapter provides a comparative evaluation of RIMS (i.e., PURE-Elsevier, Converis-Thomson Routers, and Symplectic Elements). This study contributes towards an understanding of RIMS and assists with the selection of the appropriate software application for implementation of a RIMS system in universities and libraries.

This chapter presents the findings of an online survey that was carried out to assess research data accessibility at research and academic institutions in Zimbabwe. The study primarily sought to ascertain the custodianship, storage and accessibility of research data at these institutions. The chapter also highlights the challenges associated with accessing research data in Zimbabwe and proposes mechanisms that can be put in place to address these challenges.

Research-related publications and articles have flooded the internet, and researchers are in the quest of getting better tools and technologies to improve the recommendation of relevant research papers. Ever since the introduction of research paper recommender systems, more than 400 research paper recommendation related articles have been so far published. These articles describe the numerous tools, methodologies, and technologies used in recommending research papers, further highlighting issues that need the attention of the research community. Few operational research paper recommender systems have been developed though. The main objective of this review paper is to summaries the state-of-the-art research paper recommender systems classification categories. Findings and concepts on data access and manipulations in the field of research paper recommendation will be highlighted, summarized, and disseminated. This chapter will be centered on reviewing articles in the field of research paper recommender systems published from the early 1990s until 2017.

In this chapter, the authors give an overview of the main data mining techniques that are utilized in the context of research paper recommender systems. These techniques refer to mathematical models and tools that are utilized in discovering patterns in data. Data mining is a term used to describe a collection of techniques that infer recommendation rules and build models from research paper datasets. The authors briefly describe how research paper recommender systems' data is processed, analyzed, and then, finally, interpreted using these techniques. They review different distance measures, sampling techniques, and dimensionality reduction methods employed in computing research paper recommendations. They also review the various clustering, classification, and association rule-mining methods employed to mine for hidden information. Finally, they highlight the major data mining issues that are affecting research paper recommender systems.

Academic libraries are looking for ways to grow their involvement in and scale-up their support for research activities. The successful transition depends to a large extent on the library's ability to systematically manage data, break down information silos and unify workflows across the library, research office and researchers. Data repositories are at the heart of this challenge, yet often institutional repositories are not built to address the needs of modern research data management due to inability to store all research assets, lack of consistent data models, and insufficient workflows. This chapter will present a new approach to research data management that ensures visibility of research output and data, data coherency, and compliance with open access standards. The authors will discuss a 'Next-Generation Research Repository' that spans multiple data management activities, including automated data capture, metadata enrichment, dissemination, compliance-related workflows, automated publication to scholarly profiles, as well as open integration with the research ecosystem.

The emergence of open access has opened a world of opportunities for academic and research institutions. One of such opportunities is the establishment of institutional repositories (IRs). This chapter examined the emergence and creation of IRs and trends in Africa. It noted that the development of IRs in most African countries is still at the infancy stage. The chapter highlighted the important role of libraries in the management of IRs. The Chapter also identified and discussed important issues and challenges of IRs in Africa. The identified challenges include lack of awareness, lack of required funding to establish and manage IRs, lack of Information and communication technology infrastructure, among others. It concluded that the establishment of IRs is a compulsory venture for institutions of higher learning in Africa.

The chapter focuses on the exploration and elucidation of the open access concept, with the main emphasis on open access journals, their types and features, etc. Similarly, the thrust was also given to acquaint the audience with the open access journal publishers, in order to aware them about the availability of open access literature and the opportunities where open access research can be published by the authors or scientists. In order to give some practical flavors to the readers of this study, the focus of the study was also made towards gauging the active open access journals indexed by the Scopus database. Moreover, particular emphasis was given to check the distribution of active open access journals indexed by it in the fields of life sciences, social sciences, physical sciences, and health sciences. The purpose was to ease the users to search and use the open access journal literature as per the subject taste.

With information explosion, there has been a rapid increase in the number of e-resources published across the world. In addition to this, the cost of e-resources has risen steeply. This has resulted in libraries finding it difficult to acquire all the required information resources from the budget available from its parent body. The problem of libraries is compounded by the growing costs of maintaining both print and online subscription and issues related to 'perpetual' electronic access to back files. The print industry in the world is said to be on the decline. People prefer the electronic versions of the reading materials, because they are more portable, accessible and affordable. But there are many challenges/hurdles to this path, which we have to overcome with time, effort and ingenuity. There are certain challenges

The aim of this chapter is to provide a detailed empirical example of autoregressive conditional heteroskedasticity (ARCH) model and selected generalized ARCH models. Before the ARCH/GARCH models are estimated, several calculations and tests should be done. The mean model is determined using the autocorrelation function and partial autocorrelation function and also the unit root test. The existence of ARCH effect is tested using ARCH-LM test. After these steps are done, then ARCH/GARCH models can be estimated. All these theoretical aspects are applied to Sofia Stock Indexes (SOFIX) using EViews 9 software package. The windows and output of EViews are presented. To show the output's academic writing format researchers' outputs are presented in a table.

The world is hungry for knowledge and quickly-producing researchers of varying caliber who are less dependent on the physical space than ever before. This presents a number of challenges to librarians, out of which issues related to technology stand out prominently. How can the library pave roads to curated digital content and make it easily accessible from any location? How does it remain relevant in the age of Google, sophisticated piracy and the open access movement? The chapter begins with an overview of IP-based and federated access technologies, touching on less-used methods as well. Personally-conducted interviews with library industry experts aim to determine current trends in order to provide a collective insight into future developments. These include the widespread migration towards cloud-based services, the global RA21 initiative, the open access movement, the need for better statistics, and new ways of content delivery, all of which affect libraries' demands for remote access in different ways.

The chapter aims to ascertain the ranks of 10 universities on the basis of participative index (PAI), average publications per faculty member (APPFM), and combined arithmetic mean (CAM). The data used for the present study was obtained by an online questionnaire. However, detailed information regarding their research output was collected directly from them. A total of 971 publications were published by LIS faculty till 31st December 2014. The results found that the position of some universities goes up and the position of some universities fall down when evaluated on different parameters. PU has the 2nd rank as per PAI but on the basis of other two parameters (i.e., on the basis of APPFM and CAM, it has 1st rank whereas BHU has the 1st rank as per PAI, but on the basis of APPFM it has 4th rank, and on the basis of CAM, it has the 3rd rank).

Foreword

The research landscape is changing rapidly. Researchers no longer have to wait for the publication process, including printing and mailing of journal issues, for their research to be shared with their colleagues. Today, the work carried out in a remote lab in a low-population density area of the world can influence a researcher's peers almost immediately thanks to the affordances of the web. The Invisible College or the relationships between individual researchers sharing their ideas and discoveries within a closed group of like-minded members, was once supported by written correspondence, in-person discussions (at conferences, in recent years), and in modern times, the occasional phone call. With the rise of web-based communication technologies, the interactions of the Invisible College are now largely mediated by technology, making communication instantaneous. And, with the open and transparent nature of many web-based communication technologies such as Twitter, Facebook, and blogs, the discoveries made by that remote researcher can effectively be available immediately for all the world to see and consider, when mediated by electronic communications and social media.

If the old publishing paradigm infused quality throughout the publishing process, and if the Invisible College relied on relationships, reputation, and the quality of the ideas put forth, new web-based communications of discoveries and novel ideas have also evolved mechanisms for indicating the accepted quality of work. For example, new metrics have emerged to assess the quality of these contributions to the scholarly record, including social media metrics (also known as altmetrics) whereby the reactions of web-based peers are counted and assessed. The number of downloads of an electronic article can replace the relative prestige of the journal in which the work is published (who will read the other articles published in that issue, anyway?), and a researcher's activity in research-based for-profit forums like ResearchGate can yield a numeric score to quantify that engagement.

In a world where scientific truths are called into question, transparency in the research enterprise has rightly become a focus. Both researchers and the public at large increasingly demand the right to access the products of research, and to evaluate these resources for themselves. Transparency is facilitated by the web and web-based communications as never before. But, as platforms for sharing come and go, as trends in access evolve and change, how can this record of research products, one that supports advancement in the current era of transparency, be preserved and made available – across disciplines, across regions, and across time? The answer resides in the work of the information professional, the focus of this book.

From the researcher's perspective, to participate in this global research conversation and to do so in a way that is transparent suddenly requires access to expertise not only in the area of study, but also in the ways of making their data available for public scrutiny and re-use. For example, Australia is reportedly investing millions of dollars leading up to 2020 to support data sharing initiatives. Many major funding organizations around the world such as the United States's National Institutes of Health (NIH) and the Wellcome Trust in the United Kingdom require that researchers receiving funding have *data management plans*. There are many reasons for this but one of the most prominent ones is that many of the organizations that fund research are governmental organizations or otherwise have a public-focused mission. These funders believe that in order for the funding organization and the public to get the largest return on investment (ROI), data must be properly managed and available to other researchers, either by request or as openly available datasets.

Publishing data makes it *open*. Open data is the concept that some data should be freely available without restrictions imposed by copyright, patents, licenses, or other means. Not all data can become open for various reasons. For example, some data may be purchased or licensed, and may not have been created by the researchers themselves – in these cases, the data is not the property of the researchers and cannot be shared without permission. In the social sciences or medical sciences especially, data collected by researchers may contain Personally Identifiable Information (PII). Although in some cases data can be properly anonymized, this is not always the case. A given dataset, for example, may just not be large enough to be effectively anonymized, or, in other cases, anonymizing the data may require significant resources that are not readily available. Therefore, it is important for researchers (and the information professionals supporting them) to understand the nature of the datasets and potential implications if the data is released as open data.

Reuse of data is not as uncommon as one might think, and services to support data sharing have, in some cases, been around for a long time. One noteworthy example of a very successful and longstanding data publishing initiative is the ICPSR (Inter-university Consortium for Political and Social Research) (https://www.icpsr.umich.edu/icpsrweb/), a depository of social sciences dataset that are freely available for reuse. Dryad (https://datadryad.org/) makes available the datasets that have been shared through its service, providing Digital Object Identifiers (DOIs) so that the datasets may be more easily cited. Google's Dataset Search (https://toolbox.google.com/datasetsearch) is an example of a commercial initiative providing access to open data for end-users.

Other researchers may want to use original datasets in order to test the robustness of the conclusions in the original research or the validity of the conclusions. Do a set of conclusions seem impossible? Examine the data yourself to find out the real story. If there are lies, damn lies, and statistics, then researchers should have access to original datasets to confirm the underlying analyses, assumptions, and calculations that went into producing the final, published results. In addition, longitudinal studies can theoretically be carried out if the original researchers share both their methodology and their data, thereby increasing the value (and potential for usefulness) of the original dataset Having access to open data can also help situate reproducibility and replication efforts. Researchers also may desire to utilize data for a different purpose then what it was originally intended to be used for, combine datasets to carry out different analyses, or isolate different variables for whatever reason.

In order for the data to be reused to confirm results, to enhance replicability or reproducibility, or for something new altogether, the data needs to be properly managed and made available to others in the appropriate formats and with the necessary accompanying documentation. One way to enable data to be reused is by following data sharing practices that enable or support data reuse. The provenance of the data also needs to be maintained and documented so that other researchers can be confident that the data is what they believe it is. If specialized software, algorithms, or other techniques were used to interpret the data they need to be described and, in order to enable reuse, it may be necessary to make them available as well. It is necessary to document all of the above and more. Even when all of these things and more are adequately performed, the data still cannot be reused unless a researcher can discover and access the data, so the data needs to be published in a way that it will be findable.

Some of this may sound vaguely familiar to information professionals. Many of the tasks associated with research data management and data curation are duties that librarians and other information professionals have been carrying out for years – but with monographs, serials, and artifacts in archival collections. It only makes sense that libraries would be involved with supporting research and with data publishing and sharing initiatives, too. Although many researchers may already have many of the skills related to good internal data management practices, managing, preserving, and sharing data is generally not their main focus. Researchers are often very busy and have a multitude of other tasks they need to perform or new research that that want to engage with – preparing data for sharing and for despot into a repository is an operation that is both time-consuming (especially when starting out) and not well-recognized by traditional faculty and researcher reward systems used for promotion and tenure or when making hiring decisions. Having good data sharing practices is not rewarded the same way as a well-received new paper. Enter the information professional.

Scholarly communication is complex, and the research process requires expertise, tenacity, and skill to navigate. There is seemingly no end to the ways in which information professionals can support scholars throughout the research process, and focus their many areas of expertise on the research data management enterprise with great success. Knowing how to manage research data is a logical next step for many librarians – but transferring skills might not be intuitive without training and guidance. We might argue that research data management is in a librarian's DNA, but expressing those traits, and harnessing that expertise, will actually take some work.

Research Data Access and Modern Libraries, edited by Raj Kumar Bhardwaj and Paul Banks, is a timely publication. As librarians are increasing being called upon to apply their skills, knowledge, and expertise to assist researchers and institutions in efforts related to research data management initiatives, we need to understand which skills will need to be developed, and how they will be applied. Librarians are not born experts at everything, but they know when and where to look up information. And continuing education has become the norm in the profession. Now is the time, if ever there were, for librarians supporting research to learn what they need to know, and reading a book on the topic is arguably one of the best ways to do just that.

Edward M. Corrado
Dudley Knox Library, Naval Postgraduate School, USA

Heather Moulaison Sandy
University of Missouri – Columbia, USA

NOTE

Edward M. Corrado is writing in his personal capacity. The views expressed here are those of the author and do not reflect those of the U.S. Navy, Department of Defense, or any office of the U.S. government.

Preface

Research data management is the collection, processing, storage, sharing and archiving of research data. Approaches to these activities at all stages within the research data lifecycle, from handling research data at its inception through to the preservation and archiving of data in a quality-controlled manner, need to be highly professional. Researchers need to know how to document data and support its' traceability and to make it reusable and productive while institutions and funding agencies have varying requirements relating to the archiving and subsequent reuse of research data, that researchers and data managers or librarians need to meet. Research data management is the process of organising research data and administering those activities and processes designed to make the research process more efficient, in a way that meets the different standards and requirements of research institutions, funders and legislators. As such, it has gained much attention as a professional discipline from the academic and research community in recent years. This book brings together the latest thinking in research data access and management from academic and research libraries around the world with a strong focus on innovative practice, smart tools and technological solutions that will serve to guide and assist those involved in developing good research data management practices within their own libraries and institutions.

At its simplest level, research data management enables the reuse of archived research data to facilitate the verification of results and related processes, thereby ensuring the integrity of research which in turn enhances the impact of that research. Several funding agencies around the world have mandated the management of research data to ensure the integrity of the research undertaken and to avoid the unknowing duplication of research at other institutions and by other researchers, thereby saving time and money. Ensuring research data is accessible and reusable will not only save researchers' time but in addition, the sharing of research data across disciplines contributes to interdisciplinary research. With good data management practices and a data retention policy in place, researchers are obliged to follow the correct procedure for the acquisition, storage, use and sharing of research data. Good data management practices can also incentivise researchers to share their datasets with others in the public domain, promoting a culture of openness in research. Counting data citations alongside the citation of publications, increasing funding for data-managed research projects, noting data-sharing in promotions and awards and highlighting the socio-economic impact of data-driven research, can all help to incentivise excellence in data management practices, to the extent that planning research data management prior to the commencement of research work becomes imperative for both researchers and institutions.

Academic and research institutions have faced problems in establishing good research data management processes, systems and services however, due to a lack of funds, a shortage of trained staff and poor awareness among researchers and institutional leaders (LERU Advice Paper No 14, 2013). Library and information professionals have taken a lead by educating researchers about the benefits of research data and its long-term preservation but the support of institutional leaders is crucial to fostering a culture of open data. Leaders need to be aware of and engaged in debate and discussions about research data management and must engage all stakeholders in framing the data management policies of an institution in order to reap the full benefits of good research data practice and a culture of open research. Likewise researchers should clearly understand the institutional requirements for their management of research data and to ensure the visibility of their data, be able to describe this accurately in data management planning.

Beyond institutional requirements and researcher engagement, research data should also be discoverable so that it can be easily found and reused correctly. Research institutions should establish data retention policies and standards that clearly set out the types and formats of data for inclusion in their repositories; and the processes, standards and timescales that need to be adhered to in archiving and naming data. Adhering to quality standards and clear processes avoids or at least limits ambiguity so that the research community fully benefits from easily discoverable, open research data.

The technical aspects of research data management are another significant aspect for institutions to consider when designing data management services. The selection, purchase and implementation of new repository software or a research information management system involves staff from many different departments, from research managers and librarians to finance and IT staff. Institutions frequently face difficulties in finding a team leader to implement a research data management project that impacts so many areas. Libraries are undoubtedly best placed to lead such a project and to develop research data management services; librarians' understanding of the organisation of knowledge, of the research process and the importance of research outputs provides the perfect background for the generation, dissemination and preservation of research data within an academic institution.

This book serves as a much-needed, comprehensive source of information for the understanding of data access and management issues in academic and research libraries. Numerous concepts are involved including data access, data preservation, building document and data institutional repositories, the application of Web 2.0 tools, mobile technology applications in data access, conducting information literacy programmes and so on.

Chapter 1 describes the engagement of national libraries with the data community to raise awareness of the relevance of data management and to promote their role as an essential place for data repositories and the researcher community. The author emphasizes that libraries' multi-faceted and synergistic relationship with research data actors makes them a unique participant in research data management and that a national library can be vital in developing a national strategy to develop open data in the country.

Chapter 2 proposes a framework for research data management services in academic and research institutions. It discusses in detail, the challenges encountered in establishing such services and recommends that all stakeholders should be consulted at the planning stage to ensure their involvement and to reap the benefits of the new services.

Chapter 3 compares research information management systems (RIMS) and the implementation of RIMS in universities. It highlights that research data management has become a more complex process because of the range of research information types; larger data sets, multimedia formats, teaching materials and structured models etc. RIMS providers must respond to this requirement to capture and manage complex research data.

Chapter 4 discusses the results of a survey carried out to assess data accessibility at research and academic institutions in Zimbabwe. The chapter highlights the challenges associated with accessing research data and proposes mechanisms to address these challenges.

Chapter 5 summarizes the state-of-the-art research paper recommender systems' classification categories and concepts on data access and manipulations in the field of research paper recommendation.

Chapter 6 explains data mining techniques in the context of these systems, mentioning various mathematical models and tools that are utilized in discovering patterns in data and outlining critical data mining issues facing research paper recommender systems.

Chapter 7 suggests new approaches to research data management that ensure the visibility of research output and data and compliance with open access standards. It describes multiple data management activities, covering automated data capture, metadata enrichment, dissemination and compliance-related workflows as well as open integration with the research ecosystem.

Chapter 8 covers the very significant role of libraries in the management of institutional repositories and discusses important issues and challenges concerning institutional repositories in Africa. It highlights that the establishment of repositories is a compulsory venture for institutions of higher learning in Africa.

In Chapter 9, the authors discuss the availability of open access literature and the open access publishing opportunities for authors including scientists. A particular emphasis has been given to the distribution of active open access journals indexed in the fields of life sciences, social sciences, physical sciences, and health sciences. \

Chapter 10 emphasizes the challenges faced by library and information science professionals in the selection and acquisition of electronic resources in academic libraries; the authors meticulously touch on all the pertinent aspects of electronic resources.

Chapter 11 elaborates on the benefits and challenges of the digital library and of distance learning in developing countries. The authors recommend that stakeholders give attention to addressing the problems faced by distance learners in their use of the digital library so that they can reap the full benefits of digital access.

In Chapter 12, the author explores the various dimensions of metaliteracy in academic libraries through a detailed case study at Jawaharlal Nehru University, New Delhi. The author stresses the relevance of metaliteracy for students and its importance in developing digitally-aware learners who can share knowledge effectively in collaborative online communities and research networks. Goals and learning objectives are concrete competencies and metaliteracy for learning are its basic components.

Chapter 13 deliberates on the librarian's approach to innovation in library services, emphasizing that library professionals should re-think and re-invent existing technologies, services and facilities to fulfill the changing needs and demands of library users. Technological Innovation (TI) can be considered as an innovative solution for the sustenance and rejuvenation of libraries.

Chapter 14 deals with research data analysis using EViews and explains an empirical example of modeling volatility.

Chapter 15 describes the use of federated access technologies in libraries. Interviews with experts in the field were conducted to determine current trends and to provide a collective insight into future developments. The chapter also briefly discusses the widespread migration towards cloud-based services, the open access movement and new ways of delivering content.

The book finishes with Chapter 16 which tackles the challenges and issues around successfully measuring the research outcomes of academic institutions. The authors analyze the research outcomes of ten universities in India on the basis of Participative Index (PAI), Average Publications per Faculty Member (APPFM) and Combined Arithmetic Mean (CAM).

The book in its entirety serves as a comprehensive resource for all those seeking to initiate, develop or deliver research data management services within their own institutions. It will guide readers, from institutional policy makers and senior library managers through to research data service managers, researchers and new entrants, to understand the latest thinking and innovative practice in this increasingly complex but important professional discipline that is rapidly emerging as an important role for modern academic libraries.

Raj Kumar Bhardwaj
University of Delhi, India

Paul Banks
The Royal Society of Medicine, UK

Acknowledgment

The idea of this book emerged when both the editors met in London two years ago. However, this book would not have been possible without kind support, encouragement and spirit of several professional friends who contributed and shared their expertise. Editors acknowledge the contribution of all the contributors, members of editorial advisory board and reviewers for their suggestions. Editors are also express their gratitude to all members of publishing team for their support and encouragement time to time. Editors are also express profound gratitude to Prof. Edward M. Corrado and Dr. Heather Moulaison Sandy for writing forward of this book.

A special thanks goes to Dr. Shikha and Advvay for their affection.

Chapter 1
Research Data Access and Management in National Libraries

Enrique Wulff
Marine Sciences Institute of Andalusia (CSIC), Spain

ABSTRACT

National libraries have developed research data responsibilities for reasons of data ownership and cost-efficiency. Due to their multi-faceted and synergistic relationship with research data actors (publishers and researchers), their leadership in publication standards makes them a unique participant as advisors on research data archiving and citation, as much as for their discovery and licensing expertise. National libraries engage with the data community to raise awareness of the relevance of data management and so promote themselves as an essential place for data repositories and the researcher community. This chapter introduces a framework of five national libraries: the British Library, the Library of Congress, the National Library of Medicine, the German National Library of Science and Technology, and the German National Library of Medicine.

INTRODUCTION

This chapter provides an overall description of data access and management in a variety of national libraries, in search of key trends in research data management (Ray, 2014). Emerging facilities have a significant impact on library strategies, operations and services while trends like open access and research data management reveal new challenges (Collins, 2012). Based on major national libraries and

DOI: 10.4018/978-1-5225-8437-7.ch001

institutional discussions, recommendations are proposed with respect to services to users, interoperability, enhancing discovery, improving interaction with research data national library labs and enhancing data quality. Libraries include the British Library, the Library of Congress, the National Library of Medicine, the German National Library of Science and Technology, and the German National Library of Medicine.

To best serve users and communities, research institutions rely on their academic libraries to provide persistent and secure access to, and management of, their research data (Ayris et al., 2013). A group of five national libraries (from Europe and the US) offering open research data are examined. These five national libraries have the customer base, already offer research data services and have the technical expertise required to manage research data. Their research data roles are determined by the decentralization of the web, distributed computing and storage, data analytics, artificial intelligence and knowledge graph infrastructures. Therefore, these national libraries are keen to be part of major developments in the research data area (Kruse & Thestrup, 2017).

The key to taking an intentional leadership role in the field will be achieving the necessary consensus to create and maintain an environment fostering trust, with the primary objective of recruiting and preparing librarians to purposefully enter the field and demonstrate to management that they are equipped to do the job. By selecting a network of actors and analyzing the systematic exchange of their strategic experiences, services, preservation, and lifelong education, library values are emphasized. In spite of the fact that technology is heavily involved in data management, there are also issues of selection and collection, curation, description, citation, and legislation. Under this premise, and taking into account the extent to which librarians, information technology professionals, and researchers come into this field as accidental data managers, whether this job is an information professional role rather than a technology position, poses a challenging question.

There is a need for guidelines to inform institutions about key trends in managing research data in library services, for unusual or complex tasks attached to the data life cycle. Planning for research data management, financed in whole or in part, from public funding, should be able to provide a framework to understand the stages of the data cycle and identify what services can be provided, to whom and at what stage of the cycle. National libraries cannot provide research data management services alone and it is essential to be proactive in working with the full range of stakeholders and interested parties. This chapter explores the relationships between data libraries and institutional data repositories. In this respect, knowledgeable librarians are essential and details are provided for issues relating to data management plans, guidelines for working with digital research data, quality control of digital data, data file management policies and standards, intellectual property management, metadata guidelines, ingest guidelines and other tools.

GOALS AND OBJECTIVES

To meet the theme of this book, this section aims to help practitioners understand the mix of scholarly and technological challenges that national libraries face while searching for a new cross-border research data infrastructure. In these national libraries the method of study is based on:

- The relationships between the library and the computer and data centre that may exist within the organizations which serve as its model;
- All the data policies and plans prepared at the organization to develop and exploit strategies for research data management.

This chapter relates what librarians need to know about managing research data and data management plans; the operational availability of multidisciplinary datasets will remain critical for the next generation and cross-domain data management tools will benefit both national libraries and the institutional data repositories closely linked to their regular work.

In terms of takeaways for the national libraries this chapter seeks to answer the following questions:

- What do recent studies reveal current thinking around policy and guidelines that will assist with the definition of a research data system for the library?
- How many good practices and technologies derived from research data have received serious consideration by national libraries?
- Do national libraries experience increased use by developing their research data management roles? The objective is to encourage national libraries to become involved in research data literacy programs. Lessons are drawn from the study of these access and training technologies provided by national library services and a proposal is made to consider how the international exchange of information between national libraries would be useful to avoid the expurgation of important research data.

The contribution of this chapter to the professional practice of research data management and planning derives from the analysis and evaluation of major national libraries engaged in data management. To manage research data files, institutional data repositories and professional society's data resources, national libraries actively work to integrate them with their resources and collections. This enables the regular tracking of scholarly impact and key trends of potential importance to research data management while metadata are exposed as opportunities for national libraries in an increasingly globalized world.

The results and outputs that can be expected from this chapter are:

- To identify key trends in national libraries approach to research data;
- To improve guidelines on managing data from research projects and literature, and from resources in other data repositories; the results of which will enhance sound research data management and planning;
- To examine research data management practices, employing common data life cycle models in ways that promote the growth and advancement of a national library's data services;
- To describe the inventory characteristics of data stores currently managed by national libraries;
- To offer recommendations for additional national library projects on research data.

LITERATURE REVIEW

National libraries capture an amount of research data, primarily associated with research articles. The data generated by researchers is not sufficiently interoperable because of the absence of intelligent and machine-interpretable metadata, as a global agreement on concepts and relationships is difficult even within a single scientific domain. Data annotation involves appending descriptive information to experimental data with the intention of creating a digital data object that can be intelligently linked or integrated with other data (Berman, 2003). Of course, an understanding of the data sources, access to these sources and analytical skills to process the raw data are all possible career choices for librarians (Davenport & Cronin, 1994).

The national library positions the data lifecycle within a larger circle, thus opening the door for virtual research environments (VREs) where researchers can explore hypotheses using data gathered and shared for diverse projects. For example, the integration of European holocaust research as a part of a German national library digital preservation strategy was made possible through a refugee data VRE, linking research data via annotations and linking created entities with other created entities (Ell, 2015). Similarly, the British Library developed a Research Information Centre

(RIC) for Bioscience Researchers as a VRE (Barga et al., 2007) which helped researchers utilize various research tools, communicate with colleagues and develop information communication technology infrastructures (Kwon, 2017).

The ways in which national libraries are involved with research data also include developing and using comprehensive knowledge tools that facilitate information retrieval, natural language processing and other vocabulary services for biomedical research data. For example, the US National Library of Medicine's Unified Medical Language System (UMLS) (Bodenreider, 2004). A global registration agency for research data that uses Digital Object Identifiers (DOIs), a unique and persistent identifier that facilitates data citation, was developed by the German National Library of Science and Technology (TIB), from 2005; and in 2009, TIB, the British Library, and other academic libraries and national data services agreed to improve access to research data on the internet (Brase, 2009).

Moreover, institutions require appropriate control of their data repositories and in some cases, policies and procedures are available for research data management implemented by the academic library (Ray, 2014). National and academic library holdings can be integrated with research data repositories by applying semantic technologies to support data representation, discovery, and sharing. To make data usable in a tangible way, it must be accompanied by appropriate documentation, i.e. protocols, reports, grey literature, and published papers. Data policies from published data libraries, which allow automatic retrieval of datasets based on queries using the author field, mention a specific interest in supplying data to industry and the wider public (Collins, 2012).

The provision of training in Research Data Management (RDM) at national libraries is an idea with antecedents in higher education; it was supported in the UK by the Society of College, National and University Libraries' *Seven Pillars of Information Literacy* (SCONUL, 2011). RDM training allows librarians to develop skills in data creation, preservation, and dissemination. The US National Library of Medicine has offered courses in RDM since 2014 and its potential audience for staff goes beyond subject consultants.[1] The course topics include an overview of data management, choosing appropriate metadata descriptors or taxonomies for a dataset, addressing privacy and security issues with data and creating data management plans. Training and consultancy for data management of digital content is also a service provided by TIB both for ongoing research projects and for finished projects (Kraft et al., 2017).

Good research data management is not a goal in itself however and for this reason, the European Commission (EC) decided to help Horizon 2020 beneficiaries make their research data findable, accessible, interoperable and reusable (FAIR) (European Union, 2016). It makes sense to focus on national libraries as the correct forum to discuss research data licenses (Gooding et al., 2018). The British Library Data Strategy 2017 has been developed to move forward in this area and it includes unlocking thesis data as a new service for researchers. This policy, combined with the inherent knowledge of librarians, curators, and technologists at the library, provides researchers with the opportunity to rethink the management of their scientific data in a national context (Kruse & Thestrup, 2017).

RESEARCH DATA SYSTEMS FROM THE NATIONAL LIBRARY: SELECTED LITERARY CRITERIA

National libraries have an important role to play with regard to research data infrastructure components and the British Library in particular, embodies key trends in the identification of datasets. The British Library helped to promote the development of the DataCite UK service that provides DOIs to over 90 data centres and research organizations.[2] At the heart of national libraries preservation programs, is enabling data and web application programming interfaces (APIs) to interact with them; the Library of Congress offers a collaborative solution to national digital strategies.[3] As a unifying framework for all biomedical information, a National Library of Medicine (NLM) approach, links and make convergent, collected data. For achieving consistency in data collection within and across research, precision, reproducibility and cross-study comparisons are priorities.[4] National libraries are a context for the vision of a knowledge graph for science, within the German National Library of Science and Technology (TIB).[5] Knowledge must come from the co-development of data, its information and data analytics, collaborating with the relevant stakeholders to identify the required research outputs and support the use of new data and tools.

National libraries should contribute to the development of generic solutions for the provision, referencing and searching of research software. Tailoring software development to researcher needs and new research endeavours is part of the activities undertaken by the German National Library of Medicine's Information Centre for Life Sciences (ZB MED) at the Technical University of Cologne (TH Köln), for example. Through the creation of new roles (e.g. software librarian), science libraries can implement the FAIR data principles for research software, create (national) reference systems for research software and create metadata sets for research software. In this way libraries can become major software publishers by setting up advisory services on the licensing, persistent referencing and citation of research software.[6]

By using literary criteria, it is relatively easy to establish how these innovations might contribute to making diverse but related research data more discoverable and accessible. The number and ranking of citations received on the Web of Science

(WoS) database may indicate the extent of library involvement in research data access and management. Figure 1 shows the number of research data initiatives by libraries cited in scientific articles between 2000 and 2018.

Table I provides a comprehensive list of the record count of articles on data innovation in libraries by countries, as cited by the Web of Sciences (WoS).

Figure 1. Data innovation options used by libraries in number of citations (2000-2018) to scientific articles, based on Web of Science (WoS)

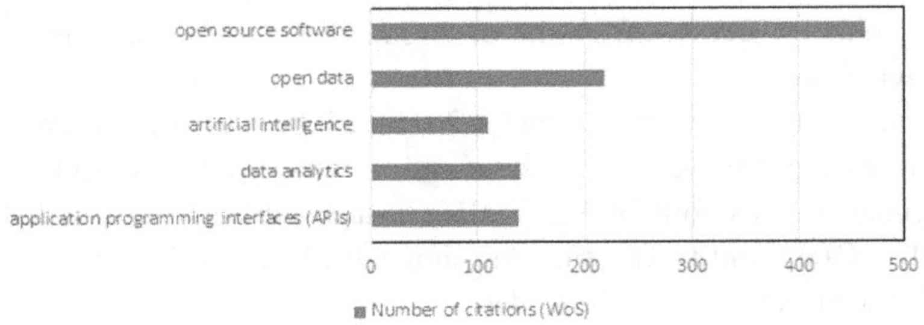

Table 1. Citations associated with the top ten countries as ranked by the number of scientific articles addressing data innovations in libraries (based on Web of Science (WoS))

Country	Number of citations
US	394
UK	136
Germany	111
Italy	65
Peoples Republic of China	57
Spain	39
France	28
Canada	14
South Korea	10
Australia	8

RESEARCH DATA MANAGEMENT PLANNING AT THE BRITISH LIBRARY

The British Library (BL) released the British National Bibliography (BNB) as Linked Open Data in July 2011. Since then, it has retained a focus on data science and artificial intelligence and is currently (since 2015), the site of the Alain Turing Institute, a major new research centre for data science backed by £42 million of public investment. The work of the Institute builds on and now complements, that of the Open Data Institute, founded in 2012 to unlock the value of data and to develop a professional network in the UK and internationally.

The first challenge to access scholarly resources from the BL is the lack of remote access to legal deposit content due to licensing restrictions. This issue goes to the heart of the heritage collections: legal deposit content (Reimer, 2018). As a legal deposit library, BL have to treat digital content like print legal deposit, i.e. content can only be accessed from the BL premises, even if it was originally open access (OA) content.

BL is aware of user expectations and in 2016 the Library set up a strategic change portfolio to enable discovery and access and to reduce data loss and the cost of managing content. This work follows the BL's inclusion in European-funded projects such as ODE, ODIN and THOR, the provision of the DataCite UK and involvement in activities such as unlocking thesis data.

British Library Research Data Strategy 2017

In the BL's data strategy, the vision of the library is that research data are as integrated into the collections, research and services as printed texts. As such, the Alan Turing Institute is based at the BL and, as AI and data-driven institutions, both the Institute and the BL are working on developing a range of collaborative research initiatives.

This strategy is structured around 4 central themes, which are enclosed in BL priorities for 2015-2023 to support the BL's research purpose (Table 2).

The BL's ambitious agenda is outlined in the recently published British Library Research Data Strategy (British Library, 2017), at the core of which is data discovery and how to increase the visibility of the complex heritage collections.

Data Creation

The BL creates datasets derived from its collections and collaborates with others in their efforts to create their own datasets derived from library collections. BL metadata is provided as open data underpinning two major initiatives:

Table 2. BL 2015-2023 priorities as consequence of data analytics revolution

Ensure that the library's on-site facilities and Reading Room services keep pace with the changing needs of researchers
Develop remote access services to become a trusted and indispensable resource for fact-finding, research, and analysis for researchers everywhere
Leverage the library's collections and expertise to drive innovation in large-scale data analytics, for the wider benefit of UK research
Work with partners to increase the Library's capacity as an independent research organization.

Source: British Library, 2015

- British Library Labs,[7] a project which supports and inspires the public use of the BL's digital collections and data and make them available as tools for the digital humanities;
- the UK Web Archive where born-digital collections are preserved as datasets.

The library also links its data collection to data held by others through the news media collections and web archive. Consequently, the role of datasets in the development of the library's collections is also considered. The library is developing a data repository (a collection of datasets released by the BL) to open its data to wider use; the site is a 'beta' (data.bl.uk). The aim is to describe collections in terms of their data format (images, full text, metadata, etc.), licenses, temporal and geographic scope, originating purpose (e.g. specific digitization projects or exhibitions) and collection and related subjects or themes.

Data Management

The BL's data strategy also sets out the creation of a data management plan ensuring that the data created as a result of the research is appropriately managed for access and reuse. This will enable the BL to meet its obligations as a recipient of research funding from Research Councils UK (RCUK), European and charitable agencies. The established practice for data management that the library has developed is designed so that it can be re-used by library staff. The library also engages with the data community to raise awareness of the services it offers that are relevant to data management.

Data Discovery, Access and Reuse

New tools and skills are developed to discover the research data held by the library (as well as by third parties); such as sentiment analysis and machine learning tools connected to the library's data via API to visualize the results as datasets. To ensure that library users can make the most of the UK's research data, new models of data access are being developed and wider access to restricted data is being offered. Moreover, DataCite UK encourages data sharing and citation.

Data Archiving and Preservation

Datasets collected and created by the library are archived and preserved in line with its other heritage collections. This presents the possibility of providing archiving services to third parties and sharing lessons learned with organizations that are just beginning to preserve their datasets. In this way, the library develops data archiving and preservation services to ensure that the UK research is available for future generations.

Other Data-Driven Activities at the BL

The library's central position in the UK's infrastructure for research and innovation ensures its digital strategy is based on activities such as:

- **DataCite:** A method by which researchers obtain credit and recognition for sharing their research data.[8] This is built on the BLs ability to assign UK organizations DOIs to their research data, software and other outputs. DOIs allow the location, identification, and citation of research data by tracking citations to the organization's data to discover their reach and impact;
- **Data Discovery Pilots:** The repository data.bl.uk is a discovery pilot where just asking to cite the data as appropriate, the library can ensure that a selected collection of datasets can be reused for research;
- **Collaborative EU-funded projects** such as *Opportunities for Data Exchange* (ODE) (based on personal interviews with leaders in scientific communities, research infrastructures, management and policy initiatives); *ORCID and DataCite Interoperability Network* (ODIN) (a two-years EC-funded FP7 project), or *Technical and Human Infrastructure for Open Research* (THOR) (a 30-months EC-funded H2020 project which permits the library to link authors, articles, theses and data).

RESEARCH DATA MANAGEMENT PLANNING AT THE LIBRARY OF CONGRESS

In August 2016, the National Digital Initiatives (NDI) division of the Library of Congress (LC), in partnership with the library's John W. Kluge Centre, examined the impact of the digital revolution using the library's collections and resources; the aim of the NDI is to explore how to deliver LC digital collections as data, to researchers.[9]

The NDI pilot and partnerships projects to be outlined included:

- Digital scholarship labs, with pilot projects to demonstrate how the collections could be used in data analysis (Mears et al., 2017);
- Using computing power to test different training models for building digital skills;
- Partnership programs with specific focus paid to residential scholars at the Kluge Centre and the LC Innovator-in-Residence Program.

This work resulted in recommendations to the library on how to set up a Digital Scholars Lab at the LC (Chudnov & Gallinger, 2016). The library also established a Plan for Digital Collecting 2017-2022 (Library of Congress, 2017a) and in August 2017, a Collections Policy Statement outlined interim guidance for datasets (Library of Congress, 2017b).

A Strategic Objective for Data Sets

Published in February 2017, and planned for the following five years, the Plan for Digital Collecting expanded the library's collection to datasets. Strategic objective 6 considered datasets as large units of content (Table 3), to be acquired as part of the LC's future acquisition of digital content.

Table 3. LC 2017-2022 Strategic Objective 6 concerning the acquisition of datasets

Selectively acquire large sets of content available in electronic format only.
Provide a datasets collecting guidelines document through a new Collections Policy Statement (CPS),
Determine the manner in which research by LC patrons using datasets will be supported, such as with special software and licensed or purchased content.
On a pilot basis, acquire sample large sets of content for the purpose of providing bulk download and text mining capabilities to the library's users.

(Library of Congress, 2017a)

The Current State of the Collecting Policy of Data Sets at the Library of Congress

The LC considers data sets as the product of scientific methods that produce massive quantitative research results, but they may also be created outside the realm of scientific research; for example, statistical tests that supply demographic or consumer information (Library of Congress, 2017b). The library has substantial experience with descriptive metadata required for library objects (Westervelt, 2015), but needs to fill gaps concerning long-term management of this content in regards to file formats, intellectual property, data sharing, funder requirements, privacy considerations, data documentation and metadata, and preservation and storage information.

Some of the efforts the LC has made with datasets are:

- By August 2017 the library limited the collecting of data sets to geospatial data acquired to support the Geospatial Hosting Environment. The library's Geospatial Hosting Environment (GHE) is an ongoing library initiative to provide coordinated resources for geospatial analysis and web mapping to Congress, Congressional Research Service (CRS) and other researchers in the library. LC provides this GIS content with collecting guidelines that can be found at the Digital Geospatial Materials Collections Policy Statement.[10]
- The deposit pilot is expanding through the Copyright Office, to acquire and make accessible content that is only available online.
- The library offers its users, databases with more than one million digital works, although these resources are not pure datasets. The dataset itself is reviewed following specific guidelines (Library of Congress, 2017b) with special consideration given to the stability and scope of the dataset and the ability to export data. Preference is given to data purchase (or perpetual access).
- Web archiving began in 2000, and harvests the Internet (Zimmer, 2015), by taking the opportunity to include all presidential and congressional elections from 2000. The library is preserving web content in the Web ARChive (WARC) format. Mandatory and recommended metadata fields refer to the WARC ISO-standard specification.

Major factors affect the current collecting of datasets, in cases where an acquisition is technically possible (Table 4).

Table 4. LC technical factors limiting the current collecting of data sets

Subject	Does the subject of the data set fall within the Library's collecting scope?
Value	Does the data set have enduring high value from a scientific or historical perspective, making it worthy of long-term preservation and access?
Documentation and metadata	Is the data set accompanied by adequate technical and descriptive information?
Format	The data set must be in a format that the Library supports. The Library's Recommended Formats Statement provides specific technical information about data sets.
Access	Does the Library have a way to provide access to the data set upon receipt? Is immediate access to the data set necessary? Has the Library defined a path to future access for this type of data set?

(Library of Congress, 2017b)

Library of Congress Lab Technical Pilot as a Site for Access to LC Collections as Data

To make it possible for the LC to explore how to deliver their digital collections as data to researchers, a variety of services and situations determine an environment that institutions call 'Labs'. From August 2016, the NDI division at LC is charged with the implementation of Labs, as a place to encourage innovation with LC digital collections.[11] The LC Lab is defined as a service centre (indeed, a service unit for the library itself) providing offerings that support the work of researchers, scholars, and other users across all the digital collections of the library (Chudnov & Gallinger, 2016).

The LC Lab Technical Pilot uses a third-party platform to analyze in-house data which was previously unavailable to the public, develops Python scripts and format conversion workflows and shows that legal issues, and cost planning problems can be successfully solved (Burton et al., 2018). The library connects scholarly digital collections, faculty teaching digital methods and curators at LC to increase pedagogical outreach.

The services workflow of the Lab defines three areas:

- LC for Robots, that allows users to gain bulk data access and application programming interfaces (APIs) as windows to the library, making collections and data more accessible to automated access via scripting and software, thus empowering developers to explore new ways to use the library's collections;

- Experiments, allowing LC to experiment with these crowdsourcing technologies, e.g. by accessing the API and analysing the colours of the thousands of digitized images put online by the library;[12]
- Events searching to empower librarians to support digital scholars.

The phases through which LC Labs have been developed are shown in Figure 2 (Chudnov & Gallinger, 2016).

RESEARCH DATA MANAGEMENT PLANNING AT THE NATIONAL LIBRARY OF MEDICINE

A growing volume of molecular biology and clinical research data is collected, organized and accessed from the National Library of Medicine (NLM). NLM sends more than 100 TB of data to more than 4 M users daily, and receives more than 10 TB of data from more than 3000 users daily. This expanding set of information resources prompted NLM to refocus on the informatics and data science research front with a specific strategic plan (National Library of Medicine, 2017).

These resources are curated and managed in digital libraries through mechanisms completely analogous to the traditional function of libraries, as libraries continue to be essential places for knowledge repositories and community gathering. Yet the NLM core functions of acquiring, collecting and disseminating the world's biomedical literature, challenge librarians and libraries to extend these skills and

Figure 2. The LC Lab Plan for Execution followed the objectives of the British Library Labs

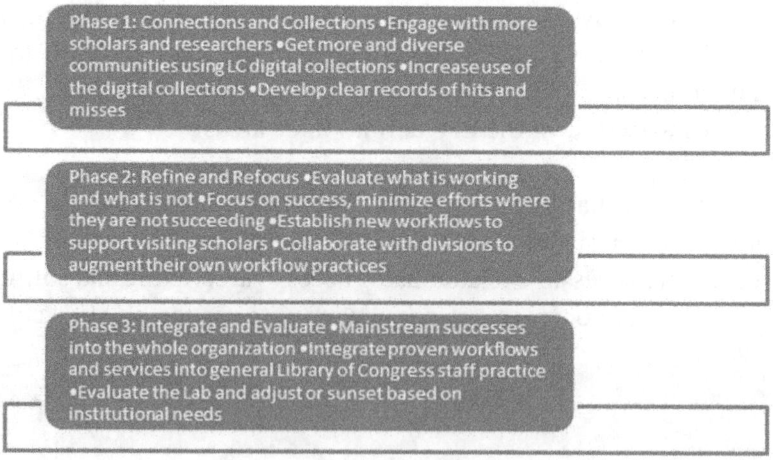

Table 5. Four themes identified as a framework for the NLM Strategic Plan Planning Process November 2016-February 2018 (National Library of Medicine, 2017)

• Advancing data science, open science, and biomedical informatics
• Advancing biomedical discovery and translational science
• Supporting the public's health: clinical systems, public health systems and services, and personal health
• Building collections to support discovery and health in the 21st century

Source: Library of Congress, 2017b

develop new ones to make data findable, accessible, interoperable, and reusable (the FAIR principles policy). As a result, the library's strategic planning initiative was begun in November 2016, with a survey based on four themes (Table 5), where the respondents included librarians, researchers, historians, nurses, informaticians, associations and the public. As a consequence, and in the context of the library leadership transition and data science positions, the NLM Strategic Plan was finally approved in February 2018.

Fostering an Ecosphere of Discovery for Digital Research Objects

The first pillar of NLM's Strategic Plan 2017-2027 (National Library of Medicine, 2017) is derived from the data demands of the research enterprise (McLaughlin, 2018). Big data for precision medicine asks about the quality of its sources, and needs to evaluate the results obtained from its uses and management; accelerating biomedical discovery and advancing health through data-driven research is the first key goal of the strategic plan.

NLM's 21st-century collection must be characterized by data discovery's continual and rapid evolution. Modern approaches to attribution must to be devised, by integrating open APIs so optimizing funder identification, content discovery and long-term accessibility. New methods of automated indexing that promote the operational efficiency and curatorial aspects of collection management are needed; in particular, by facilitating the link to resources not housed in NLM. Personalized presentation (beyond visualization) requires the availability of data, an area integrally related with the mission of the library to foster the creation of a live, comprehensive health research dataset on the order of 1% of the US population (~30 million people) (Elsevier, 2017).

Engaging Audiences to Obtain the Right Information at Near Real-Time

The value of shared learning, by rapidly assimilating data at the right-time from single-system studies, prompts a shift towards near real-time evidence-sharing aimed at changing practice and improving care (Guise et al., 2018). This shift is the second pillar of the strategic plan. Linked Data Format, RDF format, and XML standards will move to more user-centric interface formats. As the library keeps pace with these changes, this will foster the distinctiveness of NLM as a reliable, trustable source of health information and biomedical data.

Workforce Critical Re-Skilling for Data-Driven Research

Arising from this digital identity and big data analytics, a third pillar is the re-shaping of the existing workforce into a data-driven structure towards a pioneering future encompassing such topics as fostering rigor and reproducibility, thus assuring open science proficiency (Steeves, 2017). The roles of librarians must be empowered to integrate analytics, visualization, mining and other tools to use data for discoveries and to make it interoperable. Along with carrying the data-powered healthcare message to point-of-care departments (McLaughlin, 2018), this means that NLM educational services will engage in the expansion and enhancement of research training for biomedical informatics and data science.

RESEARCH DATA MANAGEMENT PLANNING AT THE GERMAN NATIONAL LIBRARY OF SCIENCE AND TECHNOLOGY (TIB)

The German National Library of Science and Technology is the Leibniz Information Centre for Science and Technology in Hannover and is Germany's National Library for all areas of engineering as well as architecture, chemistry, information technology, mathematics, and physics. It was founded in 1959, as the Technische Informationsbibliothek (TIB). At TIB, research data may be the subject of research, it may evolve during the research process or it may be the outcome of the research (Figure 3).

Depending on the method used and the specific research question, research data are available in a variety of formats, including spreadsheets, electronic text documents, photos, film and databases. Research data can be researched and supplied as knowledge objects from the TIB-portal,[13] and preserved together with

Figure 3. Research Data preservation workflow at the Alliance of German National Specialist Libraries
Source: https://www.goportis.de/en/digital-preservation/risks-relating-to-data-storagepreservation.html

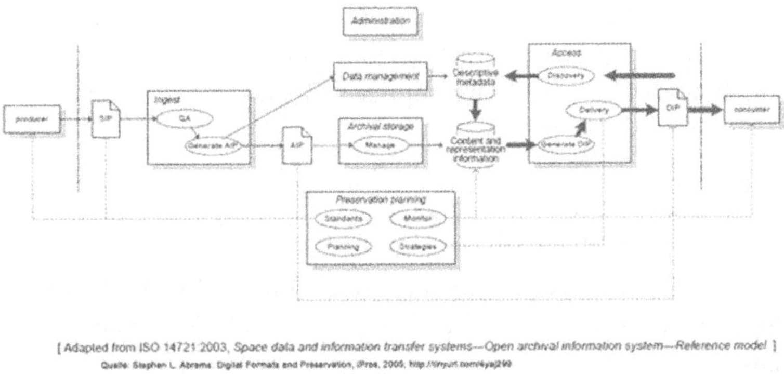

the research data from the two other German National libraries: the German National Library of Medicine in Cologne/Bonn (ZB MED) and the German National Library of Economics in Kiel/Hamburg (ZBW). All operate within the framework of the Leibniz Library Network for Research Information also known as Goportis (the Alliance of German National Specialist Libraries).[14]

In July 2017, TIB established a Data Science & Digital Libraries Research Group led by a TIB Director.[15] This Research Group is involved in three H2020 projects:

- H2020 Marie Skłodowska-Curie Innovative Training Network: WDAqua Answering Questions using Web Data (Coordinator Prof. Sören Auer, 01/2015-12/2018);
- H2020: SlideWiki – Large-scale pilots for collaborative OpenCourseWare authoring, multiplatform delivery and Learning Analytics (Coordinator Prof. Sören Auer, 01/2016-12/2018);
- H2020: IASIS Big Data for Precision Medicine (04/2017-04/2020).

TIB is active within the Research Data Alliance (RDA) with a focus on topics such as libraries for research data, the 'long tail' of research data, publishing, cost recovery for data centres, legal interoperability, metadata and PID services (Kraft et al., 2017).

TIB Open Access Policy

From December 2016, TIB's Open Access Policy established that research results generated by the library's employees should be made available as open access publications. It offers support to its employees in publishing open access with access to funds via TIB's own publishing fund and extensive advice on open access publications. In addition, the library supports Open Access for data by providing the following services:

- comprehensive advice and training on research data management, for a member of Leibniz Universität Hannover;
- strong involvement in financing and enhancing the SCOAP project;[16]
- catalogue metadata under a Creative Commons CC0 public domain license, for reuse;
- commitment to the DOI Service and to DataCite, thus ensuring the allocation of DOIs for openly accessible research data and open access publications;
- support in negotiating open access clauses in contracts with publishers.

Research Data Management

Publication and citation of research data are TIB's most singular signs of identity (Brase & Schindler, 2006) and TIB undertakes all the activities requiring the provision of data, on which a research publication is based: the creation, processing, archiving and publishing of data. TIB is one of five RADAR project partners, responsible for its sustainable data management and data publishing. RADAR, the German research data repository preserves research results for up to 15 years and started in March 2017. RADAR is a nationally recognized and certified repository for the deposition and provision of accessible, traceable and citable research data, mainly focusing on scientific specialist disciplines.[17] TIB offers RDM services to two categories of library users:

- **Services to Scientists:** Workshops offer scientists of all disciplines an overview of the topic "research data management".[18] The many challenges faced by scientists when dealing with digital data are exposed:
  - Organization and documentation fundamentals (backup and archiving, publication and reuse);
  - Data management plans (costs and benefits, implementation);
  - Repositories (data storage and publication).

- **Services to Researchers:** An advisory service was established at Leibniz Universität Hannover, working with the university's infrastructure for research data. TIB collaborates with:
    - Advanced training on data management plans within the continuing education programme of the university;
    - Assistance and individual support on research data management and publishing on research data.

Since October 2017, a Scientific Data Management Research Group has been based at the TIB, led by a Venezuelan professor at the Computer Science Department of the Simón Bolívar University.[19] The aim of the research group is to develop applications in various domains (especially biomedicine and digital libraries) turning heterogeneous research data into usable knowledge. A number of issues are faced by the research group (Table 6).

This research group participates in two H2020 projects:

- **H2020 iASiS:** Integration and analysis of heterogeneous big data for precision medicine and suggested treatments for different types of patients (4/2017 to 3/2020).
- **H2020 BigMedilytics:** Big Data for Medical Analytics (2017 to 2020)

Publishing Research Data (TIB PID Services - DOI Service, DataCite etc.)

TIB provides new digital publication and curation services for research data (Kraft et al., 2017). With the goal of the broad reuse of research data, TIB supplies German

Table 6. TIB research focus in the field of scientific data management

• Knowledge graphs encoding the meaning and connections of research data, including provenance, privacy, quality and uncertainty
• Domain-specific ontologies and link discovery techniques that promote the scalable interoperability of large and heterogenous scientific data sets
• Methods to integrate a variety of exhaustive and diverse research data sources, such as static data, continuous data streams and legacy, structured and unstructured data
• Storage and distribution of large scientific data and knowledge graphs
• Methods for access control aimed at enforcing privacy regulation for sensitive data
• Federated query engines intended for scientific knowledge graphs
• Scientific knowledge graphs to implement data analysis and methods of knowledge discovery

Source: https://www.tib.eu/en/research-development/scientific-data-management/research/

institutions with persistent identifiers (PID), support around digital resources (DOI), information infrastructure and person identifiers (ORCID) and publishes data with a DOI assignment for an unlimited period of time in RADAR.

PID Services (PIDs) are takeaways for policy actions, further analysis and technical assistance regarding (Stocker et al., 2018):

- Links with the context in which information is created and consumed;
- Deep integration with research infrastructures and VREs;
- Challenging projects with technical and social infrastructure dimensions;
- Young projects open to interested stakeholders.

DOI Services allocate DOIs for research data, so that scientific results can be referenced clearly and persistently.[20] The DOI project began at TIB in 2003 and this work led to the foundation of DataCite in 2009. TIB as a DataCite member, operates in this infrastructure through its support of simple and effective methods of data citation, discovery and access.[21]

TIB Labs develop and evaluate prototypes and beta versions while between these experimental services, lies the Leibniz Data Manager, a system for heterogenous data collections based on a CKAN distribution for RDM and supporting the management and access to heterogenous research data publications.[22]

RESEARCH DATA MANAGEMENT PLANNING AT THE GERMAN NATIONAL LIBRARY OF MEDICINE (ZB MED)

The German National Library of Medicine (ZB MED), is Germany's National Library for biological and medical sciences; the national information infrastructure and research support in the field of life sciences. Operational since 1973, the library has over 1.6 million volumes, and the journal collection contains approximately 38,400 (electronic and print) titles of which over 7,447 are current journal subscriptions. The Cologne site of the library offers literature and resources from the fields of medicine and health, and the Bonn site, those from the fields of nutritional, environmental and agricultural sciences.

ZB MED considers that in the field of life sciences, research data may include measurement data, survey data, and observational data as well as audio visual materials such as images and videos and even the development of software products (Table 7).

Research data arises during the research process and forms the basis for research results. PUBLISSO, the open access publishing portal run by ZD MED, offers a number of different ways of publishing research data.

Table 7. ZB MED research data in medicine examples

Image data from imaging techniques (e.g. MRI)
Sensor data from bio signal or vital parameter measurement (e.g. ECG, EEG)
Biomaterial data from laboratory studies (e.g. blood samples, genome data)
Diagnostic data from medical diagnostics (e.g. medical history)
Statistical data (e.g. from anonymized findings data)
Classifications and codes on diseases or materials (e.g. International Statistical Classification of Diseases and Related Health Problems (ICD))
Master data of the patient administration (e.g. from hospital information systems)

(Lindstädt, 2016)

ZB MED Data Management

At ZB MED, the guiding principles for research data management are the FAIR Data Principles; to make data findable, accessible, interoperable and reusable. The first step is to create a data management plan (DMP) that defines how the data gathered during a project should be used. An excellent guide to which aspects should be taken into account in a data management plan (a research data management plan checklist) has been created as part of the German WissGrid project.

The aim of the DMP is to ensure participants take the quality assurance steps required to assure data reusability and fitness for publication and that they consider all legal aspects (e.g. on personal data); in so doing, good scientific practices are established. In Germany, software tools have been developed to support the writing of a DMP. The Research Data Management Organiser (RDMO) assembles the relevant planning information and data management tasks along the life cycle of the research data (Figure 4).[23] For these new tasks, consideration should be given to the development and creation of new roles (e.g. software librarian) (Katerbow & Feulner, 2018).

ZB MED Data Publication

Key to publishing research data is ensuring the interoperability of that research data, through, for example, assigning PIDs. Through its DOI registration service, ZB MED promotes and facilitates research data for not-for-profit online publications in the field of medicine. PUBLISSO, its data portal, offers individual authors several different ways of publishing research data. ZB MED is a member of DataCite, as an international not-for-profit organization that promotes services and know-how

Figure 4. Life cycle of the research data: the basis for Research Data Management (Lindstädt, 2016)

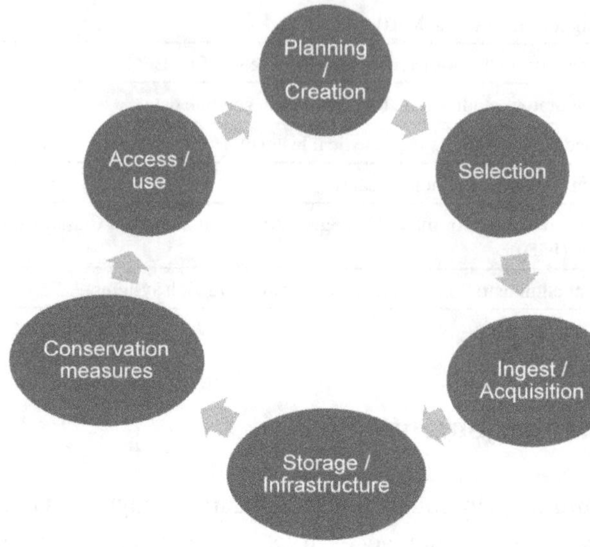

relating to the management, referencing and citation of research data. Also, ZB MED collaborates with the TIB which operates as a DOI registration agency.

ZB MED supports Open Data, and within the framework of the publishing service GMS ZB MED, cooperates with the data repository DataDryad (Arning, 2015). This means that ZB MED covers the cost of publishing the research data when authors publish an article in a GMS (German Medical Science) gGmbH journal. The data is deposited in the Dryad Research Data Repository where it is linked to the article.[24]

RECOMMENDATIONS AND CONCLUSION

The following recommendations were assembled based on discussions arising out of this chapter:

On services to users:

- A national library can advise on all steps and tasks of research data management, as the basis of a national strategy to develop Open Data;
- To continue to extend the data portals with the parameters of the FAIR policy;
- To upgrade near real-time data to set up periodically the "best copy" (validation and removing duplicates) with upgraded metadata.

On interoperability:

- To use the same standards at the international level, based on ISO regulations;
- No data should be distributed without DOI;
- The data provider codes should be able to include the monitoring institution in addition to the research institute;
- A common level of research data portals description and data repository description is advisable.

On enhancing discovery:

- To harmonize metadata information to describe catalogues of datasets and collections;
- Develop a catalogue of research data repositories, that would operate at an international level;
- Guidelines for implementation of data citation (DOI) based on international work (link to RDA).

On improving interaction with national library labs:

- To improve traceability of the use of research data;
- Feedback to the national library labs on the use of research data when an anomaly is detected;
- Visibility of the national library on the available discovery tools for researchers.

On research data quality:

- To update research data following a hierarchy of quality, from data well-described to data fully reproduced in a different environment by a different team;
- To create and recognise the documentation of research software.

This chapter concludes with the idea that national libraries have a role in actively promoting Open Data and the FAIR policy as part of good research data management practice:

- Their roles are determined by decentralization of the web, distributed computing and storage, data analytics, artificial intelligence and knowledge graphs;

- Their significant investments in data infrastructures allow them to be in leading positions in what makes for the development of a data science ecosystem;
- All sectors of the national libraries workforce are urged to help researchers with data management, sharing, and preservation;
- National library data managers must be encouraged to value in-house data decision making and enhancing services;
- The primary relationships between data libraries and institutional repositories are a substrate for innovative data science provided by national libraries' labs;
- The display of data metrics is beginning to pull data usage and citations.

REFERENCES

Anderson, M., Gallinger, M., & Potter, A. (2009). *The National Digital Stewardship Alliance Charter: Enabling Collaboration to Achieve National Digital Preservation.* In iPRES 2009: the Sixth International Conference on Preservation of Digital Objects, San Francisco, CA.

Arning, U. (2015). GMS publishes your research findings and makes the related research data available through Dryad. *GMS Zeitschrift für Medizinische Ausbildung*, *32*(3), Doc34. PMID:26413172

Auer, S., Kovtun, V., Prinz, M., Kasprzik, A., Stocker, M., & Vidal, M. E. (2018). Towards a knowledge graph for science. In *WIMS'18 Proceedings of the 8th International Conference on Web Intelligence, Mining and Semantics.* New York, NY: ACM. 10.1145/3227609.3227689

Ayris, P., Achard, P., Fdida, S., Gradmann, S., Horstmann, W., Labastida, I., & Smit, A. (2013). *LERU Roadmap for Research Data. LERU Advice Paper* (Vol. 14). Leuven, Belgium: LERU.

Barga, R. S., Andrews, S., & Parastatidis, S. (2007). A Virtual Research Environment (VRE) for Bioscience Researchers. In *Proceedings of the International Conference on Advanced Engineering Computing and Applications in Sciences*, (pp. 31-38). IEEE. 10.1109/ADVCOMP.2007.14

Berman, J. (2003). A tool for sharing annotated research data: The "Category 0" UMLS (Unified Medical Language System) vocabularies. *BMC Medical Informatics and Decision Making*, *3*(6). PMID:12809560

Bodenreider, O. (2004). The unified medical language system (UMLS): Integrating biomedical terminology. *Nucleic Acids Research, 32*(90001), 267–270. doi:10.1093/nar/gkh061 PMID:14681409

Brase, J., & Schindler, U. (2006). The publication of scientific data by the world data centers and the national library of science and technology in Germany. *Data Science Journal, 5*, 205–208. doi:10.2481/dsj.5.205

British Library. (2015). *Living Knowledge: The British Library 2015-2023*. London, UK: British Library.

Burton, M., Lyon, L., Erdmann, C., & Tijerina, B. (2018). *Shifting to Data Savvy: The Future of Data Science in Libraries*. Pittsburgh, PA: University of Pittsburgh.

Chudnov, D., & Gallinger, M. (2016). Library of Congress Lab: Library of Congress Digital Scholars Lab Pilot Project Report. Washington, DC: Academic Press.

Collins, E. (2012). The National Data Centres. In G. Pryor (Ed.), *Managing Research Data* (pp. 151–172). Facet. doi:10.29085/9781856048910.009

Davenport, E., & Cronin, B. (1994). Competitive intelligence and social advantage. *Library Trends, 43*(2), 239–252.

Ell, B. (2015). *User Interfaces to the Web of Data based on Natural Language Generation*. Karlsruhe, Germany: Scientific Publishing.

Elsevier. (2017). *Responses to NLM Strategic Vision and Plan-Related Requests for Information (RFIs)*. Retrieved from https://www.nitrd.gov/nitrdgroups/images/a/ad/ElsevierResponseNLM.pdf

European Union. (2016). *H2020 Programme: Guidelines on FAIR Data Management in Horizon 2020*. Version 3.0. Author.

Gooding, P., Terras, M., & Berube, L. (2018). Legal Deposit Web Archives and the Digital Humanities: a Universe of Lost Opportunity? In Digital Humanities 2018 (pp. 590-592). Academic Press.

Guise, J. M., Savitz, L. A., & Friedman, C. P. (2018). Mind the gap: Putting evidence into practice in the era of learning health systems. *Journal of General Internal Medicine*, 1–3. PMID:30155611

Katerbow, M., & Feulner, G. (2018). *Recommendations on the Development, Use and Provision of Research Software [Handreichung zum Umgang mit Forschungssoftware]*. Research Software Working Group, Digital Information of the Alliance of German Science Organisations.

Kraft, A., Dreyer, B., Löwe, P., & Ziedorn, F. (2017). 14 Years of PID services at the German National Library of Science and Technology (TIB): Connected frameworks, research data and lessons learned from a national research library perspective. *Data Science Journal, 16*(36), 1–10.

Kruse, F. & Thestrup, J.B. (2017). Research Data Management - A European perspective. Munich, Germany: De Gruyter Saur. doi:10.1515/9783110365634

Kwon, N. (2017). How work positions affect the research activity and information behaviour of laboratory scientists in the research lifecycle: applying activity theory. *Information Research: An International Electronic Journal, 22*(1).

Library of Congress. (2017a). *Collecting digital content at the Library of Congress*. Library Services Collection Development Office.

Library of Congress. (2017b). *Data Sets-Interim Guidance-Library of Congress*. Author.

Lindstädt, B. (2016). Management und Publikation von Forschungsdaten – Serviceleistungen einer wissenschaftlichen Bibliothek. *Bibliotheksdienst, 50*(7), 636–648. doi:10.1515/bd-2016-0078

McLaughlin, L. K. (2018). Forever agile: Hospital librarians and the NLM's Strategic Plan. *Journal of Hospital Librarianship, 18*(3), 259–265. doi:10.1080/15323269.2018.1472004

Mears, J., Potter, A., & Zwaard, K. (2017). Collections as data: preservation to access to use to impact. In *14th International Conference on Digital Preservation*, Kyoto, Japan.

National Library of Medicine. (2017). *A Platform for Biomedical Discovery and Data-Powered Health: the National Library of Medicine Strategic Plan 2017–2027*. US Department of Health and Human Services National Institute of Health.

Ray, J. M. (Ed.). (2014). *Research Data Management: Practical Strategies for Information Professionals*. West Lafayette, IN: Purdue University Press.

Reimer, T. (2018). The once and future library: the role of the (national) library in supporting research. *Insights*, 31.

SCONUL. (2011). The SCONUL Seven Pillars of Information Literacy. Core Model for Higher Education. London, UK: Society of College, National and University Libraries; Working Group on Information Literacy.

Sheehan, J., Hirschfeld, S., Foster, E., Ghitza, U., Goetz, K., Karpinski, J., & Huerta, M. (2016). Improving the value of clinical research through the use of Common Data Elements (CDEs). *Clinical Trials, 13*(6), 671–676. doi:10.1177/1740774516653238 PMID:27311638

Steeves, V. (2017). Reproducibility librarianship. *Collaborative Librarianship, 9.*

Stocker, M., Paasonen, P., Fiebig, M., Zaidan, M. A., & Hardisty, A. (2018). Curating scientific information in knowledge infrastructures. *Data Science Journal, 17*(21), 1–16.

Westervelt, T. (2015). Acquisition and management of digital content at the Library of Congress. *The Serials Librarian, 68*(1-4), 269–273. doi:10.1080/0361526X.2015.1026299

Zimmer, M. (2015). The Twitter archive at the Library of Congress: Challenges for information practice and information policy. *First Monday, 20*(7), 7. doi:10.5210/fm.v20i7.5619

ENDNOTES

1 https://nnlm.gov/classes/biomedical-and-health-research-data-management-librarians

2 DataCite – The British Library: https://www.bl.uk/datacite. Ref. in (Reimer, 2018).

3 LC Labs - Innovation with Library of Congress digital collections: https://labs.loc.gov/. Ref. in (Anderson et al., 2009).

4 Medical data analytics at NLM. Ref. in (Sheehan et al., 2016).

5 AI at TIB. Ref. in (Auer et al., 2018).

6 Research Software Working Group of the Alliance of German Science Organizations. Ref. in (Katerbow & Feulner, 2018).

7 https://www.bl.uk/projects/british-library-labs

8 https://www.bl.uk/datacite

9 http://digitalpreservation.gov/meetings/dcs16.html?loclr=blogsig

10 https://www.loc.gov/acq/devpol/anageospatial.pdf

11 http://labs.loc.gov

12 https://loc-colors.glitch.me/

13 https://www.tib.eu/en/search-discover/research-data/

14 https://www.goportis.de

15 https://www.tib.eu/en/research-development/data-science-digital-libraries/

16 https://scoap3.org/what-is-scoap3/
17 https://www.radar-service.eu/en/about-us
18 https://www.tib.eu/en/learning-working/courses-offered/on-site-training/
19 https://www.tib.eu/en/research-development/scientific-data-management/
20 https://www.tib.eu/en/publishing-archiving/doi-service/
21 https://datacite.org/board.html
22 https://datamanager.tib.eu/
23 http://rdmorganiser.github.io/en/
24 http://www.egms.de/static/en/journals/policy.htm#data

Chapter 2
A Proposed Framework for Research Data Management Services in Research Institutions in Zimbabwe

Josiline Phiri Chigwada
Bindura University of Science Education, Zimbabwe

Thembelihle Hwalima
Lupane State University, Zimbabwe

Nancy Kwangwa
University of Zimbabwe, Zimbabwe

ABSTRACT

The chapter documents the proposed framework for the establishment of research data management services in research institutions in Zimbabwe. It has been indicated that there are no formal research data management services taking place in Zimbabwe as researchers are managing their own data. It is against such a background that a literature review was undertaken to understand how research institutions in other countries are engaging in research data services. E-mails were sent to the pioneers of research data services. It was discovered that there are challenges that are faced when establishing research data management services and it is important to consult all stakeholders at the planning stage. The framework consists of strategies, policies, guidelines, processes, technologies, and services.

DOI: 10.4018/978-1-5225-8437-7.ch002

INTRODUCTION

The chapter documents a proposed framework that can be used in Zimbabwe to develop research data management (RDM) services in research institutions. Published research (Chigwada, Chiparausha and Kasiroori 2017) shows that RDM is a new concept in Zimbabwe and research institutions are working towards the establishment of RDM services. This chapter would assist in unpacking the activities and processes that should be undertaken in establishing RDM services by proposing a framework that can be used. The objectives that are addressed by this chapter are:

1. To identify the strategies that can be used to establish RDM services in Zimbabwe;
2. To identify the stakeholders that can be involved in establishing RDM services in Zimbabwe;
3. To assess the challenges faced when establishing RDM services in Zimbabwe.
4. To propose a framework that can be used to establish RDM services in Zimbabwe.

A literature survey and document analysis were carried out to obtain the information from those with experience in the establishment of RDM services. Emails were sent to RDM 'champions' to gather as much detail as possible on how research institutions in Zimbabwe might establish RDM services.

WHAT IS RESEARCH DATA MANAGEMENT?

Research data management (RDM) is the organisation and description of research data, from its entry to the research cycle to the dissemination and archiving of the results (Whyte and Tedds 2011). Pinfield, Cox, and Smith (2014) point out that RDM addresses a number of information needs and is driven by the need to provide immediate data storage facilities; to ensure the security and long term preservation of data; compliance with the requirements and policies of other agencies such as funders; the quality of the research activity and research data itself; the need to share data and make it open access; and the jurisdiction to be involved in RDM and the involvement of other players in offering RDM services. Consequently, various initiatives were carreid out in Africa to establish research data management services and some institutions are now archiving research data locally, nationally, regionally and internationally.

What is a Research Data Repository?

A research data repository is a database infrastructure set up to manage, share, access and archive researchers' datasets (Uzwyshn 2016). It can be institutional, national, regional or international and can be specialised or general. The main objective of establishing a research data repository would be to share data which would allow the examination, proof, review, transparency and validation of researchers' results by other experts, whilst allowing simultaneous access by many researchers. Uzwyshn (2016) indicates that libraries should seriously consider partnerships with national and international organisations working towards the development of research data repositories, in order to provide the required information services and infrastructure. To manage research data effectively, there is a need to comply with funders' and institutional policies. Jones, Pryor and White (2013) have written a guide, *Delivering Research Data Management Services*, for those who work in higher education institutions.

In the event that the institution does not have a data repository but wants to promote RDM services amongst its researchers, there are other avenues that can be utilised to ensure that research data is managed. In some cases, the funder might state the data repository that should be utilised by researchers when they are applying for funds. If the funder does not have a preferred repository, researchers can use discipline-specific repositories such as UK Data Archive for social sciences and humanities, arXiv for mathematics and physical science, GEO for genomic datasets, and some that are provided by PLOS journals or Scientific Data. There are general purpose repositories such as Zenodo and Mendeley data. In the absence of research data services, research institutions in Zimbabwe can encourage researchers to visit the registry of research data repositories (re3data) to find the best repository to host their data.

Initiatives to Establish RDM Services in Africa

A review of the literature indicates that efforts to establish RDM services are being undertaken in South Africa, Botswana and Zimbabwe (Chiware and Becker 2018, Peters and Hahnel 2017). The University of Cape Town, Cape Peninsula University of Technology and other institutions of higher learning in the Western Cape have taken a proactive approach in establishing RDM services, taking advantage of the open access movement. In South Africa, there is the African Open Science Platform (AOSP), managed by the Academy of Science of South Africa (ASSAf), and funded through the South Africa National Research Foundation in the Department of Science and Technology. Direction for the provision of funding is given by the International Council for Science (ICSU) Committee on Data for Science and Technology (CODATA).

The work of AOSP benefits the African content by monitoring progress in terms of open science policy, ICT infrastructure, data sharing, collaboration and capacity building. The South African National Research Foundation (NRF) policy states that research funded by public funds should be archived in trusted repositories. The Science Granting Councils Initiative (SGCI) in Sub-Saharan Africa also works with 15 science granting councils to strengthen research in the region. The Data Intensive Research in South Africa (DIRISA) was created to enable universities and research institutions to access facilities for data intensive projects. Research undertaken by Chiware and Becker (2018) indicated that there were no responses from Namibia, Malawi, Zambia, Lesotho and Swaziland in terms of reported activities relating to RDM in university and research libraries or at national level, again pointing to the need for clear national guidelines on how institutions should plan and develop this important area for research support.

Role of the Library in RDM

The role of the library and librarians has been evolving in the 21st century alomgside the increasing need to keep the library aligned to current trends in the field. Librarians have adopted a more outgoing approach in their service delivery and have started to support research undertaken within their institutions so as to remain relevant to their users. To fully understand the thrust of RDM, it is important to relate to the definition of RDM services by Whyte and Tedds (2011). It is easy to understand the increasing prominence and importance of RDM but this has come with a diverse or rather transformed the role that librarians play within their research institutions. Cox and Pinfield (2014) observe that RDM consists of a number of different activities and processes associated with the data lifecycle, involving the design and creation of data, storage, security, preservation, retrieval, sharing and reuse, all taking into account technical capabilities, ethical considerations, legal issues and governance frameworks.

The debate about the library's involvement in data management has been conducted at both strategic and operational levels. Lewis (2010) argues that data from academic research projects represents an integral part of the global research knowledge base and managing data should be a natural extension of the library's current role in providing access to the published part of that knowledge base, while also noting the scale of the challenge in terms of infrastructure, skills and culture. Consequently, librarians are encompassing new RDM responsibilities which involve being asked to do things which at present are beyond their usual expertise (Chiware & Mathe, 2015). This has been posited by Nitecki & Davis (2017) who point out that librarians, given their long experience with information organisation and documentation, are becoming more involved in the development of principles and best practices for managing digital data for long term use. In some research institutions a new role of 'data librarian' is emerging, but there can be ambiguity over the meaning of this designation: does it embody a librarian with a particular skill set, or is it more of a description of new duties? In the case of the latter, a data librarian may be someone who takes on a new role and must acquire a range of new skills on the job, as posited by Pinfield (2014).

Librarians' Response to RDM Services

Hey and Hey (2006) suggest that if librarians can respond effectively to the challenge by engaging the e-science revolution which will put libraries and repositories center stage in the development of the next generation research infrastructure, then RDM will become very prevalent. Services and tools often managed by libraries are now becoming more widespread. It is clear that at certain institutions librarians are playing significant and growing roles in the RDM process. Recognising the potential that librarians can offer and the need to develop skills, there are a growing number of online training courses being developed at national and institutional levels such as Data Scientist Training for Librarians, DIY RDM Training Kit for Librarians, Data Intelligence for Librarians (DCC 2017). It is also evident that there is much collaborative work in institutions between libraries and IT departments, the latter dealing with the technical aspects of handling petabytes of data, the former developing the organisational and service aspects of data management (Chiware & Mathe, 2015).

As approaches to RDM develop in research institutions, different stakeholders have become involved, including support services staff and faculty. University libraries have moved into this space and are increasingly seen as major contributors to RDM activity in general and in the design of research data services in particular (Pinfield, Cox & Smith, 2014). In this context, it is pivotal to train librarians so as to fully align them to this changing spectrum of RDM.

Swan and Brown (2008) see data management as a strategic issue for libraries and librarians and point out that the role of the library in data-intensive research is important and a strategic repositioning of the library with respect to research support is now appropriate. They add that three main potential roles for the library could be increasing data-awareness amongst researchers; providing archiving and preservation services for data within the institution through institutional repositories; and developing a new professional strand of practice in the form of data librarianship. Figure 1 summarises the role of the librarian in RDM services.

The diagram indicates that RDM challenges librarians to become self-motivated, research-grounded, intellectual entrepreneurs and more specifically: to become proactive designers of services that enable productive knowledge workers, to partner in knowledge-generating activities bringing understanding of the information and data

Figure 1. The role of the librarian in RDM services

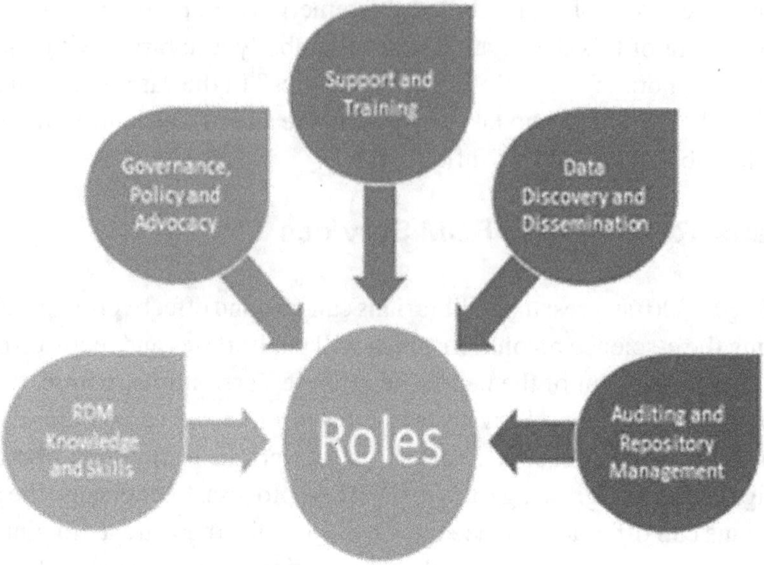

landscape and its tools for discovery and utilization; to share project management roles; to increase research team productivity; and be change agents that build evidence to monitor efficiencies and gauge impact (Nitecki & Davis, 2017).

ESTABLISHING RESEARCH DATA MANAGEMENT SERVICES

Shen and Varvel (2013) point out that human, financial and technological resources should be available for the RDM services to be successful. When establishing a research data repository, institutions should develop an RDM infrastructure profile (Davidson 2015). The profile would help to provide a better understanding of the infrastructure that is available to avoid duplication of effort by providing an inventory of the existing services. Davidson (2015) suggested the following components as the desirable scope of RDM infrastructure provision:

- A means of raising staff awareness of funders' research data requirements
- Research data policy
- Strategy or implementation plan for research data services
- RDM advice and support services
- Active data storage
- Persistent identification for datasets

- Data register or catalogue
- Data access procedures
- Secure data access
- Institutional publications repository (if it includes research data or metadata)
- Data repository for longer term access and preservation

There is a need to determine the software that would be used for archiving data. Several possibilities can be used whereby research data repository software specifically created for data or other digital library software can be used. According to Uzwyshn (2016) software specifically created for data are Dataverse, HUBzero and Chronopolis while those for general digital libraries are DSpace, Fedora and Hydra. The institution can install the software on its servers or it can be hosted by other organisations. The size of the data determines the information, communication technology (ICT) infrastructure that would be chosen for establishing a research data repository. The data sizes can be divided into three, that is, small/medium, large and very large (Uzwyshn 2016). Small to medium sized datasets can be stored on the researcher's computer and can be uploaded by a researcher, emailed or transferred through university network drives to a server or the cloud. Data from medium to large projects require special back-end storage systems while very large projects can be preserved and archived in consortial or national research data repositories. In Zimbabwe, research institutions should choose the software that matches their needs together with the available resources and IT experts should be responsible for choosing and maintaining the software.

Human and financial resources must also be available for the RDM services to flourish. RDM experts should be able to offer guidance on how best to tackle such a project and be available to train the stakeholders involved, as a way of capacity building. Financial resources and costs include the cost of setting up and managing a research data repository, the payment of expertise needed to set up and run the repository and further variable costs associated with the longevity of storage and requirments for the preservation and security of the data.

Reliable ICT infrastructure is fundamental to achieve the aim of archiving research data both at institutional and national level. In Africa, research intensive institutions are connected through the National Research and Education Network (NREN) and some institutions in Kenya, South Africa, Uganda and Zambia are running data-intensive applications and sharing high end computing assets (Adam 2016). This shows that Zimbabwe is not yet in the picture and should work towards the development of good ICT infrastructure to enable the development of RDM services.

STAKEHOLDERS IN ESTABLISHING RDM SERVICES

Stakeholders that should be involved in establishing RDM services are librarians, records managers, research institutions, research administration, researchers, library schools, IT specialists, funders, government and other RDM providers (Ingram 2016). It has been suggested that roles and responsibilities for establishing RDM services be shared among university management, support and administrative services and researchers (Jones, Pryor and Whyte 2013, Cox and Verbaan 2016, Latham 2017) while librarians should work with IT staff and research administrators to offer RDM services (Latham 2017).

It is clear that when establishing RDM services a minimum of the following offices should be involved: the research office, library, IT, researchers and the ethics committee. For this chapter, the stakeholders are divided into three i.e. management, support and administrative services and researchers. Management would define expectations, support staff would deliver the services while the researchers would create and use research data.

Management

Management should ensure that a project for establishing RDM services is feasible by providing support and ensuring that the resources are available and the infrastructure is working. According to Jones, Pryor and Whyte (2013), the roles of senior management are to provide an RDM 'champion' at the level of a Pro Vice-Chancellor Academic to chair the working group; ensure that all the stakeholders are represented in the working group including the library, research office, IT office and the researchers; approve proposals and endorse RDM budgets; and policy ratification and implementation. In addition to providing policies on how research data can be managed, research institutions must ensure that researchers have educational and support services aligned with RDM as a way of encouraging data sharing (Tenopir, Birch, & Allard, 2012; Tenopir, Sandusky, Allard, & Birch 2013).

Researchers

Conrad, Shorish, Whitmire, and Hswe (2017) state that some researchers do not receive formal training on RDM and as a result are not able to personally manage their own data. Researchers are one of the major stakeholders in the development of research data services and are crucial since they are the major provider and consumer of research data. Researchers can be from universities, think tanks, institutes, organisations or companies which have dedicated research and development departments. They collect, analyse, find and reuse data. They collect data from interviews or surveys which they deposit in the research data repository. Whyte and Wilson (2010) point out that researchers are data creators and are responsible for providing enough information that would enable other researchers to assess the quality of that data and whether it complies with the ethics of the subject. The research would also indicate the users who are permitted to access the data and any access requirements or constraints. The research data would be provided in the recommended formats and the metadata requested by the repository is also provided by the researcher.

Support and Administrative Staff

Support staff include those employed by the library, information technology, records management, research administration and any other external RDM service providers or networks. The research office plays a key role as the link between researchers, management and the funders and should work together to establish the team that would be in the working group. Administrative support staff would do the groundwork to understand the policy requirements and also have a bigger role to play in the development and implementation of proposals, plans and budgets needed for RDM services. As a result, capacity building is core to the needs of support staff and they are key advocates for the establishment of RDM services at their research institutions.

Data curators can be the library or the research office and are responsible for digital archiving, ensuring that digital objects are selected for the repository, according to an established policy. The repository should be able to house data in all the formats be it audio, video, audio visual, tif, gif, tsv or scanned documents. The curator has a duty to ensure the authenticity and integrity of the data and that the repository complies with legal regulations. A data curator also plans for the long term preservation of the data and would assume responsibility for ensuring that the data is accessible and available to the approved users.

Conrad, Shorish, Whitmire, and Hswe (2017) observe that libraries and records centres are routinely assigned responsibility to assist researchers in managing and curating research data, despite limited training. Librarians are now partners in the research data life cycle and are actively involved in curating, advising, and preserving research data. Libraries are assuming additional duties of creating awareness amongst researchers, archiving and preserving data and training researchers in RDM best practice. Peters and Dryden (2011) found that the researchers, are mostly interested in obtaining assistance with their grant proposals such as the process of data management planning, locating research data and other data related services, publication support and dealing with specific data during data collection.

In order to successfully assist the researchers, librarians must understand the researchers' needs so that the services provided would meet the research data requirements by these researchers. Librarians contribute to RDM from the proposal writing stage where they assist in creating a data management plan. During the project start-up stage, librarians help develop the data model and appropriate standards and recommended tools and resources for organising and sharing data, complying with requirements. At the end of the project, librarians support efforts to archive data by placing it in repositories for preservation and assist researchers in locating existing public data that answers their research questions.

In Zimbabwe, there are various stakeholder institutions that could be involved in the development of RDM services. These institutions play a major role in research and development activities within the country and, as the literatire review suggests, would be in an excellent position to develop RDM services, nationally. Figure 2 is a diagrammatic indications of those who could be involved in RDM services.

The diagram indicates that all institutions involved in research should take part in the development of RDM services, both those in the public and the private sector. Various ministries including the Ministry of Information Communication Technology (ICT) and Cyber security, Ministry of Higher and Tertiary Education, Science and Technology Development and Ministry of Information, Media and Broadcasting Services should be actively involved as they are responsible for

Figure 2. RDM stakeholders in Zimbabwe

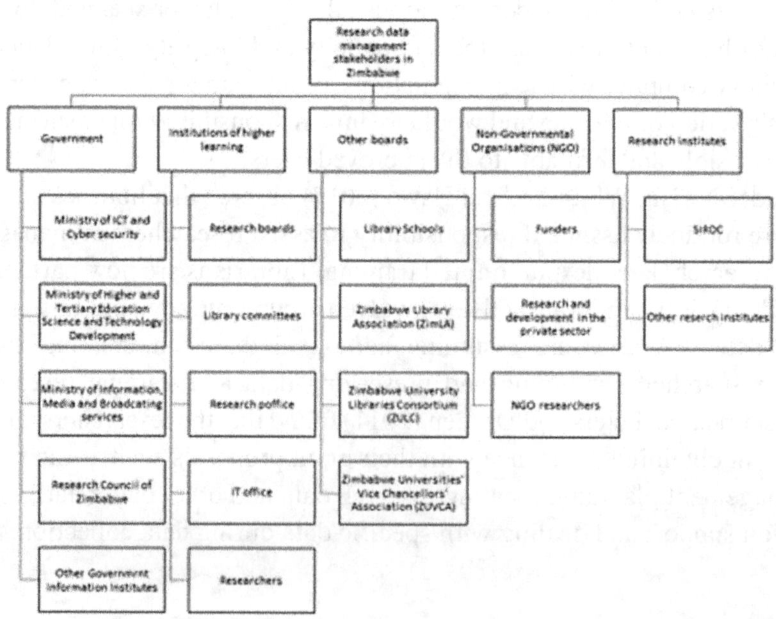

providing the infrastructure and the resources that are needed for the development of RDM services. The Research Council of Zimbabwe is ultimately responsible for all research activities and funding in the country and would assist in ensuring that research data is available for archiving.

The growing number of institutional reposiotries established to archive research outputs suggests that considerable research is being carried out in institutions of higher learning in Zimbabwe. These institutions are well-placed to develop RDM services at an institutional level where they have the resources. Another option is to develop RDM services at a national level so that there is a large pool of resources and an infrastructure to support RDM at an institutional level. Within the institutions of higher learning, there are already established boards that can be used to develop national RDM services. The Research Board deals with all the research activities of a college or university and their expertise can be used to develop policies and guidelines that would enable the archiving of research data in Zimbabwe. There are some research and development departments within the private sector and other research institutes such as Scientific and Industrial Research and Development Centre (SIRDC) which would play a very crucial role in the development and management of RDM services in Zimbabwe. Figure 2 indicates that the development of RDM services is a team effort which require the joint effort of both the private and public sector.

STRATEGIES FOR CREATING AWARENESS AMONGST RESEARCHERS

As the creators and users of research data, researcher engagement is crucial in the development of RDM services (Jones, Pryor and Whyte, 2013; Wilson and Jeffrey 2013; Buchhorn and McNamara 2010). Furthermore, Sompel et al. (2004) aptly reminded "Like any technology, success will depend not only on technical soundness but on the willingness of the participants in the system that is publishers, scholars, academic institutions, funding institutions and others, to adopt new tools and develop new organisational models on top of them." It is therefore imperative to have strategies in place to raise RDM awareness to researchers. The strategies include advocacy and training, use of social media tools and embedding RDM in existing research support activities.

Advocacy and training programmes have proven to be on top of the list in promoting new initiatives in the library and information science fraternity. In the recent past when institutional repositories and electronic resources were introduced in academic libraries in Zimbabwe, advocacy and training were central in raising awareness among researchers. A study by Chigwada et al. (2017) on RDM services in research institutions in Zimbabwe revealed that research data management is still a relatively new concept compared to other institutions in the developed countries. It is therefore, pertinent to have RDM advocacy and training programmes in place to bring researchers on board. The training programmes should target all RDM stakeholdres, not just researchers, as data management is a relatively new concept in the country.

The use of social media in promotional and advocacy initiatives cannot be over-emphasised. Social media tools provide an opportunity to reach out to a wider audience at a very low cost. There are several research tools and social media channels that can be utilized in raising RDM awareness amongst researchers. These include Researchgate, Academia.edu, Mendeley, LinkedIn, Facebook, YouTube and Twitter. Libraries in Zimbabwe have made commendable progress in the use of social media to promote their collections and they also act as an online noticeboard for announcements. Some researchers utilize platforms such as Researchgate and Academia.edu to disseminate their research findings. Librarians should maximize the opportunity to make use of these platforms to reach out to researchers.

Libraries need to provide support for the complete research cycle and to analyse what researchers require to manage their data, from creation or compilation to archive and preservation. In this context, many university libraries are seeking to enhance their support for research (Digital Curation Centre, 2016). Hence, they are rethinking the roles of their collection-based services, changing the roles of liaison librarians and developing new services for researchers including advice on scholarly communications and open access, bibliometrics services, research data management and library-led publishing services. RDM services can be embedded in the existing research support services currently being offered by libraries. There is commendable progress in research support services in academic libraries and henceforth, it should be easier to incorporate RDM in research methods courses and information literacy courses given their popularity in the research landscape.

CHALLENGES IN ESTABLISHING RDM SERVICES

Establishing a research data repository is a complex issue involving multiple activities carried out by various actors, addressing a range of drivers and influenced by a large number of factors (Pinfield et al., 2014). Given this complexity, establishing a research data service is bound to face some challenges that include, skills, costs, policies, infrastructure and sustainability. This section will provide a highlight of some of the challenges which are likely to be faced when setting up RDM services.

The success of RDM programmes partly depends on the skills and knowledge of the people involved. Henderson and Knott (2014) observe that the introduction and success of RDM services in academic libraries calls for the need to hire new staff or re-skilling and up skilling of librarians to take up new roles and responsibilities. Many librarians especially those who trained in Zimbabwe did not have any courses or formal training in data management because the subject was not covered in the Library and Information Science curriculum. A study by Nhendodzashe (2017) on the feasibility of offering RDM services at the University of Zimbabwe revealed that only a handful of librarians had knowledge of RDM. This lack of knowledge and skills presents a hurdle in the establishment of research data repositories in Zimbabwe. Interestingly, there is now a course in RDM offered as part of a graduate Library and Information Science programme at the National University of Science and Technology. In addition there are other free online RDM courses such as MANTRA and free reference material provided by the Digital Curation Centre.

The content of any research data repository obviously depends on the willingness of researchers to submit their data to the repository. Research has shown that there are mixed views from researchers regarding their willingness to submit research data to data repositories (Wilson et al., 2010; Buchhorn and McNamara 2010). Keil (2014) in a study of academic libraries' research data needs, taking the perspective of the faculty researchers revealed that sharing data can be particularly unnerving to scientists who may perceive a loss of a competitive edge for their next follow-up manuscript or grant proposal. Similarly, Kennan and Markauskaite (2015) conducted a study of RDM and the sharing practices of academics at ten universities in New South Wales, Australia. Researchers were asked whether, once they had collected their own data, they would be willing to share them outside of their research team or project. While more than half (54.7%) indicated that they would not be prepared to share any of their data, 36.4% indicated they would be prepared to share some of their data and 8.9% indicated that they would be prepared to share most of their data. On the same note, a study by Buchhornand and McNamara (2010) revealed that researchers are often reluctant to share their data. Data is viewed as a personal good, created by researchers and to be exploited by them. While many researchers feel data should be available to the research community there is a very strong and unanimous view that researchers should be able to exclusively exploit 'their' data for a period of time before it becomes available to others. In the South Africa, a study by Kennan and Markauskaite (2015) showed that the majority 73% of the researchers were willing to submit their research data to data repositories. It is discouraging to note that in institutions that have established institutional repositories, some researchers still resist submitting their research articles for archiving.

Another challenge regularly encountered in establishing a research data repository is metadata interoperability. Repositories often include metadata from a range of disciplines, each with different citation traditions and different emphases on the type of information they share (Chapman et al., 2009). Given the diversity of metadata origins, it may be difficult to enforce consistent use of metadata and entry of metadata values. Metadata can be sparse or lack important contextual information particularly when that context is held at a collection level. The breadth and depth of disciplines across an academic institution means that use of controlled subject terms is possible only at the highest levels.

The long term preservation of research data in a repository should be sustainable. A study by Chapman et al (2009) showed that responsibility for the long-term management of research data is ill-defined. This is a challenge especially for researchers who conduct research for different organisations because the responsibility for research data management will be scattered. Gold (2007) argues that it is fair to say there is still substantial uncertainty about the roles libraries can play in scientific data management, reflecting an environment of ongoing experimentation and negotiation. In addition to responsibilities, most institutions lack clear guidelines and policies that govern the operations of the data repository leading to a situation where obligations for data retention may not always be met and longer-term access may not be possible. In the Zimbabwean context, most institutions that have established institutional repositories are operating without policies which makes their operations difficult.

The establishment of a research data repository calls for a conduicive legal environment. Understanding the legal obligations around RDM is crucial as it guides the preservation and access of research data. Fitzgerald and Pappalardo (2007) assert that to achieve seamless access to data, it is necessary not only to adopt appropriate technical standards, practices and architecture but also to develop legal frameworks that facilitate access to and use of research data, whether on an inter-organisational basis or across national borders. The UK Data Archive (2015) emphasises that before embarking on a RDM project, it is imperative to know your legal, ethical and other obligations regarding research data, towards research participants, colleagues, research funders and institutions. RDM legal obligations broadly include intellectual property rights which encompass trademarks, design rights, patents and copyright. Trade secrets protect confidential business information.

Incurring costs when setting up a research data repository is inevitable. Hole et al. (2010) assert that predicting the costs of long-term digital collection, storage, preservation of and access to research data is a crucial yet complex task for even the largest repositories and institutions. Costs are incurred in acquiring hardware and software for the repository, hiring staff, staff training costs and costs associated with the maintenance of the repository. Most Zimbabwean institutions are hit by economic challenges to the extent that they are failing to recruit staff with the requisite skills to run data repositories. Additionally, foreign currency shortages is another stumbling block as some software programmes require import from other countries.

Davidson et al. (2014) assert that preserving research data for the long term has a cost; although the infrastructure itself is costly, more significant is the cost associated with human resources, such as personnel to manage and maintain the archive. Storage costs for digital data are decreasing, but costs related to storage, such as power, data curation and annotation and personnel, are not (Berman 2008 as cited by Strasser, 2014). Increasing amounts of digital data, and the need to comply with regulations regarding backup and monitoring, emphasise that these costs should not be underestimated or overlooked. Strasser (2014) posits that short-term costs for data preservation are primarily those related to storing data rather than archiving it. This may include software or hardware for backing up data or personnel costs for managing and organising data for storage. Longer-term preservation costs are associated with archives. Many repositories and archives use annual pricing schemes for a set amount of data; this situation is changing, however, to better meet the needs of researchers whose costs are intertwined with grant cycles.

Another challenge that is likely to be encountered in establishing a data repository is poor technological infrastructure; most importantly the ability to integrate the repository with existing systems. Most institutions in Zimbabwe rely on an outside vendor to update the programming of their IT systems, a costly approach and unsustainable given the financial challenges highlighted above. This is coupled by lack of institutional support especially if the project is not well-articulated and advocated for. In some institutions, the relationship of libraries with other departments is not good; this can be a result of the perceived role of the librarians in the research life cycle where librarians are not seen as partners. That negative attitude towards the librarians' role in RDM activities would mean that researchers would not look to the library for research support.

CONCLUSION, SOLUTIONS AND RECOMMENDATIONS

To counter the challenges highlighted in the preceding section, there is a need for training in data repositories. There should be training and mentorship programmes to upskill the people who will be responsible for RDM in research institutions and Zimbabwe can take advantage of the courses highlighted above, to create data experts. The use of free and open source software by organisations that plan to establish data repositories cannot be overruled; they help reduce set up and operational costs and software programmes such as Fedora, DSpace, DataVerse are freely available. There is also a need to develop clear guidelines for operational and administrative responsibilities for the data repository. Research institutions should establish strategic partnerships with other institutions that have well established data repositories. There is need to engage in fundraising activities for the setting up of data repositories. Research institutions should develop multidisciplinary metadata standards and address copyright policy which was noted by Terroir (2016) as being undeveloped, inefficient, expensive and unenforced.

The authors recommend that research institutions in Zimbabwe should develop an RDM workgroup to help establish and implement RDM policies and services. In the process, the workgroup should be able to match best practices with practical realities. The workgroup should engage and advocate for RDM both at institutional and national levels with stakeholder communities. At an institutional level, if it is a university, the working group can take advantage of established committees such as the senate, library committee, research board, faculty boards and research units such as the research office and library, to advocate for RDM services. At a national level, there are various government bodies that should be involved such as Universities, Research institutes, Scientific and Industrial Research and Development Centre (SIRDC), Research Council of Zimbabwe, Ministry of Higher and Tertiary Education Science and Technology Development, Ministry of ICT and Cyber Security, Ministry of Information, Media and Broadcasting Services and Zimbabwe Universities' Vice-Chancellors' Association.

During implementation, research institutions can start small by piloting one department and then continue collaborating with other departments whilst building capacity. When other researchers register strategic interest in managing their research data, they can be included thereby increasing the number of datasets in the repository. There is a need for capacity-building to skill the librarians and other stakeholders so that they are able to assist lecturers throughout the research data life cycle. Librarians can then support researchers and develop the expertise that is needed to deliver RDM services to the researchers. Shipman, Martin, Kaplan, and Albright (2018) emphasised the importance of training librarians.

Research institutions in Zimbabwe can build a community of practice for RDM, composed of researchers, institutions, and a network of RDM experts. Researchers would be from academic institutions, government and other research institutes. Institutions would provide liaison librarians, IT specialists, University research offices, ethics boards and other stakeholders. This would help to facilitate and provide leadership in the development of RDM infrastructure. Institutions should also develop their RDM policies and funding agencies should ensure that researchers who receive public funds should manage and share publicly their research data. Library schools should be actively involved in RDM services since they are responsible for the curriculum development of the programmes that are offered in colleges and universities; involving them would ensure that students are taught how to manage research data. There should be international collaboration both for training and infrastructure development. Research institutions in Zimbabwe should also register their presence on the registry of open data repositories when they establish research data repositories.

There are various strategic approaches that can be used to establish RDM services in Zimbabwe. RDM services can be established at institutional level or at national level or researchers can be encouraged to use well-established research data repositories, both subject specific or more general repositories. In Zimbabwe various stakeholders such as the Government, institutions of higher learning, research institutes, non-governmental organisations, funders and other boards should be involved in the establishment of RDM services. A working group should be formed to steer the process of establishing RDM services in Zimbabwe. It was noted that a number of challenges are encountered when working towards the development of RDM services. These include but are not limited to, lack of skills, lack of resources, poor ICT infrastructure and unwillingness of researchers to submit their research data for archiving. Consequently, there is also a need to develop capacity and advocate for the development of RDM services at every level to ensure that RDM is supported by all the stakeholders. A proposed framework consisting of strategies, policies, guidelines, processes, technologies and services should be followed when establishing RDM services in Zimbabwe.

FRAMEWORK FOR ESTABLISHING RDM SERVICES

The digital revolution has made it easier to store, share and re-use data, and scientific research data is almost universally created and collected in digital form. Data sharing increases the potential return on the large investments in research by reducing costly data duplication. But data sharing also requires data to be stored efficiently, maintained and preserved for re-use, discovered by secondary users and used with confidence in its authenticity and integrity; libraries and librarians need to align themselves with this fundamental change n their roles. Repositories are combinations of software and hardware that together provide a set of services that manage and disseminate digital works (Lynch, 2003; Jantz and Wilson, 2008) and in which authors are encouraged to deposit copies of their own work. The term commonly used for depositing ones' work is to 'self-archive' (Xia and Sun, 2007). Repositories come in two main types; institutional and disciplinary. There are many disciplinary repositories, some of which are very successful in covering, preserving and making accessible the literature of their discipline.

In an effort to come up with a viable framework for data repositories, there is need to borrow ideas from other frameworks that have been used and relate these to an institutions' current context or setting. Kennan (2011), in relation to an institutional repository program, identifies some components that can make up a tangible framework and these are shown in Figure 3.

Strategies

Research institutions in Zimbabwe must decide whether to develop institutional or national research data services. They have to define a vision for RDM within the institution and how it relates to the institutional mission and priorities so that it can work towards meeting the institution's long term strategy. There is a need to outline major developmental goals and principles which inform RDM activities both at institutional and national level. Research institutions must understand their current position and where they want to be so that they are in a position to define their strategy.

Figure 3. Proposed framework for research data management in Zimbabwe

Policies

There is a need to specify how those strategies are to be operationalised through regular procedures and how RDM would be incorporated into other policies such as open access and intellectual property. These policies should complement each other and cannot be considered in isolation. In Zimbabwe, research institutions deal with copyright issues in relation to the use of institutional repositories established in institutions of higher learning.

Guidelines

Detailed guidelines would outline how the policies will be implemented. These would be directed to a particular user group and would help to pin point the roles, responsibilities and activities that would be carried out by different stakeholders. The guidelines for institutional RDM services would be different from those of a national one.

Processes

There is a need to specify and regulate activities within the research data life-cycle including RDM planning for individual projects, data processing, ingesting data into central systems, selecting data for preservation and involving the use of standards and standardised procedures wherever possible. This can encompass the roles and responsibilities of the stakeholders involved in deciding on, setting up, maintaining and managing the research data repository as suggested by Flores, Brodeur, Daniels, Nicholls and Turnator, (2007). The processes would point out the steps that should be taken when establishing RDM services in Zimbabwe.

Technologies

Research institutions in Zimbabwe should ensure that there are functional data repositories and networking infrastructures to allow the storage and transport of data. A major consideration for all of those offering, or planning, a repository service is selecting an appropriate software platform. They should choose whether to use open source or proprietary software considering the cost implications.

Services

Research institutions should ensure that there is end-user access to systems and support for research data life-cycle activities. The activities of a research data service include supporting the creation of data management plans, providing skills training and delivering helpdesk services to encourage researchers to archive their research data. There is need to demonstrate the value of the research data repository to the research community. Flores et al (2007) mentions that it is one thing to have the support of senior administrators who can see the practical value of providing access to research outputs and research resources, but it is another to convince people to go through the necessary steps to ensure their materials are deposited.

FURTHER RESEARCH DIRECTIONS

A study could be carried out on the willingness of Zimbabwean researchers to archive their research data in data repositories. It was indicated that researchers are not at ease when they are asked to contribute their research data since it can be prone to abuse by other researchers.

REFERENCES

Adam, L. (2016). *Riding the National Research and Education Networking Train in Africa*. Retrieved from http://africanopenscience.org.za/wp-content/uploads/2018/01/AAURiding-the-NREN-Train-final-draft-.pdf

Brown, E. (2010). "I know what you researched last summer": How academic librarians are supporting researchers in the management of data curation. *The New Zealand Library & Information Management Journal, 52*(1), 55–69. Retrieved from http://www.lianza.org.nz/sites/lianza.org.nz/files/nzlimj_vol_52_issue_no_1_oct_2010.pdf

Buchhorn, M., & McNamara, P. (2006). *Sustainability Issues for Australian Research Data. The Report of the Australian e-Research Sustainability Survey Project*. Retrieved from http://www.apsr.edu.au

Chapman, J. W., Reynolds, D., & Shreeves, A. (2009). Repository metadata: Approaches and challenges. *Cataloging & Classification Quarterly, 47*(3-4), 309–325. doi:10.1080/01639370902735020

Chigwada, J., Chiparausha, B., & Kasiroori, J. (2017). Research Data Management in research institutions in Zimbabwe. *Data Science Journal, 16*(0), 31. doi:10.5334/dsj-2017-031

Chiware, E., & Becker, D. A. (2018). Research Data Management services in Southern Africa: A readiness survey of academic and research Libraries. *African Journal of Library Archives and Information Science, 28*(1), 1–16.

Conrad, S., Shorish, Y., Whitmire, A. L., & Hswe, P. (2017). Building professional development opportunities in data services for academic librarians. *IFLA Journal, 43*(1), 65–80. doi:10.1177/0340035216678237

Corrall, S., Keenan, M. A., & Afzal, W. (2013). Bibliometrics and research data management services: Emerging trends in library support for research. *Library Trends, 61*(3), 636–674. doi:10.1353/lib.2013.0005

Cox, A. M., & Pinfield, S. (2014). Research Data Management and libraries: current activities and future priorities. *Journal of Librarianship and Information Science*. Retrieved from http://lis.sagepub.com/cgi/doi/10.1177/0961000613492542

Cox, A. N., & Verbaan, E. (2016). How academic librarians, IT staff and research administrators perceive and relate to research. *Library & Information Science Research, 38*(4), 319–326. doi:10.1016/j.lisr.2016.11.004

Creamer, A., Morales, M. E., Crespo, J., Kafel, D., & Martin, E. R. (2012). An assessment of needed competencies to promote the data curation and management librarianship of health sciences and science and technology librarians in New England. *Journal of Escience Librarianship, 1*(1), 18–26. doi:10.7191/jeslib.2012.1006

Davidson, J. (2015). *Developing an organisational profile for research data management services - a guide for HEIs*. Edinburgh, UK: Digital Curation Centre. Retrieved from http://www.dcc.ac.uk/projects/opd-for-rdm

Davidson, J., Jones, S., Molloy, L., & Kejser, U. B. (2014). Emerging good practice in managing research data and research information within UK Universities. *Procedia Computer Science, 33*, 215–222. doi:10.1016/j.procs.2014.06.035

Digital Curation Centre. (2016). *Data lifecycle model*. Retrieved from http://www.dcc.ac.uk/resources/curation-lifecycle-model

Fitzgerald, A., & Pappalardo, K. (2007). *Building the infrastructure for data access and reuse in collaborative research: an analysis of the legal context*. Retrieved from http://eprints.qut.edu.au/8865/1/8865.pdf

Flores, J. R., Brodeur, J. J., Daniels, M. G., Nicholls, N., & Turnator, E. (2007). *Libraries and the Research Data Management landscape.* Retrieved from https://www.clir.org/wp-content/uploads/sites/9/RDM.pdf

Goben, A., & Nelson, M. S. (2018). Teaching librarians about data: The ACRL Research Data Management RoadShow. *College & Research Libraries News*, *79*(7), 354. doi:10.5860/crln.79.7.354

Gold, A. K. (2007). Cyber infrastructure, data, and libraries, Part 1: A cyber infrastructure primer for librarians. *D-Lib Magazine*, *13*(9/10). Retrieved from http://digitalcommons.calpoly.edu/cgi/viewcontent.cgi?article=1015&context=lib_dean

Henderson, M. E., & Knott, T. L. (2015). Starting a Research Data Management program based in a University Library. *Medical Reference Services Quarterly*, *34*(1), 47–59. doi:10.1080/02763869.2015.986783

Henty, M. (2007). Ten major issues in providing a repository service in Australian Universities. *D-Lib Magazine*, *13*(5/6). doi:10.1045/may2007-henty

Hey, T., & Hey, J. (2006). E-science and its implications for the library community. *Library Hi Tech*, *24*(4), 515–528. doi:10.1108/07378830610715383

Hole, B., Lin, L., McCann, P., & Wheatley, P. (2010). LIFE3: A Predictive costing tool for digital collections. *New Review of Information Networking*, *15*(2), 81–93. doi:10.1080/13614576.2010.526014

Ingram, C. (2016). *How and why you should manage your research data: a guide for researchers.* Retrieved from https://www.jisc.ac.uk/guides/how-and-why-you-should-manage-your-research-data

Jantz, R. C., & Wilson, M. C. (2008). Institutional repositories: Faculty deposits, marketing, and the reform of scholarly communication. *Journal of Academic Librarianship*, *34*(3), 186–195. doi:10.1016/j.acalib.2008.03.014

Jones, S., Pryor, G., & Whyte, A. (2013). *'How to Develop Research Data Management Services - a guide for HEIs'. DCC How-to Guides*. Edinburgh, UK: Digital Curation Centre. Retrieved from http://www.dcc.ac.uk/resources/how-guides

Keil, D. E. (2014). Research data needs from academic libraries: The perspective of a faculty researcher. *Journal of Library Administration*, *54*(3), 233–240. doi:10.1080/01930826.2014.915168

Kennan, M. A. (2011). Learning to share: Mandates and open access. *Library Management*, *32*(4/5), 302–318. doi:10.1108/01435121111132301

Kennan, M. A., & Markauskaite, L. (2015). Research data management practices: A snapshot in time. *International Journal of Digital Curation, 10*(2), 69–95. doi:10.2218/ijdc.v10i2.329

Latham, B. (2017). Research Data Management: Defining roles, prioritizing services, and enumerating challenges. *Journal of Academic Librarianship, 43*(3), 263–265. doi:10.1016/j.acalib.2017.04.004

Lynch, C. A. (2003). Institutional repositories: Essential infrastructure for scholarship in the digital age. *Portal (Baltimore, MD), 3*, 327.

Nitecki, D. A., & Davis, M. E. (2017). *Expanding Librarians' roles in the research life cycle*. IFLAWLIC Satellite Meeting. Retrieved from http://library.ifla.org/1798/1/S06-2017-nitecki-en.pdf

Peters, C., & Dryden, A. R. (2011). Assessing the academic library's role in campus-wide research data management: A first step at the University of Houston. *Science & Technology Libraries, 30*(4), 387–403. doi:10.1080/0194262X.2011.626340

Peters, D., & Hahnel, M. (2017). *A National Research Data Management strategy for South African Universities*. Retrieved from https://conference.eresearch.edu.au/2017/08/a-national-research-data-management-strategy-for-south-african-universities/

Pinfield, S., Cox, A. M., & Smith, J. (2014). Research Data Management and libraries: Relationships, activities, drivers and influences. *PLoS One, 9*(12), e114734. doi:10.1371/journal.pone.0114734 PMID:25485539

Rieh, S. Y., Markey, K., Jean, B., Yakel, E., & Kim, J. (2007). Census of institutional repositories in the U.S.: a comparison across institutions at different stages of IR development. *D-Lib Magazine, 13*(11/12). Retrieved from http://www.dlib.org/dlib/november07/rieh/11rieh.html

Shen, Y., & Varvel, V. E. Jr. (2013). Developing data management services at the Johns Hopkins University. *Journal of Academic Librarianship, 39*(6), 552–557. doi:10.1016/j.acalib.2013.06.002

Shipman, J., Martin, E., Kaplan, R., & Albright, E. (2018). *Exploring the need for a research data management librarian academy*. Retrieved from https://libraryconnect.elsevier.com/articles/exploring-need-research-data-management-librarian-academy

Smith, I., & Veldsman, S. (2018). Data driving sustainability: the African Open Science Platform Project. *ELPUB 2018*. Retrieved from https://elpub.episciences.org/4610/pdf

Sompel, H. V. D., Payette, S., Erickson, J., Lagoze, C., & Warner, S. (2004). Rethinking scholarly communication: Building the system that scholars deserve. *D-Lib Magazine*, *10*(9). Retrieved from http://dlib.org/dlib/september04/vandesompel/09vandesompel.html

Strasser, C. A. (2014). *Data Management for Libraries: A LITA guide*. Chicago, IL: ALA TechSource.

Swan, A., & Brown, S. (2008). *The Skills, Role and Career Structure of Data Scientists and Curators: An Assessment of Current Practice and Future Needs.* Truro: Key Perspectives. Retrieved from http://www.jisc.ac.uk/publications/documents/dataskillscareersfinalreport.aspx

Tenopier, C., Sandusky, R. J., Allard, S., & Birch, B. (2014). Research Data Management services in academic research libraries and perceptions of librarians. *Library & Information Science Research*, *36*(2), 84–90. doi:10.1016/j.lisr.2013.11.003

Tenopir, C., Birch, B., & Allard, S. (2012). Academic libraries and research data services: current practices and plans for the future. *Association of College and Research Libraries.* Retrieved from http://www.ala.org/acrl/sites/ala.org.acrl/files/content/publications/whitepapers/Tenopir_Birch_Allard.pdf

Tenopir, C., Sandusky, R. J., Allard, S., & Birch, B. (2013). Academic librarians and research data services: Preparation and attitudes. *IFLA Journal*, *39*(1), 70–78. doi:10.1177/0340035212473089

UK Data Archive. (2015). *Create and manage data: research data lifecycle.* Retrieved from http://www.data-archive.ac.uk/create-manage/life-cycle

Uzwyshyn, R. (2016). Research data repositories: The what, when, why, and how. *Computers in libraries*, *36*(3). Retrieved from http://www.infotoday.com/cilmag/apr16/Uzwyshyn--Research-Data-Repositories.shtml

Whyte, A., & Tedds, J. (2011). *Making the case for Research Data Management. DCC Briefing Papers*. Edinburgh, UK: Digital Curation Centre. Retrieved from http://www.dcc.ac.uk/resources/briefing-papers

Whyte, A., & Wilson, A. (2010). *How to appraise and select research data for curation. DCC How-to Guides*. Edinburgh, UK: Digital Curation Centre. Retrieved from http://www.dcc.ac.uk/resources/how-guides

Wilson, J. A., Fraser, M. A., Martinez-Uribe, L., Jeffreys, P., Patrick, M., Akram, A., & Mansoori, T. (2010). *Developing infrastructure for Research Data Management at the University of Oxford.* Retrieved from http://www.ariadne.ac.uk/issue65/wilson-et-al

Xia, J., & Sun, L. (2007). Factors to assess self-archiving in institutional repositories. *Serials Review*, *33*(2), 73–80. doi:10.1080/00987913.2007.10765100

KEY TERMS AND DEFINITIONS

Community of Practice: An informal, self-organized, network of peers with diverse skills and experience in an area of practice or profession. Such groups are held together by the members' desire to help others by sharing information and the need to advance their own knowledge by learning from others.

Data Librarian: Data librarians are professional library staff engaged in managing research data, using research data as a resource or supporting researchers dealing with data. They equip participants with the necessary knowledge to develop and implement services for research data management.

Research Data Management: Covers the planning, collecting, organising, managing, storage, security, back-up, preservation and sharing data. It ensures that research data are managed according to legal, statutory, ethical and funding body requirements.

Research Data Repository: A database infrastructure that is set up to manage, share, access and archive researchers' datasets.

Workgroup: Two or more individuals who routinely function like a team and are interdependent in achievement of a common goal.

Chapter 3
Research Information Management Systems:
A Comparative Study

Manu T. R.
Central University of Gujarat, India & Adani Institute of Infrastructure Management, India

Minaxi Parmar
Central University of Gujarat, India

Shashikumara A. A.
Dhirubhai Ambani Institute of Information and Communication Technology, India & Central University of Gujarat, India

Viral Asjola
Indian Institute of Technology Gandhinagar, India

ABSTRACT

Research information management systems (RIMS) are the emerging new service in academic and research libraries. RIMS support universities and libraries in managing their institute, faculty, and researcher information through a single interface. They also allow the researcher to deposit and share their research with the public and enable the reuse of that research. An implementation of RIMS in universities or libraries ensures the proper management of research information for future use. RIMS disseminates research information and publications and supports data, academic, and administrative work by faculty and researchers. Traditionally, an institutional repository, digital library, and research data management software were used to manage research information as part of an institutional repository, but these applications have failed to manage more specialist researcher information and more detailed faculty profiles, etc. Consequently, various specialist software companies have brought RIMS onto the market with applications and products that meet the requirements of individual researchers, libraries, and universities in the management of research information. This chapter provides a comparative evaluation of RIMS (i.e., PURE-Elsevier, Converis-Thomson Routers, and Symplectic

DOI: 10.4018/978-1-5225-8437-7.ch003

Elements). This study contributes towards an understanding of RIMS and assists with the selection of the appropriate software application for implementation of a RIMS system in universities and libraries.

INTRODUCTION

Research Information Management Systems (RIMS) are the platforms or database systems hosting research information, faculty and researcher profiles. A RIMS is an integrated system of research information, research outputs, grants, research funds and research support. Research information may be research outputs, patents, grants and projects, impact statements, media reports, activities, services, awards, instructional history and researcher affiliations. The researcher has a very little scope when their research data is made openly available alongside their research publication and it is very important to factor in accountability and transparency when the data is deposited in a data repository. Information management is a key part of the research process and good practice in managing research data will allow that data to meet funding and regulatory body requirements, avoid duplication of effort in reproducing the data; research data thereby keeps its integrity and it remains accurate, authentic and reliable. Individual researchers can also exploit the value of RIMS to manage their research outputs, to showcase and publicize their research more effectively, to share publications with others and to partner and collaborate on further research more effectively.

RIMS provide the central repository for information relating to an institution's faculty, researchers and their research activities. It provides the solution for the many requirements of academic and research universities and is efficient and effective in widening the dissemination of the research activities. RIMS connects faculty research with related funding opportunities, identifies subject experts for grants, research collaboration and campus communications. Common standards are used by RIMS: *Common European Research Information Format (CERIF)* and *Consortia Advancing Standards in Research Administration Information (CASRAI)* standards supports the interoperability of RIMS while AGROVOC, GEMET, LCSH, UMLS etc. are used to describe the subject keywords; ORCID, Altmetric, Snowball Metrics and Thomson Reuters Research Analytics standards are available for research analysis and metrics.

The major common features supported by RIMS are: researcher profiles and curriculum vitaes; a web interface with external data sources; discovery and search facilities; integration with author and researcher identifiers; faculty and researcher connection and collaboration; bibliography import and export; an integrated or linked institutional repository; impact analysis tools; reporting and dashboard facilities;

online guides and user manual of RIMS software; current version details of the system; authentication and system administration etc. *OCLC Research* (OCLCResearch, 2014) and UNESCO (Bankier, Gleason, & UNESCO, 2014).

LITERATURE REVIEW

A review of the literature points to several previous studies on the comparative evaluation of research data management (RDM) platforms and research publication and data repositories. For example, there are a number of case studies on the comparison, critical evaluation, features, advantages and disadvantages of using various research data repositories to store, archive and share research data with other researchers. Most of these studies focus on the comparison and critical analysis of open source data repositories and software such as DataVerse, CKAN, Digital commons, Dspace, ePrints, EUDAT, Fedora, Figshare, Greenstone, Invenio, Omeka, SciFLOW and Zenodo.

Clements, A., and McCutcheon, V. (2014), carried out case studies on the implementation of a RIMS at two universities in the UK. The University of St Andrews and University of Glasgow worked over several years to implement and develop their RIMS using the Pure CERIF-CRIS and EPrints software. The authors explain the strategies and systems they used and the issues that arose during the implementation process. Austin, C. et al., (2015) surveyed 32 online research data and data sharing platforms to provide a broad overview of the current features of data repositories and data sharing platforms. The authors studied selected research data platforms comparing data criteria and functionality such as cloud services, free to access, download data, and deposit data, publishing charges, the size of the repository, integration with ORCID ID, Scopus ID etc.

Amorim, R.C. et al., (2016) conducted a comparative study of various research data management (RDM) platforms, i.e. *DSpace, CKAN, Figshare, Zenodo, ePrints and EUDAT.* The platforms are compared in respect of their system architecture, metadata support, user interfaces and programming languages, search mechanisms and community acceptance around the world. Mahato, S.S. and Gajbe, S.B. (2018) produced a comparative study of two open sources of data repository software, Dataverse and CKAN. Pampel, H., et al., (2013) carried out a case study of re3data.org. The *Registry of Research Data Repositories* provides detailed information about data repositories and offers the service to the institutes, researchers, funding organizations, libraries and publishers etc. There were 400 research data repositories indexed in 2013; there are now more than 2000.

Witt, M. (2012) examined the research data repository infrastructure of the University of Purdue libraries which interconnected with multiple repositories containing different types of content, workflow, organizational units and system. Jacobs, N., Thomas, A. and Mcgregor, A. (2008) described the key areas of activities at the institutional and national levels initiatives in the UK to make efficient networked repositories that supported faculty research and showcased the contribution of JISC-funded projects. The authors highlight that JISC had been encouraged to fund new projects in the UK, by the creation of several repositories such as EThOS (http://www.ethos.ac.uk/), JorumOpen (http://www.jorum.ac.uk/) and Depot (http://depot.edina.ac.uk/) etc. Moreover, JISC funds supported work on scoping the university sector's needs regarding curation of research data and developing strategies for managing research data effectively. In a case study in 2015, Meyer, D. (2015) explored the possibility of using the open source DSpace repository as a RIMS in the South African National Research Foundation. 14 participants from the DSpace community completed a survey and the results found that using DSpace as a RIMS was both feasible and would be useful to the DSpace community. The author states that DSpace software can be developed to act more like a RIMS, by first identifying the features that Dspace has and then providing add-ons to transform the DSpace from an institutional repository into a RIMS software tool. Feldman, Craig and Meyer, Darryl (2015) described the process for the migration of two projects funded by the National Research Foundation (NRF), to the DSpace digital repository system converted to a RIMS; with a customized user interface, a converted DSpace successfully met the requirements of the NRF.

This literature review has found that most of the studies are concerned with the comparison and critical evaluation of research data repositories, software and platforms among open source repositories. Thus there is an apparent gap in the range of comparative and critical evaluation studies, with few making particular reference to RIMS.

OBJECTIVES OF THE STUDY

- To study and analyse the uses, benefits, standards and characteristic features of RIMS;
- To recognize individual RIMS capabilities, including the specific characteristics of RIM modules;
- To conduct a comparative study of PURE, Converis and Symplectic Elements;
- To suggest the significant features of RIMS that can help identify the most suitable RIMS for implementation in specific circumstances.

SCOPE AND LIMITATION OF THE STUDY

In the literature reviewed above, the researcher found that most of the studies used critical evaluation, comparative studies and case studies to survey the best practices of RDM repositories while studies of RIMS implementation focused on open source software and freely available platforms. Research studies have concentrated on assessing the features of Dataverse and CKAN, DSpace, Figshare, Zenodo, ePrints, EUDAT, re3data.org etc. software. There are hardly any studies concerning proprietary data repository software and RIMS, and it is clear that there is a gap in research focusing on the critical evaluation of RIMS and comparative studies of proprietary RIMS software. Consequently, the researcher has undertaken research to compare and critically evaluate RIMS and proprietary RIMS software, i.e. *PURE-Elsevier, Converis- Thomson Routers and Symplectic Elements.*

METHODOLOGY

The purpose of this chapter is to critically evaluate the software available for implementing RIMS, and thus requires a study of the selected research RIMS proprietary platforms. In the literature review, the researcher found a variety of institutional repository software, digital library software, institutional archive software and collection management systems widely considered for the implementation of RDM repositories. Digital commons, ContentDM, DSpace, ePrints, Fedora, Greenstone, Omeka etc. software were often used, alongside open source and proprietary software specifically intended for research data and information management. This study considers PURE, Converis and Symplectic Elements looking at their fundamental features such as content organization and control, content discovery, publication tools, reporting, multimedia supports, social functions and notifications, installation, hosting and customer support options, accessibility, preservation and data security etc.

A web survey took place to evaluate the RIMS based on different criteria used for evaluating data repositories and the minimum features the RIMS has. The study testesd whether requirements are satisfied by the selected RIMS or not, and the results have been presented in the form of Yes (satisfying) and No (not satisfying). The study also considered the literature, cases studies and implementation practices for the selected software to determine impact.

THE CASE OF THREE RIMS SOFTWARE TOOLS

The authors have selected the three commercial software tools for comparison and offer a critical evaluation of their features and support.

CONVERIS[1]

Converis is a research information management and research analytics tools developed by Thomson Reuters. Converis allow universities to manage research outputs and the entire research lifecycle including funding opportunities, grant applications, ethical approval, research projects and publications. It can be integrated with any other inbuilt internal and external systems and with University practices and standards. Converis has a strong internet security system for research information management and provides web tools to allow the extraction of publication data from the scholarly databases such as *Web of Science, Scopus, PubMed* and *DNB*.

SYMPLECTIC ELEMENTS[2]

Symplectic Elements is a single point research information management system developed by the Symplectic Lt. It helps to collect and manage information about a research project and to re-purpose and re-use that information, to make it more valuable to the institution and other researchers. Users can easily identify faculty, researchers and authors and can seek corrections of their research through internal HR and research management services data sources. Symplectic Elements integrates with other institutional systems including digital repositories, HR systems, finance systems and other applications, to reduce the administrative burden of manually re-entering information into each system. An automated facility captures research information from multiple external and internal sources and from scholarly databases.

PURE[3]

PURE is a research information management system developed by the Elsevier. PURE allows the building of a researcher's profile and website including a CV, researcher reports, expertise identification and performance assessments and manages the funding discovery process by showcasing the researcher's achievements. Pure connects multiple forms of data and captures data from citation and bibliographical databases (*Scopus, PubMed, Embase, CAB Abstracts, Web of Science),* reference management (*Mendeley*), union catalogue (*WorldCat*, preprint archives (*arXiv, SAO/ NASA Astrophysics Data System*), journal TOC and CrossRef Repository.

COMPARISON OF RIMS SOFTWARE

The following criteria are some of those that have been used to evaluate and compare the features of the three RIMS. The criteria have been selected, based on the general features, facilities and support that a RIMS should have. This section gives a general idea of the benefits of RIMS to individual researchers and to institutions preparing to implement a RIMS at the institutional level.

Researcher Profile and Research

The main objective of a RIMS is to showcase researcher profiles and their research to public from a single point. Researcher profiles disseminate the research to the wide community and create impact. RIMS facilitate the creation of researcher profiles including a researcher's CV, education, research interests, working professional experience, research publication details etc. Through a RIMS, the researcher can promote their webpage which helps to disseminate knowledge of their research to users and funding organizations. The different researcher profile creation functions available can be seen in Table 1.

Table 1 show that different functions available to researchers to enable them to create a profile and add their publications, research interest and a full CV. Converis, Symplectic Elements and PURE all have the facility to generate a researcher profile as a personal webpage, but Converis & Symplectic Elements have an additional facility that integrates with their institute HR system. This helps HR to obtain an updated researcher profile for annual performance assessment. PURE enables the universities to build analytics reports and carry out performance assessments through the researcher profiles.

Web Interface with External Data Sources

Data acquisition and collection are essential tasks for a RIMS, core to managing an institution's research information in a single system; obtaining research data

Table 1. Creation of researcher profiles and CV

Sr. No.	Functions	Converis	Symplectic Elements	PURE
1	CV creation and sharing	Yes	Yes	Yes
2	Personal webpage	Yes	Yes	Yes
3	Publication list	Yes	Yes	Yes
4	Integration with HR System	Yes	Yes	-

from each researcher would be a difficult task. A RIMS system has an interface with external data sources, search engines, citation and bibliographical database, pre-print servers, etc, This facilitates the import of research information directly through web interfaces into the RIMS. The different external data sources available, can be seen in Table 2.

Table 2, explains RIMS web integration with other bibliographical and citation databases, search engines, catalogs and other scholarly profiles where RIMS can directly fetch researcher information into their system, reducing manual data entry time for the administrator. All RIMS have integrated with ORCID, Scopus, Web of

Table 2. Web interface with external data sources

Sr. No.	Data Sources	Converis	Symplectic Elements	PURE
1	arXiv	-	Yes	Yes
2	CAB Abstracts	-	-	Yes
3	CiNii	-	Yes	-
4	CrossRef	Yes	Yes	Yes
5	DBLP	-	Yes	-
6	Dimensions	-	Yes	-
7	Embase.com	-	-	Yes
8	Europe PubMed Central	-	Yes	-
9	Figshare	-	Yes	-
10	Google Books	-	Yes	-
11	Journal TOC	-	-	Yes
12	MathSciNet	-	Yes	-
13	Mendeley	Yes	-	Yes
14	MLA Bibliography	-	Yes	-
15	MS Academic Search,	Yes	-	
16	ORCID	Yes	Yes	Yes
17	PubMed	Yes	Yes	Yes
18	RePEc	-	Yes	-
19	SAO/NASA Astrophysics Data System	-	-	Yes
20	Scopus	Yes	Yes	Yes
21	Sharpa	-	Yes	-
22	SSRN	-	Yes	-
23	Web of Science	Yes	Yes	Yes
24	WorldCat	-	-	Yes

Science and PubMed. Symplectic Elements has combined with the most external sources and databases followed by the PURE and Converis.

Discovery and Search Facilities

A further aim of a RIMS is to enable the easy retrieval of research content by the user and the discovery of that research content at as wide a level as possible. Providing flexibility in the searching, filtering, and discovery of research content, through discovery search engines and search features like advanced search, full-text search, browsing facilities, are essential characteristics of a RIMS. The different content discovery and search facilities available can be seen in Table 3.

Table 3 illustrates the content features available in the RIMS; all RIMS have search engines and single search discovery tools which through a reader can search and find information about researchers. Advanced search and full-text search facilities are available but Symplectic Elements does not index the full record; users can search bibliographical details only.

Integration with Author and Researcher Identifiers

A unique author identifier connects the researcher with their complete list of research publications alongside details of educational, history of the affiliation, institutional and biographical information etc. Standardized unique author identifiers are widely used by the academic institutions, universities, research organizations, publishers, institutional digital repositories, funding agencies, etc. Some publishers such as Thomson Reuters (Web of Science), Elsevier (Scopus) and ORCID have started assigning a single identifier to their researcher profile and to their research. RIMS

Table 3. Discovery and search facilities

Sr. No.	Discovery	Converis	Symplectic Elements	PURE
1	Integrated search engine	Yes	Yes	Yes (with Elsevier Fingerprint Engine)
2	Advanced search facilities	Yes	Yes	Yes
3	Full-Text search indexing	Yes	Not full text records indexed	Yes
4	Browse options	Yes	Yes	Yes
5	Discovery tool	Yes	Yes	Yes (Pure hosted edition)

have also integrated with other systems that manage researcher information. The different integrations that are available for author and researcher identifiers can be seen in Table 4.

Table 4 shows that all three selected RIMS has provided researcher ID, ORCID and Persistent/Handle URLs and Scopus ID integration with the exception of Converis RIMS; as Converis is more integrated with *Web of Science* databases, it uses their proprietary researcher identifier. Author and research identifiers help to identify the author, resolving name ambiguity while a persistent/handle URL provides the unique identifier/URL for each researcher's records as well as for their researcher profile.

Research Connection and Collaboration

An interesting feature of a RIMS is that one particular researcher profile and their research data can be validated by other subject experts across the institutions. This helps a researcher to establish a research network and collaborate with others carrying out similar research. The various connection and collaboration facilities available can be observed in Table 5.

Table 5 shows where a RIMS has the functionality to enable a researcher to network and collaborate with other researchers with similar interests and to seek funding opportunities related to their research interest. The table shows that Converis,

Table 4. Integration with author and researcher identifiers

Sr. No.	Researcher Identifiers	Converis	Symplectic Elements	PURE
1	Researcher ID	Yes	Yes	Yes
2	ORCID	Yes	Yes	Yes
3	Scopus ID	-	Yes	Yes
4	Persistent/Handle URLs	Yes	Yes	Yes

Table 5. Connect and collaboration

Sr. No.	Research Connection & Collaboration	Converis	Symplectic Elements	PURE
1	Identify subject experts	Yes	Yes	Yes
2	Expertise across institutions	Yes	Yes	Yes (SciVal & DIRECT2Experts connects)
3	Track funding opportunities	Yes	Yes	Yes (over 20,000 active grants)

Symplectic Elements and PURE all allow the researcher to identify subject experts and expertise across an institution and to track funding opportunities for their research. A worthy feature of these RIMS is finding relevant funding organization around the world; with this facility, researchers gets to know the funding organizations that are willing to fund projects related to their research.

Bibliography and Reference Management Systems

A RIMS system interfaces through various programming languages with bibliographic databases, to enable the import of research information in other citation formats such as BibTeX, RIS. Bibliographic data can also be retrieved from reference management systems such as RefWorks, EndNote, Reference Manager, Mendeley and Incites. A RIMS also provides bibliographic export facilities through reference management software in various citation styles. The different bibliography and reference management system integration facilities available can be seen in Table 6.

Table 6 describes the facilities available for importing and exporting bibliographic data through various reference management software, tools and search engines such as Ref work, Endnote, RIS, Mendeley, Incites, Reference Manager and others. Endnote and BibTex file format also support all three RIMS. These tools and facilities help researchers to obtain citations from researcher profiles.

Connecting to Institutional Repositories

As many institutions have associated their institutional repositories with a research management system, they have been using institutional repository software such as Dspace, ePrints, Fedora, etc. to manage research information through a single system. Some institutions have made use of VIVO, a graphical research presentation

Table 6. Bibliography import and export

Sr. No.	Software/Tools	Converis	Symplectic Elements	PURE
1	RefWorks	-	-	Yes
2	EndNote	Yes	Yes	Yes
3	BibTex	Yes	Yes	Yes
4	RIS (Reference Information System)	-	Yes	-
5	Reference Manager	Yes	Yes	-
6	Google Scholar	-	Yes	-
7	Mendeley	-	Yes	Yes
8	InCites	Yes	-	-

and networking analysis software and Figshare, an online digital repository to preserve research information. Some RIMS have established connections with major repository software and the principle institutional repository tools integration can be viewed in Table 7.

The institutional repository software listed here is open access and provides an excellent infrastructure to manage research information. Table 7 outlines the facilities, that our selected RIMS provide, to connect to institutional repositories built through DSpace, ePrints, Fedora, VIVO and Figshare. Symplectic Elements only provides the facility for an institutional repository to connect with VIVO and Figshare.

Research Impact Analysis

Another significant advantage of a RIM system is its ability to present research impact analysis data on the researcher's profile. A RIMS ranks the researcher by the total number of publications, citations, *h*-index and their visibility through social media, etc. Some of RIMS integrate with Altmetrics which measure the impact of research articles through their online attention; bibliometrics indicators include the number of citations, self-citation, *h*-index, multiple author articles etc. The different impact analysis tools available can be seen in Table 8.

Table 8 presents the RIMS features that help to researchers and administrators to analyse their research impact through Altmetrics and bibliometrics indicators including citation, *h*-index and other tools for ranking the research. Bibliometrics

Table 7. Connect to the institutional repositories

Sr. No.	Institutional Repositories	Converis	Symplectic Elements	PURE
1	DSpace	Yes	Yes	Yes
2	ePrints	Yes	Yes	Yes
3	Fedora	Yes	Yes	Yes
4	Figshare for Institutions	-	Yes	-
5	VIVO	-	Yes	-

Table 8. Impact analysis tools

Sr. No.	Analysis Tools	Converis	Symplectic Elements	PURE
1	Altmetrics	-	Yes	Yes
2	Bibliometrics indicators	Yes	Yes	Yes
3	Research ranking	Yes	Yes	Yes

indicators and the ranking of research are features common to all RIMS, but Symplectic Elements and PURE provide the Altmetrics integration to enable the evaluation of research impact over social networking and online attention.

Reporting and Dashboard

Flexible dashboard and multiple report options contribute towards a full assessment of the most appropriate RIMS for an institution. An attractive dashboard presents statistics relating to research information and research reports help to significantly reduce administrative time for both faculty and research administrative staff in maintaining researcher profiles. RIM systems have significant roles to play in the generation of accurate statistics from the available data using various statistical data analysis tools. The different reporting facilities available can be seen in Table 9.

Table 9 presents RIMS reporting and dashboard facilities where researchers can view and browse statistics and reports generated by the RIMS. The administrator will also have the full credentials to download all types of reports in XML, Excel, HTML and PDF etc. Symplectic Elements has an additional separate reporting tool database which helps to download a multiple number of reports using reporting tools.

Online Support

A RIM system will usually provide online support for institutions, researchers and librarians to implement and maintain the RIM system database easily and effectively. Online guides help the researcher to create awareness of the features and facilities available in a RIMS. Different types of online support ware provided with users rights, navigation, workflow and a user manual. The various online guides and user manuals available can be seen in Table 10.

Table 9. Reporting and dashboard facilities

Sr. No.	Reporting and Dashboard Facilities	Converis	Symplectic Elements	PURE
1	Dashboard	Yes	Yes	Yes
2	Data export MS Excel (CERIF)XML)	Yes	Yes	Yes
3	Network reports	Yes	-	Yes
4	Standard reports per module*	Yes	-	-
5	HTML files	-	-	Yes
6	Adobe® PDF	-	Yes	Yes
7	Reporting tools database	-	Yes	-

Table 10. Online guides and user manual of RIMS software

Sr. No.	Online Supports	Converis	Symplectic Elements	PURE
1	User Rights	Yes	Yes	Yes
2	Navigation & data quality	Yes	Yes	Yes
3	Online help	Yes	Yes	Yes
4	Workflows	Yes	Yes	Yes
5	User Manual	Yes	Yes	Yes

Table 10 shows the online support, user and administrator guidelines, workflows, user navigation and rights facilities, etc. Since the selected RIMS are commercial products, they all provide end-user services including training for administrator and research staff.

Regular Updating

Software capabilities of RIMS are built on regular updates with the latest technologies and facilities. Supporting software and hardware also require regular updating to maintain security and functionality. The current versions available are illustrated in Table 11.

Table 11 shows the latest version and regular update status of the selected RIMS; all systems have been updated regularly with additional features and latest technology.

Technologies of RIM System

As the popularity of RIMS has increased so too have their technological requirements, developed; the latest technologies, architecture and applications are now required to establish a RIMS. As a Software as a Service (SaaS), RIMS have the stability to host applications under any platform with minimum requirements. RIM systems have a strong technological architecture including database support, programming languages, data backup, web servers, application interfaces, search engines. RIMS

Table 11. Current version details of RIM system

Sr. No.	Version Details	Converis	Symplectic Elements	PURE
1	Version update	Yes	Yes	Yes
2	Latest version release	-	December 2017	October 5, 2017
3	Latest version number	6.0	5.9	5.10

are browser agnostic with standards to make for a stable and robust institutional RIMS. The different technological features available can be seen in Table 12.

Table 12 explains the technical proposition of selected RIMS. All three RIMS have stable core architectures built using Java and PHP programming languages;

Table 12. Technologies of RIMS software

Sr. No.	Areas	Converis	Symplectic Elements	PURE
1	Core architecture	Java EE	JDK	JDK
2	Programming language	Java 5	Java & c++	Java/PHP
3	Database engine	PostgreSQL or Oracle	Oracle JDK	Oracle
4	Application server	GlassFish v2	-	-
5	Reporting engine	XSL / FOP	XSL	XSL
6	Web interface	JSF RI 1.2, Rich Faces, Ajax4JSF	-	-
7	Web Server	Apache	Apache	Apache
8	XML	Xquare	XSLT	
9	Utilities	PD4ML for PDF generation	PDF generation	PDF generation
10	Data access	TopLink	-	-
11	Operating System	Linux	Linux	Linux
12	Application Interface	API	API	API
13	Browser support	Google Chrome, Mozilla Firefox, Internet Explorer, Safari	Google Chrome, Mozilla Firefox & Internet Explorer	Mozilla Firefox, Google Chrome & Internet Explorer
14	Harvesting	OAI-PMH	Symplectic-Harvester	-
15	Server platform	Cloud & Server	Cloud & Server	Cloud
16	Standards	-	-	Z39.50 Protocol Compliant
17	Remote access	VPN Connection	VPN Connection	VPN Connection

these can be easily installed, customized and other technical support included. All provide database engines, application servers, data harvesting, server platforms, remote access facilities etc while PURE is also Z39.50 protocol compliant. All search engines and web browsers are supported and the XSL reporting engine is widely used. A Linux operating system is recommended for the installation of RIMS and the server can be either server-based or cloud-based. Converis, Symplectic Elements and PURE systems are all user-friendly and customizable as per system administrator requirements.

Authentication and System Administration

Authentication is required to verify and authenticate user access to the system. An authentication process always proceeds through system administration and system administrators have full rights to assign user privileges to access, edit, add, modify and delete researcher credentials. All RIM systems have a Single Sign On (SSO) server configuration for single user authentication. Further, the ability to register and verify new users, limit access by user types and limit access at file/object level are also facilities that are available in a RIMS. The various authentication and system administration facilities available can be seen in Table 13.

Table 13 summarizes the user and administrator rights, login services and other access limitation characteristics. All RIMS have system administration and login services; Converis and Symplectic Elements have SSO for security purposes. New user registration, editing user profile rights and limiting access by user types and file/record levels are available for all RIMS. In addition to the list above, all RIMS have content management features, metadata standard support, infrastructure features, file format support and user interface facilities.

Table 13. Authentication and system administration

Sr. No.	Authentications	Converis	Symplectic Elements	PURE
1	System administration	Yes	Yes	Yes
2	Login servers	Yes (Shibboleth, Kerberos, CAS, often with Single Sign-On (SSO)	Yes (Webauth/ SSO)	Yes
3	User registration verification/ Other security mechanisms	Yes	Yes	Yes
4	Edit user profile	Yes	Yes	Yes
5	Limit access by user type	Yes	Yes	Yes
6	Limit access at file/object level	Yes	Yes	Yes

All RIMS offer various features, tools and support services many of them outlined above, with particular strengths and weakness. This comparative study highlights the primary publication management, faculty profile, grant management, reports and collaboration facilities of the selected software.

SUGGESTIONS

Based on the above comparison of RIMS features and scope, this section will suggest the major features and scope of the RIMS which can help in selecting the best RIMS for an institutions' research information management requirements. Such features can be grouped in the three categories:

1. *Architecture*, for structural related characteristics;
2. *Metadata and preservation* for those related to flexible description
3. *Interoperability research dissemination* for research collaboration and wide distribution of research information.

Architecture

There are several aspects to consider in connection with a RIMS technical architecture, some of which are outlined below:

- Easy to install and customize to satisfy the needs of users
- User authentication, federated user account access management system
- User interface and the development of data visualization plug-ins
- Data storage capacity, locations (local and remote) and standard backup facilities
- Ongoing maintenance costs for supporting the infrastructure
- Large supporting community to assist in tackling issues and obstacles
- Internationalization support of RIMS
- Handling identifiers and persistent identifiers including Pre-reserving DOI supports
- A user-friendly interface to enable their use as part of researcher's daily activities
- Providing full API

Metadata and Preservation

- Compatible with several metadata schemas and domain (subject)-specific metadata schemas
- It should have the ability to use multiple metadata schemas which can be set up by a system administrator
- Support for metadata exporting schemas
- Dublin Core, MARC, MARCXML schema flexibility
- Content validation and OAI-PMH supports
- Record license specification
- Support for descriptive and structural metadata

Interoperability and Research Dissemination

- Connecting with other RIMS, intuitional repositories, national registries and funding agencies
- Research collaborative environment and network
- Support an institutions' research workflows
- Embargo facility, which allows researcher to make data available to the community after the expiry of an embargo period
- Allow the exposing of research information to the outside community
- User-friendly searching to find research information
- Effective research facilities including full-text searches
- Multiple search engine and browser compatibility
- Effective collaborative data management

SCOPE FOR FURTHER STUDIES

Institutions may implement RIMS for several reasons: to create and maintain researcher profiles, generate faculty CV/webpages, create an institutional repository to manage faculty research outputs and to assess researcher performance and research outputs. The major RIMS are commercial products and institutions and libraries must contract with dedicated company service providers to secure regular troubleshooting assistance and support. Several volunteer communities and their supporters have also been contributing to open source software solutions as an alternative to commercial RIMS and their development and additional plug-ins may also meet an institutions' research management needs; it may be difficult to select the best RIMS application without further comparative study and an assessment of institutional research management needs and requirements.

This study helps universities, institutions and libraries to select the most suitable RIMS application tools for their research management needs at their institutions. It should encourage researchers, librarians and authors to undertake further studies and surveys with existing RIMS users and researchers, to understand their research management needs and practices, and their opinions of RIMS. A survey analysis and further study would enable librarians and institutes to select the most suitable RIMS for their researcher's use; studies in the best practice in technical procedures and applications could also be undertaken.

CONCLUSION

The key finding of this study is that the various RIMS are capable of supporting all the major research information management functions of an academic institution with their major features and tools (Annex I) enabling institutional publications management, research dissemination, faculty profile creation, research analytics etc.

In addition, they also support the establishment of institutional publications and data repositories. Research data management used to mean managing publications but today, managing research data is a much more complex process due to the range of research information types; larger data sets, multimedia formats, teaching materials and structured models etc. RIMS providers must respond to this requirement to capture and manage much more complex research data.

Finally, academic and research libraries have been and will continue to be closely involved in the implementation of research information management systems and in the provision of extensive scholarly communication services.

REFERENCES

Amorim, R. C. (2016). *A Comparison of research data management platforms: architecture, flexible metadata and interoperability*. Univ Access Inf Soc.

Austin, C. E. (2015). Research Data Repositories: A review of current features, gap analysis, and recommendations for minimum requirements. *IASSIST Quarterly*.

Avedas. (2017). *CONVERIS. Managing the Research Life Cycle*. Karlsruhe, Germany: Avedas AG. Retrieved from https://www.campus-innovation.de/fileadmin/dokumente/Loesungen_und_Praxis/CONVERIS_Produktbeschreibung_Details.pdf

Bankier, J. G., Gleason, K., & UNESCO. (2014). *Institutional Repository Software Comparison.* Retrieved from http://www.unesco.org/new/en/ communication-and-information/resources/publications-and-communication-materials/publications/full-list/institutional-repository-software-comparison/

Bryant, R., Oxnam, M., & Mangiafico, P. (2017). *The Emergence of Research Information Management (RIM) within US libraries.* CNI Spring Meeting, Albuquerque, NM.

Clements, A., & McCutcheon, V. (2014). Research data meets research information management: Two case studies using (a) Pure CERIF-CRIS and (b) EPrints repository platform with CERIF extensions. *Procedia Computer Science*, *33*, 199–206. doi:10.1016/j.procs.2014.06.033

Elsevier. (2014). *Pure Hosted Edition.* Retrieved from https://www.elsevier.com/__data/assets/pdf_file/0004/53437/pure-hosted-edition-brochure-version2.01August2014.pdf

Elsevier. (2018). *Elsevier PURE-Features*. Retrieved from https://www.elsevier.com/solutions/pure/features

Feldman, C., & Meyer, D. (2015). *IR to RIMS: Transforming an institutional repository into a Research Information Management System.* IFLA.

Gramstadt, M.-T. (2018). Kultivating Kultur: Increasing arts research deposit. *Ariadne*.

Hawks, J. (2015). Research Information Management: making sense of it all. London, UK: Digital Science.

Ibberson, P. (2010). Symplectic Elements research information software. In *UAS Conference 2010.* The University of Oxford, Oxford, UK.

JISC. (2010). *Research information management: Developing tools to inform the management of research and translating existing good practice*. Imperial College London.

Kissling, A. D., & Ballinger, K. D. (2018). Implementation of a Research Information Management System in a Pediatric Hospital. *Medical Reference Services Quarterly*, *37*(2), 184–197. doi:10.1080/02763869.2018.1439224 PMID:29558332

Meyer, D. (2015). *Transforming DSpace into a Research Information Management System: Ingestion Manager and Report Writer Components*. Computer Science Honours Final Paper, University of Cape Town.

Morton, J., Rasins, R., & Bubalo, V. (2016). *Implementing Symplectic elements at Macquarie University as a hosted publication sourcing solution*. Prezi.

Nyirenda, M. (2017). *Issues and challenges of research information management in higher education institutions – and possible solutions*. The Association of Commonwealth Universities.

OCLC: Lorcan Dempsey's Weblog. (2014, October 14). *Research Information Management Systems – A New Service Category?* Retrieved from http://orweblog.oclc.org/research-information-management-systems-a-new-service-category/

Pampel, H., Vierkant, P., Scholze, F., Bertelmann, R., Kindling, M., Klump, J., ... Dierolf, U. (2013). Making Research data repositories visible: The re3data.org Registry. *PLoS One*, *8*(11), 78080. doi:10.1371/journal.pone.0078080 PMID:24223762

Rau, H., Goggins, G., & Fahy, F. (2018). From invisibility to impact: Recognising the scientific and societal relevance of interdisciplinary sustainability research. *Research Policy*, *47*(1), 266–276. doi:10.1016/j.respol.2017.11.005

Stvilia, B., Wu, S., & Lee, D. J. (2018). Researchers' participation in and motivations for engaging with research information management systems. *PLoS ONE, 13*(2), e0193459.

Symplectic. (2016). *The Wealth of Institutions: understanding research information.* Symplectic. Retrieved from https://symplectic.co.uk/wp-content/uploads/The_Wealth_Of_Institutions_White_Paper.pdf

Witt, M. (2008). Institutional repositories and research data curation in a distributed environment. *Library Trends*, *57*(2), 191–201. doi:10.1353/lib.0.0029

KEY TERMS AND DEFINITIONS

Altmetric: Altmetrics are metrics and qualitative data that that complement traditional, citation-based metrics.

API: An application program interface (API) is a code that allows two software programs to communicate with each other.

Authentication: The process of determining whether someone or something, is who or what it declares itself to be.

Author Name Ambiguity: The author name can't be used to reliably identify all scholarly authors, thus making it impossible to unanimously associate all scholarly works with their authors.

Bibliography: A list of books, scholarly articles, speeches, private records, diaries, interviews, laws, letters, websites, and other sources that are used when researching and writing a paper.

Citations: A reference to the source of information used in research work.

Collaboration: In academic research, collaboration is usually taken to mean an equal partnership between two academic faculty members who are pursuing mutually beneficial research.

Harvesting: A process where a small script, also known as a malicious bot, is used to automatically extract a large amount of data from websites and use it for other purposes.

Interoperability: Refers to the essential ability of computerized systems to connect and readily communicate with each other, even if different manufacturers developed them in various industries.

Metadata: A set of data that describes and gives information about other data.

ORCID: A persistent digital identifier that identifies and distinguishes individual researchers thereby resolving author ambiguity.

Preservation: Action taken to prevent damage occurring, for example by packing and storing documents in a suitable environment.

SaaS: Software as a service. A software distribution model in which a third-party provider hosts applications and makes them available to customers over the internet.

ENDNOTES

1 https://clarivate.com/products/Converis/

2 https://symplectic.co.uk/products/elements/

3 https://www.elsevier.com/solutions/pure

APPENDIX A Overall Findings

Table 14.

Criteria and Features, Supports	Converis	Symplectic Elements	PURE
Creation of Researcher Profiles and CV			
Researcher CV creation and sharing	Yes	Yes	Yes
Researcher Personal webpage	Yes	Yes	Yes
Publications list	Yes	Yes	Yes
Web Interface with External Data Sources			
arXiv	-	Yes	Yes
CAB Abstracts	-	-	Yes
CiNii	-	Yes	-
CrossRef	Yes	Yes	Yes
DBLP	-	Yes	-
Dimensions	-	Yes	-
Embase.com	-	-	Yes
Europe PubMed Central	-	Yes	-
Figshare	-	Yes	-
Google Books	-	Yes	-
Journal TOC	-	-	Yes
MathSciNet	-	Yes	-
Mendeley	Yes	-	Yes
MLA Bibliography	-	Yes	-
MS Academic Search,	Yes	-	
ORCID	Yes	Yes	Yes

continued on the following page

Table 14. Continued

Criteria and Features, Supports	Converis	Symplectic Elements	PURE
PubMed	Yes	Yes	Yes
RePEc	-	Yes	-
SAO/NASA Astrophysics Data System	-	-	Yes
Scopus	Yes	Yes	Yes
Sharpa	-	Yes	-
SSRN	-	Yes	-
Web of Science	Yes	Yes	Yes
WorldCat	-	-	Yes
Discovery and Search Facilities			
Integrated Search Engine	Yes	Yes	Yes (with Elsevier Fingerprint Engine)
Advanced Search facilities	Yes	Yes	Yes
Full Text Search Indexing	Yes	Not full text Records Indexed	Yes
Browse options	Yes	Yes	Yes
Discovery tool	Yes	Yes	Yes (Pure hosted edition)
Integration with Author and Researcher Identifiers			
Researcher ID	Yes	YES	Yes
ORCID	Yes	YES	Yes
Scopus ID	-	YES	Yes
Persistent/Handle URLs	Yes	Yes	Yes
Connection and Collaboration			
Subject experts	Yes	Yes	Yes
Expertise across institutions	Yes	Yes	Yes (SciVal and DIRECT2 Experts connects)

continued on the following page

Table 14. Continued

Criteria and Features, Supports	Converis	Symplectic Elements	PURE
Track funding opportunities	Yes	Yes	Yes (over 20,000 active grants)
Bibliography Import and Export			
RefWorks	-	-	Yes
EndNote	Yes	Yes	Yes
BibTex	Yes	Yes	Yes
RIS (Reference Information System)	-	YES	-
Reference Manager	Yes	YES	-
Google Scholar	-	Yes	-
Mendeley	-	Yes	Yes
InCites	Yes	-	-
Connect to Institutional Repositories			
DSpace	Yes	Yes	Yes
ePrints	Yes	Yes	Yes
Fedora	Yes	Yes	Yes
Figshare for Institutions	-	Yes	-
VIVO	-	Yes	-
Impact Analysis Tools			
Altmetrics	-	Yes	Yes
Bibliometrics	Yes	Yes	Yes
Research ranking	Yes	Yes	Yes
Reporting and Dashboard Facilities			
Dashboard	Yes	Yes	Yes
Data export MS Excel (CERIF)XML)	Yes	Yes	Yes
Network Reports	Yes	-	Yes
Standard Reports per module*	Yes	-	-
HTML files	-	-	Yes
Adobe® PDF	-	Yes	Yes
Reporting Tools database	-	Yes	-

Table 15.

Criteria and Features, Supports	Converis	Symplectic Elements	PURE
Online Guides and User Manual of RIMS Software			
User rights	Yes	Yes	Yes
Navigation & Data quality	Yes	Yes	Yes
Online help	Yes	Yes	Yes
Workflows	Yes	Yes	Yes
User manual	Yes	Yes	Yes
Current Version Details of RIM System			
Regular updates	Yes	Yes	Yes
Latest version release	-	December, 2017	October 5, 2017
Latest version number	6	5.9	5.1
Technologies of RIMS Software			
Core architecture	Java EE	JDK	JDK
Programming language	Java 5	Java & c++	Java/PHP
Database engine	PostgreSQL or Oracle	Oracle JDK	Oracle
Application server	GlassFish v2	-	-
Reporting engine	XSL / FOP	XSL	XSL
Web interface	JSF RI 1.2 Rich Faces Ajax4JSF	-	-
Web server	Apache	Apache	Apache
XML	Xquare	XSLT	
Utilities	PD4ML for PDF generation	PDF generation	PDF generation
Data access	TopLink	-	-
Operating System	Linux	Linux	Linux
Application Interface	API	API	API
Search browser	Internet Explorer, Mozilla Firefox, Safari & Google Chrome	Internet Explorer, Mozilla Firefox & Google Chrome	Internet Explorer, Mozilla Firefox, & Google Chrome
Harvesting	OAI-PMH	Symplectic-Harvester	-
Server platform	Cloud & Server	Cloud & Server	Cloud
Standards	-	-	Z39.50 Protocol Compliant

Table 16.

Criteria and Features, Supports	Converis	Symplectic Elements	PURE
Authentication & System Administration			
System administration	Yes	Yes	Yes
Login servers	Yes (Shibboleth, Kerberos, CAS, often with Single Sign On (SSO)	Yes (Webauth/SSO)	Yes
User registration verification/Other security mechanisms	Yes	Yes	Yes
Edit user profile	Yes	Yes	Yes
Limit access by user type	Yes	Yes	Yes
Limit access at file/object level	Yes	Yes	Yes

Chapter 4
Accessibility of Research Data at Academic Institutions in Zimbabwe

Blessing Chiparausha
Bindura University of Science Education, Zimbabwe

Josiline Phiri Chigwada
Bindura University of Science Education, Zimbabwe

ABSTRACT

This chapter presents the findings of an online survey that was carried out to assess research data accessibility at research and academic institutions in Zimbabwe. The study primarily sought to ascertain the custodianship, storage and accessibility of research data at these institutions. The chapter also highlights the challenges associated with accessing research data in Zimbabwe and proposes mechanisms that can be put in place to address these challenges.

INTRODUCTION

Research data is "any information collected, stored, and processed to produce and validate original research results" (Macalester College 2018). Research data is therefore critical to the research process. Research data can be in the form of text, figures, audio, video, graphs, specimens, software etc. DePaul University Library (2018) defines research data management (RDM) as the "care and maintenance of the data that is produced during the course of a research cycle". RDM involves file naming, data access, data documentation, metadata creation and controlled

DOI: 10.4018/978-1-5225-8437-7.ch004

vocabularies, data storage, data archiving and preservation, data sharing and reuse, data privacy, data rights and data publishing (Henderson 2017). RDM is a key component of the research process as it helps to ensure that data is properly organized, described, preserved and shared (DePaul University Library 2018). This chapter presents findings of an online survey that was carried out to assess research data accessibility at academic institutions in Zimbabwe. The academic institutions surveyed included universities, polytechnics, research institutions, libraries, records centres and archival institutions. Sixty-one responses were received from participating institutions and respondents included librarians, researchers, record managers, archivists, information technology experts and research officers. The study was aimed at ascertaining the custodianship, storage and accessibility of research data at these institutions and highlighting the challenges associated with accessing research data at academic institutions in Zimbabwe.

OBJECTIVES OF THE STUDY

The study sought to specifically answer the following research questions:

1. Who is responsible for managing the data?
2. Where is the research data stored?
3. Who can access the research data?
4. What are the challenges associated with accessing the research data?

Research Data Custodianship

Whyte, Jones and Pryor (2014) and Corrall (2012) observe that although roles and responsibilities in RDM have not yet been clearly spelt out, libraries and librarians are taking a leading role in assuming responsibility for research data. She points out that university librarians are participating in activities that assist researchers in accessing research data. Corrall (2012), however, notes that apart from librarians, there are other key players who have been involved in RDM; information and computer scientists, database and software engineers and programmers, disciplinary experts, curators and expert annotators and archivists. In the context of RDM, these professionals are collectively referred to as 'data scientists' and the same study also confirms collaboration amongst the various professionals in RDM (Corrall 2012:106). Some researchers however, continue to prefer keep research data themselves on their desktops, laptops and other devices at their disposal (Procter, Halfpenny and Voss 2012).

Figure 1. Research data management responsibilities

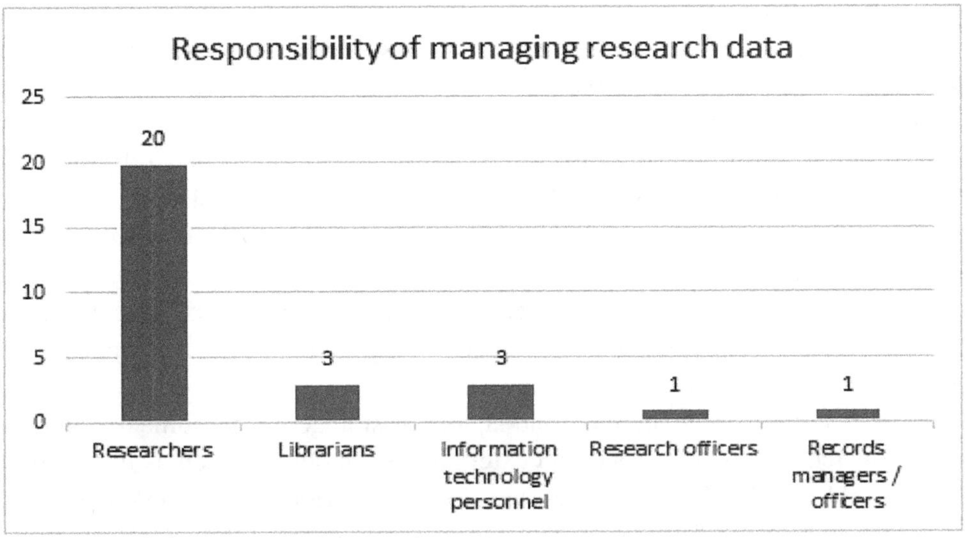

Findings from the survey show that researchers are primarily responsible for managing their own research data in academic institutions in Zimbabwe as shown in Figure 1; this is in line with what was stated by Procter, Halfpenny and Voss (2012). Figure 1 also shows that other stakeholders such as librarians, information technology personnel, research officers and records managers are also involved in RDM in Zimbabwe; RDM calls for a team effort to ensure that the data is accessible and reusable. Collaboration is also important to ensure that that there is no duplication of effort. The FAIR principle calls on the research community to ensure that research data is Findable, Accessible, Interoperable and Reusable (GO FAIR International Support and Coordination Office 2018). The FAIR principle can only be applied if all stakeholders are involved in ensuring that data is archived correctly and securely.

Research Data Storage

Henderson (2017) observes that there are several options for research data storage, these include:

1. Personal computers and laptops;
2. Network storage especially for researchers who are collaborating;
3. External storage devices such as hard drives;
4. Removable storage devices such as flash drives and compact discs;
5. Remote storage such as cloud services; and,

6. Physical storage like physical paper copies and physical specimens.

Libraries, especially at academic institutions, are setting up repositories to store research data (Corrall 2012). The repositories operate in the same way as institutional repositories used for collecting, preserving and disseminating the intellectual research output of an institution, in a digital format. Whereas Ray (2014) concurs with Corrall (2012) that library and information professionals are taking responsibility for managing the storage of research data by using software (such as DSpace and Fedora, Procter), Halfpenny and Voss (2012) report that researchers who are storing the research data by themselves are using their desktops and laptops as storage media. The research data is therefore kept in folders on a computer with specialised software to manage the data.

Instead of just using computers and laptops as storage media, some researchers store research data on the cloud and external storage devices such as hard drives (Wiley and Kerby 2018). Researchers are also using various online RDM platforms to store their research data (University of Warwick Library 2018). Such platforms include Figshare, Zenodo and Mendeley Data. Researchers create personal accounts on these platforms and log in to upload their research data for archiving and sharing with others.

The responses in this study showed that most of the researchers keep their research data on their hard drives and other external storage devices though some indicated that they use external data repositories such as Mendeley Data since their institutions do not have facilities to archive research data. This is prompted mainly by a lack of skills within institutions and a lack of knowledge of best practice in dealing with research data as it is such a new concept in Zimbabwe. This was supported by Wiley and Kerby (2018) in their study, when they discussed where researchers archive their research data. Figure 2 indicates the various formats that are used by researchers to store research data. The formats are mainly determined by the data collection instruments that are used during the research process; most research data is in graphics, spreadsheets and text documents.

Research Data Accessibility

As henderson (2017) suggests, making research accessible to others is important as it promotes research transparency and reproducibility of research. Besides, some funders also require research data to be publicly available; this is an accountability issue and facilitating public access promotes maximum use of the research data. Procter, Halfpenny and Voss (2012) report that when requested, some researchers share their research data with colleagues using email. However, the authors point

Figure 2. Formats for storing research data

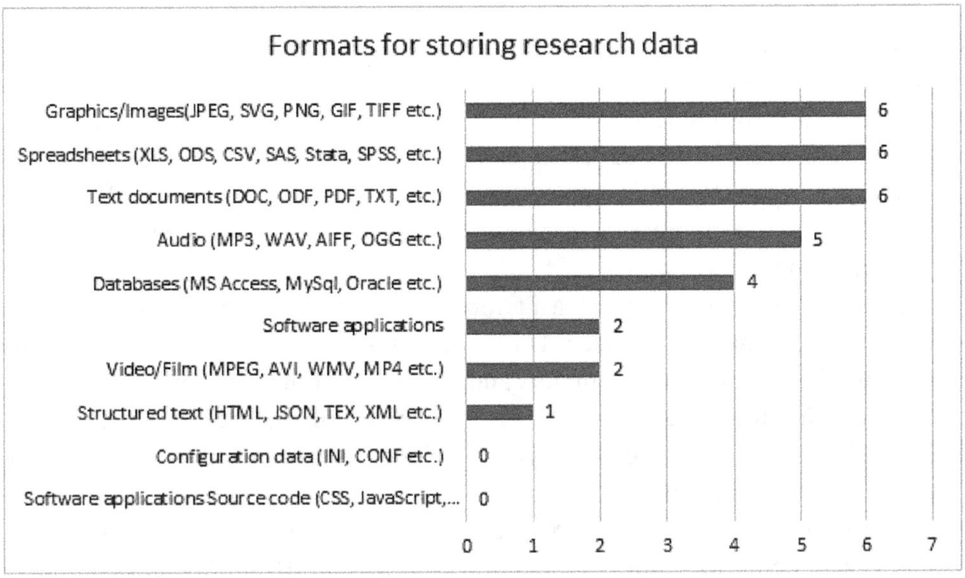

out that researchers prefer to share their research data with colleagues they know and trust.

Many research institutions use digital repository software such as Fedora, Islandora and DSpace to ensure their data repositories are open access; research data is fully accessible and can be retrieved by other interested researchers worldwide (Ray 2014). Ray (2014) also points out that there are researcher software applications such as VIVO that are being used to facilitate research data sharing. VIVO, for instance, is a social networking platform that researchers can use to connect and share their research outputs. Researchers also use various online RDM platforms to make their research data accessible.

The findings showed that in Zimbabwe, research data is not easily accessible since researchers are mainly the custodians of their research data. As a result, data reuse is not possible until the data is shared and researchers decide whom to share their research data with (Procter, Halfpenny and Voss 2012). Most researchers fear that their data would be abused and other researchers would benefit by reusing the research data generated by others. If researchers are not willing to share their research data, then no one will have access to it. There are no policies in place at research institutions in Zimbabwe to ensure that research data is accessible and reusable.

Research Data Access Challenges

Research data can be more valuable if it is properly managed, accessible and reusable. It is difficult however, to ensure that data is "systematically organized, securely stored, fully described, easily locatable, accessible on appropriate authority, shareable, archived and curated" (Procter, Halfpenny and Voss 2012:135). A number of players are required to achieve these. Procter, Halfpenny and Voss (2012) observe that researchers lack interest in sharing their research data with other researchers they are not familiar with.

Lack of policy framework at a national level has deterred efforts to ensure data access and sharing (Procter, Halfpenny and Voss 2012). As a result, the responsibilities of researchers, funders and research institutions may not be clearly outlined making it difficult for these key players to collaborate. Besides, without a clear policy framework in place, it is difficult for research institutions to enforce research data archiving and sharing.

Some research data contains personal information and sensitive issues that make it challenging to share (Figueiredo 2017; Tsang 2014; Procter, Halfpenny and Voss 2012). Balancing openness and confidentiality is not easy and there is a need to anonymize the data by removing personal details that may link the data to an individual or an organisation.

Facilitating access to research data also comes with a cost. Procter, Halfpenny and Voss (2012) stress that implementing and maintaining research data services require information and communication technology (ICT) infrastructure and human capital. Hardware, software and the network infrastructure required to facilitate research data archiving and subsequent access is not cheap and then there is also a need to invest in the human capital responsible for managing the research data.

Despite having the required human capital, hardware, software and networking infrastructure available, some research institutions are opposed to sharing research data (Tsang 2014). If there is no support from management, it would be difficult to implement the archiving of research data within an institution, to promote RDM activities and to build RDM capacity amongst those who would benefit from the process.

The findings indicated that the challenges that are experienced by researchers in accessing research data include a lack of guidance on good RDM practices, technological obsolescence leading to some data not being accessible when there is a hardware or software upgrade, security issues, inadequate financial and human resources, poor infrastructure to archive research data and use of different vocabulary among those who use research data. This is documented in Figure 3.

Figure 3. Challenges experienced in accessing research data

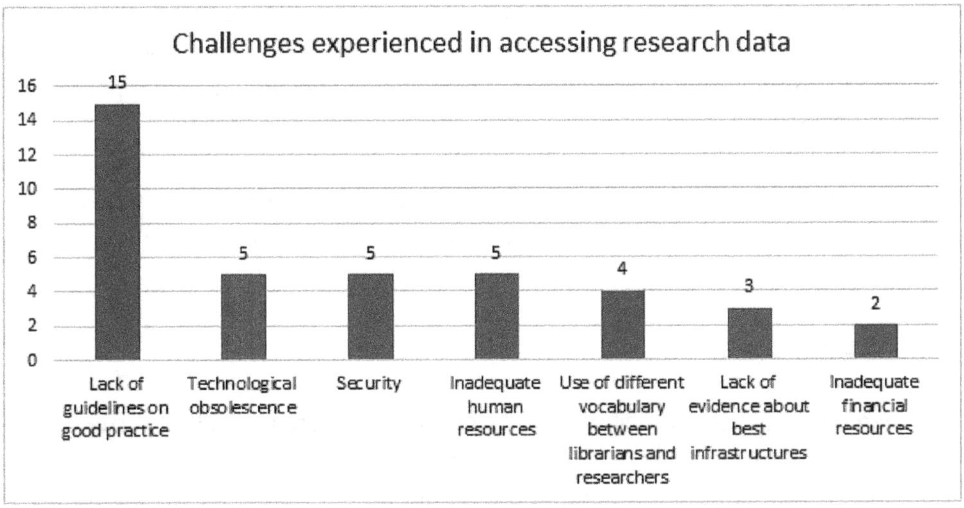

SOLUTIONS AND RECOMMENDATIONS

Henderson (2017) emphasizes that where required, research data anonymization and de-identification should be carefully planned and executed as a means of protecting the privacy and confidentiality of individuals and organisations. This would also be another measure mitigating some of the security issues that are seen as a threat to accessibility and reuse of research data.

Research data and public access policies are required to ensure that individuals privacy is upheld (Henderson 2017). Governments therefore need to work with various stakeholders in developing a policy framework governing RDM. Research institutions would then craft their own policies that dovetail into the national policy framework. In Zimbabwe, the African Open Science Platform can be engaged when drafting the national policy, to provide the guidelines to be followed to ensure that all the stakeholders are involved.

The respondents indicated that there is need to conduct training sessions and workshops to teach RDM and ensure researchers and institutional management understand the need to have a research data repository within the institution. In the absence of managerial support for an institutional data repository, creating an awareness of external data repositories is necessary to ensure that researchers are aware of other platforms that they can use to archive their research data. It would be easier to advocate for institutional support when the researchers are knowledgeable of how to archive research data and when they are aware of the benefits.

The authors recommend that policy makers should ensure that the infrastructure is sufficient and viable to promote the archiving of research data so that it is accessible and reusable. Policies should also be enacted at a national level and those who receive public funds should be mandated to archive the research data in open access repositories so that it is accessible to others. It would be difficult to plan and develop research data repositories in research institutions if there is no enabling legislation. Librarians and other keen researchers should also continuously build their capacity so that they keep pace with the ever changing technologies of open data.

FUTURE RESEARCH

As research data is largely inaccessible in Zimbabwe, there is need for further study to discover and promote institutional best practices in archiving research data in a resource constrained environment; and to find out if researchers are aware of the current trends in RDM and identify what might be done to make research data more discoverable and usable.

CONCLUSION

It can be concluded that accessibility of research data in research institutions in Zimbabwe remains a significant challenge; researchers are managing their own research data and some are unwilling to share that data. Currently, there is no institution with a research data repository though most institutions of higher learning are now working towards the development of repositories. The major challenge experienced is a lack of expertise and enabling policies to support RDM and repository initiatives. As a result, capacity building, and engaging some institutions who have 'walked the journey' is encouraged to ensure that research data is archived, made accessible and reusable.

REFERENCES

Corrall, S. (2012). Roles and responsibilities: libraries, librarians and data. In G. Pryor (Ed.), *Managing Research Data* (pp. 105–134). London, UK: Facet Publishing. doi:10.29085/9781856048910.007

DePaul University Library. (2018). *Research Data Management (A How-To Guide): Research Data Management Definition*. Retrieved from https://libguides.depaul.edu/c.php?g=620925&p=4324498

Figueiredo, A. S. (2017). Data sharing: Convert challenges into opportunities. *Frontiers in Public Health*, *5*, 327. doi:10.3389/fpubh.2017.00327 PMID:29270401

GO FAIR International Support and Coordination Office. (2018). *FAIR Principles - GO FAIR*. Available at: https://www.go-fair.org/fair-principles/

Henderson, M. E. (2017). *Data Management: A Practical Guide for Librarians*. Lanham, MD: Rowman & Littlefield Publishers.

Macalester College. (2018). *Defining Research Data - Data Module #1: What is Research Data?* Retrieved from http://libguides.macalester.edu/data1

Procter, R., Halfpenny, P., & Voss, A. (2012). Research data management: opportunities and challenges for HEIs. In G. Pryor (Ed.), *Managing Research Data* (pp. 135–150). London, UK: Facet Publishing. doi:10.29085/9781856048910.008

Ray, J. M. (2014). *Research Data Management: Practical Strategies for Information Professionals*. West Lafayette, IN: Purdue University Press.

Rice, R. (2009). *DISC-UK DataShare project: Final report*. Available at http://ie-repository.jisc.ac.uk/336/1/DataSharefinalreport.pdf

Tsang, D. C. (2014). *Research Data Management: Challenges and Opportunities*. Presentation at Singapore Management University, Li Ka Shing Library, Singapore. Available at: https://ink.library.smu.edu.sg/lib_events/2/

University of Warwick Library. (2018). *Accessing Research Data*. Available at: https://warwick.ac.uk/services/library/staff/research-data/accessing-research-data/

Whyte, A., Jones, S., & Pryor, G. (2014). *Delivering Research Data Management Services: Fundamentals of Good Practice*. London, UK: Facet Publishing.

Whyte, A., & Tedds, J. (2011). *Making the Case for Research Data Management. In DCC Briefing Papers*. Edinburgh, UK: Digital Curation Centre. Available at http://www.dcc.ac.uk/resources/briefing-papers

Wiley, C. A., & Kerby, E. E. (2018). Managing Research Data: Graduate Student and Postdoctoral Researcher Perspectives. *Issues in Science and Technology Librarianship*. Available at http://www.istl.org/18-spring/refereed1.html

Chapter 5
Information Processing in Research Paper Recommender System Classes

Benard M. Maake
Tshwane University of Technology, South Africa

Sunday O. Ojo
Tshwane University of Technology, South Africa

Tranos Zuva
Vaal University of Technology, South Africa

ABSTRACT

Research-related publications and articles have flooded the internet, and researchers are in the quest of getting better tools and technologies to improve the recommendation of relevant research papers. Ever since the introduction of research paper recommender systems, more than 400 research paper recommendation related articles have been so far published. These articles describe the numerous tools, methodologies, and technologies used in recommending research papers, further highlighting issues that need the attention of the research community. Few operational research paper recommender systems have been developed though. The main objective of this review paper is to summaries the state-of-the-art research paper recommender systems classification categories. Findings and concepts on data access and manipulations in the field of research paper recommendation will be highlighted, summarized, and disseminated. This chapter will be centered on reviewing articles in the field of research paper recommender systems published from the early 1990s until 2017.

DOI: 10.4018/978-1-5225-8437-7.ch005

INTRODUCTION

The volume of web-based literature skewed towards scientific research is growing at an exponential rate and better tools and methodologies to effectively manage these documents are required. Academic search engines, archives, and digital libraries have been developed and improved to save the worsening web search situation, and for that reason, better information filtering mechanisms are being introduced daily. To easily access relevant and high-quality research papers from the Internet and other repositories, research paper recommender systems (RPRS) have been developed and integrated with information search and retrieval systems. Regrettably, the state-of-the-art RPRS has not received the much-needed attention to improve on its search, retrieval and recommendation capabilities. This chapter reviews and highlights important classification aspects concerning the recommender system in the field of research papers.

RPRS have been enabled by technologies in Information Retrieval (IR), Databases, the Web and many other technologies as depicted in Table 1. Recommender Systems (RecSys) and Search Engines (SE) are technologies that help users filter information that is found on the Web. They also help retrieve relevant and comprehensive information that is personalized based on the user's needs, bringing more benefit to users of the World Wide Web (WWW). RecSys, unlike SE, is a subclass of information filtering systems that predict ratings or make a preference that users will

Table 1. Research paper recommender systems' enabling technologies

Technology	Description
Predictive analytics	Branches of advanced analytics that uses techniques from data mining, statistics, modeling, machine learning, and artificial intelligence to make a prediction about the future of an unknown event (i.e. predictive ratings for recommending research papers in a collaborative topic modeling approach (Wang & Blei, 2011)).
Distribute file systems	A file system that processes data that is stored on a server as if it were on the local client machine (i.e. using the web search engine that spans multiple file systems to recommend documents, (Brin & Page, 1998)).
Stream analytics	Perform real-time stream processing of your data (i.e. extracting relevant records from a stream on incoming records (Bollacker, Lawrence, & Giles, 2000)).
Databases	Various structure of data held in computers that can be accessed in various ways (i.e. CiteSeer and the Papists RPRS query databases for related research papers (Watanabe, Ito, Ozono, & Shintani, 2005; Zarrinkalam & Kahani, 2012)).
Web Technologies (Internet)	Infrastructural building blocks of computer networks (i.e. enables researchers to publish and access research results as soon as it is obtained (Lopes, Souto, Wives, & de Oliveira, 2008)).

give to an item (Shinde & Potey, 2016). Most popular RecSys approaches include Collaborative Filtering (CF), Content-Based Filtering (CBF), Demographic-Filtering and Knowledge-Based Filtering. A combination of one or more approaches makes the Hybrid recommender system. The use of the term "article" in this chapter refers to research papers or journals articles. The objectives of this chapter are to highlight the various methods that are used to recommend research papers from the domain, highlight RPRS enabling technologies and suggest future directions in research paper access and management.

BACKGROUND

Research paper recommendation survey articles have not been undertaken comprehensively in the past, but the work done by (Beel, Langer, Genzmehr, Gipp, et al., 2013) turns out to be the most extensive one so far in the field of research paper recommendation. In their work, they presented a detailed descriptive statistic of major concepts in RecSys, various definitions used in the field of RecSys and highlighted the various fields that are related to research paper recommendation. They went further and conducted various mini-surveys to completely understand various aspects that were being investigated by authors in this field. Firstly, they conducted a survey of evaluations exploring various evaluation methods and metrics in RPRS. Secondly, they did a survey of recommendation classes that are used in RPRS. Thirdly, they surveyed the major research fields and shortcoming in RPRS, and finally, they gave their summary and outlook regarding the field of research paper recommendation.

Our work is a complement of their work in that, it extends the various concepts and approaches that have been used in RecSys recommendation classes. We identify selected concepts and map them to authors, topics and classes. Secondly, we provide basic selected formulae of metrics used in the processing of recommendation, also representing concepts that are used in RPRS in other new perspectives and paradigms and finally, we discuss future directions that are promising if well pursued in this field of RPRS. (Smeaton & Callan, 2005) is another survey paper in a digital library that investigates how personalization can be identified, examined and then implemented into digital libraries. They highlighted the various potentials that personalization brings into digital libraries, further explaining the active role of recommender systems in ensuring that digital library users are satisfied with the recommendations they receive. In their work, a wide range of potential personalization techniques and methods in digital libraries were discussed, further highlighting the various research challenges in the personalisation of digital libraries. They concluded their work by giving-out a perspective on possible future directions on better techniques if implemented in digital libraries.

METHODOLOGY

A thorough review of the literature was conducted in the field of research paper recommendation systems and the articles were obtained through a variety of scholarly databases. This was done through downloading articles using the keywords, "research paper recommender systems", "scientific-paper recommender systems", "academic paper recommendation" and "academic publication recommendation". Closely related to research paper recommendation was "citation recommendation", which also recommended both citation and research papers to users. We, therefore, did further exploration of articles having the keywords "citation recommendation", "citation metrics" and "citation analysis", and all the papers that were relevant based on the keywords, abstract and title were saved and used in this mini-review work. A further selection of the papers for this review was conducted based on the following criterion:

Paper Selection Criteria

Articles were accessed for downloading, reading, viewing and printing through scholarly databases and repositories that are linked to the university's website and library. These articles collected were further classified as per their importance. Articles that were left out are those that were repeated in more than one database, or those that were written in foreign languages like Chinese, Arabic or Germany (Gillitzer, 2010; Kuberek & Mönnich, 2012; Mönnich & Spiering, 2008; Naak, 2009) and could not be translated because of time and cost implications that were to be encountered. We also encountered in our paper selection process articles that were full of grammatical errors which made comprehending the contents of the paper very difficult, they were left out.

Our paper selection criterion was aimed at having a chapter that will inform readers of (a) the major classes in the field of research paper recommender systems, (b) the subject categories or fields that research-paper recommendation technologies are highly related to, (c) provide insights of the possibilities and opportunities of applying these techniques in various fields, (d) briefly describe how various methods, measures, and metrics have been used in the recommendation of research papers and finally, (e) to encourage the research community to venture into other promising fields with the goal of solving problems arising in the field. RPRS articles were found in wide-ranging subjects as depicted in Table 2. Both backward and forward chronological search was conducted on both the references and the authors of the articles, and this was done to identify how the field developed over time. These methods helped in understanding the origins and developments of various theories, models and constructs of interests in the field of RPRS. The reference list of the downloaded papers especially the survey paper done by (Beel, Gipp, Langer, & Breitinger, 2015) was examined to lead to other important papers.

Data Source and Formula of Mining for Relevant Articles

The articles used in this research were all gathered from open access portals, university library subscriptions and peer sharing platforms like ResearchGate and Academic. edu. The following sources were greatly used to download the articles: IEEE Xplore digital library, Association for Computing Machinery (ACM), ScienceDirect, Springer, Emerald, Elsevier, CiteSeer, ResearchGate, Wiley and Academia.edu online databases. The main academic search engines that were employed included the Google Scholar and Microsoft Academic Search. For the few articles that were not accessed from the above-mentioned repositories, a search into researchers'

Table 2. Online digital repositories and topics

Online database	Topics
Association for Computing Machinery (ACM)	Recommender systems Digital libraries Context-aware in retrieval and recommendation Adaptive and convergence systems Iniquitous information management and communication Human factors in computing Information retrieval Information systems World Wide Web (WWW)
ScienceDirect/ Elsevier	Information processing and management E – Technologies Artificial intelligence Natural language processing User modeling and adaptability
Wiley	Computational intelligence Intelligence systems
IEEE Xplore	Computing and networking technology Enterprise computing, E-Commerce, and E-Services Behavioral, Economic and Social Cultural Computers (BESC) Social networking analysis and mining Data mining Application of digital information and web technologies Advanced computer theory and engineering

website, webpage, blog posts or institutional repositories yielded rewards. In general, the process of mining for relevant articles from the above online databases took the form described by Figure 1.

Classification of Articles by Publication Year

The articles used in this review were classified according to the years that they were published. The rationale for selecting the range of years starting from 1990 – 2017 is that; the first research paper recommender system was developed in the mid-'90s by (Giles, Bollacker, & Lawrence, 1998), and from then till present, we have observed enormous growth and development of new-featured research paper recommender systems. Cumulatively, we have been having more and more research papers recommender systems associated articles over the years, consequently attesting that there is a constant need for better methods to retrieve and recommend research papers.

Classification of Articles by an Online Database

Most of the articles that were used for this research were downloaded from various online databases and repositories. These online repositories had copies of the same articles, thus ensuring easy access to the articles for the review process. We selected the articles that were readily available for download through the university's online subscriptions, and the abstract, title and reference lists of papers were used to further

Figure 1. The formula for mining relevant articles

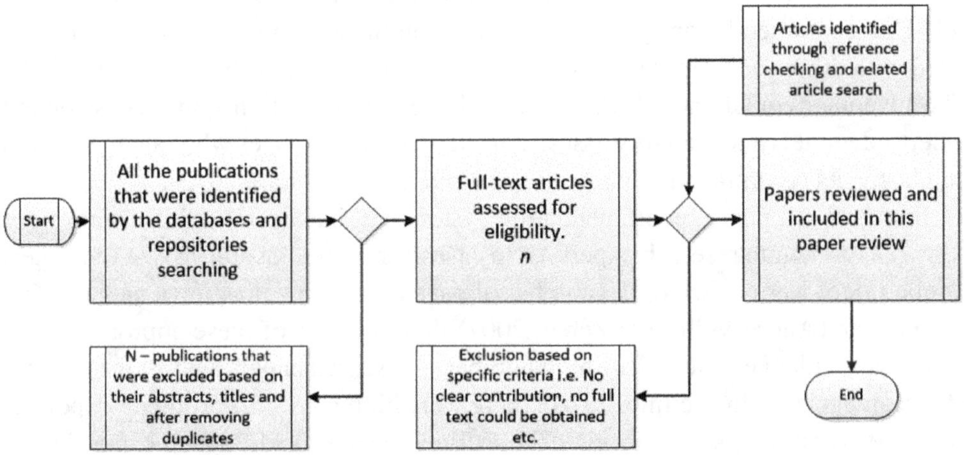

refine our search for articles stored in the event the repositories required payments to be completed before accessing articles.

Classification of Articles by Journal Database

Not all the articles downloaded were published journals, but we also downloaded conference papers and proceedings, patents, dissertations and other types of scientific publications. These articles were all kept by different databases and journal repositories thus demonstrating that most of the repositories published articles relevant to the field of recommender systems. We reviewed approximately 39% of the total articles from the ACM journal repositories. This was followed closely by the Springer journal repository archiving 31% of papers relevant to our study, then the IEEE Xplore contained 12% of relevant articles, Wiley approximately 3%, Elsevier approximately 3%, Emerald nearly 3% and other journals about 9%.

Classification of Articles Based on Recommendation Classes

There are many types of recommendation classes in research paper recommendation, but in this chapter, we choose to focus on; collaborative filtering, content-based filtering, graph-based, and the hybrid approach.

Collaborative Filtering

Collaborative Filtering (CF) is an approach that is utilized by recommender systems for making predictions to interested users based on a collected and analyzed preference of many other users. In a CF approach, the following sequence of steps is followed: (i) A user rates an item based on the preference. (ii) The recommendation system matches this user's ratings against other different users, to search for similar preferences. (iii) The recommendation system will then recommend items to you that have been rated with other users similar to your preference (Ricci, Rokach, & Shapira, 2011). The advantages of CF include the fact that the recommendation approach is content independent, it is a real quality assessor as humans are the ones who rate the system and lastly, its recommendations are serendipitous (Beel et al., 2015).

In a research paper recommendation system, CF has been used in a variety of ways, i.e. users rate research papers, or in case users were not able to rate the pages, implicit rates were inferred, i.e. number of pages read, downloading a paper, citing a paper, etc.(Andre Vellino & Zeber, 2007) though some of these approaches had their own challenges. Due to the high number of research papers against the number of researchers (André Vellino, 2010), there were high *cold start* problems reported, because several papers were not rated (Gipp, Beel, & Hentschel, 2009), nor considered for download or opening. In (Naak, Hage, & Aïmeur, 2008), different parts of an article are rated depending on how interesting they are to the user, and those ratings are used for recommendation. Implicit ratings were considered in some situations which have privacy issues due to constant monitoring of user behavior (Naak et al., 2008), they could also be misinterpreted (Beel et al., 2015). To use CF, one needs the user-item matrix, and (Lee, Lee, Kim, & Kim, 2015) considered authors as users, and papers as items, while (Dong, Tokarchuk, & Ma, 2009) considered research papers as users and citations as items that had been rated. However, the user-item matrix is plagued by the data sparsity problem (André Vellino, 2010). Fortunately, (Sugiyama & Kan, 2015) alleviated the sparsity problem by identifying potential citation papers using CF. (McNee et al., 2002) utilized citation graphs to seed a CF recommender system for journal articles. (Guan et al., 2010) utilized a collaborative filtering method on tagging data to recommend documents. (McNee, Kapoor, & Konstan, 2006) utilized user-based collaborative filtering (user-user CF or Resnick's algorithm) to generate recommendations that were serendipitous to the users.

(Torres, McNee, Abel, Konstan, & Riedl, 2004) developed two collaborative filtering techniques (Pure-CF & Denser-CF) that took in citations of a paper as input, and gave out a list of recommended citations as output. Mendeley uses usage-data to develop research paper recommendations based on collaborative filtering principles (Jack, 2012). (McNee et al., 2002) recommended research papers by applying collaborative filtering innovatively on the citation web, users and on the prediction of which values to appear on blank spots on the user-item matrix. (Chen, Kuo, & Liao, 2015) utilized the collaborative filtering approaches together with the Personal Ontology Model to determine like-minded users in a digital library. (Mishra, 2012) utilized a Neighbour-weighted Collaborative Filtering (NwCF) approach to both enhance the ranking and filter out potential noise in their research paper recommender system. In the CF algorithm, finding out the similarity between two users is done by calculating the Pearson correlation measure of the rating of the common users. Once the similarity measure has been established, the items are ranked so that they may be recommended to the center user using the predicted rating with the average adjusted rating of a user (Schafer, Frankowski, Herlocker, & Sen, 2007). Using CF for recommending research papers amidst the many criticisms and issues that are associated with CF, i.e. implicit ratings can be interpreted wrongly whereas explicit ratings can be manipulated or abused. Also, using implicit user behavioral patterns such as users search, views on a page, or the number of clicks on a document, usually convey weak signals and most times it accounts to too much noise in the data used for recommending purposes (Xue, Guo, Lan, & Cao, 2014).

Content-Based Filtering

Content-Based Filtering (CBF) is another type of approach that is used to design recommender systems. In this approach, recommendations are based on the description of the item matched against the description of the user's profile (Brusilovski, Kobsa, & Nejdl, 2007). An important element of the CBF is the user modeling process that infers the user's interests based on the items features used to describe an item or type of interaction between a user and items (Beel et al., 2015). In the research paper recommendation system field, CBF is more dominant compared to the CF because of the rich textual features available in articles (Alzoghbi, Ayala, Fischer, & Lausen, 2016). Articles and researchers were represented as feature vectors whose similarities are computed, and articles having the highest resemblance to the user's profile formed part of the recommended list (Tran, Huynh, & Hoang, 2015). CBF was used to generate to a user a list of recommended papers in (M. Zhang, Wang, & Li, 2008). Researcher's features (researcher's interests and their search query histories) were compared with paper's features (titles, abstracts, keywords and year of publication) to find out articles which closely matched and were recommended (Alotaibi & Vassileva, 2015). (Beel & Langer, 2015) utilized a term-based CBF and a citation-based CBF during their experiments of evaluating evaluation-measures in RPRS. (Ekstrand et al., 2010) located similar papers by matching text acquired from titles, abstracts, and keywords using the CBF algorithm. (Alotaibi & Vassileva, 2015) used CBF to judge the relevance of a research paper, while (Xue et al., 2014) matched user's research interests against candidate papers to come up with a recommendation list.

The CBF approach extracts key phrases to produce a rich description of user profiles and contents of the article (Ferrara, Pudota, & Tasso, 2011). In (Beel, Langer, Genzmehr, & Nürnberger, 2013; Sugiyama & Kan, 2010) selected words and textual data are used in building a user model, and these terms contained in the research paper are tokenized using a process known as stop-word removal, then stemmed, transforming the tokens further into n-grams using the stemming algorithms (Lovins, 1968). Then lastly, the n-grams are processed using the Term Frequency-Inverse Document Frequency (TF-IDF) to reflect which words are important in a particular document. CBF has shortcomings, for instance, it ignores the quality and popularity of an item, and it is dependent on features of items without which, it cannot make recommendations (Dong et al., 2009). CBF systems were utilized to rank keywords with TF-IDF in order of their importance (Nascimento, Lavender, da Silva, & Gonçalves, 2011). With the power that TF-IDF comes with, it did not solve the problem of synonymy or polysemy in RPRS (Zhao, Wu, Dai, & Dai, 2015). Parts of speech tags were used to discover concepts present in text/phrases (Nascimento et al., 2011).

Since research papers have text as their main content, measures to find the importance of terms in a document is very important (Alotaibi & Vassileva, 2015; Alzoghbi et al., 2016; Dong et al., 2009). The Term Frequency-Inverse Document Frequency (TF-IDF) is one of the metrics that was commonly used in CBF. TF-IDF was used weigh terms and citations that were present in a research paper (Beel & Langer, 2015), to represent all resources used in the recommender system as vectors (Ferrara et al., 2011), to give added weights to words that were used for searching and to calculate the importance and similarity between documents (Watanabe et al., 2005). (Tran et al., 2015) built new feature vectors by combing the of-IDF vector with other vectors in the research paper. (Nascimento et al., 2011) ranked research papers using the if-idf. (Danesh, Sumner, & Martin, 2015; Ohta, Hachiki, & Takasu, 2011; Wang & Blei, 2011) utilized to-IDF to select distinct words that formed a corpus that was used during recommendation. (Kodakateri Pudhiyaveetil, Gauch, Luong, & Eno, 2009) utilized to-idf to find top-n words to be used for recommendation. (Guan et al., 2010) used to-IDF to measure user-user similarity in a tag user-based CF approach. (Ohta et al., 2011) scored technical feature extracted from a research paper while (Achakulvisut, Acuna, Ruangrong, & Kording, 2016) used to-IDF to remove terms that did not meet a quantified threshold. (Danesh et al., 2015) Utilized the of-IDF on n-grams to find the similarity of words that had a threshold determined by the length of the document. The TF-IDF can be understood by the following basic form.

Given a corpus of articles that are going to be processed, the *tf-idf* weight of term *t* in document *d* is statistically expressed as:

$$tf - idf(t,d) = tf(t,d) * idf(t)$$

Where the *tf(t,d)* represents the frequency of the term *t* in document *d*, and the *idf(t)* represents:

$$idf(t) = \log\left(\frac{N}{df(t)}\right)$$

Where *N* describes all the documents in the corpus in their total number, and *df(t)* the number of documents containing term *t*.

Graph-Based Approach

When graphs and citation structures were used to represent academic papers, they formed an acyclic graphic which took the form: $G = \langle V, E \rangle$ where *V* represents the research paper, and *E*, represents the citation link (Liang, Li, & Qian, 2011). In RPRS, citation analysis was utilised to come with network diagrams that showed connections between research papers based on various criterions and features, i.e. visual representations of connections between research paper authors, venues, publishing years, genes and proteins etc. (Beel et al., 2015). Textual features of a recommender system can also be used to show how closely one document is connected with another, and it can be done through a graph. In the work done by (Gupta & Varma, 2017), scientific articles were recommended using a distributed representation of text and graphs. On the other hand, Bi-partite graphs linked papers to technical terms (Ohta et al., 2011), and citations generated domain specific articles network graphs (McNee et al., 2002; Paraschiv, Dascalu, Dessus, Trausan-Matu, & McNamara, 2016). In (Kapoor et al., 2007), paper votes were used to build a citation graph. (Strohman, Croft, & Jensen, 2007) measured the relevance between articles by linearly combining textual features and citation graph features like the Katz distance and the citation count. (Z. Huang, Chung, Ong, & Chen, 2002) developed a graph-based recommender systems for a digital library by combining CBF and CF approaches, where books and users were represented in an extended graph, book-book, user-user and user-book correlations were incorporated. (McNee et al., 2002; West, Wesley-Smith, & Bergstrom, 2016) utilised a citation graph to seed in a journal recommender system. (Ferrara et al., 2011) utilised a graph-based ranking approach that extracted keyphrases from documents that were represented as term graphs. (Paraschiv et al., 2016) created graphs based on semantic relatedness between abstracts using network graph visualisation representations. (Guan et al., 2010) recommended web pages and research papers using tagging data. Similarity was measured between three bi-partite graphs that represented tags, users and documents. An affinity graphs that represented the similarity between documents that were to be recommended.

The researcher (M. Zhang et al., 2008) modeled users and paper profiles using concept graphs to semantically extend these profiles for CF operations. (West et al., 2016) utilised the citation graph to partition a research papers' network by taking advantage of scholarly literature domain-specific properties like fields, subfields and sub-subfields. (Jiang, Jia, Feng, & Zhao, 2012) utilised a paper citation graph to generate a set of possible relevant papers for a target paper. (Ekstrand et al., 2010) utilised three graph ranking algorithms (PageRank, HITS and SALSA) to compute the importance of a research paper based on their connectivity on the citation web. (Liu, Zhang, & Guo, 2016) enhanced citation recommendation by utilising proximity-based citation contexts and publication topic distributions to generate citation graphs that were used to calculate the importance of topics in publications. (Z. Huang et al., 2002) built a graph-based book recommender system that modeled a two-layered graph from books, customers and their purchase information. (Chakraborty, Modani,

Narayanam, & Nagar, 2015) utilised keywords and a Vertex Reinforced Random Walk (VRRW) algorithm on citation graphs to search for semantically relevant research papers. (Bollacker et al., 2000) built a full graph of citing and cited papers so that titles could be automatically matched to their citations during a search.

(Woodruff, Gossweiler, Pitkow, Chi, & Card, 2000) represented a citation index as a directed graph whereby the edges represented a citation relationship between papers, i.e. one paper being referenced by another paper. (Shimbo, Ito, & Matsumoto, 2007) compared graph-mining approaches (kernel-based measures) no graph nodes after seeding a research paper to evaluate their advantages as recommendation systems for articles. (Küçüktunç, Kaya, Saule, & Çatalyürek, 2012) utilised hypergraphs to recommend citations on bibliographic networks, where citation graphs were used to generated sparse matrices. (Chakraborty et al., 2016) constructed multi-faceted filtered graph-based recommender systems to improve the overall accuracy of the system. (Liang et al., 2011) developed a method that utilized graphs and links to capture the global relevance between two articles in the entire citation graph. (Xia, Asabere, Liu, Deonauth, & Li, 2014) described folksonomies as hypergraphs in a socially-aware research paper recommender system for conference participants. (Tang & Zeng, 2012) utilized weighted research paper keywords that were represented as a bipartite graph to extend the subject ontology in a paper recommender system. (Zhou et al., 2008) combined multiple graphs to measure document similarities.

(Ohta et al., 2011) recommended related papers by using the technical terms that were appearing in the papers. They assumed that each paper had a link to the technical terms, and a bipartite graph generated was then analyzed by the HITS algorithm to rank the papers based on their hubs scores. (Lao & Cohen, 2010) represented scientific literature meta-data as a labeled directed graph to better retrieve and recommend venues, genes, reference lists and experts in a scientific literature domain. (Zhao et al., 2015) utilized a weighted undirected graph to bridge the knowledge gap between a researcher's background knowledge and their research target. (Gori & Pucci, 2006) proposed a random-walk based research paper algorithm to recommend related papers based on a set of relevant-papers selected by users. (Küçüktunç, Saule, Kaya, & Çatalyürek, 2013) employed graphs to diversify their results in a citation recommendation system. (Xia, Liu, Lee, & Cao, 2016) utilized graphs to exploit common authors relationships and historical preferences in their scientific article recommender system. (Le Anh, Hai, Tran, & Jung, 2014) utilized graphs to rank and determine relationships between keywords in recommending papers. (Zarrinkalam & Kahani, 2013) utilized graphs to generate research paper candidate set. Finally, (Dattolo, Ferrara, & Tasso, 2009) utilized multigraphs in the organization of user concept spaces in their publication sharing system.

Hybrid Recommendation Approaches

Hybrid research paper recommendations systems usually combine two or more techniques to improve the performance of the overall system. They are meant to make obsolete the disadvantages that exist in either CF or CBF or any other recommendation approaches if they were to run as silos without being combined with any other approaches (Gipp et al., 2009). Table 3 elucidates the various hybridization methods and their descriptions which are applied to various research paper recommendation systems.

(Joseph, 2013) combined impact-based and conceptual recommender systems to have a hybrid system. (Z. Huang et al., 2002) proposed a graph-based recommendation system that naturally combined the CBF and the CF algorithms. (Andre Vellino & Zeber, 2007) combined a hybrid CF and CBF with multi-dimensional meta-data features such as subject categories and journal clusters to enhance the recommendation system. (Zarrinkalam & Kahani, 2012) used CBF and a multi-criteria CF with multiple data sources to provide a rich source of recommendation data. (M. Zhang et al., 2008) utilized CF tagging data to compute semantic similarities while CBF to generate recommendations. (Lopes et al., 2008) combined user-user correlation details (CF) with a book-book and book-user details (CBF) to make recommendations

Table 3. Recommender systems hybridization methods

Hybridization method	Description
Weighted	The scores (votes) of several recommendation techniques are combined to produce a single recommendation, i.e. (Joseph, 2013), (Y.-c. Huang, 2007)
Switching	The system switches between recommendation techniques depending on the current situation, i.e. (Y.-c. Huang, 2007)
Feature combination	Features from different recommendation data sources are thrown together into a single recommendation algorithm, i.e. (Ma et al., 2015)
Cascade	One recommender refines the recommendations given by another, i.e. (Naak et al., 2008), (Ekstrand et al., 2010)
Fusion	Computes two parallel recommendation approaches and then merges their final recommendation lists to generate their recommendations, i.e. (Ekstrand et al., 2010), (Y.-c. Huang, 2007), (Torres et al., 2004)
Mixed	Recommendations from several different recommenders are presented at the same time (Gipp et al., 2009)
Feature augmentation	The output from one technique is used as an input feature to another (Burke, 2002; Z. Zhang & Li, 2010)
Meta-level	The model learned by one recommender is used as input to another (Torres et al., 2004)

to users. (Z. Zhang & Li, 2010) created a target user profile based on the content of documents, then the spreading activation algorithm was used to search for users with similar interests like the target user. (Ferrara et al., 2011) combined tag, domain ontologies and keyphrase extraction techniques and tools to retrieve relevant items. (Ekstrand et al., 2010) generated automatically a reading list after augmenting CF and CBF approaches with measures of the influence of a research paper in the web of citations.

A graph-based recommender system was utilized to combine the content and collaborative filtering approaches by (Z. Huang et al., 2002). On one hand, (H. Zhang, Ni, Zhao, Liu, & Yang, 2014) used a hybrid recommendation to recommend resources in a Technologically Enhanced Learning (TEL) environment. (Zarrinkalam & Kahani, 2012) combined CBF and multi-criteria CF to develop a hybrid system based on linked data where the user and item profiles were selected using CF, then CBF was used to generate the recommendation list. (Y.-c. Huang, 2007) used the switching hybrid approach between content-based filtering and social network-based approach. (Torres et al., 2004) combined the CF and CBF approach to their TechLens system to enhance and recommend relevant papers to users. (West et al., 2016) developed a hybrid system that suggested topics based on the text from documents. (Uchiyama, Nanba, Aizawa, & Sagara, 2011) combined author-based CF and a keyword-based CBF approach to developing a cross-lingual research paper recommender system. (Naak et al., 2008) developed a hybrid research paper management system that combined a bibliography management system, a research paper recommender system and an enterprise content management system to enhance research paper management and recommendation. (Wang & Blei, 2011) combined a probabilistic topic modeling with collaborative filtering to effectively recommend existing and recently published papers. (Yin, Zhang, & Li, 2007) combined hybrid methods for representing user interests with user-user CF approaches to recommend research papers in a CF tagging environment. (Shinde & Potey, 2016) proposed a hybrid approach that combined the Mahout and Lenski frameworks in evaluating the coverage of a research paper recommender system. (Gipp et al., 2009) developed the first hybrid research paper recommender system that combined various tools and techniques (i.e. author analysis, citation analysis, implicit ratings, explicit ratings, and source analysis) to the traditional keyword-based recommender system.

Classification of Articles Based on Evaluation Methods in Research Paper Recommender Systems

The work of evaluating RPRS is aimed at defining what constitutes a good research paper recommender system and to determine the suitability of the system. Three major approaches used include user studies, online evaluations, and offline evaluations. The goal of evaluating research paper recommender systems is to measure the quality of recommendations and the performance made by the systems. Each of the evaluation methods discussed below has its benefits and limitations to the recommendation process. The evaluation approaches differed from one experiment to another due to the fact that different features, recommendation tasks, data preprocessing methods and etc. were used in the process of evaluation (Beel & Langer, 2015).

Firstly, user studies evaluations were used to measure the satisfaction levels of the system users through the recommendations received, i.e. (Konstan et al., 2006; Lee et al., 2015; McNee et al., 2006; Torres et al., 2004), and this was done by both qualitative and quantitative methods. Online evaluations, i.e. (Lee et al., 2015; Tran et al., 2015; Xue et al., 2014) though expensive when compared to offline experiments (Tran et al., 2015) was used to measure the user acceptance degree and impact of recommendations from the system being evaluated. This was achieved through online surveys (Baez, Mirylenka, & Parra, 2011; McNee et al., 2002) or explicit and implicit measures such as click-through-rates (Beel, Langer, Genzmehr, & Nürnberger, 2013) and web usage information. Lastly, offline evaluations are the experiments that were used to measure the accuracy of research paper recommender systems using datasets presented for the experiment. Therefore, the goal of this section is to identify and highlight the various approaches that have been used to evaluate research paper recommender systems. It should be noted that some of the authors did use all the three evaluation methods to test their systems, i.e. (McNee et al., 2002), (Torres et al., 2004) and (Liang et al., 2011). The expert evaluation was also conducted by (Liang et al., 2011).

EVALUATION METRICS USED IN RPRS

Online Evaluation Metrics

Online evaluation measures for RPRS are not common since very few online experiments were conducted according to the outcome of the review of articles. When evaluating online studies, special metrics are used to mine and interpret usage data from the retrieval systems. Methods such as click-through-rate (CTR), link-through rate (LTR) and annotate-through rate (ATR), download-through rate (DR) and transition-through rate (DR) are used to find information about how online recommendation takes place. CTR is defined as the ratio of users who click on a specific link to the number of total users who view a page, email or advertisement.

$$CTR = \frac{clicks}{impression} * 100\%$$

Where the *impression* is the delivered recommendations. In the work done by (Joseph, 2013), the time spent on an online document, including the clicks determined the user activity of the user, thus they aided in building a user profile. Other online measures used in helping in the discovery of research paper include download through rates (DR), transition through rate (TR) by (Wesley-Smith & West, 2016) who chose user-centric measures took into consideration whether a user viewed and downloaded a paper.

$$DR = \frac{downloads}{impressions} * 100\%$$

$$TR = \frac{downloads}{clicks} * 100\%$$

The downside of CTR is that it cannot be predicted through offline evaluations (Beel, Genzmehr, Langer, Nürnberger, & Gipp, 2013; Wesley-Smith & West, 2016), also, both click rates and page view rates on research papers presents a very weak signal, thus they convey a lot of noise (Xue et al., 2014). However, click streams could be used to help rank recommendation results (Andre Vellino & Zeber, 2007). All these online approaches are very expensive as they require live users (Wesley-Smith & West, 2016).

Offline Evaluation Metrics

Offline evaluation metrics were dominantly used among all the evaluation types used in RPRS, and this is because they are convenient and easy to conduct due to the availability of datasets and affordability when it comes to costing matters. The evaluation metrics that were used include but are not limited to the following metrics: precision, recall, F-Measure, Discounted Cumulative Gain (DCG), Mean Average Precision (MAP) and Mean Reciprocal Rank (MRR). In this chapter, we categorize these evaluation metrics into three classes namely:

1. Rating and usage prediction accuracy: (precision, recall, F-Measure, Mean Average Precision (MAP), Root Mean Square Error (RMSE) and the Mean Absolute Error (MAE).
2. Ranking metrics that show how good a recommender system ranks its recommendations: (Discounted Cumulative Gain (DCG), Mean Reciprocal Rank (MRR), the area under the curve (ROC – receiver operating characteristic).
3. Metrics that quantify subjective recommendation qualities: (novelty, serendipity, diversity).

There are authors who used some of them, while other authors used most of them. The choice of metric depended on various reasons that the authors were trying to measure, and below are the measures used in the context of RPRS. Since offline evaluation is the most popular method of research paper recommender system, we provide details of metrics and category of the authors who implemented it in Table 4.

Table 4. Offline recommendation

Evaluation Class	Category	Metric	References
Offline evaluation	Accuracy metrics	Precision	(Choochaiwattana, 2010), (Ohta et al., 2011), (Zhao et al., 2015), (Bogers & Van den Bosch, 2008), (Kodakateri Pudhiyaveetil et al., 2009), (Hwang, Hsiung, & Yang, 2003),(H. Zhang et al., 2014), (Nanba & Okumura, 2005), (Z. Huang et al., 2002), (Baez et al., 2011), (Takano & Li, 2009), (Caragea, Silvescu, Mitra, & Giles, 2013), (Woodruff et al., 2000), (Arnold & Cohen, 2009), (Gipp & Beel, 2009), (McNee et al., 2002), (Uchiyama et al., 2011), (Liang et al., 2011), (Strohman et al., 2007), (Wu, Hua, Li, & Pei, 2012), (J. He, Nie, Lu, & Zhao, 2012), (Danesh et al., 2015), (Beel, 2017), (Gupta & Varma, 2017), (Guan et al., 2010), (H. Zhang et al., 2014), (Q. He, Pei, Kifer, Mitra, & Giles, 2010)
		Recall	(Xue et al., 2014), (Choochaiwattana, 2010), (Nascimento et al., 2011), (Zarrinkalam & Kahani, 2012), (Hwang et al., 2003), (H. Zhang et al., 2014), (Nanba & Okumura, 2005), (Z. Huang et al., 2002), (Baez et al., 2011), (Caragea et al., 2013), (Arnold & Cohen, 2009), (McNee et al., 2002), (Strohman et al., 2007), (Wu et al., 2012), (Danesh et al., 2015), (Zarrinkalam & Kahani, 2013), (Fujii, 2007), (Beel, 2017), (Liang et al., 2011), (Hanyurwimfura, Bo, Havyarimana, Njagi, & Kagorora, 2015), (Q. He et al., 2010)
		F-Measure	(Choochaiwattana, 2010), (Arnold & Cohen, 2009), (McNee et al., 2002), (Liang et al., 2011), (Danesh et al., 2015)
		MAE	(Shinde & Potey, 2016)
		MAP	(Bogers & Van den Bosch, 2008), (Martín, Schockaert, Cornelis, & Naessens, 2010), (Arnold & Cohen, 2009), (Jiang et al., 2012), (Strohman et al., 2007), (J. He et al., 2012), (Bethard & Jurafsky, 2010), (Fujii, 2007), (Joseph, 2013), (Gupta & Varma, 2017), (Guan et al., 2010), (Pohl, Radlinski, & Joachims, 2007)
		RMSE	(Shinde & Potey, 2016)
	Ranking metrics	nDCG	(Tran et al., 2015), (Xue et al., 2014), (Nascimento et al., 2011), (Pijitra Jomsri, Siripun Sanguansintukul, & Worasit Choochaiwattana, 2009), (P Jomsri, S Sanguansintukul, & W Choochaiwattana, 2009), (Zarrinkalam & Kahani, 2012), (Jiang et al., 2012), (Liang et al., 2011), (Wu et al., 2012), (Zarrinkalam & Kahani, 2013), (Beel, 2017), (Gupta & Varma, 2017), (Guan et al., 2010), (Hanyurwimfura et al., 2015), (Q. He et al., 2010)
		MRR	(Tran et al., 2015), (Bogers & Van den Bosch, 2008), (Martín et al., 2010), (Liang et al., 2011), (Wu et al., 2012), (Beel, 2017)
		ROC	(Zhao et al., 2015)

FUTURE DIRECTION

With the increase in data on the internet, better methods and tools are required that will aid in recommending relevant research papers to user. Below are few suggestions that might be followed.

1. Bisociation and research paper recommender systems (Maake, Ojo, & Zuva, 2019; Magara, Ojo, & Zuva, 2018), where by unrelated domains are processed to find out related concepts and topics that can be used in a research paper recommender system.
2. There is need for a thorough exploitation of user observations from applications like click data, eye tracking to enable the system model a user's precise activity on the research paper. These models when semantically enriched will yield better recommendations (Abel, Celik, Hauff, Hollink, & Houben, 2011). Similarly, users can be grouped together to improve the quality of recommendations on users or groups (M. Zhang et al., 2008)
3. Privacy and data security measures need to be implemented to facilitate trust-based recommendation. Adding trust value to each semantic individual is possible so that the items (research papers) that have been disliked by users are not used for recommendation again. (Lémdani, Polaillon, Bennacer, & Bourda, 2011).

REFERENCES

Abel, F., Celik, I., Hauff, C., Hollink, L., & Houben, G.-J. (2011). *U-sem: Semantic enrichment, user modeling, and mining of usage data on the social web.* arXiv preprint arXiv:1104.0126

Achakulvisut, T., Acuna, D. E., Ruangrong, T., & Kording, K. (2016). Science Concierge: A fast content-based recommendation system for scientific publications. *PLoS One, 11*(7), e0158423. doi:10.1371/journal.pone.0158423 PMID:27383424

Alotaibi, S., & Vassileva, J. (2015). *Multi-dimensional Ratings for Research Paper Recommender Systems: A Qualitative Study.* Paper presented at the International Symposium on Web AlGorithms, Deauville, France.

Alzoghbi, A., Ayala, V. A. A., Fischer, P. M., & Lausen, G. (2016). *Learning-to-Rank in Research Paper CBF recommendation: Leveraging Irrelevant Papers.* Paper presented at the CBRecSys@ RecSys, Boston, MA.

Arnold, A., & Cohen, W. W. (2009). *Information extraction as link prediction: Using curated citation networks to improve gene detection.* Paper presented at the International Conference on Wireless Algorithms, Systems, and Applications. 10.1007/978-3-642-03417-6_53

Baez, M., Mirylenka, D., & Parra, C. (2011). Understanding and supporting the search for scholarly knowledge. *Proceeding of the 7th European Computer Science Summit*, 1-8.

Beel, J. (2017). *Towards effective research-paper recommender systems and user modeling based on mind maps.* arXiv preprint arXiv:1703.09109

Beel, J., Genzmehr, M., Langer, S., Nürnberger, A., & Gipp, B. (2013). A comparative analysis of offline and online evaluations and discussion of research paper recommender system evaluation. *Proceedings of the international workshop on reproducibility and replication in recommender systems evaluation.* 10.1145/2532508.2532511

Beel, J., Gipp, B., Langer, S., & Breitinger, C. (2015). Research-paper recommender systems: A literature survey. *International Journal on Digital Libraries*, 1–34.

Beel, J., & Langer, S. (2015). *A comparison of offline evaluations, online evaluations, and user studies in the context of research-paper recommender systems.* Paper presented at the International Conference on Theory and Practice of Digital Libraries. 10.1007/978-3-319-24592-8_12

Beel, J., Langer, S., Genzmehr, M., Gipp, B., Breitinger, C., & Nürnberger, A. (2013). Research paper recommender system evaluation: a quantitative literature survey. *Proceedings of the International Workshop on Reproducibility and Replication in Recommender Systems Evaluation.*

Beel, J., Langer, S., Genzmehr, M., & Nürnberger, A. (2013). Introducing Docear's research paper recommender system. *Proceedings of the 13th ACM/IEEE-CS joint conference on Digital libraries.* 10.1145/2467696.2467786

Bethard, S., & Jurafsky, D. (2010). Who should I cite: learning literature search models from citation behavior. *Proceedings of the 19th ACM international conference on Information and knowledge management.* 10.1145/1871437.1871517

Bogers, T., & Van den Bosch, A. (2008). Recommending scientific articles using CiteULike. *Proceedings of the 2008 ACM conference on Recommender systems.* 10.1145/1454008.1454053

Bollacker, K. D., Lawrence, S., & Giles, C. L. (2000). Discovering relevant scientific literature on the web. *IEEE Intelligent Systems & their Applications*, *15*(2), 42–47. doi:10.1109/5254.850826

Brin, S., & Page, L. (1998). The anatomy of a large-scale hypertextual web search engine. *Computer Networks and ISDN Systems*, *30*(1), 107–117. doi:10.1016/S0169-7552(98)00110-X

Brusilovski, P., Kobsa, A., & Nejdl, W. (2007). The adaptive web: methods and strategies of web personalization (Vol. 4321). Berlin, Germany: Springer Science & Business Media. doi:10.1007/978-3-540-72079-9

Burke, R. (2002). Hybrid recommender systems: Survey and experiments. *User Modeling and User-Adapted Interaction*, *12*(4), 331–370. doi:10.1023/A:1021240730564

Caragea, C., Silvescu, A., Mitra, P., & Giles, C. L. (2013). Can't see the forest for the trees?: a citation recommendation system. *Proceedings of the 13th ACM/IEEE-CS joint conference on Digital libraries*. 10.1145/2467696.2467743

Chakraborty, T., Krishna, A., Singh, M., Ganguly, N., Goyal, P., & Mukherjee, A. (2016). *Ferosa: A faceted recommendation system for scientific articles*. Paper presented at the Pacific-Asia Conference on Knowledge Discovery and Data Mining. 10.1007/978-3-319-31750-2_42

Chakraborty, T., Modani, N., Narayanam, R., & Nagar, S. (2015, April). *Discern: a diversified citation recommendation system for scientific queries*. Paper presented at the 2015 IEEE 31st International Conference on Data Engineering (ICDE). 10.1109/ICDE.2015.7113314

Chen, L.-C., Kuo, P.-J., & Liao, I.-E. (2015). An ontology-based library recommender system using MapReduce. *Cluster Computing*, *18*(1), 113–121. doi:10.100710586-013-0342-z

Choochaiwattana, W. (2010). *Usage of tagging for research paper recommendation*. Paper presented at the 2010 3rd International Conference on Advanced Computer Theory and Engineering (ICACTE). 10.1109/ICACTE.2010.5579321

Danesh, S., Sumner, T., & Martin, J. H. (2015). SGRank: Combining Statistical and Graphical Methods to Improve the State of the Art in Unsupervised Keyphrase Extraction. In *Proceedings of the fourth joint conference on Lexical and Computational Semantics (SEM 2015),* (pp. 117-126). Academic Press.

Dattolo, A., Ferrara, F., & Tasso, C. (2009). *Supporting personalized user concept spaces and recommendations for a publication sharing system.* Paper presented at the International Conference on User Modeling, Adaptation, and Personalization. 10.1007/978-3-642-02247-0_31

Dong, R., Tokarchuk, L., & Ma, A. (2009). Digging friendship: paper recommendation in the social network. *Proceedings of Networking & Electronic Commerce Research Conference (NAEC 2009)*, 21-28.

Ekstrand, M. D., Kannan, P., Stemper, J. A., Butler, J. T., Konstan, J. A., & Riedl, J. T. (2010). Automatically building research reading lists. *Proceedings of the fourth ACM conference on Recommender systems*. 10.1145/1864708.1864740

Ferrara, F., Pudota, N., & Tasso, C. (2011). *A keyphrase-based paper recommender system. Digital Libraries and Archives* (pp. 14–25). Springer. doi:10.1007/978-3-642-27302-5_2

Fujii, A. (2007). Enhancing patent retrieval by citation analysis. *Proceedings of the 30th annual international ACM SIGIR conference on Research and development in information retrieval, 793-794.*

Giles, C. L., Bollacker, K. D., & Lawrence, S. (1998). CiteSeer: An automatic citation indexing system. *Proceedings of the third ACM conference on Digital libraries*. 10.1145/276675.276685

Gillitzer, B. (2010). Der Empfehlungsdienst BibTip—Ein flächendeckendes Angebot im Bibliotheksverbund Bayern. *BIT Online*, *13*(1), 47.

Gipp, B., & Beel, J. (2009). Citation Proximity Analysis (CPA)-A new approach for identifying related work based on Co-Citation Analysis. *Proceedings of the 12th International Conference on Scientometrics and Informetrics (ISSI'09),* 571-575.

Gipp, B., Beel, J., & Hentschel, C. (2009, January). Scienstein: A research paper recommender system. *Proceedings of the international conference on Emerging trends in computing (ICETiC'09), 309-315.*

Gori, M., & Pucci, A. (2006). *Research paper recommender systems: A random-walk based approach.* Paper presented at the 2006 IEEE/WIC/ACM International Conference on Web Intelligence, Hong Kong, China.

Guan, Z., Wang, C., Bu, J., Chen, C., Yang, K., Cai, D., & He, X. (2010). Document recommendation in social tagging services. *Proceedings of the 19th international conference on World wide web*. 10.1145/1772690.1772731

Gupta, S., & Varma, V. (2017). Scientific Article Recommendation by using Distributed Representations of Text and Graph. *Proceedings of the 26th International Conference on World Wide Web Companion*. 10.1145/3041021.3053062

Hanyurwimfura, D., Bo, L., Havyarimana, V., Njagi, D., & Kagorora, F. (2015). An effective academic research papers recommendation for non-profiled users. *International Journal of Hybrid Information Technology*, *8*(3), 255–272. doi:10.14257/ijhit.2015.8.3.23

He, J., Nie, J.-Y., Lu, Y., & Zhao, W. X. (2012). *Position-aligned translation model for citation recommendation.* Paper presented at the International Symposium on String Processing and Information Retrieval. 10.1007/978-3-642-34109-0_27

He, Q., Pei, J., Kifer, D., Mitra, P., & Giles, L. (2010). Context-aware citation recommendation. *Proceedings of the 19th international conference on World wide web*. 10.1145/1772690.1772734

Huang, Y.-C. (2007). *Combining Social Networks and Content for Recommendation in a Literature Digital Library*. Taiwan: National Sun Yat-Sen University.

Huang, Z., Chung, W., Ong, T.-H., & Chen, H. (2002). A graph-based recommender system for digital library. *Proceedings of the 2nd ACM/IEEE-CS joint conference on Digital libraries*. 10.1145/544220.544231

Hwang, S.-Y., Hsiung, W.-C., & Yang, W.-S. (2003). A prototype WWW literature recommendation system for digital libraries. *Online Information Review*, *27*(3), 169–182. doi:10.1108/14684520310481436

Jack, K. (2012). *Mendeley: recommendation systems for academic literature. Presentation at Technical University of Graz, Graz, Austria.*

Jiang, Y., Jia, A., Feng, Y., & Zhao, D. (2012). Recommending academic papers via users' reading purposes. *Proceedings of the sixth ACM conference on Recommender systems*. 10.1145/2365952.2366004

Jomsri, P., Sanguansintukul, S., & Choochaiwattana, W. (2009). *A comparison of search engine using "tag title and abstract" with CiteULike—An initial evaluation.* Paper presented at the International Conference for Internet Technology and Secured Transactions (ICITST 2009), London, UK.

Jomsri, P., Sanguansintukul, S., & Choochaiwattana, W. (2009). *Improving research paper searching with social tagging—A preliminary investigation.* Paper presented at the Eighth International Symposium on Natural Language Processing (SNLP'09), Bangkok, Thailand.

Joseph, A. S. (2013). *Conceptual, impact-based publications recommendations.* University of Arkansas.

Kapoor, N., Chen, J., Butler, J. T., Fouty, G. C., Stemper, J. A., Riedl, J., & Konstan, J. A. (2007). Techlens: a researcher's desktop. In *Proceedings of the 2007 ACM conference on Recommender systems (pp. 183-184).* ACM. 10.1145/1297231.1297268

Kodakateri Pudhiyaveetil, A., Gauch, S., Luong, H., & Eno, J. (2009). Conceptual recommender system for CiteSeerX. In *Proceedings of the third ACM conference on Recommender systems, (pp. 241-244).* ACM.

Konstan, J. A., McNee, S. M., Ziegler, C.-N., Torres, R., Kapoor, N., & Riedl, J. (2006). Lessons on applying automated recommender systems to information-seeking tasks. In *AAAI* (Vol. 6, pp. 1630-1633). Academic Press.

Kuberek, M., & Mönnich, M. (2012). *Einsatz von Recommender systemen in Bibliotheken.* Recommender systems in libraries: Presentation.

Küçüktunç, O., Kaya, K., Saule, E., & Çatalyürek, Ü. V. (2012, August). Fast recommendation on bibliographic networks. In *2012 IEEE/ACM International Conference on Advances in Social Networks Analysis and Mining* (pp. 480-487). IEEE. 10.1109/ASONAM.2012.82

Küçüktunç, O., Saule, E., Kaya, K., & Çatalyürek, Ü. V. (2013). Result diversification in automatic citation recommendation. *Proceedings of the iConference workshop on Computational scientometrics: theory and applications,* 1-4.

Lao, N., & Cohen, W. W. (2010). Relational retrieval using a combination of path-constrained random walks. *Machine Learning, 81*(1), 53–67. doi:10.100710994-010-5205-8

Le Anh, V., Hai, V. H., Tran, H. N., & Jung, J. J. (2014). Scirecsys: A recommendation system for scientific publication by discovering keyword relationships. In *International Conference on Computational Collective Intelligence* (pp. 72-82). Cham, Switzerland: Springer. 10.1007/978-3-319-11289-3_8

Lee, J., Lee, K., Kim, J. G., & Kim, S. (2015). *Personalized Academic Paper Recommendation System.* Academic Press.

Lémdani, R., Polaillon, G., Bennacer, N., & Bourda, Y. (2011). A semantic similarity measure for recommender systems. *Proceedings of the 7th International Conference on Semantic Systems.* 10.1145/2063518.2063545

Liang, Y., Li, Q., & Qian, T. (2011). *Finding relevant papers based on citation relations.* Paper presented at the International Conference on Web-Age Information Management. 10.1007/978-3-642-23535-1_35

Liu, X., Zhang, J., & Guo, C. (2016). Citation recommendation via proximity full-text citation analysis and supervised topical prior. *Proceedings of IConference 2016.*

Lopes, G. R., Souto, M. A. M., Wives, L. K., & de Oliveira, J. P. M. (2008). A personalized recommender system for digital libraries. *Proceedings of the 14th Brazilian Symposium on Multimedia and the Web.* 10.1145/1666091.1666103

Lovins, J. B. (1968). *Development of a stemming algorithm.* Academic Press.

Ma, L., Zhang, Y., Sunderraman, R., Fox, P. T., Laird, A. R., Turner, J. A., & Turner, M. D. (2015). Hybrid feature selection methods for online biomedical publication classification. In *2015 IEEE Conference on Computational Intelligence in Bioinformatics and Computational Biology (CIBCB)* (pp. 1-8). IEEE. 10.1109/CIBCB.2015.7300320

Maake, B. M., Ojo, S. O., & Zuva, T. (2019). A Serendipitous Research Paper Recommender System. *International Journal of Business and Management Studies, 11*(1), 38–53.

Magara, M. B., Ojo, S. O., & Zuva, T. (2018). Towards a Serendipitous Research Paper Recommender System Using Bisociative Information Networks (BisoNets). In *2018 International Conference on Advances in Big Data, Computing and Data Communication Systems (icABCD)* (pp. 1-6). IEEE.

Martín, G. H., Schockaert, S., Cornelis, C., & Naessens, H. (2010). *Metadata impact on research paper similarity.* Paper presented at the International Conference on Theory and Practice of Digital Libraries, Glasgow, UK.

McNee, S. M., Albert, I., Cosley, D., Gopalkrishnan, P., Lam, S. K., Rashid, A. M., ... Riedl, J. (2002). On the recommending of citations for research papers. *Proceedings of the 2002 ACM conference on Computer supported cooperative work.* 10.1145/587078.587096

McNee, S. M., Kapoor, N., & Konstan, J. A. (2006). Don't look stupid: avoiding pitfalls when recommending research papers. *Proceedings of the 2006 20th anniversary conference on Computer supported cooperative work.* 10.1145/1180875.1180903

Mishra, G. (2012). Optimised research paper recommender system using social tagging. *International Journal of Engineering Research and Applications, 2*(2), 1503–1507.

Mönnich, M., & Spiering, M. (2008). Erschließung. Einsatz von BibTip als Recommender system im Bibliothekskatalog. *Bibliotheksdienst*, *42*(1), 54–59. doi:10.1515/bd.2008.42.1.54

Naak, A. (2009). *Papyres: un système de gestion et de recommandation d'articles de recherche*. Academic Press.

Naak, A., Hage, H., & Aïmeur, E. (2008). *Papyres: A research paper management system*. Paper presented at the 2008 10th IEEE Conference on E-Commerce Technology and the Fifth IEEE Conference on Enterprise Computing, E-Commerce and E-Services. 10.1109/CECandEEE.2008.132

Nanba, H., & Okumura, M. (2005). *Automatic detection of survey articles*. Paper presented at the International Conference on Theory and Practice of Digital Libraries, Vienna, Austria.

Nascimento, C., Laender, A. H., da Silva, A. S., & Gonçalves, M. A. (2011). A source independent framework for research paper recommendation. *Proceedings of the 11th annual international ACM/IEEE joint conference on Digital libraries*. 10.1145/1998076.1998132

Ohta, M., Hachiki, T., & Takasu, A. (2011). *Related paper recommendation to support online-browsing of research papers*. Paper presented at the 2011 Fourth International Conference on the Applications of Digital Information and Web Technologies, University of Wisconsin, Madison, WI.

Paraschiv, I. C., Dascalu, M., Dessus, P., Trausan-Matu, S., & McNamara, D. S. (2016). *A Paper Recommendation System with ReaderBench: The Graphical Visualization of Semantically Related Papers and Concepts. In State-of-the-Art and Future Directions of Smart Learning* (pp. 445–451). Springer.

Pohl, S., Radlinski, F., & Joachims, T. (2007). Recommending related papers based on digital library access records. *Proceedings of the 7th ACM/IEEE-CS joint conference on Digital libraries*. 10.1145/1255175.1255260

Ricci, F., Rokach, L., & Shapira, B. (2011). Introduction to recommender systems handbook. Boston, MA: Springer. doi:10.1007/978-0-387-85820-3

Schafer, J., Frankowski, D., Herlocker, J., & Sen, S. (2007). Collaborative filtering recommender systems. In *The adaptive web* (pp. 291-324). Berlin, Germany: Springer.

Shimbo, M., Ito, T., & Matsumoto, Y. (2007). Evaluation of kernel-based link analysis measures on research paper recommendation. *Proceedings of the 7th ACM/IEEE-CS joint conference on Digital libraries*. 10.1145/1255175.1255245

Shinde, S. B., & Potey, M. M. (2016). Research Paper Recommender System Evaluation Using Coverage. *International Research Journal of Engineering and Technology, 3*(6).

Smeaton, A. F., & Callan, J. (2005). Personalisation and recommender systems in digital libraries. *International Journal on Digital Libraries*, *5*(4), 299–308. doi:10.100700799-004-0100-1

Strohman, T., Croft, W. B., & Jensen, D. (2007, July). Recommending citations for academic papers. In *SIGIR (Vol. 7, pp. 705-706)*. ACM.

Sugiyama, K., & Kan, M.-Y. (2010). Scholarly paper recommendation via user's recent research interests. *Proceedings of the 10th annual joint conference on Digital libraries*. 10.1145/1816123.1816129

Sugiyama, K., & Kan, M.-Y. (2015). A comprehensive evaluation of scholarly paper recommendation using potential citation papers. *International Journal on Digital Libraries*, *16*(2), 91–109. doi:10.100700799-014-0122-2

Takano, K., & Li, K. F. (2009). *An adaptive personalized recommender based on web-browsing behavior learning.* Paper presented at the 2009 International Conference on Advanced Information Networking and Applications Workshops. 10.1109/WAINA.2009.160

Tang, X., & Zeng, Q. (2012). Keyword clustering for user interest profiling refinement within paper recommender systems. *Journal of Systems and Software*, *85*(1), 87–101. doi:10.1016/j.jss.2011.07.029

Torres, R., McNee, S. M., Abel, M., Konstan, J. A., & Riedl, J. (2004). Enhancing digital libraries with TechLens+. In *Proceedings of the 4th ACM/IEEE-CS joint conference on Digital libraries (pp. 228-236). ACM.*

Tran, H. N., Huynh, T., & Hoang, K. (2015). *A Potential Approach to Overcome Data Limitation in Scientific Publication Recommendation.* Paper presented at the 2015 Seventh International Conference on Knowledge and Systems Engineering (KSE). 10.1109/KSE.2015.76

Uchiyama, K., Nanba, H., Aizawa, A., & Sagara, T. (2011). OSUSUME: cross-lingual recommender system for research papers. *Proceedings of the 2011 Workshop on Context-awareness in Retrieval and Recommendation.* 10.1145/1961634.1961642

Vellino, A. (2010). A comparison between usage-based and citation-based methods for recommending scholarly research articles. *Proceedings of the American Society for Information Science and Technology*, *47*(1), 1–2. doi:10.1002/meet.14504701330

Vellino, A., & Zeber, D. (2007). A hybrid, multi-dimensional recommender for journal articles in a scientific digital library. *Proceedings of the 2007 IEEE/WIC/ACM international conference on web intelligence and international conference on intelligent agent technology.* 10.1109/WI-IATW.2007.29

Wang, C., & Blei, D. M. (2011). Collaborative topic modeling for recommending scientific articles. *Proceedings of the 17th ACM SIGKDD international conference on Knowledge discovery and data mining.* 10.1145/2020408.2020480

Watanabe, S., Ito, T., Ozono, T., & Shintani, T. (2005). A paper recommendation mechanism for the research support system papits. *Proceedings of the 2005 International Workshop on Data Engineering Issues in E-Commerce.* 10.1109/DEEC.2005.3

Wesley-Smith, I., & West, J. D. (2016). Babel: a platform for facilitating research in scholarly article discovery. *Proceedings of the 25th international conference companion on world wide web.* 10.1145/2872518.2890517

West, J. D., Wesley-Smith, I., & Bergstrom, C. T. (2016). A recommendation system based on hierarchical clustering of an article-level citation network. *IEEE Transactions on Big Data, 2*(2), 113–123. doi:10.1109/TBDATA.2016.2541167

Woodruff, A., Gossweiler, R., Pitkow, J., Chi, E. H., & Card, S. K. (2000). Enhancing a digital book with a reading recommender. *Proceedings of the SIGCHI conference on Human factors in computing systems.* 10.1145/332040.332419

Wu, H., Hua, Y., Li, B., & Pei, Y. (2012). *Enhancing citation recommendation with various evidences.* Paper presented at the 2012 9th International Conference on Fuzzy Systems and Knowledge Discovery. 10.1109/FSKD.2012.6234002

Xia, F., Asabere, N. Y., Liu, H., Deonauth, N., & Li, F. (2014, April). Folksonomy based socially-aware recommendation of scholarly papers for conference participants. In *Proceedings of the 23rd International Conference on World Wide Web* (pp. 781-786). ACM.

Xia, F., Liu, H., Lee, I., & Cao, L. (2016). Scientific article recommendation: Exploiting common author relations and historical preferences. *IEEE Transactions on Big Data, 2*(2), 101–112. doi:10.1109/TBDATA.2016.2555318

Xue, H., Guo, J., Lan, Y., & Cao, L. (2014). *Personalized paper recommendation in online social scholar system.* Paper presented at the 2014 IEEE/ACM International Conference on Advances in Social Networks Analysis and Mining. 10.1109/ASONAM.2014.6921649

Yin, P., Zhang, M., & Li, X. (2007). *Recommending scientific literatures in a collaborative tagging environment.* Paper presented at the International Conference on Asian Digital Libraries. 10.1007/978-3-540-77094-7_60

Zarrinkalam, F., & Kahani, M. (2012). *A multi-criteria hybrid citation recommendation system based on linked data.* Paper presented at the 2012 2nd International eConference on Computer and Knowledge Engineering. 10.1109/ICCKE.2012.6395393

Zarrinkalam, F., & Kahani, M. (2013). SemCiR: A citation recommendation system based on a novel semantic distance measure. *Program, 47*(1), 92–112. doi:10.1108/00330331311296320

Zhang, H., Ni, W., Zhao, M., Liu, Y., & Yang, Y. (2014). *A hybrid recommendation approach for network teaching resources based on knowledge-tree.* Paper presented at the 2014 33rd Chinese Control Conference. 10.1109/ChiCC.2014.6895511

Zhang, M., Wang, W., & Li, X. (2008, December). *A paper recommender for scientific literatures based on semantic concept similarity. In 2008 11th International Conference on Asian Digital libraries (pp. 359-362). Berlin, Germany:* Springer. doi:10.1007/978-3-540-89533-6_44

Zhang, Z., & Li, L. (2010). *A research paper recommender system based on spreading activation model.* Paper presented at the 2010 2nd International Conference on Information Science and Engineering. 10.1109/ICISE.2010.5689417

Zhao, W., Wu, R., Dai, W., & Dai, Y. (2015, November). Research Paper Recommendation Based on the Knowledge Gap. In *2015 IEEE International Conference on Data Mining Workshop* (pp. 373-380). IEEE.

Zhou, D., Zhu, S., Yu, K., Song, X., Tseng, B. L., Zha, H., & Giles, C. L. (2008). Learning multiple graphs for document recommendations. *Proceedings of the 17th international conference on World Wide Web.* 10.1145/1367497.1367517

KEY TERMS AND DEFINITIONS

Algorithm: A process or set of rules to be followed in calculations or other problem-solving operations, especially by a computer.

Citation: A way in which you inform your reader that certain materials in your work came from another source. It is a quotation from a book, paper, or author.

Collaborative Filtering: A filtering and evaluation process that is utilized by recommendation systems for making predictions to interested users based on a collected and analyzed preference of many other users.

Content-Based Filtering: An approach that recommends items based on the descriptions of that item matched against the description of the user profile.

Data Mining: This is the process of sorting through databases to identify patterns and establish relationships to solve problems through data analysis.

Information Retrieval: A process of obtaining information system resources relevant to an information need from a collection.

Recommender System: A computerized systems that suggest goods and service by predicting user's preference and ratings.

Scientific Paper: A written report describing original research present on printed paper or electronically using editorial formats and ethics that have been developed.

Chapter 6
A Survey on Data Mining Techniques in Research Paper Recommender Systems

Benard Magara Maake
Tshwane University of Technology, South Africa

Sunday O. Ojo
Tshwane University of Technology, South Africa

Tranos Zuva
Vaal University of Technology, South Africa

ABSTRACT

In this chapter, the authors give an overview of the main data mining techniques that are utilized in the context of research paper recommender systems. These techniques refer to mathematical models and tools that are utilized in discovering patterns in data. Data mining is a term used to describe a collection of techniques that infer recommendation rules and build models from research paper datasets. The authors briefly describe how research paper recommender systems' data is processed, analyzed, and then, finally, interpreted using these techniques. They review different distance measures, sampling techniques, and dimensionality reduction methods employed in computing research paper recommendations. They also review the various clustering, classification, and association rule-mining methods employed to mine for hidden information. Finally, they highlight the major data mining issues that are affecting research paper recommender systems.

DOI: 10.4018/978-1-5225-8437-7.ch006

1. INTRODUCTION

Recommender systems are lately gaining significant roles in information filtering search. In the field of research paper recommender systems, various data mining techniques have been utilized to perform various tasks. This chapter intends to highlight the use of data mining and associated methods that have been used in research paper recommendation. We partly adopt the data mining steps and methods for recommender systems as highlighted by (Amatriain, Jaimes, Oliver, & Pujol, 2011) in the recommender systems handbook by (Ricci, Rokach, & Shapira, 2011) to represent the various data mining methods and technologies that were employed at various levels of computing research paper recommendations. Data mining in this context consists of three main steps namely: Data preprocessing stage, Data analysis stage and the Result interpretation stage. We may not have a crisp separation and categorization of some of the methods and algorithms since most of them overlap.

This review chapter is organized according to the following sections: The chapter introduction and overview is presented in Section 1. A summary of data preprocessing methods and measures as utilized in research paper recommender systems is presented in Section 2. Classification algorithms utilized by research paper recommender systems are highlighted in Section 3. Section 4 presents clustering algorithms, while Section 5 presents other approaches to classification. Section 6 presents the main data mining issues facing research paper recommendation, whereas Section 7 concludes the chapter.

Figure 1 highlights data mining features, approaches, and processes utilized in research paper recommender systems (RPRS). It represents the three main data mining steps which are consecutively applied during the processing of data, and they include data preprocessing step, data analysis step and finally, the results interpretation step. This chapter, however, dwell much on the first two steps, data preprocessing and data analysis steps since they actively utilize various data mining techniques.

2. DATA PREPROCESSING IN RPRS

Data preprocessing is an important step in machine learning and information retrieval because it screens data for any problems to prevent the possibility of producing misleading results after the processing process. Real-world datasets in the field of RPRS were generally incomplete (Gupta & Varma, 2017), noisy (Bogers & Van den Bosch, 2008; Bollen & Van de Sompel, 2006; Dong, Tokarchuk, & Ma, 2009; J. He, Nie, Lu, & Zhao, 2012; Y. Liang, Li, & Qian, 2011; McNee et al., 2002; Torres, McNee, Abel, Konstan, & Riedl, 2004; Tran, Huynh, & Hoang, 2015; Wu, Hua, Li,

Figure 1. Data Mining in RPRS

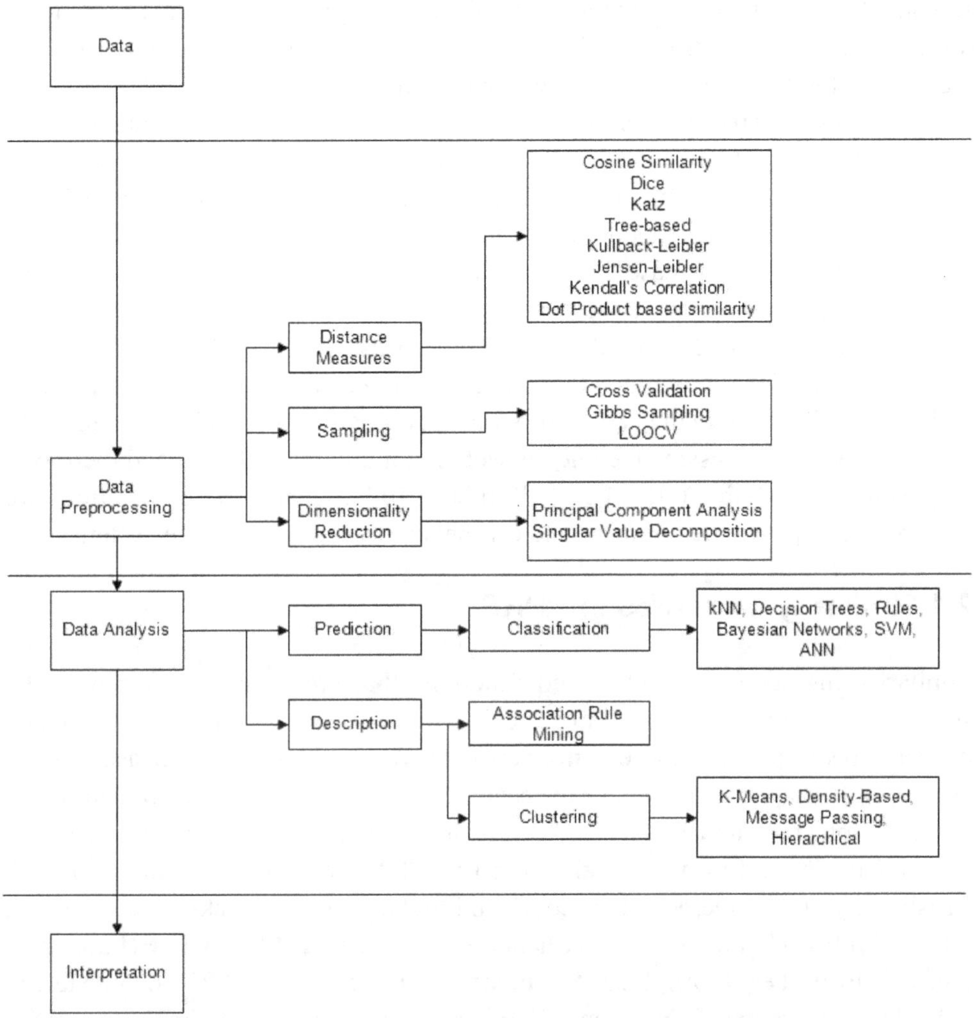

& Pei, 2012; Xue, Guo, Lan, & Cao, 2014) and inconsistent (Capocci & Caldarelli, 2008) and thus required tasks that will transform them (Nascimento, Laender, da Silva, & Gonçalves, 2011). These preprocessing tasks include: data cleaning (Ferrara, Pudota, & Tasso, 2011), data integration (Hwang, Hsiung, & Yang, 2003; Mönnich & Spiering, 2008; Wu et al., 2012; Zarrinkalam & Kahani, 2012), data transformation (Joran Beel & Gipp, 2009), data reduction and data discretization. Data cleaning ensures that missing values are filled, noisy data is smoothed, outliers are removed (T.-P. Liang, Yang, Chen, & Ku, 2008) and all inconsistencies are resolved. Data integration ensures integration of all necessary files or databases (Zarrinkalam & Kahani, 2012). Data transformation normalises and aggregates the data going to be used for analysis. Data discretization ensures that some parts of numerical attributes are replaced with nominal ones, when the need arises.

Before research paper recommender systems datasets were used in analysis, they were preprocessed (Avancini, Candela, & Straccia, 2007; Guan et al., 2010; Gupta & Varma, 2017; Lee, Lee, Kim, & Kim, 2015; Paraschiv, Dascalu, Dessus, Trausan-Matu, & McNamara, 2016; Zarrinkalam & Kahani, 2013) to remove special characters, transform the text to one case, i.e. the lower case (Gupta & Varma, 2017), remove available stop words, remove tab character or overlap vacancy characters and get keywords (Hong, Jeon, & Jeon, 2012). Text preprocessing was performed to improve the efficiency of the recommendation algorithm (Zarrinkalam & Kahani, 2013), and then finally, to stem the keywords with relevant algorithms (Nascimento et al., 2011). These preprocessing techniques were not mutually exclusive and therefore, they were used together (Han, Pei, & Kamber, 2011). Finally, these operations are designed to improve the accuracy and efficiency of recommendation systems.

2.1 Similarity measures in RPRS

Similarity measures are real-valued functions that are utilized to quantify the similarity between two objects, and in the field of RPRS they were utilized as distance measures between two or more terms/ concepts. Variety of similarity measures were used to define appropriate distance measure/ similarity, i.e. the cosine similarity measure (Jomsri, Sanguansintukul, & Choochaiwattana, 2009), asymmetric, Jaccard & extended Jaccard measure (Takano & Li, 2009), Pearson correlation (Parra & Brusilovsky, 2009), tree-edit distance (Chandrasekaran, Gauch, Lakkaraju, & Luong, 2008), Kullback-Leibler measure (Chandrasekaran et al., 2008), CCIDF (Lawrence, Giles, & Bollacker, 1999), katz (Strohman, Croft, & Jensen, 2007), dice (Martín, Schockaert, Cornelis, & Naessens, 2010), etc. for instance, the simplest distance measure used is the Euclidean distance (Guan et al., 2010).

$$d(x,y) = \sqrt{\sum_{k=1}^{n} (x_k - y_k)^2}$$

Where n is the number of dimensions (attributes), x_k and y_k are the kth attributes of data objects x and y, respectively. Most research papers recommender systems used the cosine similarity which considered articles as document vectors that were being projected to an n-dimensional space. The similarity of the documents was computed as the cosine of the angles formed between those two objects. The cosine similarity measure takes this form:

$$\cos(x, y) = \frac{(x \cdot y)}{\|x\|\|y\|}$$

Where • was the vector dot product, and ||*x*|| was the norm vector *x*.

In RPRS, the vector cosine similarity was used in various ways, i.e. cosine similarity was used to measure: the semantic similarity between two research paper tags (M. Zhang, Wang, & Li, 2008), the terms in documents (Nascimento et al., 2011), the semantic similarity of research paper keywords (Hong, Jeon, & Jeon, 2013), the ranking of research papers (Jiang, Jia, Feng, & Zhao, 2012; Nascimento et al., 2011; Sugiyama & Kan, 2010), retrieve and rank search results (Jomsri et al., 2009), matching categories of n-gram features (Ferrara et al., 2011), measure semantic relatedness of words, tags and documents (Paraschiv et al., 2016), similarity between a paper and a researcher (Tran et al., 2015), used as a recommendation strategy (Nascimento et al., 2011), performed indexing for each paper and constructed an inverted index file in the databases (Hong et al., 2013), measure likeness between web documents and a thesaurus (Takano & Li, 2009) and measure relevance of a candidate paper (Hanyurwimfura, Bo, Havyarimana, Njagi, & Kagorora, 2015).

On the other hand, the generalized and extended Jaccard similarity coefficients were used to measure the similarity of the users (Dattolo, Ferrara, & Tasso, 2009) and of terms coming from paper abstracts (Martín et al., 2010). The Dice similarity measured papers represented as vectors in the vector space model (Dattolo et al., 2009), then the Katz distance measured the similarity between nodes in a graph (Y. Liang et al., 2011), and unique paths on a citation graph (Strohman et al., 2007), greatly increasing the performance of their model. Tree-edit distance measure computed the similarity between user profiles and paper profile (Chandrasekaran et al., 2008).

The Pearson similarity measure was used to calculate the similarity between the target paper and the candidate papers (Lee et al., 2015), i.e. in Papyres, it calculated the similarity between the researcher and his neighbours (Naak, Hage, & Aïmeur, 2008). It (Pearson similarity measures) also calculated the similarity between original datasets and manually built datasets (Tran et al., 2015), further again calculating the similarity between users and items (Mishra, 2012; Pan & Li, 2010), and neighbourhood between users (Tang & McCalla, 2003). Finally, the Pearson measure was used to conduct a correlation of different evaluation metrics that were used in RPRS (Joeran Beel, 2017).

The Kullback-Leibler distributional similarity measure was used to measure how redundant one document was from another (Y. Zhang, Callan, & Minka, 2002), and how topics were distributed in documents (Bethard & Jurafsky, 2010).

The Jensen Shannon divergence similarity measure also measured topic distribution in a document (Bethard & Jurafsky, 2010; Paraschiv et al., 2016). The Kendall's Spearman's and the Pearson were all used to evaluate between manually built and original datasets (Tran et al., 2015). The dot-product based similarity score was used to compute the information retrieval score of documents in a search engine (Brin & Page, 1998). A cosine dot product similarity between two documents pairs were used to make recommendations (Woodruff, Gossweiler, Pitkow, Chi, & Card, 2000). Lastly, the dot product similarity measure computed the similarity between user-interest tags of the literature' selected keywords (Yin, Zhang, & Li, 2007).

Not all authors prepared their data for analysis, and the few preprocessing methods that were conducted lacked measurable standards and substantial details as to why they chose those methods, and how they performed the process. Whenever users realize that the data had lots of noise, then the results of the algorithms is not going to be trusted. Figure 2 represents a comparison on the popularity of similarity measures that were utilised in RPRS. The cosine similarity was the most popular measure used by most authors.

Figure 2. Similarity measures used in RPRS

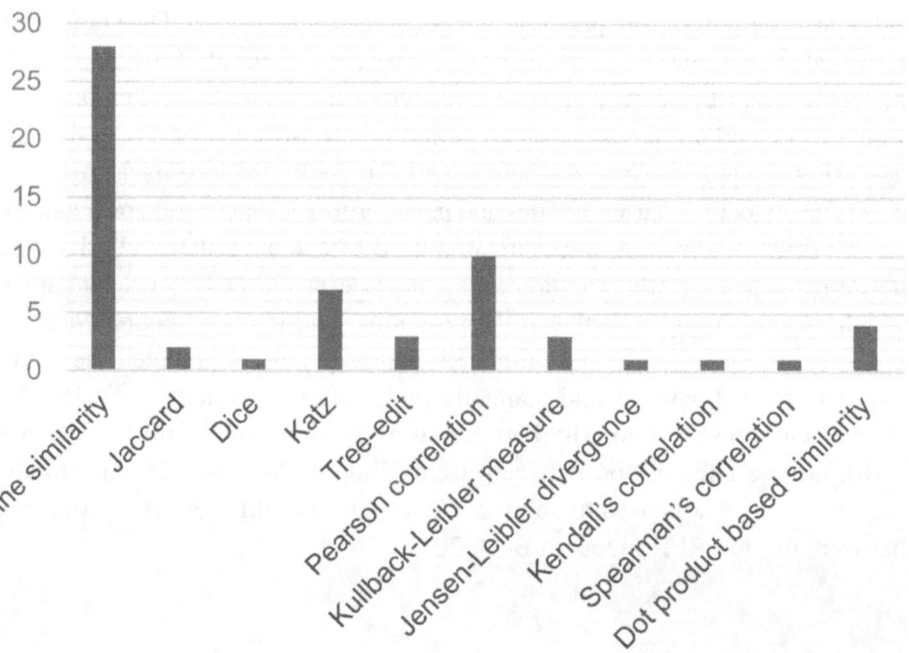

2.2 Sampling

Sampling helps the researchers select a subset of relevant data ensuring the cost of computation complexity is not very expensive given that there is a very large dataset. It is applied at both the preprocessing stage as well as the data interpretation stage. It is therefore used to get the representative dataset to perform various experiments. Sampling in (Xue et al., 2014) was used to generate dynamically research paper recommendations to users and add uncertainty to represent non-interesting papers to candidates. To test the algorithm, citation datasets were divided into training and test data, and a 10-fold cross-validation was done (Dong et al., 2009; McNee et al., 2002; Torres et al., 2004), cross-validation was used to prevent overfitting of several parameters used in predicting papers (Bogers & Van den Bosch, 2008). 4-fold cross-validation was conducted on research papers having tags (Yin et al., 2007). 10-fold cross validation was utilized on reference list (Gori & Pucci, 2006); on a query set (Strohman et al., 2007); on bibliographic collection (André Vellino, 2009); on user book-purchase history data (Huang, Chung, Ong, & Chen, 2002) et cetera. Gibbs sampling, on the other hand, was used to analyze topics (words in documents/ research papers) in (Pan & Li, 2010; Zhao, Wu, Dai, & Dai, 2015).

2.3 Dimensionality reduction

High dimensional features or very sparse matrices need to be reduced so that efficiency can be realized when recommending research papers. Even as the reduction of data happens, the integrity of the original data should always be closely maintained (Han et al., 2011). Preprocessing data through stemming is one of the very first steps that dramatically reduces the dimensionality of data (Lee et al., 2015). The Principal Component Analysis (PCA) and the Singular Value Decomposition (SVD) are the two most frequently used methods for transforming high dimensional spaces into low dimensional spaces. Funk-SVD was used by (Guan et al., 2010) to approximate the original data in the user-item matrix. (Caragea, Silvescu, Kataria, Caragea, & Mitra, 2011) utilized the SVD on the graph formed by citation data. (Zhou et al., 2008) used citation graphs and author graphs to construct an author-document matrix that they optimized with the SVD. (Bollen & Van de Sompel, 2006) mapped journals onto a 2-dimensional location based on their usage data.

2.4 Denoising

Data that needs to be analyzed has so much noise such as missing values, outliers, etc. and denoising is used to remove unwanted data so as to prevent unwanted effect in analysis and interpretation. In RPRS, depending on what was being investigated missing abstracts or portions of the article were enough to warrant the paper to be dropped from the dataset of the ones going to be processed, i.e. (Gupta & Varma, 2017) pre-filtered incomplete records and documents that had less than ten citations from the dataset. Papers that cited less than two other papers were removed, and citations were removed from papers that were dropped (Dong et al., 2009). Torres et al., 2004 removed papers with less than two citations and also papers that did not have full text (Torres et al., 2004), while others removed papers with less than four citations (Daud, Shaikh, & Rajpar, 2009), (Caragea, Silvescu, Mitra, & Giles, 2013; Gupta & Varma, 2017) removed all papers that had more than one hundred citations and less than 10 citations. Publications that had missing values, and ones that had no title and abstracts were also filtered out (Zarrinkalam & Kahani, 2012), user sessions considered as robots were removed (Hwang et al., 2003), duplicate and near duplicate papers were removed (Nascimento et al., 2011), self-citations (Baez, Mirylenka, & Parra, 2011), inadequate queries that can retrieve irrelevant paper were removed (Hanyurwimfura et al., 2015), bookmarks with no tags were removed (Guan et al., 2010). Other features that were also considered as noise or outliers are extremely high citations.

3. CLASSIFICATION ALGORITHMS

In data mining, a classifier maps a feature space to a label space, whereby a feature space includes all the relevant characteristics of the object, and a label space is the classes that the items are going to be classified into. There are many types of classifiers namely: supervised and unsupervised and they are all used in RPRS. Supervised classifiers in RPRS include: *k*-Nearest neighbours (*k*-NN), Decision trees, Rule-based, Bayesian classifiers, Artificial Neural Networks (ANN), Ensembles of classifiers. On the other hand, unsupervised classifiers include: cluster analysis (k-means, density based, hierarchy and message passing) and Association Rule Mining.

The *k*-NN algorithm was used to find neighbourhood between users, as articles having references to other articles were considered as "*users*" (André Vellino, 2009). The *k*-NN was also used to find user ratings neighborhood (Pan & Li, 2010), it was used to suggest citations in a content-based approach (Nascimento et al., 2011), but on the other hand, it was used to output an ordered list of citations as its recommendation (Chandrasekaran et al., 2008). The *k*-NN algorithm was further used to classify tags (Guan et al., 2010; Kodakateri Pudhiyaveetil, Gauch, Luong, & Eno, 2009; Yin et al., 2007), used the cosine similarity measure to create a neighbourhood of highly similar papers to the target paper given by a user-item rating matrix (McNee et al.,

2002), it took citations of active papers as input and gave out a list of recommended citations as output (Torres et al., 2004), compared document vectors to user profile vector to rank documents (Joseph, 2013), measured researchers highest ratings and also predicted researchers ratings to an unrated resource (Naak et al., 2008), and even it recommended papers to the user (Lee et al., 2015). In (McNee, Kapoor, & Konstan, 2006) it was used to generate a recommendation for specific users. In (Xue et al., 2014) it was used in a typical user-based Collaborative Filtering to recommend papers that were similar to other profiles that were not within the author's interest profile. In (Pan & Li, 2010) *k*-NN was used to establish the similarity between the user needs, while in (Gipp, Beel, & Hentschel, 2009) it was used to classify and analyze text along with other features in a hybrid recommender system.

(Joeran Beel, Langer, Genzmehr, & Nürnberger, 2013) utilized a tree-like data structure (mind maps) to manage its information. (Huang et al., 2002) used a PAT-tree to efficiently access large corpus of data, while (Martín et al., 2010) utilized the ACM classification tree structure to store and manipulate the papers. (Chandrasekaran et al., 2008) utilized trees to represent user profiles, while (H. Zhang, Ni, Zhao, Liu, & Yang, 2014) represented network teaching resources as knowledge trees that are organized with decision trees. Related concepts and relationships were represented as semantic trees (T.-P. Liang et al., 2008), and finally, the rule-based structure was used to reduce the size of candidate phrase sets (Ferrara et al., 2011).

Probabilistic models were the most common classification algorithms used in RPRS. In the work done by (J. He et al., 2012), the model tried to accurately align queries probabilistically to relevant parts of a document. (Danesh, Sumner, & Martin, 2015) sought higher transition probability of terms with higher statistical weights than those with lower weights. (Zarrinkalam & Kahani, 2013) designed a system that would accept text as input and then recommend publications that should be cited by it using co-citation probabilities. (Bethard & Jurafsky, 2010) developed a system with topical features that inspected probability distributions of topics in a particular document. (Gori & Pucci, 2006) used PageRank to sort out papers according to the expected liking of a user, as higher PageRank position implied a higher probability of a paper being a valuable suggestion to a user. (Shimbo, Ito, & Matsumoto, 2007) utilised the Hofmann's probabilistic Latent Semantic Indexing on citation to determine distinct topics, (Gipp & Beel, 2009) developed a citation proximity analysis approach which gave probability weights to citations depending on how close they were to each other, i.e. citations within same sentences received different weights compared to the ones within the same paragraph. (Jiang et al., 2012) proposed to satisfy users specific reading purpose and tasks by recommending the most problem and solution related papers using the topic modeling algorithm

– Latent Dirichlet Allocation (LDA) model. (Zarrinkalam & Kahani, 2012) used co-cited probability to measure the quality of recommendations from their citation based systems enhanced with multiple linked data sources. (Wang & Blei, 2011) recommended online user by combining collaborative filtering and probabilistic topic models, (Paraschiv et al., 2016) proposed a model that suggested similar, semantically related, and highly relevant papers using LDA, Latent Semantic Analysis (LSA). (Zhao et al., 2015) utilized concept maps to establish the knowledge gap of the user, and topic modeling algorithm LDA extracted topics that reflected certain domains. (Pan & Li, 2010) utilized LDA to perform thematic similarity of papers and to alleviate the cold start problem in RPRS, while (Bogers & Van den Bosch, 2008) calculated the similarity of items (papers) using conditional probability among other similarity metrics. (McNee et al., 2002) used the Naïve Bayes based classifier as one of the algorithms used to select citations. (Lee et al., 2015) utilized the Naïve Bayes assumptions of the position and proximity independence of words, and (Arnold & Cohen, 2009) used probabilistic social network link models to predict connections between authors and genes.

(Gipp et al., 2009) used the Support Vector Machines (SVM) to analyze and classify input text for recommendation purposes, (Xue et al., 2014) utilized the Ranking SVM to their ranking model. (Bethard & Jurafsky, 2010) utilized an SVM-MAP classifier to optimize the Mean Average Precision (MAP) when retrieving a list of references as recommendations in response to an abstract input. (Strohman et al., 2007) used the SVM to train all the features that were going to be used for recommendation computation. (Krallinger, Erhardt, & Valencia, 2005) used SVM to estimate the dependencies that existed between their data. (Ferrara et al., 2011) utilized a rule-based engine to reduce and filter out the size of candidate phrases during the preprocessing stage. (Krallinger et al., 2005) used an ad hoc rule-base classifier to tag genes and proteins.

4. CLUSTERING AND CLUSTERING ALGORITHMS

Clustering is a process that groups a set of similar objects together (cluster) through the assessment of attribute values that are describing the objects. In RPRS, clustering may be used for various functions, i.e. clustering documents into topics or concepts (Han et al., 2011), preceding other classification algorithms as a preprocessing function, and, candidate research papers were clustered to the most similar papers using the K-Means algorithm (Lee et al., 2015). Grouping together of users of a similar research paper can also be done by clustering (Tang & McCalla, 2003).

(Huang et al., 2002) weighted and classified key phrase features extracted from the title, keywords, and authors. (Hwang et al., 2003) utilized the Association Rule Hyper-graph Partitioning clustering technique to analyze web usage logs in order to identify article clusters and discover relevant article association rules. (Andre Vellino & Zeber, 2007) recommended the approach of profiling user behaviors into clusters, then cluster them according to some similarity measure. (Bollen & Van de Sompel, 2006) mapped journals to user interest clusters, (Bollacker, Lawrence, & Giles, 1998) clustered identical citations together for automatic similarity retrieval of documents. The PLSI in (McNee et al., 2006) "acted" as a soft cluster algorithm that grouped latent classes into clusters. (Capocci & Caldarelli, 2008) utilized clustering coefficients to analyze and uncover hidden semantic relationships between tags. (J. He et al., 2012) clustered together specific topics that were in a document. In (Ohta, Hachiki, & Takasu, 2011), all the training documents were clustered into three topical groups, and in each cluster, a ranking algorithm was used to rank the tags, further clustering concepts according to user preferences. (Tang & McCalla, 2003) utilized browsing sequences and active assessment of research papers to cluster together users with similar interests. (Krallinger et al., 2005) clusters words and genes into relevant clusters. In (West, Wesley-Smith, & Bergstrom, 2016) clustering was used to perform three major tasks namely: clustering citation networks (graphs), ranking of nodes, and finally, establishing and defining the boundaries between domains, subdomain, and fields. (Bancu et al., 2012) performed citation matching through clustering articles into groups that would cite the same paper. (Q. He, Kifer, Pei, Mitra, & Giles, 2011) used each citation as a bag-of-words, and the title and abstract features were clustered into relevant topics. (Küçüktunç, Saule, Kaya, & Çatalyürek, 2012) used clustering to differentiate between old and new research papers, as new papers had fewer neighbors compared to the old papers. They also clustered similar keywords to enable them expand their query generation mechanism. CiteSeer a scientific literature repository which by design clusters together interests of its users (Bollacker, Lawrence, & Giles, 2000).

5. OTHER APPROACHES TO CLASSIFICATION

Many data mining classification approaches were also encountered in RPRS. (Bethard & Jurafsky, 2010) used two variants of a logistic classifier to train the data, while (Ekstrand et al., 2010) used logistic classifier to train his data and test the text similarity of the algorithms. (Gori & Pucci, 2006) presented a random-walk scoring algorithm that recommended papers based on few papers selected by the user, Random walking may also be used to classify text through graphs. (Arnold & Cohen, 2009) used random walks to calculate the proximity of nodes in a paper graph to lead to better recommendations.

The concept-tree algorithm outperformed traditional keyword matching algorithms during the recommendation of articles (Chandrasekaran et al., 2008). (Bethard & Jurafsky, 2010) used the Pointwise Mutual Information (PMI) algorithm to select important citing terms in article recommendation. (Zarrinkalam & Kahani, 2013) used Genetic Algorithm to assign proper weights to features in the citation recommender system. (Xue et al., 2014) provided a personalised paper recommender system by employing a learning to rank algorithm. In various experiments, PageRank was used for various reasons, for instance, in (Andre Vellino & Zeber, 2007), it was used to give weights to citation-based ratings, in (Brin & Page, 1998) it prioritized web-based keyword results, in (Gori & Pucci, 2006). PageRank assigned preference scores to documents in a digital library, while in (Ekstrand et al., 2010) it measured the influence of a paper within citation networks (graphs) using PageRank and Hyperlink-Induced Topic Search (HITS) algorithms. (Bollen & Van de Sompel, 2006) used a PageRank variation called *Usage PageRank* to rank journals based on their usage data. (Bethard & Jurafsky, 2010) used PageRank as a scoring function to calculate and normalize the popularity of articles. (Xue et al., 2014) described the quality of a candidate paper using the articles static features, while (André Vellino, 2009) attempted to improve journal recommendations through PageRank ratings, unfortunately, the performance was very poor. (Fujii, 2007) used PageRank with text-based retrieval methods to enhance patent retrieval. Finally, the HITS algorithm was used to rank related papers (Ohta et al., 2011), and automatically detect survey papers (Nanba & Okumura, 2005).

Association rules are created by analyzing data for frequency of if-then patterns using the support and confidence criterions to identify the most important relationships. In RPRS, association rules were used by a few authors. (Bollen & Van de Sompel, 2006) recommended papers based on the relationship between papers and usage data collected for accessing those papers. (Hwang et al., 2003) used usage logs on their electronic thesis and dissertation database to discover article clusters and then utilized association-rule-based recommendations to recommend top-N articles relevant to users (H. Zhang et al., 2014).

From Sections 3, 4 and 5 when analyzing the data, probabilistic methods were more favorable than other algorithms during the process of computing recommendation in research paper recommender systems. Figure 3 represents a summary of the data mining algorithms used in research paper recommender systems. Some authors utilized many data mining techniques to achieve various goals in their systems whereas other utilized few.

Figure 3. Data mining algorithms used in RPRS

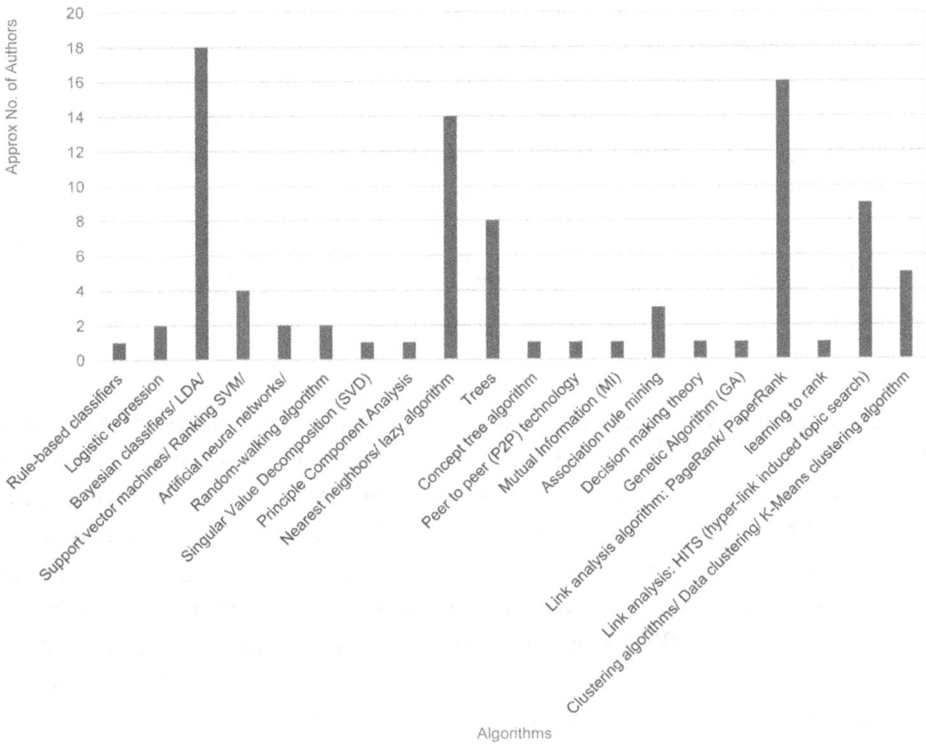

6. DATA MINING ISSUES FACING RESEARCH PAPER RECOMMENDER SYSTEMS

There are many benefits that have been brought about by the data mining technology in research paper recommendation which makes then still usable and adoptable by these information filtering and search systems. However, there are also many issues and challenges related to this data mining technology that the research paper recommendation systems' field has encountered. They include:

6.1 Data Sparsity

Data sparsity can be caused by a limited number of users to rate items or, development of recommender systems for particular areas or fields that do not support rating of the system (Andre Vellino & Zeber, 2007). RPRS does not have rating features, and due to the nature of research papers, they take long before they are discovered online or even before they start getting citation counts, thus data sparsity becomes a problem if the citation counts are going to be taken or used as ratings. The situation is exacerbated when the article is not even seen, or downloaded or even receive any act of recognition for its presence. Large number of ratings are required to be able to make better recommendations – thus chances are there to have millions of papers not rated thus not having any ratings. Items are more compared to users and the likelihood of users not willing to rate all papers is high, and manipulations are very common (André Vellino, 2010), (Kodakateri Pudhiyaveetil et al., 2009), (Arnold & Cohen, 2009), (Dong et al., 2009). Due to data sparsity in (Guan et al., 2010), the algorithm completely fails to run on CiteULike datasets. (Torres et al., 2004).

6.2 Overspecialization in CBF

Overspecialization occurs when items like the first one are recommended again and again to the user, saturating him with very similar items. In RPRS overspecialization will be seen when similar research papers are proposed to users again and again (Dong et al., 2009; Andre Vellino & Zeber, 2007) making the user experience lower serendipity on the recommendations received (Dong et al., 2009), and this is the disadvantage of using content-based filtering algorithm for paper recommendation (Andre Vellino & Zeber, 2007). However, approaches like randomness and bisociation in recommendation can generate serendipitous research papers (Maake, Ojo, & Zuva, 2019; Magara, Ojo, & Zuva, 2018).

6.3 Privacy Issues

Implicit rating requires that the users are constantly monitored, thus raising privacy issues of current activities of the user (Bollen & Van de Sompel, 2006; Mönnich & Spiering, 2008). Since the user is tracked on a real-time basis, then even his activities can be inferred by interpreting patterns formed from his online activities while reading and searching for research papers (Geyer-Schulz, Hahsler, Neumann, & Thede, 2003). Users that never registered themselves to online research paper recommender systems were thought to be concerned about their privacy (Joeran Beel & Langer, 2015), and there were forces between getting good recommendations versus remaining anonymous (Geyer-Schulz, Hahsler, & Jahn, 2001; Jack, 2012). Sharing and collaborating in research while maintaining privacy is a challenging balance to strike (Smeaton & Callan, 2005).

6.4 Reproducibility

Most of the experiments that were conducted in the articles reviewed could hardly be reproduced since the presence of various challenges like inaccessible datasets, different ways and methods of processing the data, etc. lack of a standard method of evaluation methods and the temporal state of datasets and specific features that keeps changing from time to time like in the case of online experiments make it hard to reproduce those experiments (Joeran Beel, Langer, Genzmehr, Gipp, et al., 2013).

6.5 Cold Start

The ratio of users (researchers) to that of articles (research papers) is so large and there is a chance that some of the work done by many researchers will go unnoticed for a couple of days. If some new researchers or one that is coming from a different field altogether comes to access a recommender system, chances are that the recommender systems might not have any recommendation for such a person - cold start could be very high. Requires user's participation, and if the users are very few, then the cold start problem faces the approach (Jiang et al., 2012; McNee et al., 2002).

6.6 Computational Complexity

The task of recommending research paper and utilizing all features will require more computing power than most types of approaches since each item's features must be analyzed, made into a model and then the similarity measures performed (Joeran Beel, Gipp, Langer, & Breitinger, 2015). Better and efficient data mining and processing methods need to be discovered to ensure efficiency during recommendation.

6.7 Synonym and Polysemy

Problems caused due to synonymies and unclear nomenclatures in research paper recommendation (Gipp et al., 2009) make recommendation of research papers inaccurate. Better technologies need to be used to be able to differentiate words synonymous works, and also exploit the context of works in a document.

6.8 Manipulation of Research Paper Recommendation Engines

During research paper recommendation using the state of the art research paper recommender systems, it is possible to manipulate features and tools that are used to recommend papers, i.e. the Google Scholar can be manipulated to give false information about a particular paper without being detected (Lopez-Cozar, Robinson-Garcia, & Torres-Salinas, 2012).

7. CONCLUSION

This chapter was dedicated to identifying the various data mining techniques and methodologies that are used in the domain of research paper recommender systems. Variety of methods used have been identified and we propose further research into establishing better techniques to handle this data through a combination of an existing technologies, and development of new techniques. Critical data mining issues facing research paper recommender systems were also heightened and they provide a guide for further research.

REFERENCES

Amatriain, X., Jaimes, A., Oliver, N., & Pujol, J. M. (2011). Data mining methods for recommender systems. In Recommender systems handbook (pp. 39–71). Boston, MA: Springer. doi:10.1007/978-0-387-85820-3_2

Arnold, A., & Cohen, W. W. (2009). *Information extraction as link prediction: Using curated citation networks to improve gene detection.* Paper presented at the International Conference on Wireless Algorithms, Systems, and Applications. 10.1007/978-3-642-03417-6_53

Avancini, H., Candela, L., & Straccia, U. (2007). Recommenders in a personalized, collaborative digital library environment. *Journal of Intelligent Information Systems*, *28*(3), 253–283. doi:10.100710844-006-0010-3

Baez, M., Mirylenka, D., & Parra, C. (2011). Understanding and supporting the search for scholarly knowledge. *Proceeding of the 7th European Computer Science Summit.*

Bancu, C., Dagadita, M., Dascalu, M., Dobre, C., Trausan-Matu, S., & Florea, A. M. (2012). ARSYS--Article Recommender System. In *2012 14th International Symposium on Symbolic and Numeric Algorithms for Scientific Computing*(pp. 349-355). IEEE.

Beel, J. (2017). *Towards effective research-paper recommender systems and user modeling based on mind maps.* arXiv preprint arXiv:1703.09109

Beel, J., & Gipp, B. (2009). Google Scholar's ranking algorithm: the impact of citation counts (an empirical study). In *2009 Third International Conference on Research Challenges in Information Science* (pp. 439-446). IEEE.

Beel, J., Gipp, B., Langer, S., & Breitinger, C. (2015). Research-paper recommender systems: A literature survey. *International Journal on Digital Libraries*, 1–34.

Beel, J., & Langer, S. (2015, September). A comparison of offline evaluations, online evaluations, and user studies in the context of research-paper recommender systems. In *International Conference on Theory and Practice of Digital Libraries* (pp. 153-168). Cham, Switzerland: Springer. 10.1007/978-3-319-24592-8_12

Beel, J., Langer, S., Genzmehr, M., Gipp, B., Breitinger, C., & Nürnberger, A. (2013, October). Research paper recommender system evaluation: a quantitative literature survey. In *Proceedings of the International Workshop on Reproducibility and Replication in Recommender Systems Evaluation* (pp. 15-22). ACM.

Beel, J., Langer, S., Genzmehr, M., & Nürnberger, A. (2013). Introducing Docear's research paper recommender system. *Proceedings of the 13th ACM/IEEE-CS joint conference on Digital libraries*. 10.1145/2467696.2467786

Bethard, S., & Jurafsky, D. (2010). Who should I cite: learning literature search models from citation behavior. *Proceedings of the 19th ACM international conference on Information and knowledge management*. 10.1145/1871437.1871517

Bogers, T., & Van den Bosch, A. (2008). Recommending scientific articles using citeulike. *Proceedings of the 2008 ACM conference on Recommender systems*. 10.1145/1454008.1454053

Bollacker, K. D., Lawrence, S., & Giles, C. L. (1998). CiteSeer: An autonomous web agent for automatic retrieval and identification of interesting publications. *Proceedings of the second international conference on Autonomous agents*. 10.1145/280765.280786

Bollacker, K. D., Lawrence, S., & Giles, C. L. (2000). Discovering relevant scientific literature on the web. *IEEE Intelligent Systems & their Applications*, *15*(2), 42–47. doi:10.1109/5254.850826

Bollen, J., & Van de Sompel, H. (2006). An architecture for the aggregation and analysis of scholarly usage data. *Proceedings of the 6th ACM/IEEE-CS joint conference on Digital libraries*. 10.1145/1141753.1141821

Brin, S., & Page, L. (1998). The anatomy of a large-scale hypertextual web search engine. *Computer Networks and ISDN Systems*, *30*(1), 107–117. doi:10.1016/S0169-7552(98)00110-X

Capocci, A., & Caldarelli, G. (2008). Folksonomies and clustering in the collaborative system CiteULike. *Journal of Physics. A, Mathematical and Theoretical*, *41*(22), 224016. doi:10.1088/1751-8113/41/22/224016

Caragea, C., Silvescu, A., Kataria, S., Caragea, D., & Mitra, P. (2011, December). *Classifying scientific publications using abstract features*. In Ninth Symposium of Abstraction, Reformulation, and Approximation, Catalonia, Spain.

Caragea, C., Silvescu, A., Mitra, P., & Giles, C. L. (2013). Can't see the forest for the trees?: a citation recommendation system. *Proceedings of the 13th ACM/IEEE-CS joint conference on Digital libraries*. 10.1145/2467696.2467743

Chandrasekaran, K., Gauch, S., Lakkaraju, P., & Luong, H. P. (2008). Concept-based document recommendations for citeseer authors. *Proceedings of the Adaptive hypermedia and adaptive web-based systems*. 10.1007/978-3-540-70987-9_11

Danesh, S., Sumner, T., & Martin, J. H. (2015). SGRank: Combining Statistical and Graphical Methods to Improve the State of the Art in Unsupervised Keyphrase Extraction. *Lexical and Computational Semantics (* SEM 2015)*, 117.

Dattolo, A., Ferrara, F., & Tasso, C. (2009). Supporting personalized user concept spaces and recommendations for a publication sharing system. *Proceedings of the International Conference on User Modeling, Adaptation, and Personalization*. 10.1007/978-3-642-02247-0_31

Daud, A., Shaikh, A. M. A. R., & Rajpar, A. H. (2009). Scientific reference mining using semantic information through topic modeling. *Research Journal of Engineering & Technology*, *28*(2), 253–262.

Dong, R., Tokarchuk, L., & Ma, A. (2009). Digging friendship: paper recommendation in the social network. *Proceedings of Networking & Electronic Commerce Research Conference (NAEC 2009)*.

Ekstrand, M. D., Kannan, P., Stemper, J. A., Butler, J. T., Konstan, J. A., & Riedl, J. T. (2010). Automatically building research reading lists. *Proceedings of the fourth ACM conference on Recommender systems*. 10.1145/1864708.1864740

Ferrara, F., Pudota, N., & Tasso, C. (2011). A keyphrase-based paper recommender system. In Digital Libraries and Archives (pp. 14–25). Berlin, Germany: Springer. doi:10.1007/978-3-642-27302-5_2

Fujii, A. (2007). Enhancing patent retrieval by citation analysis. In *Proceedings of the 30th annual international ACM SIGIR conference on Research and development in information retrieval* (pp. 793-794). New York, NY: ACM.

Geyer-Schulz, A., Hahsler, M., & Jahn, M. (2001). Educational and scientific recommender systems: Designing the information channels of the virtual university. *International Journal of Engineering Education, 17*(2), 153–163.

Geyer-Schulz, A., Hahsler, M., Neumann, A., & Thede, A. (2003). Behavior-based recommender systems as value-added services for scientific libraries. *Statistical Data Mining & Knowledge Discovery*, 433-454.

Gipp, B., & Beel, J. (2009). Citation Proximity Analysis (CPA)-A new approach for identifying related work based on Co-Citation Analysis. *Proceedings of the 12th International Conference on Scientometrics and Informetrics (ISSI'09).*

Gipp, B., Beel, J., & Hentschel, C. (2009). Scienstein: A research paper recommender system. *Proceedings of the international conference on Emerging trends in computing (ICETiC'09).*

Gori, M., & Pucci, A. (2006). *Research paper recommender systems: A random-walk based approach.* Paper presented at the IEEE/WIC/ACM International Conference on Web Intelligence.

Guan, Z., Wang, C., Bu, J., Chen, C., Yang, K., Cai, D., & He, X. (2010). Document recommendation in social tagging services. *Proceedings of the 19th international conference on World wide web*. 10.1145/1772690.1772731

Gupta, S., & Varma, V. (2017). Scientific Article Recommendation by using Distributed Representations of Text and Graph. *Proceedings of the 26th International Conference on World Wide Web Companion*. 10.1145/3041021.3053062

Han, J., Pei, J., & Kamber, M. (2011). Data mining: concepts and techniques. Amsterdam, The Netherlands: Elsevier.

Hanyurwimfura, D., Bo, L., Havyarimana, V., Njagi, D., & Kagorora, F. (2015). An effective academic research papers recommendation for non-profiled users. *International Journal of Hybrid Information Technology*, *8*(3), 255–272. doi:10.14257/ijhit.2015.8.3.23

He, J., Nie, J.-Y., Lu, Y., & Zhao, W. X. (2012). Position-aligned translation model for citation recommendation. *Proceedings of the International Symposium on String Processing and Information Retrieval*. 10.1007/978-3-642-34109-0_27

He, Q., Kifer, D., Pei, J., Mitra, P., & Giles, C. L. (2011). Citation recommendation without author supervision. *Proceedings of the fourth ACM international conference on Web search and data mining*. 10.1145/1935826.1935926

Hong, K., Jeon, H., & Jeon, C. (2012). *UserProfile-based personalized research paper recommendation system.* Paper presented at the 2012 8th International Conference on Computing and Networking Technology (ICCNT).

Hong, K., Jeon, H., & Jeon, C. (2013). Advanced personalized research paper recommendation system based on expanded userprofile through semantic analysis. *International Journal of Digital Content Technology and its Applications, 7*(15), 67.

Huang, Z., Chung, W., Ong, T.-H., & Chen, H. (2002). A graph-based recommender system for digital library. *Proceedings of the 2nd ACM/IEEE-CS joint conference on Digital libraries*. 10.1145/544220.544231

Hwang, S.-Y., Hsiung, W.-C., & Yang, W.-S. (2003). A prototype WWW literature recommendation system for digital libraries. *Online Information Review*, *27*(3), 169–182. doi:10.1108/14684520310481436

Jack, K. (2012). *Mendeley: recommendation systems for academic literature. Presentation at Technical University of Graz, Graz, Austria*.

Jiang, Y., Jia, A., Feng, Y., & Zhao, D. (2012). Recommending academic papers via users' reading purposes. *Proceedings of the sixth ACM conference on Recommender systems*. 10.1145/2365952.2366004

Jomsri, P., Sanguansintukul, S., & Choochaiwattana, W. (2009). *A comparison of search engine using "tag title and abstract" with CiteULike—An initial evaluation.* Paper presented at the International Conference for Internet Technology and Secured Transactions, 2009. ICITST 2009.

Joseph, A. S. (2013). Conceptual, impact-based publications recommendations. Fayetteville, AR: University of Arkansas.

Kodakateri Pudhiyaveetil, A., Gauch, S., Luong, H., & Eno, J. (2009). Conceptual recommender system for CiteSeerX. *Proceedings of the third ACM conference on Recommender systems.*

Krallinger, M., Erhardt, R. A.-A., & Valencia, A. (2005). Text-mining approaches in molecular biology and biomedicine. *Drug Discovery Today, 10*(6), 439–445. doi:10.1016/S1359-6446(05)03376-3 PMID:15808823

Küçüktunç, O., Saule, E., Kaya, K., & Çatalyürek, Ü. V. (2012). *Direction awareness in citation recommendation*. Academic Press.

Lawrence, S., Giles, C. L., & Bollacker, K. (1999). Digital libraries and autonomous citation indexing. *Computer, 32*(6), 67–71. doi:10.1109/2.769447

Lee, J., Lee, K., Kim, J. G., & Kim, S. (2015). *Personalized Academic Paper Recommendation System*. Academic Press.

Liang, T.-P., Yang, Y.-F., Chen, D.-N., & Ku, Y.-C. (2008). A semantic-expansion approach to personalized knowledge recommendation. *Decision Support Systems, 45*(3), 401–412. doi:10.1016/j.dss.2007.05.004

Liang, Y., Li, Q., & Qian, T. (2011). Finding relevant papers based on citation relations. *Proceedings of International Conference on Web-Age Information Management*. 10.1007/978-3-642-23535-1_35

Lopez-Cozar, E. D., Robinson-Garcia, N., & Torres-Salinas, D. (2012). *Manipulating Google Scholar citations and Google Scholar metrics: Simple, easy and tempting*. arXiv preprint arXiv:1212.0638

Maake, B. M., Ojo, S. O., & Zuva, T. (2019). A Serendipitous Research Paper Recommender System. *International Journal of Business and Management Studies, 11*(1), 38–53.

Magara, M. B., Ojo, S. O., & Zuva, T. (2018, August). *Towards a Serendipitous Research Paper Recommender System Using Bisociative Information Networks (BisoNets)*. Paper presented at the 2018 International Conference on Advances in Big Data, Computing and Data Communication Systems (icABCD).

Martín, G. H., Schockaert, S., Cornelis, C., & Naessens, H. (2010). *Metadata impact on research paper similarity*. Paper presented at the International Conference on Theory and Practice of Digital Libraries.

McNee, S. M., Albert, I., Cosley, D., Gopalkrishnan, P., Lam, S. K., Rashid, A. M., ... Riedl, J. (2002). On the recommending of citations for research papers. *Proceedings of the 2002 ACM conference on Computer supported cooperative work.* 10.1145/587078.587096

McNee, S. M., Kapoor, N., & Konstan, J. A. (2006). Don't look stupid: avoiding pitfalls when recommending research papers. *Proceedings of the 2006 20th anniversary conference on Computer supported cooperative work.* 10.1145/1180875.1180903

Mishra, G. (2012). Optimised research paper recommender system using social tagging. *International Journal of Engineering Research and Applications*, *2*(2), 1503–1507.

Mönnich, M., & Spiering, M. (2008). Adding value to the library catalog by implementing a recommendation system. *D-Lib Magazine*, *14*(5/6), 1082–9873. doi:10.1045/may2008-monnich

Naak, A., Hage, H., & Aïmeur, E. (2008). Papyres: A research paper management system. *Proceedings of 2008 10th IEEE Conference on E-Commerce Technology and the Fifth IEEE Conference on Enterprise Computing, E-Commerce and E-Services.* 10.1109/CECandEEE.2008.132

Nanba, H., & Okumura, M. (2005). *Automatic detection of survey articles.* Paper presented at the International Conference on Theory and Practice of Digital Libraries.

Nascimento, C., Laender, A. H., da Silva, A. S., & Gonçalves, M. A. (2011). A source independent framework for research paper recommendation. *Proceedings of the 11th annual international ACM/IEEE joint conference on Digital libraries.* 10.1145/1998076.1998132

Ohta, M., Hachiki, T., & Takasu, A. (2011). *Related paper recommendation to support online-browsing of research papers.* Paper presented at the 2011 Fourth International Conference on the Applications of Digital Information and Web Technologies (ICADIWT).

Pan, C., & Li, W. (2010). *Research paper recommendation with topic analysis.* Paper presented at the 2010 International Conference on Computer Design and Applications (ICCDA).

Paraschiv, I. C., Dascalu, M., Dessus, P., Trausan-Matu, S., & McNamara, D. S. (2016). *A Paper Recommendation System with ReaderBench: The Graphical Visualization of Semantically Related Papers and Concepts. In State-of-the-Art and Future Directions of Smart Learning* (pp. 445–451). Springer.

Parra, D., & Brusilovsky, P. (2009). Collaborative filtering for social tagging systems: an experiment with CiteULike. *Proceedings of the third ACM conference on Recommender systems*. 10.1145/1639714.1639757

Ricci, F., Rokach, L., & Shapira, B. (2011). Introduction to recommender systems handbook. Berlin, Germany: Springer. doi:10.1007/978-0-387-85820-3

Shimbo, M., Ito, T., & Matsumoto, Y. (2007). Evaluation of kernel-based link analysis measures on research paper recommendation. *Proceedings of the 7th ACM/IEEE-CS joint conference on Digital libraries*. 10.1145/1255175.1255245

Smeaton, A. F., & Callan, J. (2005). Personalisation and recommender systems in digital libraries. *International Journal on Digital Libraries*, *5*(4), 299–308. doi:10.100700799-004-0100-1

Strohman, T., Croft, W. B., & Jensen, D. (2007). Recommending citations for academic papers. *Proceedings of the 30th annual international ACM SIGIR conference on Research and development in information retrieval*.

Sugiyama, K., & Kan, M.-Y. (2010). Scholarly paper recommendation via user's recent research interests. *Proceedings of the 10th annual joint conference on Digital libraries*. 10.1145/1816123.1816129

Takano, K., & Li, K. F. (2009). An adaptive personalized recommender based on web-browsing behavior learning. *Proceedings of the International Conference on Advanced Information Networking and Applications Workshops, 2009. WAINA'09*. 10.1109/WAINA.2009.160

Tang, T. Y., & McCalla, G. (2003). *Smart recommendation for an evolving e-learning system*. Paper presented at the Workshop on Technologies for Electronic Documents for Supporting Learning, AIED.

Torres, R., McNee, S. M., Abel, M., Konstan, J. A., & Riedl, J. (2004). Enhancing digital libraries with TechLens+. *Proceedings of the 4th ACM/IEEE-CS joint conference on Digital libraries*.

Tran, H. N., Huynh, T., & Hoang, K. (2015). A Potential Approach to Overcome Data Limitation in Scientific Publication Recommendation. *Proceedings of 2015 Seventh International Conference on Knowledge and Systems Engineering (KSE)*. 10.1109/KSE.2015.76

Vellino, A. (2009). Recommending journal articles with pagerank ratings. *Recommender Systems, 2009*.

Vellino, A. (2010). A comparison between usage-based and citation-based methods for recommending scholarly research articles. *Proceedings of the American Society for Information Science and Technology*, *47*(1), 1–2. doi:10.1002/meet.14504701330

Vellino, A., & Zeber, D. (2007). A hybrid, multi-dimensional recommender for journal articles in a scientific digital library. *Proceedings of the 2007 IEEE/WIC/ACM international conference on web intelligence and international conference on intelligent agent technology.* 10.1109/WI-IATW.2007.29

Wang, C., & Blei, D. M. (2011). Collaborative topic modeling for recommending scientific articles. *Proceedings of the 17th ACM SIGKDD international conference on Knowledge discovery and data mining*. 10.1145/2020408.2020480

West, J. D., Wesley-Smith, I., & Bergstrom, C. T. (2016). A recommendation system based on hierarchical clustering of an article-level citation network. *IEEE Transactions on Big Data*, *2*(2), 113–123. doi:10.1109/TBDATA.2016.2541167

Woodruff, A., Gossweiler, R., Pitkow, J., Chi, E. H., & Card, S. K. (2000). Enhancing a digital book with a reading recommender. *Proceedings of SIGCHI conference on Human factors in computing systems*. 10.1145/332040.332419

Wu, H., Hua, Y., Li, B., & Pei, Y. (2012). Enhancing citation recommendation with various evidences. *Proceedings of 2012 9th International Conference on Fuzzy Systems and Knowledge Discovery (FSKD).* 10.1109/FSKD.2012.6234002

Xue, H., Guo, J., Lan, Y., & Cao, L. (2014). Personalized paper recommendation in online social scholar system. *Proceedings of 2014 IEEE/ACM International Conference on Advances in Social Networks Analysis and Mining (ASONAM).* 10.1109/ASONAM.2014.6921649

Yin, P., Zhang, M., & Li, X. (2007). Recommending scientific literatures in a collaborative tagging environment. *Proceedings of International Conference on Asian Digital Libraries*. 10.1007/978-3-540-77094-7_60

Zarrinkalam, F., & Kahani, M. (2012). A multi-criteria hybrid citation recommendation system based on linked data. *Proceedings of 2012 2nd International eConference on Computer and Knowledge Engineering (ICCKE).* 10.1109/ICCKE.2012.6395393

Zarrinkalam, F., & Kahani, M. (2013). SemCiR: A citation recommendation system based on a novel semantic distance measure. *Program*, *47*(1), 92–112. doi:10.1108/00330331311296320

Zhang, H., Ni, W., Zhao, M., Liu, Y., & Yang, Y. (2014). A hybrid recommendation approach for network teaching resources based on knowledge-tree. *Proceedings of 2014 33rd Chinese Control Conference (CCC).* 10.1109/ChiCC.2014.6895511

Zhang, M., Wang, W., & Li, X. (2008). A paper recommender for scientific literatures based on semantic concept similarity. In Digital libraries: Universal and ubiquitous access to information (pp. 359–362). Berlin, Germany: Springer. doi:10.1007/978-3-540-89533-6_44

Zhang, Y., Callan, J., & Minka, T. (2002). Novelty and redundancy detection in adaptive filtering. *Proceedings of the 25th annual international ACM SIGIR conference on Research and development in information retrieval.* 10.1145/564376.564393

Zhao, W., Wu, R., Dai, W., & Dai, Y. (2015). *Research Paper Recommendation Based on the Knowledge Gap.* Paper presented at the 2015 IEEE International Conference on Data Mining Workshop (ICDMW).

Zhou, D., Zhu, S., Yu, K., Song, X., Tseng, B. L., Zha, H., & Giles, C. L. (2008). Learning multiple graphs for document recommendations. *Proceedings of the 17th international conference on World Wide Web.* 10.1145/1367497.1367517

KEY TERMS AND DEFINITIONS

Algorithms: A process or set of rules to be followed in calculations or other problem-solving operations, especially by a computer.

Classification: The action or process of categorizing or grouping something.

Data Mining: The practice of examining large pre-existing databases in order to generate new information.

Recommender System: A subclass of information filtering system that seeks to predict the rating and preference a user would give to an item.

Similarity Measure: The measure of how much alike two data objects are. In data mining context, it is a distance with dimensions representing features of the objects.

Chapter 7
Delivering the Next-Generation Research Repository:
The Challenges of Institutional Repositories and the Need for a New Approach

Adi Alter
Ex Libris, Israel

Eddie Neuwirth
Ex Libris, USA

Dani Guzman
Ex Libris, Israel

ABSTRACT

Academic libraries are looking for ways to grow their involvement in and scale-up their support for research activities. The successful transition depends to a large extent on the library's ability to systematically manage data, break down information silos and unify workflows across the library, research office and researchers. Data repositories are at the heart of this challenge, yet often institutional repositories are not built to address the needs of modern research data management due to inability to store all research assets, lack of consistent data models, and insufficient workflows. This chapter will present a new approach to research data management that ensures visibility of research output and data, data coherency, and compliance with open access standards. The authors will discuss a 'Next-Generation Research Repository' that spans multiple data management activities, including automated

DOI: 10.4018/978-1-5225-8437-7.ch007

data capture, metadata enrichment, dissemination, compliance-related workflows, automated publication to scholarly profiles, as well as open integration with the research ecosystem.

INTRODUCTION

Institutional repositories that collect a university's research assets in one place and make them publicly available, serve an important role. These repositories, which are usually managed by the library, help disseminate the work of faculty members to a broader academic community, making it easier for other researchers to find, use, and build on the knowledge generated by a university. They also help universities comply with rules requiring research funded with public tax money, to be made publicly available. But in many ways, the institutional repositories that exist today are not meeting the needs of libraries or the research community effectively. For instance, they often lack a clear and cohesive structure, which makes research assets hard to find. They are also largely cumbersome to maintain, with inefficient workflows that make it difficult to deposit new research outputs, link publications with their underlying data sets, and add comprehensive metadata to make these assets discoverable.

As a result, the research assets of universities are not being showcased as well as they could be and staff is spending too much time on these labor-intensive tasks.

In this white paper, we will make the case for how a next-generation research repository can solve these challenges. With input from research universities around the world, we will outline a vision for a next-generation research repository that meets the needs of both researchers and institutions far more effectively ("Implementing FAIR Data Principles", n.d.).

The Limitations of Current Repositories

Institutional repositories can mean different things to different universities but generally, they are intended to store the content created by scholars at the university and make this material accessible to a wider audience. In most cases, university libraries are tasked with managing these repositories, sometimes with the help of their IT department.

Here are some of the many ways the repositories being used today fall short of meeting institutional needs:

Lack of a Clear Strategy

Many universities have no clear strategy for how they will store and manage their research assets. This often results in the creation of multiple repositories within the same institution.

According to one research article, "Many institutions describe a situation where they have as many as five different platforms … that have characteristics of [an institutional repository]." This "fragmented environment" results in a duplication of effort across the university and means that "standards are often implemented a little differently from one repository to another." (Arlitsch et al, 2018).

In some cases, universities have lost sight of what the goals for their institutional repository were in the first place; or else these goals have evolved over time. In other cases, the personnel who created the institutional repository might not be the same people who manage it today, and so the policies defining what belongs in the repository may not be clear.

At some institutions, the repository began as a way of showcasing only open-access materials, which make up a just small fraction of their research assets. As leaders looked to expand the types of research assets they were collecting and managing, they developed additional repositories for other kinds of works. Sometimes, universities are forced to create multiple repositories because the systems they are using will not support new asset types; a university might have one repository for publications, another for data sets, and so on.

Instead of having a single, unified place where all research assets are stored, universities frequently end up with separate silos of research content. Not only are the data in these silos disconnected, but having disparate systems makes it harder to standardize the collection of research assets and apply metadata to these assets consistently. Managing multiple repositories also takes more time and effort.

And even when institutions don't have multiple repositories, the lack of a clear strategy can be problematic and can result in a repository that is a confused mixture of unrelated content, thus undermining the value of the repository and its content.

Inefficient Workflows

Populating an institutional repository can be a challenge. Typically, faculty are encouraged to deposit their research outputs by filling out an online form but many researchers don't follow through on this step, either because they don't have the time or they don't see the value in doing so.

Even where faculty do deposit their research outputs, they might add the wrong version of their publication or they are likely to upload it with incomplete metadata. Library staff frequently have to fix incorrect entries or enrich the metadata associated with these entries to ensure that research assets are easily discoverable. With no easy, systematic way to do this, the process can take several hours of staff time.

Incomplete and Disconnected Data

Inefficient processes tend to discourage researchers from uploading their work into an institutional repository and this results in the omission of many research assets. Even when articles or publications *are* deposited, there is seldom an easy way to add metadata or link to the data this work derives from. This means other researchers cannot easily verify or build on this scholarship; and if metadata are incomplete, research assets are less likely to be discovered.

Why Does This Matter?

These shortcomings in how research outputs are collected, stored and managed have important implications for everyone involved in the research lifecycle.

- *For researchers*, not promoting their work as effectively as possible in a research repository means they could be missing opportunities for professional recognition, connecting with colleagues at other institutions who are doing similar research and even securing future grant funding;
- *For research librarians*, having to spend countless hours manually updating the institutional repository and adding or enriching metadata, takes away from the time they could be spending on more strategic work instead, such as scaling up their activities to support more researchers and projects, helping researchers develop data management plans and advising on, and ensuring compliance with, open-access policies;
- *For universities*, when assets are missing from a repository, leaders have an incomplete picture of what their university's research outputs are. If the institution is not showcasing its work effectively for potential students, donors, or faculty, this could make fundraising, student recruitment and attracting and retaining talent more difficult. Non-compliance could also become an issue in cases where grant programs require research results to be made publicly available;

- *For the research community and the public as a whole*, when a university's research outputs are not easily discoverable, this deprives researchers from other institutions of the opportunity to validate, challenge, support or expand on this body of knowledge, as well as the opportunity to find collaborators for their own work. It also prevents the public from engaging in "citizen science" and even just learning about the work of academics. The entire sum of knowledge is less rich as a result.

Use Case: University of Surrey

The University of Surrey's experience shows the challenges that are common amongst research institutions as they try to archive, manage, and promote faculty research.

A public research university in England, the University of Surrey has had an institutional repository showcasing faculty research papers for more than a decade, says Fiona Greig, Head of E-Strategy and Resources for the university's library. But when the U.K. government stipulated a new rule requiring universities to make the data from research projects publicly available, Greig and her colleagues realized this system would not be sufficient to meet their needs.

"Any data set produced with government funding must be made publicly available when a research article is published and the data have to be reusable and accessible for at least 10 years," Greig explains. But the repository that Surrey was using was not designed to store data sets as well as journal articles. This forced the university to use a separate repository for its research data. Managing the original repository was challenging enough from a resource standpoint, without adding a second one to manage.

Because academics were often confused about how to deposit their research and add the proper metadata, the library had made this a fully mediated service for faculty. But this resulted in a significant workload for library staff; "I have three team members whose job is to upload open-access materials," Greig says.

Having a separate repository for research data adds to this work and the systems' shortcomings create further challenges. For instance, it is not easy to link data sets with the journal articles they accompany and there is no hierarchical structure to these repositories; "our existing repositories are just flat boxes with metadata," Greig observes. "They take everything as non-relational documents."

In addition, these repositories do not have advanced metrics for measuring the impact of the university's research. With time spent uploading and maintaining research assets, librarians can't focus on this task themselves. As a result, "we are not measuring our outputs very well," she says.

Faced with all these challenges, Greig and her colleagues are looking for a new approach to managing research assets. "We need to be smarter about the technologies we use," she concludes. "It's too big a risk for institutions like ours *not* to comply with open-access requirements. The current workload needed to ensure compliance is not sustainable, and we need something that is easier and more efficient moving forward."

What an Ideal Research Repository Should Look Like

A next-generation research repository can solve these challenges by making it much easier to collect, manage, promote, and track the impact of a university's research outputs. The entire research community would benefit from these improvements.

Here are the key characteristics that we believe such a repository should include:

Comprehensiveness

A next-generation research repository should enable universities to collect, manage and showcase *all* of their faculty outputs and data within a single repository. To meet this requirement, it must be able to support a wide variety of asset types across a full range of academic disciplines. The repository should not be limited to publications but should also include pre-prints, data sets, audiovisual media, creative works, computer code, blog posts and other kinds of materials.

Connectedness

The ideal research repository would give universities an easy way to link research outputs with the data sets, presentations, blog posts, press coverage, social media mentions, awards and other materials and activities associated with these outputs. That way, anyone who is reading a faculty member's research paper would have access not just to the paper itself, but to a wide range of information that could help them better understand and make use of this scholarship. Users would be able to navigate easily from one related asset to another.

Openness

The ideal research repository would apply the FAIR Data Principles to make data findable, accessible, interoperable and reusable by other researchers and institutions.[1] It should also integrate seamlessly with a university's existing workflows and technology systems through application programming interfaces (APIs) and well-known standards.

Automation

A next-generation research repository would use automated processes to capture information and make it easier to deposit research assets wherever possible, thus reducing the workload on librarians and faculty. For instance, it should be able to identify journal articles published by faculty, capture the metadata associated with these articles and add this research to the repository automatically. By using flexible data models to support various asset types, a next-generation research repository would give faculty and librarians a very structured way of adding metadata to ensure that research outputs are fully discoverable.

Advanced Analytics

The ideal research repository should use advanced analytics to give leaders greater insight into the impact of their institution's research. Provosts, deans, research office staff and others should be able to glean insights that go beyond just how many papers their faculty have published in academic journals and how often these papers have been cited. For instance, leaders should also be able to track faculty publications in non-academic channels, such as traditional and social media. They should be able to measure the impact of a variety of asset types and get an accurate picture of the research collaboration that is occurring.

Easy to Scale and support

A next-generation research repository must be easy to scale and support. It must be able to grow with the institution as needs change. Ideally, it should be cloud-based, so universities are automatically using the latest version without having to upgrade or re-implement the repository over time. In essence, the solution should allow library and IT staff to work more efficiently by focusing their efforts on supporting researchers instead of managing and maintaining the technology.

Use Case: Drexel University

As the University of Surrey, Drexel University has been using an institutional repository that was not intended to store and manage research data. As a result, Drexel faculty and curators have maintained research data in separate collections but the university did not have a way to make these data collections searchable. Drexel librarians wanted to adopt a more thoughtful, integrated approach to managing research assets in a way that would ensure regulatory compliance, while also making *all* assets easily discoverable.

Recognizing the need for a more strategic approach, stakeholders from Drexel's research office, compliance and security officers, graduate school, IT and libraries engaged in conversations to address these challenges. Their discussions focused on three areas in particular: the policies, communication, and socio-technology needed for success. "Managing research outputs is not a solo activity," says Dean of Libraries Danuta Nitecki. "It takes a collaborative village."

With respect to the technology that Drexel would use for this task, university leaders hope to implement a system that can integrate research outputs with their underlying data sets, while also making the data discoverable. A key consideration is that the system must be easy for faculty to use in promoting their research to a global community. "If you make the process too complicated, nobody is going to do it," Nitecki says.

Nitecki and her colleagues believe they have found such a system in Esploro, a new cloud-based research services platform from Ex Libris.

How Esploro Meets the Need for a Next-Generation Research Repository

In consultation with library and research staff at universities around the world, Ex Libris has developed a next-generation research repository that meets these key criteria. Named Esploro, this cloud-based solution helps universities showcase their research and measure its impact by systematically capturing, managing and disseminating research outputs and data using a unified repository, integrating research evidence from diverse systems.

Esploro is based on open standards, so that it integrates easily with other existing research systems; and it includes automated processes to save time and simplify data capture for librarians and researchers. For example, by leveraging integrated researcher profiles and Ex Libris' discovery services, Esploro can automatically identify research published by faculty in journals, external repositories, and other sources; capture the relevant metadata associated with a source; and create a record within Esploro for that research asset. This saves librarians and researchers from having to manually enter all of this information for themselves.

Esploro also broadens the scope of research assets that can be stored in a research repository. The solution's flexible data model supports a wide variety of research assets, including data sets, creative works and other materials. Each type of asset has its own unique schema for capturing metadata with data fields that are relevant to that particular asset type. Having a unique schema for each asset type helps institutions add these various research assets to the repository easily, while also capturing rich, high-quality metadata to ensure discoverability.

In addition, Esploro contains built-in metrics to demonstrate the use and impact of research outputs in much more sophisticated ways. The solution does this in two ways: (1) by broadening the traditional impact metrics such as h-index to take into account multiple asset types, and (2) by measuring impact across both academic publications and traditional and social media.

One of the guiding principles in developing Esploro was that universities are not going to change the habits of their researchers. If a faculty member is already depositing her research into Arxiv, for instance, because that is where all of her peers are working, she is not likely to repeat this step in an institutional repository. With Esploro, she won't have to; the system can capture information about her research directly from Arxiv and create a record for that research automatically. In this way, populating the research repository is no longer dependent on the actions of researchers themselves.

With rule-based workflows that universities can customize according to their needs, Esploro is intuitive out of the box, yet highly configurable for each institution, helping librarians and researchers alike, work much more effectively and efficiently.

Use Case: University of Denver

The University of Denver has a Digital Commons system to store faculty research, as well as faculty profile pages to highlight their work, but these two systems are not connected, which requires faculty to enter their research in two different places. Not surprisingly, "we have had very slow uptake in faculty wanting to engage with that," says Dean of Libraries Michael Levine-Clark. Even faculty who were depositing their research were doing so inconsistently, often with incomplete metadata. University leaders also wanted the ability to capture a broad range of faculty outputs, including creative works; something that wasn't easy with the systems they had in place ("The Need for Next Generation Research Repository", n.d.).

Levine-Clark and his colleagues were determined to find a better solution. "Esploro happened to come along at just the right time, as we were beginning those conversations," he says ("The Need for Next Generation Research Repository", n.d.).

The University of Denver has joined Surrey, Drexel and other leading research universities from around the world in becoming early adopters of Esploro. Levine-Clark is looking forward to having a single, unified system for storing and disseminating many different kinds of faculty outputs, with automated processes for capturing information.

"It's important for us to present this as less work for our faculty, not more," he says. "If we can tell them that we'll automatically populate their faculty profile pages with information generated by the system, and all they have to do is review and approve this information, that's a key way we can provide value for them." ("The Need for Next Generation Research Repository", n.d.).

Besides simplifying workflows, Esploro will improve the university's ability to measure the impact of its research. "We are currently tracking the number of articles our faculty publish and the number of citations their work receives," Levine-Clark says. "But we would like to have a much better picture of the full scholarly and social impact of their work." He concludes: "We expect Esploro to give us a much more efficient way to showcase faculty research to colleagues, students, and the media, while also measuring our results in richer ways. This puts the library at the center of things that are a high priority for the university and helps us demonstrate real value for the institution." ("The Need for Next Generation Research Repository", n.d.).

CONCLUSION

Collecting evidence of a university's research outputs in one place and making them easily discoverable is an important goal. But there are many challenges that stand in the way of achieving this goal, and current institutional repositories are limited in how effectively they can resolve these challenges. A next-generation research repository holds the answer. By automating workflows, broadening the scope of research assets that can be stored and managed, making assets more discoverable, and measuring the impact of research in new and exciting ways, a next-generation research repository can transform how universities manage and promote critical outputs, leading to benefits for everyone involved.

REFERENCES

Arlitsch, K., & Grant, C. (2018). Why So Many Repositories? Examining the Limitations and Possibilities of the Institutional Repositories Landscape. *Journal of Library Administration*, *58*(3), 264–281. doi:10.1080/01930826.2018.1436778

Implementing FAIR Data Principles: The Role of Libraries. Retrieved from the Association of European Research Libraries: https://libereurope.eu/wp-content/uploads/2017/12/LIBER-FAIR-Data.pdf

The Need for Next Generation Research Repository. (n.d.). Retrieved from https://www.exlibrisgroup.com/wp-content/uploads/The-Need-for-a-Next-Gen-Research-Repository-Ex-Libris-Paper.pdf

Chapter 8
Institutional Repositories in Africa:
Issues and Challenges

Felicia O. Yusuf
Covenant University, Nigeria

Goodluck Ifijeh
Covenant University, Nigeria

Sola Owolabi
Landmark University, Nigeria

ABSTRACT

The emergence of open access has opened a world of opportunities for academic and research institutions. One of such opportunities is the establishment of institutional repositories (IRs). This chapter examined the emergence and creation of IRs and trends in Africa. It noted that the development of IRs in most African countries is still at the infancy stage. The chapter highlighted the important role of libraries in the management of IRs. The Chapter also identified and discussed important issues and challenges of IRs in Africa. The identified challenges include lack of awareness, lack of required funding to establish and manage IRs, lack of Information and communication technology infrastructure, among others. It concluded that the establishment of IRs is a compulsory venture for institutions of higher learning in Africa.

DOI: 10.4018/978-1-5225-8437-7.ch008

INTRODUCTION

The importance of scholarly communication in an academic environment cannot be overemphasized. The American Library Association, ALA (2015) defined scholarly communication as the system through which research and other scholarly writings are created, evaluated for quality, disseminated to the scholarly community, and preserved for future use. Various media of scholarly communication abound which according to ALA (2015) may be through formal or informal channels. The formal and informal channels according to ALA include publication in peer-reviewed journals and electronic listservs respectively.

As important as scholarly communication is to the scholarly environment, it has been observed that most of the outlets used for communication such as journals, online databases etc. are beyond the reach of the scholarly community in terms of the cost of subscription which has led to the expression of dissatisfaction by scholars. Ogbomo and Muokebe (2015) observed the increasing dissatisfaction expressed by scholars and researchers with the existing model of scholarly communication where they lamented that subscription rates for journals were high and the fear that universities may lose their print materials if not properly archived was on the increase.

Abubakar (2010) noted a profound and progressive change across various disciplines as occasioned by the rapid development and advancement of information and communication technology (ICT). The ICT era has indeed heralded a new way of preserving scholarly communications making them available and accessible on the web without any form of restriction. This is a total departure from the traditional way of preservation. Digital preservation of such scholarly communications has become widely accepted hence the introduction of repositories. Bailey (2005) observed that repositories are an essential component in reforming the system of scholarly communication. Institutional Repositories (IR) provide an alternative model of scholarly communication that is less cumbersome when compared with the traditional publishing model (John-Okeke, 2008). Commenting on the importance of repositories especially to higher institutions of learning, the Alpha Babel Library (2007) observed that "the institutions of higher education all over the world are experiencing the necessity of managing their education, research and resources in a more effective and open way. By making the research and scientific output easily available, they will support the development of new relationships between the academicians and both national and international research centres".

A lot of researches go on in higher institutions of learning which according to Ogbomo and Muokebe (2015) have led to the increased quest for alternative modes of preserving and disseminating findings of the research. Ivwighreghweta (2012) also noted that the emergence of IR has revolutionized the methods of preserving as well as communicating research outputs in academic and research institutions.

Nkiko, Bolu and Michael-Onuoha (2014) opined that IRs provide a strong basis for the crystallization of open access to intellectual outputs and enrichment of scholarship in the universities. According to them, IRs confer institutional prestige and global visibility on the institutions hosting them. Repositories are an essential component in reforming the system of scholarly communication and they serve as tangible indicators of a university's quality while also demonstrating the scientific, societal and economic relevance of its research activities, thus increasing the institution's visibility, status and public value (Crow, 2002; Bailey, 2005).

The need to maintain an IR by universities across the globe in the era of Information and Communications Technology cannot be over-emphasized. Commenting on the impact of technology on scholarly communication, Davis and Connolly (2007) observed that the digital revolution has affected how scholars create, communicate and preserve new knowledge. An IR provides a platform for showcasing the research output of universities and faculty members across the world thereby enhancing their web visibility. Jain, Bentley, and Oladiran (2008) noted that recognition of the importance of IR as an essential infrastructure of scholarly dissemination in the universities in this electronic age has been on the increase. Livingston and Naltasie (2009) also recognized that the creation of IR is a huge support to academic activities in higher institutions. They however pointed out that the challenges associated with sustaining, preserving, securing and interoperability are capable of undermining the entire project if not clearly articulated and resolved.

Institutional repositories have been found to serve as checks to publishers who because of the economic gains expected from sales of intellectual content of authors, deny scholars free access to literature. There exist two divergent perspectives on the justification for IRs. One of the perspectives views IRs as competing with traditional publishing, while the other sees it as a supplement to traditional publishing.

One of the proponents of IRs as competing with traditional publishing is Crow. Crow (2002) believes that increasing access to the literature is but one goal of IRs. Crow posits that by taking at least some control over the dissemination of scholarship, repositories can increase competition in the market place thereby reducing the monopoly power of journals. Furthermore, the author believes that there is no reason that IRs cannot provide all of the functions of traditional publishing, thereby taking over the role of scholarly publishing completely from the hands of third party publishers and placing it back in the hands of the academy.

Sternly opposing this view is Lynch (2003) who views IRs as mere supplements, and not primary avenues for scholarly publishing and further warns against assuming the role of certification in the scholarly publishing process. Lynch argues that IRs are not journals or a collection of journals and should not be managed like one. Furthermore, Lynch expressed fears that viewing IRs as instruments for undermining the economics of the current publishing system discounts their importance and reduces their ability to promote a broader spectrum of scholarly communication. The author however, advised that IRs may better be useful in disseminating grey literature; documents such as pamphlets, bulletins, visual conference presentations and other materials that are typically ignored by traditional publishers. Davis and Connolly (2007) noted that IRs help to reduce the power wielded by publishers who they claimed have built economic barriers to limit scholars' access to the literature.

Libraries have always been engaged in managing their institutional collections, and possess accumulated abundant expertise in collection assessment, organization and development. Libraries have a key role to play in building IRs as their roles are becoming more deeply engaged with the broader vision of the institution by being more intertwined and interdependent with other stakeholders, such as the university administration, faculty, and other departments.

Faculty need to stay abreast of changes in information technology but considering their tight schedule, they may consider self-archiving as extra administrative work. The library comes to play a cardinal role in this respect. Institutional repositories have been argued to be best domiciled in libraries because librarians by professional standing strategically occupy the role of educating faculty and researchers on metadata uploading to maintain consistency of uniformity. Technical services librarians are very relevant in this respect. Most African libraries are currently embracing the idea of digital library which coincides with the period of deployment of institutional repository. Apart from academic qualifications of librarians, they are engaging in special trainings which are prerequisite to successful deployment of institutional repositories. It may be unrealistic to keep on training all members of faculty, students and researchers successively. Even when this is possible, the knowledge garnered soon fades because uploading of papers and other institutional documents are not their primary assignments.

Institutional Repository Defined

Several authors have defined institutional repositories. Ware (2004) defined an IR as a web-based database of scholarly material which is institutionally defined; cumulative and perpetual; open and interoperable; and thus collects, stores and disseminates. In addition, most would include long-term preservation of digital materials as a key function of IRs. Giesecke (2011) also defined IR as a set of services that are offered by an institution for the management and dissemination of digital materials created by the members of the institution or scholarly community. For McCord (2003), an institutional repository is a storehouse of digital content produced by faculty, staff and students of an institution.

To Harnard, Brody, Vallieres, Carr, Hitchcock, Gingras, and Hilf, (2008) an IR is a digital archive of the intellectual product created by the faculty, research staff and students of an institution and made accessible to end users both within and outside the institution with few or no barriers to access. Alpha Network Babel Library (2007) sees IR to mean an electronic archive of the scientific and scholarly output of an institution, stored in digital format where search and recovery are allowed for its subsequent national and international use.

Jain, Bentley, and Oladiran (2008) defined an IR as a digital research archive consisting of accessible collections of scholarly work that represent the intellectual capital of an institution. According to them, it is a means for institutions to manage the digital scholarship their communities produce, maximize access to research outputs both before and after publication and also to increase the visibility and academic prestige of both the institution and authors.

The most comprehensive and widely used definition is the one by Lynch (2003). Lynch defined a university-based IR as a set of services that a university offers to the members of its community for the management and dissemination of digital materials created by the university and its community members. It is most essentially an organizational commitment to the stewardship of these digital materials, including long-term preservation where appropriate, as well as organization and access or distribution.

Furthermore, Lynch described IR as a new channel for structuring the university's contribution to the broader world. According to Lynch, it is a recognition that the intellectual life and scholarship of our universities will increasingly be represented, documented and shared in digital form and that a primary responsibility of our universities is to exercise stewardship over these riches; both to make them available and to preserve them.

Open Access Movement and the Emergence of Institutional Repository

Open access movement according to Christian (2008) is traceable to the 1960s but gained momentum in the 1990s with the growth of modern information and communication technology especially the internet as well as the ability to copy and distribute electronic data at little or no cost. The development of institutional repositories according to John-Okeke (2008) was the outcome of several open access initiatives and movements made to salvage the dwindling scholarly communication. The open access movement according to Christian (2008) seeks to use the internet to provide free access to research and scholarly output to people irrespective of their physical or geographical location or other social and economic means.

A defining moment in the history of the open access movement came in 2001 at a landmark meeting initiated by the Open Society Institute in Budapest which resulted in the adoption of the Budapest Open Access Initiative (BOAI) (Christian, 2008). The Budapest Open Access Initiative defines Open Access as "free availability on the public internet, permitting any user to read, download, copy, distribute and/or print, with the possibility to search or link to the full texts of these articles, crawl them for indexing, pass them as data to software, or use them for any other lawful purpose, without financial, legal or technical barriers other than those inseparable from gaining access to the internet itself".

According to John-Okeke (2008), the major initiatives that gave rise to open access institutional repositories include the Budapest open access initiative, the Bethesda statement on open access publishing and Berlin open access initiative which later led to the development of open access journals and digital archives/institutional repositories. Other such initiatives as identified by Alpha Network Babel Library (2007) are the Welcome Trust about Open Access, the Valparaiso Declaration, the IFLA Statement on Open Access to Scholarly Literature and Research Documentation and the Washington D.C. Principles for Free Access to Science.

Similarly, Christian (2008) explained that the open access movement emerged in response to increasing legal and economic barriers by commercial scholarly publishers which invariably has made access to research output and information a difficult task especially to those in developing countries. Giesecke (2011) on the other hand linked the development of IR to the development of the Internet and the World Wide Web. According to the author, the first discipline archive launched in 1991 was the physics repository now known as arXiv which began as a server for articles on theoretical physics by Paul Ginsberg. The emergence of these open access initiatives, as well as information and communication technologies, have provided a veritable medium to address the problem of poor visibility of academic research information emanating from developing countries like Nigeria (Christian, 2008).

Benefits of Institutional Repositories

The recognition of institutional repositories as essential infrastructures of scholarly dissemination by academic institutions has been on the increase (Jain, Bentley & Oladiran, 2008). They have become veritable tools for enhancing the visibility of universities and researchers all over the world. Swan (n.d) explained the importance of repositories to the university noting that it fulfills a university's mission to engender, encourage and disseminate scholarly work while also serving as a marketing tool for them thereby providing maximum web impact for the institution.

For the researcher, Swan also noted that IR provides a platform for them to disseminate the outcome of their researches at no cost to the entire world. This, Swan further observed serves as a location for supporting data that are unpublished while also providing a platform for personal marketing. In line with this thought, literature has also revealed that articles and research findings disseminated on the platform of IRs enjoy wider coverage and circulation thereby increasing the level of citation of such articles and authors. It has been observed that the citation impact of research findings in IRs have significantly higher citation impact than those in restricted access (Jones, Andrew & MacColl, 2006; Harnard et al., 2008).

Bolu (2011) as cited in Nkiko, Bolu and Michael-Onuoha (2014) also captured the benefits of IRs to include: IR provides multiple access to documents, it requires no physical space for storage, easy retrieval of documents, increased global visibility of content, secure storage of documents, excellent search capabilities, controlled environment for updates to content, complex security rules to control access, reduced time and effort spent on document management and ability to maintain document history to meet legal requirements.

Greater speed of knowledge dissemination, citation advantage, advancement of science, access to scientific information, increase in audience among others are also some of the benefits of IRs (Alpha Babel Library, 2007; Fry, Lockyer, Oppenheim & Houghton, 2009). Commenting on the importance of the institutional repository, the Alpha Network Babel Library (2007) noted that access to full text of the content of a repository makes it a fundamental support tool for teaching and research while at the same time multiplying the institution's visibility in the international community.

Caution, however, needs to be maintained in running an institutional repository. Singh (2005) sounded a note of warning on the thoroughness of the peer- review process. Singh cautioned that peer review may be undermined which in turn reduces the authenticity of research papers published in the institutional repository.

Requirements for Setting up an IR/Policy

Certain things must be put in place in order to ensure a smooth hosting and sustenance of an institutional repository. Nkiko et al. (2014) observed that requirements for setting up an institutional repository vary according to the size and nature of the repository. Jain et al. (2008) mentioned the following as basic requirements for setting up an IR:

Software and Hardware Requirements: Though many IRs employ free open source software like Eprints and DSpace, the provision still needs to be made for modifications to the repository software. The Hardware requirements, on the other hand, involve having a dedicated server with sufficient capacity.

Staffing: Which include an administrator and other supporting personnel for populating the IR and developing several policies to manage the system.

Running costs which include how the IR would be operated and maintained. Issues such as system maintenance, upgrades, and training of staff feature under running cost.

The Internet has been recognized as the platform for all virtual activities of which institutional repositories also enjoys hosting. There cannot be successful deployment of institutional repositories without the use of the internet. Okoye & Ejikeme (2011) distinguished the role of the internet deployment of Institutional Repository. They recommended that institutions should place a premium on the provision of the internet before embarking on the institutional repository as a project.

Nkiko et al. (2014) also highlighted the following as minimum hardware requirements for setting up an IR: repository servers, 24-port Cisco switch, 26U cabinet, internet radio, content server-HP Pc4GB RAM, A3 scanner with feeder-network, barcode scanner, cache server- HP Pc 4GB RAM, network printer, 5KVA inverter and 5KVA UPS, back-up server-HP BL 380 G6 and KVM switch- 8 port. They observed that the equipment are expensive to procure.

Institutions around the world have policies and guidelines regulating the upload of content into their repositories and preservation of the content. The first step in setting up a repository as identified by Koulouris, Kyriaki-Mamessi, Giannakopoulos and Zervos (2013) is to set up policies with respect to the content, self-archiving procedure, use of personalized services for users and the introduction of relevant routines. Li and Banach (2011) noted that strategies for preserving IR content and the decisions about what content requires short, medium or long term preservation should be driven by preservation policies.

Trends in Africa

Chisenga (2006) observed that institutional repositories are valuable for research and development because they can offer instant access to information and knowledge resources being generated on the continent. The universities and research institutions in Africa are the major centers of research and consequently the major generators of research-based data, information and knowledge. The scientific and technological information and knowledge which they are generating should be easily accessible, and the creation and use of institutional repositories could be the first step in this process.

The first attempt to launch an institutional repository in Africa was made in the year 2000. University of Pretoria, South Africa established the first repository in Africa in the year 2000, concentrating mainly on theses and dissertation. In 2006 they expanded their sources to include all publication output from the university as well as digitize historical and archival materials donated to the university (Van Deventer & Pienaar 2008).

An attempt was made in 2002 by the University of Zimbabwe Library when they started participating in Database of African Theses and Dissertations (DATAD). Items uploaded on this platform were, however, limited to titles, abstracts and the names of authors and their supervisors, and were made accessible on the World Wide Web (Thata, 2007). Sustaining the repository was however an issue of concern as reported by Nyambi (2011). Ghana's first institutional repository came into being in 2008 with the establishment of Kwame Nkrumah University of Science and Technology's (KNUST) institutional repository. Six months later and with 560 postgraduate theses entered, KNUST appeared on the Webometrics ranking for 100 best universities in West Africa. Similarly, in Nigeria, the move towards open access repositories began in 2008 at an international workshop held in Ahmadu Bello University, Zaria (Okoye & Ejikeme, 2011). At the workshop, Bozimo (2008) emphasized the need for Nigerian universities and research libraries to organize their scholarly outputs into repositories in order to make them visible and available nationally and internationally without restrictions. Following this workshop, in 2009, University of Jos took the first step towards launching an institutional repository and the University is reputed to be the first to take such initiative in Nigeria and the second in West Africa after the University of Science & Technology, Ghana (Akintunde & Anjo, 2010). This move, according to Akpokodje and Akpokodje (2015) catapulted the University of Jos to the 4th, 70th and 7000th position in Nigeria, Africa, and the world respectively in the January 2010 Ranking Web of World Universities.

In 2009, the University of Botswana also established its own institutional repository known as the University of Botswana Research, Innovation and Scholarship Archive (UBRISA). UBRISA's strategic aim is to capture and preserve the institution's intellectual output and other digital assets in perpetuity, in pursuance of research excellence to which the university has committed itself (University of Botswana, 2009). In Uganda, Makerere University took the first step in setting up an institutional repository in 2009 which they referred to as Uganda Scholarly Digital Library (Namaganda, 2012).

At the later part of 2010, Covenant University Ota and the University of Nigeria Nsukka became registered with DOAR while the Federal University of Technology Akure followed suit in 2011. As at October 27, 2015, there are ten universities in Nigeria whose institutional repositories are listed in openDOAR. These include; Ahamdu Bello University, Covenant University, Landmark University, Federal University of Technology Akure, Federal University Oye Ekiti, University of Jos, University of Lagos, University of Ilorin, University of Nigeria Nsukka and Federal University Ndufu-Alike Ikwo (www.opendoar.org).

Akintunde and Anjo (2012) also described the state of institutional repositories in Nigeria with respect to posting digital content on the web, which they noted does not appear to follow any standards, while also using diverse output platforms. According to them, some of these institutions use open source software such as Eprints and DSpace, while others simply post into their institutional web content management systems which are not necessarily open sources.

It is, however, saddening to note that the development of IRs in Africa has been adjudged to be very slow and discouraging. Apart from challenges such as lack of ICT infrastructure, paucity of funds, lack of human capacity and skills to establish and maintain the repositories, African researchers by nature have been found to be unfavourably disposed to sharing their research with foreigners for fear that the information will be stolen and used by outside sources (Ford, 2005; Jain et al., 2008). This disposition has constituted a huge setback to the development of IR in Africa. Currently, out of the 54 countries in Africa, only 22 have been found to have a presence in the Directory of Open Access Repositories (DOAR) (www.opendoar.com, 2015). Out of the 22 countries only 4, namely South Africa, Kenya, Nigeria, and Algeria have institutional repositories in more than ten institutions. Botswana, Cameroon, Lesotho, Mozambique, Rwanda, Tunisia and Zambia have the least representation. South Africa has 24 institutional repositories, which is the highest number in Africa, followed by Kenya with 20. Nigeria and Algeria have 11 each while countries like Botswana, Cameroon, Lesotho, Mozambique, Rwanda, Tunisia, and Zambia have the least number with just 1 each. The current state of institutional repositories in Africa as reflected in Table 1 below is not encouraging as only a few nations in Africa have fully embraced the idea of hosting one.

It is evident that the establishment of institutional repositories in academic and research institutions in Africa is undergoing a serious developmental issue that requires urgent attention. van Wyk and Mostert (2012) lamented that open access IRs in the developing world especially Africa is far from ideal as only few academic institutions have taken up the challenge of making available their internally stored research output to the global market. From the foregoing, the noticeable trend among most institutions in Africa who have embraced IR is their initial focus on electronic theses and dissertations. In South Africa, van Deventer and Pienaar (2008) observed that this trend has changed as most institutions make readily available their special collections to researchers all around the globe.

Furthermore, they noted that beyond textual artefacts, some repositories now host videos, sound and datafiles. Nkosi (2008) also observed that the initial resistance to publishing research work in IRs by academics is fast fading as they are becoming increasingly aware that publishing in a reputable journal is not the only option to introduce new research work or be discovered by the academic community. This awakening has helped to enhance the development of IRs in Africa. It has been

Table 1. Distribution of institutional repositories in Africa

S/N	Country	No. of IRs
1.	South Africa	24
2.	Kenya	20
3.	Algeria	11
4.	Nigeria	11
5.	Tanzania	10
6.	Zimbabwe	8
7.	Sudan	5
8.	Egypt	4
9.	Ghana	4
10.	Cape Verde	2
11.	Ethiopia	2
12.	Morocco	2
13.	Namibia	2
14.	Senegal	2
15.	Uganda	2
16.	Lesotho	1
17.	Mozambique	1
18.	Rwanda	1
19.	Botswana	1
20.	Cameroon	1
21.	Tunisia	1
22.	Zambia	1

Source: www.opendoar.org

however noted that despite the fact that institutions are beginning to experience positive response from members of faculty, the self-archiving policy has not found a fertile ground to thrive among academics. Canadian Association of Research Libraries (2014) observed that institutions are settling down with the fact that self-archiving policy as laudable as it is, has the tendency to cause a draw back in populating their repositories. The current trend, therefore, favors central archiving process with the library serving as the coordinating body.

A major gap observed in the development of IRs in Africa has to do with the issue of copyright. Nkosi (2008) noted that the period it takes authors to obtain copyright clearance is quite significant and delays prompt submission to repositories, making particular reference to the University of South Africa Institutional Repository.

Libraries and Librarians are the major drivers of IRs, Morris (2002) also emphasized this. Most librarians are however not formally trained to take on this responsibility as noted by van Deventer and Pienaar (2008); this constitutes a major setback to the urgency required to set-up and successfully host an IR. They claimed that the creation of the various digital repositories has had a huge influence on the working lives of many librarians as many had to be trained or had to train themselves in order to fit into the new environment.

Issues and Challenges of Institutional Repositories in Africa

Very little research outputs find their way into the world's well-established international scientific journals due to various problems among them because publications in mainstream journals face the problems of over-subscription and recorded prejudice against submissions from developing country scientists. Additionally, local journals, in general, have poor distribution and visibility. This situation results in research from developing countries not being indexed in major international databases which have the capacity to increase the visibility of these research outputs. The author further noted that much of the research generated in research institutions are not being shared or developed further beyond field and laboratory research. Very useful and valuable technological and scientific information and knowledge remain unexploited and in some cases are lost.

Nyambi (2011) observed the challenges encountered when the University of Zimbabwe embarked on the institutional repository project. The author noted that sustaining the repository was a major issue of concern due to the high cost of bandwidth required to host the repository, political issues, brain drain among others. Also, in a communique at the end of the 2012 Standing Conference of Eastern, Central and South Africa Library and Information Association (SCECSAL), in Nairobi, Kenya, some of the challenges encountered in deploying IRs were highlighted. They include the following:

- Lack of motivation and incentives for researchers/academicians to submit their works to the institutional repositories;
- Absence of institutional policies and strategies to support open sharing of information resources;
- Inadequate bandwidth in institutions;
- Fear of the un-known resulting in resistance to open access initiatives by researchers, academicians, and librarians;
- Conflicts/differences between information technology specialists and information/library professionals in the institutions regarding the approaches and software tools to be used;

- The unstable power supply in some countries impact on 24/7 provision of access to institutional repositories;
- Open access and institutional repository initiatives are seen as additional responsibilities to normal library duties and do not receive the attention required;
- Absence of appropriate skills, especially IT skills, in libraries and documentation centres;
- Absence of clear copyright and guidelines for licensing digital content;
- Lack of knowledge about publishers' policies on open access and self-archiving.

Specifically, in Nigeria, Christian (2008) found that many academic institutions are still battling to overcome many challenging issues in an attempt to make their research outputs openly accessible by means of internet technologies like institutional repositories. Some of the issues identified in this which adversely militate against the development of institutional repositories in the country include:

- Lack of awareness of open access institutional repositories among researchers and academics in the country's academic and research institutions. More than 74% of the respondents surveyed during the course of the research were completely unfamiliar with open access institutional repository.
- Inadequate information and communication technology infrastructure. A major problem in this area is the high cost of internet bandwidth in the region. This cost results from the use of satellite infrastructure for internet connection as opposed to much efficient and cheaper fiber optic infrastructure. There is also the problem of inadequate and epileptic electricity supply to power ICT facilities in academic institutions. The long-term solution to the high cost of bandwidth lies in the development of more fiber optic infrastructure in the region as well as open access to same. The issue of poor electricity power supply will necessitate further research into eco-friendly alternative energy generating system to power ICT facilities in academic and research institutions.,
- Inadequate funding also constitutes another problem identified in the course of the research. Most of the academic and research institutions in Nigeria are funded by the government. These institutions continue to grapple with the percentage decline in budgetary allocation. Considering the fact that the development of institutional repository in this part of the world is a capital intensive project, funding constitutes another major obstacle to the development of institutional repository in the country's institutions.

The low level of awareness of open access institutional repository in Nigeria is directly linked to issues of inadequate advocacy for open access. One of the best ways to promote the development of open access institutional repository in developing countries is through advocacy. Effective advocacy presupposes that the advocates or stakeholders are very familiar with the concept. Issues related to intellectual property rights have also been a major concern to the development of institutional repositories. Christian (2008) reported that the International Institute of Tropical Agriculture (IITA) in Nigeria's institutional repository could not go public due to some copyright issues that needed to be resolved. Research works conducted by the researchers at the Institute were signed away to the journal publishers when the papers were submitted to commercial journal publishers for publication. Consequently, the Institute lost the right to make public research works it has funded and now has to negotiate the right from the journal publishers.

An intellectual property right is an aspect of the law that covers diverse legal rights that exist in creative work. Intellectual property law embraces such exclusive rights in copyright, patent, trademark, industrial designs, trade secret, trade name, etc. Copyright law determines how a person can deal with a written work such as a journal article or a research paper. Generally, a copyright holder has the exclusive right to authorize the copying, recopying or distribution of the written work. In other words, she/he has the right to determine whether the work shall be available in a closed or open access format (Christian, 2008).

Acquiring the rights from content contributors and copyright holders to distribute the content freely forms an integral part of collecting content for IRs (Li, & Banach, 2011). The issue of content has also been a major bane of the development of IRs. Between 2005 and 2010 as reported by Koulouris et al. (2013), the Technological Educational Institute of Athens attempted to flag a repository but failed due to lack of content. This according to them was due to the fact that faculty members appear to be ignorant of the benefits of pushing their publications into the repository, are suspicious of open access policies and are hesitant because publishing rights and policies are not clear. Other challenges identified include cost, difficulties in generating content, sustaining support and commitment, rights management issues, working culture and policy issues as well as lack of incentives (Pickton & Barwick, 2006).

Ezeani and Ezema (2011) also observed that inability to attract skilled personnel who possess the expertise to troubleshoot equipment such as computers, scanners, and the likes constitutes a major challenge to the development of institutional repositories, especially in the developing countries. Other challenges as identified in the literature include inadequate power supply, constant change in hardware and software, copyright issues, lack of technical support, technophobia, low bandwidth and lack of support from the academic community (Eke, 2011; Akintunde & Anjo, 2012).

Christian (2008) found that many academic institutions are still battling to overcome many challenging issues in an attempt to make their research outputs openly accessible by means of internet technologies like institutional repositories. Some of the issues identified which adversely militate against the development of institutional repositories include:

- Lack of awareness of open access institutional repositories among researchers and academics as well as research institutions.
- Inadequate information and communication technology infrastructure. A major problem in this area is the high cost of internet bandwidth in Africa. This cost results from the use of satellite infrastructure for internet connection as opposed to much efficient and cheaper fiber optic infrastructure. There is also the problem of inadequate and epileptic electricity supply to power ICT facilities in academic institutions. The long-term solution to the high cost of bandwidth lies in the development of more fiber optic infrastructure in the region as well as open access to same. The issue of poor electricity power supply will necessitate further research into eco-friendly alternative energy generating system to power ICT facilities in academic and research institutions.,

CONCLUSION

Scholarly communication in the academic environment has been limited by restraining policies of publishers who are commercial in their approach to information dissemination. The advent of Open Access Initiative which also houses institutional repositories emancipated researchers from the hold of publishers. On the global platform, IR has been a warehouse of information, especially for institutions that are interconnected, enjoying resource sharing. The development of IRs in Africa has not been very encouraging as only a few repositories are active with the largest number hosted by institutions in South Africa. Also, there appears to be no uniform standard adopted for hosting and posting information on the repository. The need to also drive interoperability of IRs among institutions in Africa is germane. This, however, is yet to be fully operational. Librarians have a key role to play in popularizing the IR as it appears that most academics do not appreciate the importance of depositing their intellectual output in the repository.

REFERENCES

Abubakar, B. M. (2010). Digital libraries in Nigeria in the Era of Global change: A Perspective of the major Challenges. *TRIM*, *6*(2), 125–131.

Akintunde, S. A., & Anjo, R. (2012). *Digitizing Resources in Nigeria: An Overview*. Retrieved from www.netlibrarynigeria.net/downloads/Akintunde.doc/pdf

Alemayehu, M. W. (2010). *Researcher's attitude to using Institutional Repositories: A case study of the Oslo University Institutional Repository.* Retrieved from http://hdl.handle.net

Alpha Network Babel Library. (2007). *Guidelines for the creation of Institutional Repositories at Universities and Higher Education Institutions*. Columbus, OH: Europe Aid Co-operation Office.

Bailey, C. W. Jr. (2005). The Role of Reference Librarians in Institutional Repositories. *RSR. Reference Services Review*, *33*(3), 259–26. doi:10.1108/00907320510611294

Canadian Association of Research Libraries (CARL). (2014). A Guide to Setting-Up an Institutional Repository. *CARL.* Retrieved from http://www.carl-abrc.ca/en/scholarly communications/carl-institutional-repository-program/a-guide-to-setting-up-an institutional-repository.html

Chisenga, J. (2006). *The development and use of digital libraries, institutional digital repositories and open access archives for research and national development in Africa: Opportunities and challenges.* WSIS Follow-up Conference on Access to Information and Knowledge for Development. Retrieved from http://www.uneca.org/disd/events/2006/wsislibrary/presentations/Development%20and20Use%20 of%20Institutional%20Repositories%20-%20Justin%20Chisenga%20 %20EN.pdf

Christian, G.M. (2008). *Issues and Challenges to the Development of Open Access Institutional Repositories in Academic and Research Institutions in Nigeria.* Academic Press.

Crow, R. (2002). *The case of Institutional Repositories: A SPARC Position Paper.* Retrieved from http://www.arl.org/sparc/bm~doc/ir_final_release_102.pdf

Crow, R. (2002). Open access and scholarly communications. *SPARC/Science Commons.* Available at http://surf.nl/download/countryupdate2005.pdf

Davis, P. M., & Connolly, M. J. L. (2007). Institutional Repositories: Evaluating the Reasons for non-use of Cornell University's Installation of DSpace. *D-Lib Magazine*, *13*(3&4). Retrieved from http://www.dlib.org/dlib/march07/davis/03davis.html

Eke, H. N. (2011). *Digitizing resources for University of Nigeria Repository: Process and Challenges.* Retrieved from http://www.webology.org/2011/v8n1/a85.html

Ezeani, C. N., & Ezema, I. J. (2011). Digitizing Institutional Research Output of University of Nigeria, Nsukka. *Library Philosophy and Practice.* Retrieved from http://unllib.unl.edu/LPP

Ford, H. (2005). *Why the Lack of Open Content in Africa?* Retrieved from http://www.culturalivre.org.br/english/index.php?option=com_content

Giesecke, J. (2011). *Institutional Repositories: Keys to Success.* Retrieved from http://digitalcommons.unl.edu/cgi/viewcontent.cgi?a

Harnard, S., Brody, T., Vallieres, F., Carr, L., Hitchcock, S., Gingras, Y., & Hilf, E. (2008). The access/impact problem and the green and gold roads to Open Access: An update. *Serials Review*, *34*(1), 36–40. doi:10.1080/00987913.2008.10765150

Ivwighreghweta, O. (2012). An Investigation to the Challenges of Institutional Repositories development in six Academic Institutions in Nigeria. *International Journal of Digital Library Services*, *2*(4), 1–16.

Jain, P., Bentley, G., & Oladiran, M. T. (2008). *The Role of Institutional Repository in Digital Scholarly Communications.* Retrieved from www.library.up.ac.za/digi/docs/jain_paper.pdf

John-Okeke, R. (2008). Developing Institutional Repositories: Considering Copyright Issues. *Journal of Applied Information Science and Technology*, *2*, 11–18.

Jones, R., Andrew, T., & McColl, J. (2006). *The Institutional Repository*. Oxford, UK: Chandos Publishing. doi:10.1533/9781780630830

Koulouris, A., Kyriaki-Mamessi, D., Giannakopoulos, G., & Zervos, S. (2013). Institutional Repository Policies: Best Practices for Encouraging Self-Archiving. *Procedia: Social and Behavioral Sciences*, *73*, 769–779. doi:10.1016/j.sbspro.2013.02.117

Li, Y., & Banach, M. (2011). Institutional Repositories and Digital Preservation: Assessing Current Practices at Research Libraries. *D-Lib Magazine*, *17*(5&6). doi:10.1045/may2011-yuanli

Livingston, H., & Nastasie, D. (2009). The Role of Academic Libraries in the Sustainability, Preservation and Access control of Digital Repositories. *Proceedings of 60 DCC State of the Art Report EDUCAUSE Australasia '09.* Retrieved from http://www.caudit.edu.au/educauseaustralasia09/authorspapers/Livingston.pdf

Lougee, W. P. (2003, May). Diffuse libraries. *The 142nd Association of Research Libraries Membership Meeting, Program Session II*. Available at http://www.arl.org/arl/proceedings/142/lougee.html

Lynch, C. (2003). Institutional Repositories: Essential infrastructure for Scholarship in the Digital Age Portal. *Libraries and the Academy, 3*(2). Retrieved from http://muse.jhu.edu/journals/portal_libraries_and_the_academy/v003/3.2lynch.html

McCord, A. (2003). Institutional Repositories: Enhancing Teaching, Learning and Research. *EDUCAUSE National Conference.*

Namaganda, A. (2012). *Institutional Repositories and Higher Education in Uganda: The Role of the Consortium of Uganda University Libraries.* Retrieved from https://www.academia.edu/3617835/Institutional_Repositories_and_Higher_Education_in-Uganda_The_Role_of_the_Consortium_of_Uganda_University_Libraries

Nkiko, C., Bolu, C. & Micahel-Onuoha, H. (2014). *Managing a Sustainable Institutional Repository: The Covenant University Experience.* Academic Press.

Nkosi, D. S. (2008). *Establishing an Institutional Repository: A UNISA Case Study*. Retrieved from http://uir.unisa.ac.za/bitstream/handle/10500/4297/22_D-S-_Nkosi-2.pdf?sequence=1&isAllowed=y

Ogbomo, E. F., & Muokebe, B. O. (2015). Institutional Repositories as Emerging Initiative in Nigerian University Libraries. *Information and Knowledge Management, 5*(1). Retrieved from http://www.iiste.org/Journals/index.php/IKM/article/view/19418/19409

Okoye, M. O., & Ejikeme, A. N. (2011). Open access, institutional repositories, and scholarly publishing: the role of librarians in South Eastern Nigeria. *Library Philosophy and Practice.*

Pickton, M., & Barwick, J. (2006). *A Librarian's guide to Institutional Repositories*. Loughborough, UK: Loughborough University. Retrieved from http://magpie.lboro.ac.uk/dspace/handle/2134/1122

Pringle, J. (2005). Partnering helps Institutional Repositories thrive. *Knowledge Link Newsletter*. Retrieved from http://scientific.thomson.com/news/newsletter/2005-02/8264025/

Standing Conference of Eastern, Central, and South Africa Library and Information Association (SCECSAL) in Nairobi, Kenya. (2012). *Challenges to Open Access and Institutional Repositories in Africa.* Author.

Swan, A. (2007). *Open Access Self-archiving: An Author Study.* Cornwall, UK: Key Perspective. Available on www.keyperspectives.co.uk

Thata, M. B. (2007). *Building a Digital Library at the University of Zimbabwe: A Celebration of teamwork and collaboration.* Retrieved from http://r4d.dfif.gov.uk/PDF/Outputs/Peri/Zimbabwe

van Deventer, M., & Pienaar, H. (2008). *South African Repositories: Bridging Knowledge Divides.* Retrieved from http://repository.up.ac.za/bitstream/handle/2263/8615/VanDeventer_South(2008).pdf?sequence=1

van Myk, B., & Mostert, J. (2012). *African Institutional Repositories as contributors to Global Information: A South African Case Study.* Retrieved from http://etd2012.unmsm.edu.pe/pdf/presentation/VWyKETD2012FT.pdf

Ware, M. (2004). *Pathfinder Research on Web-based Repositories,* Publisher and Library/Learning Solutions. Retrieved from http://www.palsgroup.org.uk/palsweb.nsf/0/8c43ce800a9c67cd80256e370051e8

KEY TERMS AND DEFINITIONS

Copyright: The exclusive and assignable legal right, given to the originator/author/creator for a fixed number of years, to print, publish, perform, film, or record literary, artistic, or musical material.

Institutional Repository: A digital archive of the intellectual product created by the faculty, research staff and students of an institution and made accessible to end users both within and outside the institution with few or no barriers to access.

Intellectual Property Right: An aspect of the law that covers diverse legal rights that exist in creative work.

Open Access: Free availability on the public internet, permitting any user to read, download, copy, distribute and/or print, with the possibility to search or link to the full texts of these articles, crawl them for indexing, pass them as data to software, or use them for any other lawful purpose, without financial, legal or technical barriers other than those inseparable from gaining access to the internet itself.

Scholarly Communication: The system through which research and other scholarly writings are created, evaluated for quality, disseminated to the scholarly community, and preserved for future use.

Chapter 9
Exploring the Concept of Open Access Journals:
Its Types and Features with an Emphasis on Identification of Active OA Journals Indexed by Scopus Database

Showkat Ahmad Wani
University of Kashmir, India

Zahid Ashraf Wani
University of Kashmir, India

ABSTRACT

The chapter focuses on the exploration and elucidation of the open access concept, with the main emphasis on open access journals, their types and features, etc. Similarly, the thrust was also given to acquaint the audience with the open access journal publishers, in order to aware them about the availability of open access literature and the opportunities where open access research can be published by the authors or scientists. In order to give some practical flavors to the readers of this study, the focus of the study was also made towards gauging the active open access journals indexed by the Scopus database. Moreover, particular emphasis was given to check the distribution of active open access journals indexed by it in the fields of life sciences, social sciences, physical sciences, and health sciences. The purpose was to ease the users to search and use the open access journal literature as per the subject taste.

DOI: 10.4018/978-1-5225-8437-7.ch009

INTRODUCTION

The knowledge is a power which enables mankind to find the core solutions to the complex social problems. Researches are conducted to find reliable answers and solutions to the problems faced by the masses in different social settings. Conducting research is heavily dependent on quality relevant literature, which is most costly in nature as it is available in subscription mode. Due to advancements in knowledge development and dissemination in an electronic mode, the concept of Open Access evolved on the horizon of scholarly communication.

The Open Access means the free and unrestricted access to full-text information especially, the journal articles, technical reports, conference papers, thesis, and other scientific literature, across the globe without any technical, legal, subscription barriers (Suber, 2007; Ghosh & Kumar, 2007; Herring, 2002). Today the concept of the OA has revolutionized the scientific communication by making access to knowledge easier and faster. It aims to make scientific knowledge universally accessible to those who need it for certain purposes. In the traditional scholarly communication model (Toll-Access model), scientific literature remained to be the property of elites (financially sound subscribers). Thus created the division within the scientific community by making the subscription group more powerful by getting the valued insights offered by Toll-Access resources and paralyzed the un-subscribed group by barring their accessibility on the same. In such a situation, the Open Access to quality scientific literature can provide a reliable solution to this problem faced by financially inefficient scholars. Most researchers try to search the scientific literature published in scientific journals to meet their literature requirements. The Toll- Access journals will meet the requirements of their subscribers only. While as, the OA journals offer free access to its scientific contents without any subscription, technical and other barriers for everyone. Thus it can become a helping tool for researchers to find the required scientific literature pertinent to their field of study.

Although the concept of Open Access has gained popularity to a greater extent still there is some lacking awareness among the literature users particularly about the concept of OA journals, its types & features? In this milieu, the study has made an endeavor to shed some light on the concept of the Open Access, its features, Open Access journals, their characteristics & types, and some OA literature publishing platforms. Besides, the study has also made an endeavor to acquaint the audience about the Scopus database & OA journals. The Scopus database is an indexing and abstracting database covering a large number of books, journals (both active and inactive, including OA & non-OA), and conference proceedings (Scopus, 2018). The prime focus of the study goes on Active OA journals indexed in Scopus data 2018, distribution of OA journals in fourtop-level subject areas viz: life sciences, social sciences, physical sciences, and health sciences. The study can help its readers to increase their knowledge pertinent to the above-mentioned concepts and will also enable them to take a comprehensive view of active Open Access journals which they can utilize for diverse purposes.

BACKGROUND

"Access to knowledge is, you know, a basic human right" (Elliot, 2014).

The humans have progressed their survival of life on earth by innovating and adopting the modern knowledge and technologies pertaining to diverse issues and problems they have countered in different situations. Many civilizations that flourished across the globe have utilized a good chunk of knowledge for their development, evidenced even in present times by observing their residual remains like Harappa Civilization, Chinese Civilization, and many others. One important point that has been marked by every person is that without the use of knowledge and technologies these civilizations might not have been developed as such as they were. Similarly, the development of present societies is not possible with applying the quality knowledge and advanced technologies for various purposes by the masses. The present societies are knowledge-driven societies, where all most all aspects are dependent on the utilization of knowledge. Knowledge is considered more important than other economic components and similarly, greater emphasis is given to generate quality scientific knowledge for which various Research & Development institutes are established covering the vast area of subject fields.

The access to knowledge is considered as the basic human right and provisions to safeguard this vital right of masses is need of the hour; its responsibility should rely on the constitutions of the states across the world (Rens and Kahn, 2009). In the present era, knowledge is generated at an enormous pace by researchers across the globe in various scientific fields, but a major portion of it remains the barred under the provision of Toll- Access or subscription model. This results in limited utilization of all the developed scientific knowledge and in turn results in the slower development of countries in general and quality-life of masses in particular. Although this is a big issue or problem faced by knowledge seekers at all levels, the scholars are major victims of this issue, because their works heavily rely upon the latest qualitative scientific literature. An old saying is that 'where there is a will there is a way'. Same is applicable here, that if the above-mentioned issue needs to be solved the solution for this problem lies in strengthening, supporting and utilizing Open Access to scientific literature.

What Open Access Means

Open Access is the free, immediate, online availability of research articles coupled with the right to use these articles fully in the digital environment. Open Access ensures that anyone can access and use these results- to turn into industries and breakthroughs into better lives. (SPARC, 2018).

The concept of Open Access means the provision of un-barred access to peer-reviewed scientific publications and often agglomerates with the calls for Open research, Open data, Open education and Open science (Terras, 2015). Open data means the research data accessible freely on the internet permitting its download, copy, use & distribution without any financial and technical barriers. While as Open Education covers all tools, practices, and resources that are free from any barrier and can be used, shared & adopted fully in an electronic environment. It makes the education of masses more affordable, accessible and effective by maximizing the power of the World Wide Web or internet (SPARC, 2018). According to open access. nl (2018), Open Access is a global academic movement that aims to offer free and instant online access to latest research findings or scholarly literature, with rights to download, distribute, copy, use and re-use them for multiple purposes in various situations. In simple terms, Open Access (OA) means the free, un-subscribed or unrestricted access to the full text of scientific articles to anyone anywhere without any hindrance (Bjo ¨rk, 2017). In the same vein, "Open Access (OA) means that electronic scholarly articles are available freely at the point of use" (Jeffery, 2006). In the same manner, Springer (2018) mentions that when the publications are freely available online without any cost to all the users it is termed as Open Access. For authors, readers and funders un-restricted distribution of research is vital because due to this the authors and funders can reach a wider audience and increase their publication impact and readers can access more literature without paying. It can also be said that Open Access is a comprehensive source of knowledge and cultural heritage that scientific community has approved and knowledge dissemination mission is half completed if it is not made readily available to widest part of the society (Berlin Declaration as cited by Redalyc, Clase & In-Com Uab, 2003; MAX-PLANCK-GESELLSCHAFT, 2018; open access.nl, 2018). The main thrust of the Open Access concept is on restriction less access to scholarly contents for everyone who is interested to use these contents.

The majority of the literature shows that Open Access means free and unrestricted access to knowledge or scientific publications, empowers the knowledge seekers to acquire the latest quality knowledge any time anywhere through the use of the internet without any constraints of finance, legal and other barriers. It is believed that Open Access has its roots in the development of the internet and modern technologies.

The internet has sped up the knowledge sharing among the masses by interlinking them across the different virtual networks throughout the globe. Similarly, scholarly communities became able to share their works by publishing them in Open Access mode via different platforms so that their objective of reaching the wider audience can get fulfilled.

Significance of Open Access

Nowadays, it is widely recognized that making research results more accessible contributes to better and more efficient science and to innovation in the public and private sectors. (European Commission, Horizon 2020 as mentioned by open access. nl, 2018)

The importance of Open Access is huge in the present era for every information user, especially to those who are mostly dependent to access the latest scientific finding in their field. Scientists who are working on different projects are constantly in search of the latest research articles for getting valuable insights to yield better results of their studies. But, as per observation that the majority of quality literature is available in subscription mode and demands a good amount of money from subscribers for granting them access on these papers. The economic divisions are prevailing between the nations, societies, institutions and particularly among the researchers as well. Thus becomes a major problem for those needy literature searchers who are inefficient to subscribe to Toll-Access knowledge resources. Open Access as already explained above removes the financial, technical and legal barriers to scientific publications and allows the users to access the quality contents without paying for it.

The public and private sectors can get advanced growth and innovation by making the research findings more accessible in Open Access mode. Literature is evident that Open Access has a lot of significance to its credit. It makes the scholarly research permanently available online without restrictions; provide benefits for all stakeholders including students, researchers, funders, librarians, scholarly societies and the general public. Thus strengthens the advancement of learning, knowledge & research worldwide and helps in achieving the objectives laid by the institution and fulfill their missions (Cambridge University Press, 2018). Similarly, Bernius (2010) opines that Open Access is the cost-efficient approach for disseminating and using scientific knowledge and accelerating the scientific creation. Similarly, Open Access reduces the cost of scholarly publishing which can be a motivation for scholars to use Open Access routes. It helps in establishing the links between the individual authors and fosters interdisciplinary research (Swan, 2010; Bernius & Hanauske, 2009; Awre, 2003). Some of the key benefits of Open Access are mentioned by open access.nl (2018) as; it enables rapid and wide dissemination of scholarly knowledge, serves as an impetus to new knowledge, helps in building the knowledge economy and increases the economic boost, helps in putting the new knowledge in teaching, and can be considered as a cost-saving approach for better developments of nations. In the same manner, the Cambridge University Press, (2018) also mentions some major benefits of Open Access as follows:

The benefits of OA include:

- **Discoverability and Dissemination:** The free & online availability of Open Access works, accessible across the globe empowers the researchers, authors and many funding agencies to enhance the visibility and discoverability of their works, thus promising them a better return on their invested resources.
- Educational and Other Re-Uses: Open Access works (Gold OA) can be re-used by anyone into any format like changes in languages, figures and texts etc. under the application of a creative commons licence. Mostly it enables these changes and re-use for educational purpose.
- Public Access and Engagement: The biggest advantage of Open Access is it offers greater access for society and facilitates the greater public engagement with research. It can help the health workers, teacher, lawyers and many others to reap the benefits of accessing the latest scientific findings.

Open Access Resources

There are various Open Access resources that facilitate the accessibility to different ideas and insights. These include Open Access e-books, ETD, e-print archive, Open Access repositorie, and OA directories. All of these aim to disseminate the scientific knowledge to the widest audience.

Open Access e-Books

The books that are available in e-format and are accessible without their subscription at anywhere in the world are termed as Open Access e-books. Today a wide amount of e-book literature is available and is disseminating knowledge to the users concerned with various subject areas. Some of the well-known sources for accessing the OA e-book contents are; Project Gutenberg (http://www.gutenberg.org), DOAB: Directory of Open Access Books (http://doabooks.org) and Open Library (https://openlibrary.org).

Electron Thesis and Dissertations

The important source of scholarly contents is Electronic Thesis and Dissertations; it enables the researchers to disseminate the knowledge to the wider user base and helps in avoiding the duplication of research in various disciplines (Sivakumaren, 2015). In the same vein, ETDS can be easily located, readily accessible, and transferred over the internet especially when it is in Open Access mode (Vijaykumar & Murthy, 2001). Similarly, Moxley (2001) views that in future the quality of the universities will be ascertained by its digital library of Electronic Thesis and Dissertations. Various sources are available by which ETDS can be accessed by the knowledge seekers, Open Access Theses and Dissertations: OATD (http://oatd.org), OpenThesis.org (http://www.openthesis.org), Open Directory Project Free Dissertations (http://www.dmoz.org/search?q=free+dissertation), ShodhGanga, India (http://shodhganga.inflibnet.ac.in), NDTLD (http://www.ndltd.org), and Mahatma Gandhi University Online Theses Library (http://www.mgutheses.in). These Open Access ETD sources can be used by the users to access the quality scientific knowledge covering the wide range of subject areas without paying any amount in terms of the subscription fee.

E-print archive

The online repository of contents freely available on the web for widest dissemination of scholarly knowledge is said to be known as e-print archive (Pinfield, Gardner & MacColl, 2002). Similarly, it is defined that "Open access e-print archives are where authors of published research papers and papers destined for peer-reviewed publication can self-archive the full texts of their work for all to see." – (OpCit Project mentioned by The Library of Congress, 2015). The well-known Open Access e-print archives that authors are using for disseminating their research findings to a large number of users are; ArXiv.org (http://arxiv.org), CERN Document Server (http://cds.cern.ch), Chemical Sciences Repository (http://www.rsc.li/repository), Cogprints (http://cogprints.org), Cryptology ePrint Archive (https://eprint.iacr.org) and Eprint Network (http://www.osti.gov/eprints) etc.

Apart from the above-mentioned e-print archives, there are various others in large number which can also be used by the knowledge seekers or information users to access the trending cutting-edge research findings at anywhere in the world through internet.

Open Access Repositories

The Open Access repositories are digital platforms of research outputs deposited by the researchers or author that re freely accessible. It allows downloading and distributing the research contents to every user (University of Bradford, 2018). Repositories can be institution-based, subject-based, funder-based or national. Repositories can hold published or unpublished articles, presentations, datasets, and/or metadata about them.

OA Directories

The Open Access directories are those directories that are listing the Open Access contents links, names and other information and are guiding the users to find the appropriate Open Access resource, which meets his taste or requirement. Directories are made to cover both the individual items and the aggregate resources depending upon the nature and purpose of it. In present ere several Open Access directories are built to strengthen the access to scientific knowledge some examples includes: Directory of Open Access Books (DOAB) (http://doabooks.org), Directory of Open Access Journals (DOAJ) (http://www.doaj.org), Free Medical Journals (http://www.freemedicaljournals.com), Institutional Archives Registry (http://roar.eprints.org), Open Access Directory (http://oad.simmons.edu/oadwiki/Main_Page), Open DOAR (http://www.opendoar.org), ROAR (http://roarmap.eprints.org) and ROAD (http://road.issn.org).

Open Access Journals and Their Advantages

Open-access (OA) literature is digital, online, free of charge, and free of most copyright and licensing restrictions. What make it possible is the internet and the consent of the author or copyright-holder. (Peter Suber, 2007)

The journals which are available in Open Access mode and are bound to provide access to quality peer-reviewed articles in various domains are called as Open Access journals. Open Access journal literature is digital, online, free of cost and free from any other restrictions like copyright and licensing etc. All readers are empowered to access these OA journals on the public internet for different purposes especially for teaching- learning and research (Deoghuria & Paul, 2018). Open Access journals have many advantages that can encourage the authors to publish their scientific findings in this mode. Such as it helps the authors to make their publications visible to the large audience and increases the chances of getting more citations for these papers. Similarly, on the other side, the literature users become able to harness the advantage of getting access to quality literature relevant to their need without any spending or free of cost. According to Xia et al. (2011) as quoted by Koler-Pov et al. (2014) Open Access articles are more citable than non-Open Access articles, as they are free to use for every at any place on the world via internet or World Wide Web. It is believed that if the authors can find improvement in the impact of their researches due to Open Access, they will prefer to publish their works through the Open Access route (McVeigh, 2004). It has been founded that the impact of Open Access is significantly positive when it comes to availability of scientific journals literature. But there is a difference between the disciplines due to lack of awareness among the researchers although results should be of general interest to all scientists (Björk, et al., 2010).

According to Lawrence (2001), the online availability of scientific papers potentially enhances its overall impact especially when it is freely available and accessible. Moreover, Hajjem, Harnad, and Gingras (2006) revealed that "Comparing OA and NOA articles in the same journal/year, OA articles have consistently more citations, the advantage varying from 36%-172% by discipline and year. Comparing articles within six citation ranges (0, 1, 2-3, 4-7, 8-15, 16+ citations), the annual percentage of OA articles is growing significantly faster than NOA". In the same vein, Björk and Solomon (2012) in his study found out that Open Access journals that were indexed by the web of science and Scopus possess the same Impact and quality, which the subscription journals have. Similarly, Antelman (2004) also founded that, the disciplines of philosophy, political science, electrical and electronic engineering and mathematics adopted Open Access at varying stages, and the Open Access articles of these disciplines have a greater impact (in terms of citations). Thus, revealed that those who adopt Open Access practices are rewarded for the same. After scrutinizing the literature pertinent to Open Access journals and their advantages it has been observed that if the journals which contain qualitative scientific literature or research findings adopt Open Access route to disseminate their latest knowledge. Then they might have a sure positive impact in terms of increased citation count, wider publicity, and significant achievements. Open Access journals are now emerging in great quantity in diverse subject areas, need is to make a strong and maximum awareness of these journal resources to the users who are major expected beneficiaries of the Open Access journals (e.g. researchers, librarians etc.).

Types of OA Journals

The concept of Open Access, particularly the Open Access journals is a broad concept encompasses various types in its domain. Various scholars have categorized these Open Access journals in varied categories like Green Open Access, Gold Open Access or Libre OA, Gratis OA, Delayed OA, Hybrid OA and so on. As evident from the literature, OA to scientific articles can be made in two way viz: Green OA- is also known as self-archiving, following this route the manuscript of the authors is deposited into a repository for making it accessible to everyone free of cost. The copyright for these papers is retained with the publisher, or affiliated society and some restrictions are posted on how the work can be reused. Simply, an embargo period is also applied to these types of Open Access articles. While the Gold OA- includes the final versions of those articles that are put to offer free and permanent access to everyone, immediately after publication. Copyright of these articles is retained by the authors with most of the permission barriers are removed. These journals are published either in fully Open Access mode or hybrid Open Access mode (Springer, 2018; Jeffery, 2006; Gargouri, et al, 2010; Harnad, et al, 2004). In the same vein, Open Access journals can follow the routes of "gratis OA (free of charge, but not free of copyright or licensing restrictions), libre OA (free of charge and expressly permits uses beyond fair use), delayed OA (paid access initially, becoming open after a set time period), green and gold OA (pay-for-production followed by delayed publication in an OA repository or gratis OA) and so on" (Suber, 2013 as cited in Rob, Sandra & Dermot, 2015). Similarly, Bjork and Solomon (2012) asserts "gold OA publishing is rapidly increasing its share of the overall volume of peer-reviewed journal publishing, and there is no reason for authors not to choose to publish in OA journals just because of the 'OA' label, as long as they carefully check the quality standards of the journal they consider".

The hybrid Open Access journals are those which provide a proportion of individual articles openly accessible within the subscribed articles in the same journal to the users by demanding an optional payment from the authors (Björk B-C as cited by Laakso & Björk, 2012). The journal literature publishers are offering the authors an option to make their scientific articles openly accessible in hybrid Open Access mode if they pay article processing charges. These articles also undergo a standard peer-review process then ask the authors to choose the Open Access option. The copyright is still retained with an author; he can publish the final version of his paper in intuitional repositories without any embargo period (Mueller-Langer & Watt, 2014). Similarly, those authors who are not able to or interested in to pay the article processing charges for making their publications in Open Access mode (hybrid-OA), but are willing to go through an embargo period then to make it Openly accessible is termed as delayed Open Access (Lin, 2006). Similarly, "the delayed access model indicates that researchers (and their libraries) place a premium on immediacy of access. This immediacy is also important for news releases, which would not be able to access these articles at the time news releases are issued. However, news releases remain online and indexed in search engines for years after they are released, as demonstrated in this study. Therefore, hyperlinking to articles will, over time and with no additional effort, facilitate access to an increasing number of the articles mentioned, from one-third to over one half" (Young, 2017). Different approaches or routes can be adopted by the authors of scientific papers to publish their findings depends upon their choice. Like, whether they are interested to publish their articles in Toll-Access mode or they will prefer to publish in OA by paying article processing charges or they will make them freely accessible after a certain period of time (embargo period) e.g. usually after six months (Mann, Walter, Hess & Wigand, 2009). Thus the literature shows that there could be different types of Open Access journals. All are named after their policy of access adopted. The access types of Open Access journals are also discussed above and reveal that these are the main routes adopted by them to disseminate the scientific literature. The vast quantity of journal literature is already available for users through different sources and platforms, but due to lesser awareness about these resources results in their insufficient utilization. The overall awareness of the Open Access movement, resources, and anything should be strengthened.

Open Access Journal literature Publisher

The Open Access journals literature is published by various publishers in different subject fields. But, the awareness pertinent to these publishers is not to all authors and knowledge seekers. There is a need to acquaint the audience with some Open Access journal content publishers concerned with different disciplines. Following publishers are concerned with OA journals.

Biomed Central

The BMC is a journal publishing platform publishing 300 peer-reviewed journals in the fields of science, technology, engineering, and medicine. Since 1999 it has made high-quality research Open to everyone by adopting the Open Access publishing model. It is also the part of Springer Nature, offers the authors an opportunity to create a connection with the research communities across the world. It adopts the policy of "Gold OA model" and gives the readers free, instant access and faster discovery of the latest research. It enabled the authors to publish 70,000 Open Access articles which contribute to more than 5-million article downloads in 2017. Some of the leading selective journals are; BMC Biology, BMC Medicine, Genome Biology, Genome Medicine, and its academic journals such as; Journal of Hematology & Oncology, Malaria Journal & Microbiome, and the BMC *series*. It has around 65 inclusive journals that are focused to meet the needs of individual research communities (BioMed Central, 2018).

PLOS

The Open Access journal literature publisher PLOS was founded in 2001 by Harold Varmus, Patrick Brown and Michael Eisen. It is a non-profit Open Access publisher, innovator and advocacy organization, missioned to accelerate progress in science and medicine by leading transformation in research communication. It believes in that Open Access is not just free and unrestricted access to research but it also indicates open data, transparency in peer review & assessment of science openly. Similarly, Open Access is a mind-set that fosters best scientific values and brings the scientists together to share works to advance science faster for the benefit of society as a whole. PLOS launched its first journal in 2003, since accelerates and innovates science & medicine, from discovery of the research to influence tracking. Its vision is that scientific concepts or ideas & discoveries are the public good. The benefit of the same will only be achieved of realized when scientists have efficient means for communicating their ideas, research results and any other discovery between the stakeholders, particularly the wider public (PLOS, 2018).

Hindawi

Another research publisher Hindawi supports Open Access research and scholarly communication enables the authors to publish their works in an Open Access mode and helps them to reach the wider user base. It collaborates with the global academic community to promote Open Access to scholarly research and offers the authors robust publishing standards and editorial integrity (Hindawi, 2018).

Copernicus.org

It is the publisher of peer-reviewed Open Access journals of high repute and is more dedicated to promoting science, technology & the humanities. Besides, it also supports the development of relevant and appropriate software solutions to achieve its objectives (Copernicus Publications, 2018). Apart from the above mentioned Open Access journal literature or OA journal publishers. There are many others which are also supporting and strengthening the Open Access to knowledge and encourage the authors to publish their research findings in Open Access mode. Like, The Winnower, figshare, MUSE OPEN, and many others. Researchers can make use of these resources to reap the benefits of Open Access and contribute to social development.

Scopus Database and Open Access

Scopus is the largest indexing and abstract database of peer-reviewed literature of books, scientific journals, and conference proceedings. It highlights and delivers the research outputs in the areas of science, technology, medicine, social sciences, and arts & humanities by adopted or featuring the smart tools analyze, track and visualize research. It is used by more than 3,000 academic, government and corporate institutions and enables its users to remain up-to-date in their fields and fosters interdisciplinary research. The Scopus database also Index the Open Access journals, as mentioned by it that out of its total active indexed journals, a good number of Open Access journals are also registered. It also indicates the listed Open Access journals in orange colour on any results list where they are available, like the Scopus source page or source details page (Scopus, 2018).

MAIN FOCUS OF THE CHAPTER

The scope of the study is limited to the concept of Open Access and its significance, concept of OA journals their types & advantages. Besides, the study had also gauged the active journals indexed by Scopus database. Moreover, the coverage of the study is further extended to check the distribution of active OA journals & active non-OA journals. The prime emphasis was given to check the distribution of active Open Access journals indexed by Scopus in its top-level subject fields viz: life sciences, social sciences, physical sciences, and health sciences.

Problem

Open Access is the trending sensation in present era throughout the globe. The more awareness about it will definitely bring positive results for the literature users, who are constantly in search of the latest scientific literature. The knowledge about the Open Access concept, its significance, OA journals, and their various types & features will significantly change the usage pattern of scholarly communication. There is a lack of knowledge among the authors about OA literature publishing platforms, results in the slow pace of Open Access literature publishing. Although there were sufficient OA journal resources available for users due to limited knowledge about their place of availability and the subject area to which they are relevant, results in scare utilization of these resources. So in this ambient, there is a need to make the literature users more aware about the whole concept of Open Access by shedding light on the OA its features, OA journals its types and characteristics. In addition to this need is to explore, identify & gauge the active OA journal resources indexed by Scopus database in various subject areas. So that the users can become aware of active OA journals in some broader subject fields to which they may be concerned.

Objectives

- To explore the concept of OA, particularly the OA journals and their varients & features.
- To accustom the audience with the OA journal literature publishers.
- To gauge the active OA journals indexed by Scopus database in the subject fields of life science, social science, physical science & health science.

Methodology

In order to achieve the objectives of the study, the relevant scientific literature has been explored pertaining to the concept of Open Access and its features with particular emphasis on the Open Access journals & their variants and characteristics. An effort was also made to identify and discuss some major OA journal literature publishers. So that the readers who are willing to share or contribute their research findings in an Open Access mode can explore and exploit them with ease. The majority of scholarly literature users are mainly concerned with major disciplines and are in search of the relevant literature for different purposes. It could be a cost-effect approach for them if they can access the required literature without paying or other restrictions usually imposed by Toll-Access model. In order to solve this issue, the study made an endeavor to access & explores the Scopus database (https://www.scopus.com/sources?zone=&origin=NO%20ORIGIN%20DEFINED). The data was harvested on 22-July-2018. The data retrieved as such was analyzed to identify the active journals indexed. The study further investigated the distribution of both active OA journals & active non-OA journals. Later on, the study was confined only to active OA journals, the subject wise distribution of active OA journals in the broader subject fields like life sciences, social sciences, physical sciences & health sciences was also checked and gauged. The purpose was to sensitize the audience about the proportion of active Open Access journals which are available for dissemination of scientific findings and use in the said disciplines.

SOLUTIONS AND RECOMMENDATIONS

The Scopus database is a very rich indexing and abstracting service of Elsevier. It indexes books, proceedings and journals. As the study was only concerned with the identification of active OA journals of the Scopus database, the study succeeded in revealing them by analysing the distribution of both active and in-active journals indexed in the Scopus database.

Distribution of Active & In-active journals in Scopus Database

The analysed data showed that there were a total of 22888 Active journals and 12589 in-active journals indexed in the Scopus database. The former constitutes 65% out of aggregate indexed journals and the later constitutes around 35% out of the same. Fig-1 offers a clear view.

Total Active OA Journals and Active Non-OA Journals in Scopus Database

The analysis of the data pertaining to active journals indexed by Scopus was further extended to achieve the objective of identifying active Open Access journals indexed by it. Results showed that out total active journals (22888), there are sizeable active Open Access journals 4073 (18%) indexed by Scopus. Although the proportion of active Open Access journals indexed by it seems to be on the lower side but given its recent origin, the growth is still phenomenal. These active OA journals can be used by knowledge seekers to achieve their desired objective in a cost-efficient manner. See Fig-2 which shows a lucid picture.

Figure 1. Distribution of journals (Active and inactive)

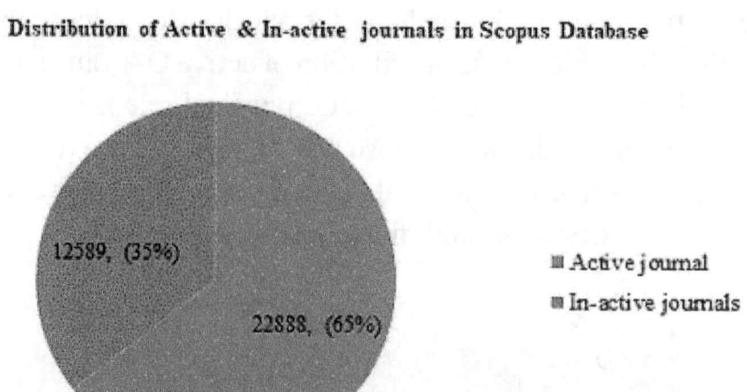

Figure 2. Total open access journals and non-open access journals in Scopus

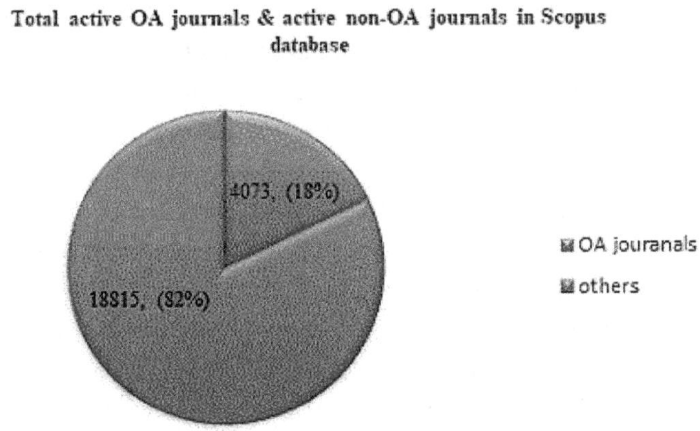

Subject-Wise Distribution of OA Journals

The study was also curious to know the subject wise distribution of Open Access journals indexed by the Scopus database. In this vein, four top-level subject areas listed by the Scopus were selected viz: Life Science, Social Science, Physical Science, and Health Science. The data sources were scrutinized and analyzed. It was found that Health Sciences leads them with highest number of active OA journals indexed by Scopus i.e. 1576 (31%), followed by Physical Sciences 1185 (24%), Social Sciences 1176 (23%), and Life Sciences 1127 (22%). It can also be noted that a good number of Open Access journals in these subject areas are interdisciplinary in nature. So the variation in the gross tally as indexed by Scopus is expected. For a comprehensive view see Fig-3.

Figure 3. Subject wise distribution of open access journals

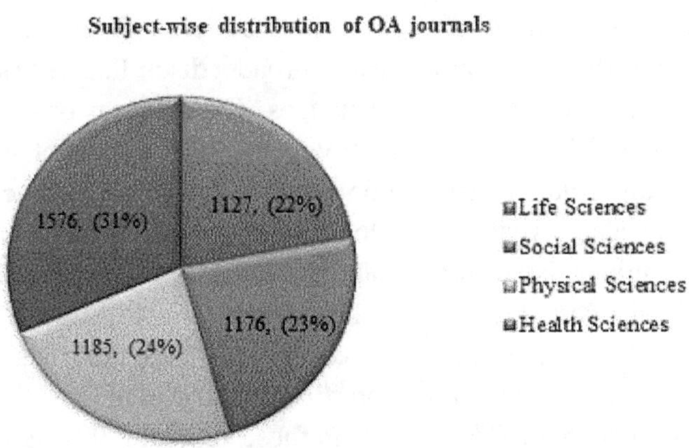

FUTURE RESEARCH DIRECTIONS

The study has only tried to discuss the concept of Open Access with particular reference to Open Access journals. Besides, it has also shed light to aware the audience about the types of OA journals, OA journal literature publishers, etc. Moreover, it has only limited its scope to identify the active OA journals indexed by the Scopus database with emphasis on the subject wise distribution of these journals and included only broader subject areas viz: life sciences, Social sciences, physical sciences, and health sciences. The vast numbers of other facets are there upon which future researches could be conducted like, the concept of Open Access books and other materials, their types, etc. Besides, some other indexing and abstracting databases other than Scopus can also be brought under research surveillance. Similarly, the other individual subject wise–distribution of OA journals or other resources can be checked and gauged. In this ambient, the study directs the interested researchers to explore the said areas with valuable efforts to find out the reliable answers to different questions or we can say to help the masses by disseminating them quality research findings covering the diverse issues.

CONCLUSION

The study succeeded in exploring the concept of Open Access and its significance, OA journals their types and advantages and Open Access journal publishers by scrutinizing the relevant literature. The literature reveals that the concept of Open Access is clearly understandable and has a vast number of advantages that are realized by many stakeholders' viz. literature users, literature publishers, and literature developers or authors across the globe. Still, more awareness is required especially about the OA resources for the benefit of socio-economic development of the general public.

As the main focus of the study was to find out active Open Access journals of Scopus database and their distribution in four broader disciplines; life sciences, social sciences, physical sciences and health sciences. The findings of the study showed that there were 35477 journals (both active and inactive) out of its total records 37537. The active journals constitute 65% and in-active journals constitute 35%. Similarly, findings also revealed that Open Access journals indexed in Scopus are 4073 and accordingly it also resulted that these OA journals covered in life sciences are 22%, social sciences- 23%, physical sciences-24%, and health sciences-31%. The study also finds out that there are certain active OA journals covering these mentioned subjects areas, which are interdisciplinary in nature. So, variations in estimating the total share of OA journals in these subject fields may be inevitable.

The study finally concludes that active Open Access journals indexed in Scopus are sufficient in number and these indexed journals can be accessed by the literature searchers throughout the globe. Besides, as indicated by the study that in each broader discipline or subject fields a good number of OA journals is available for utilization. So, those persons who interested to find and access the journal literature that is subject specific and cater to the particular needs of individual users. They are informed that your information or scientific literature search can get fulfilled easily when you will make use of indexed journals of Scopus in your subject area, depends upon whether you belong to life science field, social sciences, physical sciences or health sciences.

REFERENCES

Access, O. (2018). What is open access? *Open Access.nl.* Retrieved from http://www.openaccess.nl/en/what-is-open-access

Antelman, K. (2004). Do open-access articles have a greater research impact? *College & Research Libraries*, *65*(5), 372–382. doi:10.5860/crl.65.5.372

Awre, C. (2003). Open access and the impact on publishing and purchasing. *Serials, 16*(2), 205-208. Retrieved from https://www.researchgate.net/profile/Chris_Awre/publication/276594507_Open_access_and_the_impact_on_publishing_and_purchasing/links/5603709d08ae460e2704de31.pdf

Berlin Declaration on Open Access to Knowledge in the Sciences and Humanities. (2003). Retrieved from http://www.redalyc.org/pdf/782/78241008.pdf

Bernius, S. (2010). The impact of open access on the management of scientific knowledge. *Online Information Review*, *34*(4), 583–603. doi:10.1108/14684521011072990

Bernius, S., & Hanauske, M. (2009, January). Open access to scientific literature-increasing citations as an incentive for authors to make their publications freely accessible. In *Proceedings of 42nd Hawaii International Conference on System Sciences, 2009. HICSS'09.* (pp. 1-9). IEEE. Retrieved from http://www.is-frankfurt.de/publikationenNeu/OpenAccesstoScientificLiteratu3032.pdf

BioMed Central. (2018). About BMC: Open Access. *BMC Part of Springer Nature*. Retrieved from https://www.biomedcentral.com/about/open-access

Björk, B. C. (2017). Open access to scientific articles: a review of benefits and challenges. *Internal and Emergency Medicine, 12*(2), 247-253. Retrieved from https://link.springer.com/article/10.1007/s11739-017-1603-2

Björk, B. C., & Solomon, D. (2012). Open access versus subscription journals: A comparison of scientific impact. *BMC Medicine, 10*(1), 73. doi:10.1186/1741-7015-10-73 PMID:22805105

Björk, B. C., Welling, P., Laakso, M., Majlender, P., Hedlund, T., & Guðnason, G. (2010). Open access to the scientific journal literature: Situation 2009. *PLoS One, 5*(6), e11273. doi:10.1371/journal.pone.0011273 PMID:20585653

Cambridge University Press. (2018). *Benefits of open access.* Cambridge University Press. Retrieved from https://www.cambridge.org/core/services/open-access-policies/open-access-resources/benefits-of-open-access

DeoghuriaS.PaulG. (2018). *Open Access journals.* Retrieved from http://arxiv.iacs.res.in:8080/jspui/bitstream/10821/4052/1/Open-Access-Impact.docx

Elliot. (2014). Access to knowledge: a basic human right. *Creative Commons.* Retrieved from https://creativecommons.org/2014/01/07/access-to-knowledge-a-basic-human-right/

Gargouri, Y., Hajjem, C., Larivière, V., Gingras, Y., Carr, L., Brody, T., & Harnad, S. (2010). Self-selected or mandated, open access increases citation impact for higher quality research. *PLoS One*, *5*(10), e13636. doi:10.1371/journal.pone.0013636 PMID:20976155

Ghosh, S. B., & Kumar Das, A. (2007). Open access and institutional repositories—a developing country perspective: a case study of India. *IFLA Journal, 33*(3), 229-250. doi:10.1177/0340035207083304

Hajjem, C., Harnad, S., & Gingras, Y. (2006). *Ten-year cross-disciplinary comparison of the growth of open access and how it increases research citation impact.* Retrieved from https://arxiv.org/pdf/cs/0606079

Harnad, S., Brody, T., Valliares, F. O., Carr, L., Hitchcock, S., Gingras, Y., & Hilf, E. R. (2004). The access/impact problem and the green and gold roads to open access. *Serials Review, 30*(4), 310-314. Retrieved from https://eprints.soton.ac.uk/259940/6/34.html

Herring, S. D. (2002). Use of electronic resources in scholarly electronic journals: A citation analysis. *College & Research Libraries*, *63*(4), 334–340. doi:10.5860/crl.63.4.334

Hindawi. (2018). Open Research, Publishing with Hindawi. *Hindawi*. Retrieved from https://about.hindawi.com/

Jeffery, K. G. (2006). Open Access: an introduction. *Ercim News, 64*(3). Retrieved from https://www.researchgate.net/profile/Keith_Jeffery/publication/228635875_Open_Access_an_introduction/links/00b7d527a52273637a000000.pdf

Kitchin, R., Collins, S., & Frost, D. (2015). Funding models for Open Access digital data repositories. *Online Information Review*, *39*(50), 664–681. doi:10.1108/OIR-01-2015-0031

Koler-Povh, T., Južnič, P., & Turk, G. (2014). Impact of open access on citation of scholarly publications in the field of civil engineering. *Scientometrics*, *98*(2), 1033–1045. doi:10.100711192-013-1101-x

Laakso, M., & Björk, B. C. (2012). Anatomy of open access publishing: A study of longitudinal development and internal structure. *BMC Medicine*, *10*(1), 124. doi:10.1186/1741-7015-10-124 PMID:23088823

Lawrence, S. (2001). Free online availability substantially increases a paper's impact. *Nature*, *411*(6837), 521. doi:10.1038/35079151 PMID:11385534

Library of Congress. (2015). Selected Internet Resources Eprints: Quick Guide to Open-Access Archives in Science, Technology & Medicine. *The Library of Congress*. Retrieved from https://www.loc.gov/rr/scitech/selected-internet/eprints.html

Lin, S. K. (2006). *Delayed open access or permanent non-open access*. Retrieved from http://www.mdpi.com/1420-3049/11/7/496/pdf

Mann, F., von Walter, B., Hess, T., & Wigand, R. T. (2009). Open access publishing in science. *Communications of the ACM*, *52*(3), 135–139. doi:10.1145/1467247.1467279

Max-Planck-Gesellschaft München. (2018). Berlin Declaration on Open Access to Knowledge in the Sciences and Humanities. *Open Access*. Retrieved from https://openaccess.mpg.de/Berlin-Declaration

McVeigh, M. E. (2004). *Open access journals in the ISI citation databases: analysis of impact factors and citation patterns: a citation study from Thomson Scientific*. Philadelphia, PA: Thomson Scientific. Retrieved from http://www.academia.edu/download/39476484/openaccesscitations2.pdf

Moxley, J. M. (2001). American Universities Should Require Electronic Theses and Dissertations. *EDUCAUSE Quarterly*, *61*(3). Retrieved from http://scholarcommons.usf.edu/cgi/viewcontent.cgi?article=1112&context=eng_facpub

Mueller-Langer, F., & Watt, R. (2014). *The Hybrid Open Access Citation Advantage: How Many More Cites is a $3,000 Fee Buying You?* Retrieved from https://mpra.ub.uni-muenchen.de/61801/1/MPRA_paper_61801.pdf

Pinfield, S., Gardner, M., & MacColl, J. (2002). Setting up an institutional e-print archive. *Ariadne,* (31). Retrieved from http://www.ariadne.ac.uk/issue31/eprint-archives/intro.html

PLOS. (2018). About PLOS: who we are, our history, core principles. *Public Library of Science (PLOS).* Retrieved from https://www.plos.org/history

Publications, C. (2018). Welcome to Copernicus.org! *Copernicus Publications, Meetings and Open Access Publishing.* Retrieved from https://publications.copernicus.org/open-access_journals/open_access_journals_a_z.html

Rens, A., & Kahn, R. (Eds.). (2009). *Access to knowledge in South Africa: part of the access to knowledge research series.* Cape Town, South Africa: University of Cape Town. Retrieved from http://www.academia.edu/download/30876140/A2K-in-SA.pdf

Scopus. (2018). What is Scopus about? *Elsevier/Scopus: Access and use Support Center.* Retrieved from https://service.elsevier.com/app/answers/detail/a_id/15100/supporthub/scopus/

Sivakumaren, K. S. (2015). Electronic thesis and dissertations (ETDs) by Indian universities in Shodhganga project: a study. *Journal of Advances in Library and Information Science, 4*(1), 62-66. Retrieved from http://jalis.in/pdf/4-1/Sivamit.pdf

SPARC. (2018). Open Access. *SPARC.* Retrieved from https://sparcopen.org/open-access/

Springer. (2018). *What is Open Access?* Berlin, Germany: Springer. Retrieved from https://www.springer.com/gp/authors-editors/authorandreviewertutorials/open-access/what-is-open-access/10286522

Suber, P. (2007). *Open access overview.* Retrieved from https://www.researchgate.net/profile/Arunachalam_Subbiah/publication/48547497_Open_access_to_science_in_the_developing_world/links/09e415058b88dbf15c000000/Open-access-to-science-in-the-developing-world.pdf#page=8

Swan, A. (2010). *The Open Access citation advantage: Studies and results to date.* Retrieved from https://eprints.soton.ac.uk/268516/2/Citation_advantage_paper.pdf

Terras, M. (2015). Opening Access to collections: The making and using of open digitised cultural content. *Online Information Review*, *39*(5), 733–752. doi:10.1108/OIR-06-2015-0193

University of Bradford. (2018). *What are Open Access repositories?* Bradford, UK: University of Bradford. Retrieved from https://www.bradford.ac.uk/library/resources/open-access-publishing/what-are-open-access-repositories/

Vijayakumar, J. K., & Murthy, T. A. V. (2001). *Need of a Digital Library for Indian Theses and Dissertations: a model on par with the ETD initiatives at International Level.* Retrieved from http://eprints.rclis.org/7217/1/vijayakumarjk_06.pdf

Young, P. (2017). Research Access and Discovery in University News Releases: A Case Study. *Journal of Librarianship and Scholarly Communication*, *5*(1). doi:10.7710/2162-3309.2155

KEY TERMS AND DEFINITIONS

Active OA Journals: Those free access journals which are currently in active mode.

Biomed Central: An open access journal literature publisher.

Copernicus.org: The platform where OA journals are published.

OA Journal Publisher: Publishers who publish OA journals.

OA Journals: Those journals which are free from subscription to its users.

OA Resources: All resources that offer free access without any restrictions like, books, journals, proceedings, videos, etc.

Open Access: Unrestricted free access to knowledge means open access.

PLOS: Public Library of Science, an OA journals publisher.

Scopus-OA Journals: Scopus is an indexing and abstracting database, it also indexes open access journals.

Chapter 10
Selection and Acquisition of Electronic Resources in Academic Libraries:
Challenges

N. K. Khatri
Indian Statistical Institute New Delhi, India

ABSTRACT

With information explosion, there has been a rapid increase in the number of e-resources published across the world. In addition to this, the cost of e-resources has risen steeply. This has resulted in libraries finding it difficult to acquire all the required information resources from the budget available from its parent body. The problem of libraries is compounded by the growing costs of maintaining both print and online subscription and issues related to 'perpetual' electronic access to back files. The print industry in the world is said to be on the decline. People prefer the electronic versions of the reading materials, because they are more portable, accessible and affordable. But there are many challenges/hurdles to this path, which we have to overcome with time, effort and ingenuity. There are certain challenges relating to their selection, acquisition, maintenance and preservation, etc., which need joint efforts of library professionals and associations. Electronic publishing of scholarly journals, emerging of consortia, pricing models of the publishers give new opportunities for libraries to provide instant access to information. Consortium, formed by a group of libraries, is a unique program to facilitate electronic access to scholarly databases and journals. The beneficiaries will be faculty, researchers, students and neighbor institutes engaged in pursuing higher education. Consortia will minimize the financial burden and pave the way for an enormous amount of saving of time, money, and manpower.

DOI: 10.4018/978-1-5225-8437-7.ch010

INTRODUCTION

On the one hand there has been a remarkable increase in the number of new journals and databases advertised and published by commercial publishers; on the other, there has been the pressure on the libraries to go electronic. A few years ago the possibilities of electronically submitting a manuscript, which is then transmitted with almost no delay to referees and the wonderful feature of reading accepted papers that are yet to appear in print, were almost unheard of. Owing to growth in commercial publishing, in some areas, journal prices have spiraled out of control, forcing libraries to cut back on their holdings. The professional societies, particularly in the United States, produce many of the flagship journals of science, which have maintained their pre-eminent position over the last century. However, the ongoing electronic revolution has forced major changes (Balaram, 2000). An academic library exists to serve their students, research scholars and faculty members by providing the required information. They need information to carry out their research work. The objective of the libraries is to provide an effective combination of print and electronic resources, and the integration of the use of these resources in support of teaching, learning and research at their academic institutions. Electronic resources, however, pose challenges not encountered with the acquisitions of traditional library materials, such as access, interface, technical support and licensing. Libraries therefore need to formulate a separate electronic resource collection development policy to address these issues. The purpose of this policy is to provide guidelines in choosing appropriate electronic resources and to establish consistency and priorities in managing the important part of the libraries' collection. This chapter covers, the major steps in acquiring electronic resources; relationships among libraries, publishers and vendors; ordering, receiving, and paying for materials; and handling licensing agreements and formation of consortia etc.

"Electronic resources" according to International Federation of Library Association (IFLA, 2012) are materials that require computer access, whether through microcomputer, mainframe, or other types of computers, and they may either be accessed via the internet or locally. A large number of the earlier studies of users of electronic journals have appeared in the last few years. The pursuit of electronic resources by libraries was driven by the core values of library science. It is possible to recognize in Ranganathan's five laws of library science the motivation that drove libraries to incorporate electronic resources into services and collections. Paraphrased to better suit electronic resources, the laws read: resources are for use, every person has his or her resource, every resource its user, save the time of the user, and the library is a growing organism (Ranganathan, 1963). With the advent of e-resources, job responsibilities of selectors have changed drastically. Selection of e-resources outside the guidance of a collection development policy leads to haphazard unfocused groupings of resources that may not support the mission of the library. In the past, selectors recommended new titles on an individual basis using traditional selection criteria such as quality, relevance, use, and cost observed (Welch, 2002).

Owing to the overwhelming growth and availability of a variety of electronic products, the workflow of acquisitions has changed significantly, becoming more complex. Though the acquisitions process is closely connected to collection development in any type of library, it has distinct functions. The primary responsibility of the acquisitions department is getting the materials needed by the library's users in the most desired format and in the most efficient and economical manner. Thus, acquisition is defined as the technical process of ordering, receiving, and paying for an item after the intellectual decision to purchase an item has been made (Chapman, 2004). It can require additional budget allocations due to higher subscription costs than for print collections. Owing to the increase in the number of electronic formats, acquisition librarians are no longer just an expert in acquiring materials, having knowledge about publishers and book vendors, and identifying incomplete citations as well finding out-of-print materials. Now they are also responsible for solving more creative problems in the areas of collection development, licensing, cataloguing, technology and other issues related to e-resources (Kennedy, 2004). Kumbar & Hadagali (2007) in their paper stated that the current trends in electronic environment suggest a complete revolution in the status of collection development policy. The library of the future will be more a portal through which students and faculty will access the vast information resources of the world. It will concentrate on access and knowledge management rather than on physical ownership of materials. Joshipura (2008) mentioned that selection of information resources is the foundation of collection development function, and the main objective of the selection decision for any format is satisfying user needs. At the present time, with rapid growth of availability of e-resources, selection of e-resources becomes difficult for the selectors. Therefore, selection tools need to be consulted to make right resources available to right user with fair price. She suggested the use of various selection tools such as trail offer, demonstration from the publisher/vendor, faculty/patron suggestion, vendor exhibition at conference, consulting librarians already subscribing to a product about their experiences, publisher catalog and reviews in print and electronic sources, etc. However, those selection criteria that apply to print resources are not enough to apply for selection of e-resources. The selector must consider the other criteria in the selection process such as ease of access, content, search capability, functionality of the interface, technical support, and method of pricing and licensing agreement. Acquisition librarians to verify the license agreement with the publisher before ordering the product. She further said the selectors to consult staff responsible for technical services for legal and access issues, technology for compatibility with software and hardware and public services for training and ease of use in selection of an e-resource. Das (2010) addressed the acquisition of electronic information resources and its collection development policy. A three step strategy is put forwarded to introduce e-resources in library i.e. link of library websites to open e-resources available freely in public domain, become a part of existing library consortia and recruit an electronic resources acquisitions librarian for independent subscription. According to (Vashishth, 2011), the main problems in building collection in e-environment are quotation system, cost factor, rate of library discount, unorganized book trade and reminder books. He also pointed out that lack of ICT infrastructure, inadequate collection, and lack of mechanism for training library personnel are other major problems being faced by librarians.

Collection Development Policy

Collection Development Policy is a written statement prepared for the guidance of the librarian regarding planning, budgeting selection and acquisition of library material. It is an essential communication tool for librarians to ensure continuity and consistency in the collection development program. It is a good planning tool in the hands of librarians to safeguard or protect them against any personal pressure or influences. A policy is a set of rules or a framework which needs to be abided and followed by any institution or any organization in a timely manner. As the library grows the collection also grows. It then becomes difficult to manage the new collections and discard the old and present collections in a library. Hence, in order to take sufficient steps the Collection Development Policy (CDP) is adopted. The collection development policies are documents which define the scope of a library's existing collections, plan for the continuing development of resources, identify collection strength and outline the relationship between selection philosophy and the institutions goals, general selection criteria and intellectual freedom (ALA, 1987). Selecting and adding e-resources for the collection becomes easier for the selectors when a collection development policy is in place. Such a policy provides a framework for decision-making and is a necessary planning tool, the use of which leads to consistent, informed decisions. It is a blueprint for the selectors and helps them ensure uniformity in procedures and appropriate balance in the library collection. As more and more e-resources are acquired, it is wise to integrate these products into the library's overall policy. The three main purposes of a collection development policy include informing, directing, and protecting (Gregory & Hanson, 2006). The purpose of informing is to serve as a communications vehicle for the library's staff, administrators, and various constituencies. The purpose of directing is to serve as a guideline for the selectors to maintain balance in the collection for its users. The purpose of protecting is serve justifying of selection to the users.

The policy serves as a supporting document for the library against challenges to its procedures and resources. To maintain currency, the policy should be reviewed and revised periodically (Joshipura, 2008). These policies not only help in the selection of documents for the library collections but also help in other tasks like setting the budget, acting as a channel between the library and the suppliers, preventing censorship, intellectual copyrights assistance, helping in management of activities, selection of gifts and so.

Elements of Collection Development Policy

There are various elements to be considered in developing a collection development policy. It should take into account the aims and objectives of the academic institution, the mission of the library, existing collection and its future requirements. It should describe the community served, including students, faculty, researchers and staff, their needs, academic programs, off campus users etc. It should provide guidelines and criteria for the subject experts and selectors. It should identify selection tools for the library. A general statement regarding the parameters of collection, such as specific subject field and type of formats that the library will acquire. It should provide identification of specific clientele to be served. It should include guidelines for weeding, cancellation, renewal, retention, replacement and preservation of resources. It should include issues such as resource sharing and role of library consortia.

Policy should have proper guidelines for pricing models, price packages and licensing requirements for electronic resources. Besides this, library services such as inter-library lending activities, awareness among library users, remote access availability etc. The policy of electronic access has to be accompanied by a policy of archiving, to give future users an opportunity for an access to preserved electronic information. Training and technical support for the library staff ought to provided time to time.

Selection Criteria for E-Resources

Selection criteria need to be consistent with the libraries' plans for establishing electronic information environment. All electronic materials should be relevant and appropriate to a significant segment of the libraries' user community current academic needs and the university's mission. Special attention should be given to electronic resources that provide coverage of high priority subject areas. In the selection of electronic materials, the availability of appropriate hardware and software should be considered. For CD-ROM products, consideration also needs to given as whether the product is networkable. If additional software needs to be acquired to run the product, this factor should be noted. If the electronic resource duplicates another resource already available in the libraries, the proposed electronic resource should offer some value-added enhancement, for example, wider access or greater flexibility in searching. In addition to the cost of the product, if any, the following hidden costs need to be considered: licensing fees, hardware, software, staff training, cataloguing, duplicating support materials, updates, maintenance and any other costs. The product should be user-friendly, that is, provide ease of use and guidance for the users via appropriate menus, help screens, or tutorials.

Selection and Evaluation of Electronic Resources

All selection decisions begin with a consideration of the user community and the long-term mission, goals, and priorities of the library and its parent body. Long ago, **(Drury, 1930)** stated, "The high purpose of book selection is to provide the right book for the right reader and at the right time. The selection process can be thought of as a four-step process: (1) identification of the relevant, (2) assessment (is the item appropriate for the collection?) and evaluation (is the item worthy of selection?), (3) decision to purchase, and (4) order preparation. Identifying possible items requires basic, factual information about authors, titles, publishers, and topics. The fulfillment of university/institutions library objectives does not complete with just the acquisition of library materials. Once the resource is identified, evaluation of the material is the second most step for selectors. Evaluation helps the selectors determine the reliability of the content provider. Selection tools such as demonstration of the product, as well as reviews by experts helps in evaluating the product to subscribe. Usually selectors (Library committee members including librarian) consider the credentials of the author, reputation of the publisher, the subject, cost, accuracy, curriculum or research needs of researchers and faculty. Citation analysis and user surveys also help the selection team to evaluate the product. However, the selector must consider additional elements such as an easy access to the content/subject, search capability and functionality, technical support, method of pricing, provisions of licensing agreements. Collection evaluation according to (Spiller, 2001) is the process of identifying the strength and weaknesses of a library's resources, and attempting to correct existing weaknesses while maintaining the strength. In the library, at the end of each fiscal year or in the beginning of financial year, the library evaluates its electronic resources for replacement or de-selection. These resources acquired are continually evaluated to determine how adequately they meet the needs of the users. To do this the librarian needs to have a comprehensive data on how researchers actually work and what materials they need and use.

Selection Guidelines for Electronic Resources

Content/Subject: Electronic resource should be reviewed and evaluated for selection from a content perspective, under the same policies, criteria and guidelines that apply to print resources. The electronic resource must support the curricular and research needs of the academic institutions. The content should come from an authoritative author and or publisher on the subject, accuracy and completeness as compared with print format, if available. Electronic resource should have all the articles, illustrations, tables and graphs, as they appear in the print counterpart. Also it is important to check duplication of the content in case of journal packages.

Access and Related Technical Requirements

The electronic resource should be available for remote access. Selectors should evaluate the functionality of the electronic products, such as ease of access by comparing the electronic to the print format. Authentication: IP filtering and login with password preferred for access. The libraries prefer access via IP filtering, because it also provides access to users via a proxy server allowing authorized users to access from outside the library. The electronic resource should be compatible across different platforms (PC, Mac, etc). Though local installation and maintenance are not preferred, if they are chosen, the electronic resource must be compatible with the existing hardware and software. Obsolete formats and platforms are not supported.

- **Reputation:** Selectors should confirm the reputation of the provider before selecting a product. It is important to find out the business practices of the providers, their response to problems, and system reliability.
- **Impact Factor:** Impact factor is more important to evaluate the journal titles using journal citation reports, if available. Such sources provide systematic and objective data to evaluate the use and reputation of journals selection.
- **Functionality and System Reliability:** The electronic resource will provide sufficient added value over the print or other formats. The interface should be user-friendly. Some common user friendliness features are introductory screens, online tutorials, context-sensitive help, and pop-ups and menus. The search and retrieval software must be powerful and flexible. Some features that should be available include command search, index and title browsing, auto-stem, history and alert/SDI. The system should support multiple export, downloading, printing and email options. The system capacity and network infrastructure should be technologically up-to-date and provide for optimum response time 24/7.

- **Vendor Support:** The vendor of the electronic resource should be established and reliable. The electronic resource should be available for trial. Preferably, the vendor will provide product demonstrations if needed. If needed, the vendor should provide initial and preferably, ongoing product training. Customer and technical support should be timely, accurate and professional. The vendor should provide quality statistical reporting. Preferably, the reports should follow ICOLC (International Coalition of Library Consortia)'s Guidelines for Statistical Measures of Usage of Web-Based Information Resources. The vendor should be prepared to respond to the Libraries' requests for customization, branding and provision of MARC records and URLs. The vendor should provide advance notifications for content and platform changes, as well as system down time.
- **Pricing Consideration:** The vendor should offer a choice of pricing models from which the libraries may select. The cost may also vary according to the number of users/ ports/passwords, remote access, etc. The libraries should not be required to purchase both the print and electronic versions of a resources. The cost of the electronic resource should not exceed that of the print counterpart. An increase in price from print to electronic format, and from CD-ROM to Web, should be reflected in the increase in functionality and accessibility. Content providers may offer special deals for consortia members as a whole, and the price variations based on the number of full time researchers, budget, and authentication of users, simultaneous use, and remote access for users.
- **Licensing Consideration:** 'Authorized Users' should be defined as broadly as possible. Bona fide faculty members, students, researchers, any employees and contractors engaged by the academic institution as well as on-site users of the institution should be included as authorized users. "Authorized Sites" should be defined as broadly as possible. Authorized users should be permitted to access the electronic resource from anywhere through the use of proxy server. Access should be permitted via IP authentication for the entire institution(s), including simultaneous access for multiple users, in different geographic locations, sites. The license should permit fair use of all information for non-commercial, educational and research purposes by the libraries and authorized users. These include viewing, downloading and printing. In general, the vendor should employ a standard agreement that describes the rights of the libraries and is easy to understand.

Challenges and Role of Collections Librarians

Sottong (2001) defined eight criteria that can be used for the evaluation of e-books technology: quality, durability, initial cost, continuing cost, ease of use, features and standardized etc. He used the criteria in 2001 and concluded that e-books failed on six of the eight criteria. Evaluation criteria introduce new and unique challenges to the selectors. There are various types of e-resources and each one has different selection process. A standing committee, similar to a serials review committee, may have responsibility for reviewing e-resources, especially large, expensive electronic databases and especially those that are multidisciplinary in nature. Committees can bring together the expertise needed and might include selectors from other disciplines, catalogers and staff from information technology unit. Selectors need to understand the universe with which they are dealing- file formats, methods of access and delivery, hardware, software, pricing options, licensing and contracts - so they can test, explore, and evaluate options and involve the right people in their library. Selection decisions are never made in isolation. More than any other format, electronic information requires broad communication and cooperation of staff across various units working towards common goals. Quality assessment of e-resources is more difficult than printed materials. Therefore, collection development of e-resources is essentially more complex than the printed resources. Moreover, librarians have been dealing with print resources for centuries and are familiar with their acquisition procedure and practices which are well established and standardized, whereas acquisition of e-resources still remains fluid. Librarians alone are not in a position to take a decision in selection of serials particularly when these are being licensed under consortium pricing. The costs of e-resources are not fixed as that of printed resources which varies depending upon various variables like the number of concurrent users, level of access, nature of the institution, different renewal policies, etc.

Collection development of e-books has its own problems of acquisition due to unpopular pricing model, publishers' embargo, etc. Reading of e-books is still not as convenient as printed books. A majority of e-resources is licensed for a limited time. Thus, at the end of the license period, if the selector decides to cancel the subscription, it results in a loss of access to the content. Thus, preserving and archiving e-resources adds different problems for selectors. The content of the resource may change over time and require review and evaluation by the selectors. There can be duplication of the content across databases. Duplication and availability of content from various sources add confusion to selectors as well as users. Selectors must know the impact of these issues. Selectors have to prepare themselves to work together with librarians and to cooperate with libraries.

Suitability of pricing model is more important for selection and acquisition of electronic resources. Publishers are interested in offering bundle price for their products. It is not easy to make the exact assessment by the selectors of the usage of the package, whether to go for bundle pricing or selective titles by paying more for individual title. No doubt, pricing model gives access to big collection, but usability is not much.

There are many management issues to handle. Library softwares hardly have adequate provisions to handle e-resources except a few. The existing software are incapable of handling e-resources. It is difficult to evaluate and select the right system as per requirement of the libraries. E-resources in libraries remain unorganized and scattered on publishers' websites. Publishers management is so complex that it is difficult to find satisfactory solutions required by the users and the library staff. Students, research scholars and faculty staff have multiple approaches to access e-resources and it is expected to satisfy all possible approaches and also the requirements of the library staff.

Acquisition Policy

Acquisition policy is an integral part of collection development policy. It provides details about how the resources selected through selection process are to be acquired for the library or acquired for access by the users. The policy must be regularly reviewed and updated, at least once in two years, so as to reflect the changes taking place in procedures and responsibilities. The acquisition policy covers the following aspects:

1. Procedures to be followed.
2. Listing of jobs and responsibilities assigned to different staff members.
3. General statement, giving guidelines for making informed choices to vendors to be used for supply of different types of resources, keeping in view the different types of resources, keeping in view the different needs of the users. It should also make provision for urgent orders, providing special powers to the Chief Librarian for taking action for immediate compliance.

Acquisition Process of Electronic Resources

Though an acquisitions process for an e-resource resembles the process for a print resource, such as pre-order investigation and ordering, specific tasks vary between the two formats. Once the individual selector or selection committee has chosen a resource for the library's collection, the standard acquisition process of locating and acquiring the resource takes place (Joshipura, 2008). Acquisition of electronic resources begins after the selection of product by subject expert or selector. It needs proper planning and good management. The following considerations must be kept in view (Scammel, 2001):

- **Technical Infrastructure:** The existing technical infrastructure must be suitable. Some corporate networks have security systems, having firewalls that prevent access to some sites and downloading of certain files. This problem needs to be tackled before placing an order.
- **Licensing:** The librarians must understand how the terms and conditions of licensing should have an impact on the use of resources. What are the best practices in terms of licensing restrictions? Should e-books be purchased or licensed?
- **Copyright:** The librarian needs to understand as to how the local copyright restrictions correspond with the restrictions put by the vendor.
- **Package of Products:** Many electronic products are sold by the vendors as a package, consisting of an assortment of products. Under this, the librarian may need only a specific product, but he is forced to purchase all the products in the package, though there may be heavy discount as an incentive.
- **Vendor:** It is found to be convenient, if e-books and e-journals are purchased from the same vendor. In that case, the same password can be used to access the products and services. The users can also access directly from the same web site of the vendor. The librarian needs to understand: Should we use a vendor's platform, or should the library host its own e-book platform ?
- **Trial Basis Run:** It is always helpful to get the product on trial basis to identify and resolve problems.

E-Books

E-books are becoming increasingly popular among library users, and thus almost every library needs to ensure that the e-books available to its users meet their needs. Access to electronic books is purchased by the library directly from the publisher or the vendor. It involves initial purchase charges plus ongoing access charges. Many publishers and vendors promote purchase of collections of electronic books as a package, giving sufficient discount. In purchasing access to e-books, the librarian must take into consideration the following aspects:

1. **Length of Period for Ongoing Access:** How long will access be provided? How is ongoing access to be granted?
2. **Restrictions:** What will be the restrictions, if any, on access, downloading, copying, etc.? How many users allowed access simultaneously?

3. **Charges for Additional Titles:** In case the library purchases a collection and wants to access additional titles that are published later, will the library be charged for those additional titles?

Print vs. E-Books

Although academic libraries may be interested in moving more of their acquisitions budget to e-books, several studies have shown that only a small proportion of published academic materials are available as e-books (Jindal & Pant, 2013). A study at the Jawaharlal Nehru University Library in New Delhi compared the availability of print titles versus the e-book format and found that an average of 57.5 percent of titles were available in e-book format (availability varied depending upon subject area from a low of 39.5 percent to a high of 70 percent). The study also noted that the purchase price of print books was cheaper than that of e-books (ignoring the continuing costs to store and provide access to library physical collections) (Rao, Tripathi & Sunil Kumar, 2016).

E-Journals

Electronic journals (e-journals) are serial publications available in digital format. Serials include magazines, newsletters, newspapers, annual publications, journals, memoirs, proceedings, transactions of societies and numbered series. E-journals are available through the Internet. Some are free, and some are available only by subscription. The growth of electronic journals parallels the growth of the Web. Libraries of all types and sizes are facing unrelenting pressure to provide access to an increasing number of electronic journals and other digital resources. Users have desktop access to the electronic resources 24/7 without requiring a trip to the library. Libraries can provide access to electronic journals and to indexing and abstracting databases, as well as to other electronic content. Clearly, digital collections save the library space, but moving toward an increasing amount of digital resources will possibily require new skill sets.

Users of electronic journals typically search journal tables of contents, briefly scan the full text of the article, and then request a PDF version of the article for printing or archiving. Younger scholars report that they are frequent e-journal users; older scholars tend to be troubled by the user interface at multi journal Web sites and thus use e-journals less frequently (Institute for the Future, 2001). E-Journals are made available by publishers and vendors via their web sites. In acquiring e-journals, the librarian must carefully examine the following aspects:

1. **Archiving:** Will the back issues be accessible in future? What guarantee is provided by the publishers or Vendor? Will there be additional charges for the same?
2. **Content:** Is there any difference in the content between electronic and print versions? If any, where lies the difference.
3. **Restrictions:** What are the restrictions on access? How many users are allowed access simultaneously? What are the restrictions on copying or downloading?

Web-Based Reference Resources

Many reference resources (encyclopedias, dictionaries, yearbooks, atlases, etc are available on the web. These are often available free for a trial period and after that the library has to pay ongoing charges. One study noted that reference librarians use electronic resources six times more than print sources to respond to customer queries (Bradford, Costello & Lenholt, 2005). The top five sources used to respond to reference questions were electronic databases (24 percent), other librarians (24 percent) the library catalogue (15 percent), an internal Web page (12 percent), and reference books (9 percent). It is interesting to note that during the two semesters that the data were gathered, only 173 of the library's 9,587 reference collection titles were used - that is, less than 2 percent of the library's print reference collection. And for 75 percent of the questions, the librarians only referred to a single source for an answer. The switch by students to the direct use of Internet-based resources (search engines) and avoiding the need to visit- in any way- the library has even been noticed by the popular press (Boyle, 2000).

Consortium Purchasing: Library consortia exist for two possible reasons: to provide a set of services that are lower in cost than an individual library can provide, and to provide services collectively that a single library is unable to perform by itself. A library consortium consists of a number of libraries, preferably with some common characteristics by subject, institutional affiliation or branches/units of libraries that come together with common interest and wish to do certain job collectively. These jobs may include resource sharing, subscribe e-resources, shared cataloguing, shared infrastructure and technology solution etc. Due to financial crunch and the rising costs of e-resources, many libraries cannot subscribe to all the required e-journals, e-resources and online databases etc. To overcome this problem, "Group or branches of libraries come together with common interest" and participate in making consortia to share electronic access to journals and other e-resources. Under consortium, one library in the group subscribes to a particular product and acquires user license for other libraries, so that users of libraries in the group or consortium are able to have access to that product without any restriction. Often, the groups working together can negotiate with the publishers/vendors for higher discount as well as for

Table 1.

S.no.	Online Resources and started (Year)	Consortium Members	Journals covered under consortium	Archives	Online access
1	MathSciNet (AMS) (1999)	20 including three ISIs Kolkata,Delhi and Bangalore	Mathematical Reviews	1940 +	IPbased unlimited
2	Science Direct (Elsevier Sc.) (2003)	Three ISIs Kolkata,Delhi,Bangalore	127	1995 +	IPbased unlimited
3	Springer Link (Springer Group) (2005)	Three ISIs Kolkata,Delhi, Bangalore	96	1997 +	IPbased Unlimited
4	J-STOR (2008)	Three ISIs Kolkata, Delhi, Bangalore	184	1872 +	IPbased Unlimited
5	OxfordUniv.Press. Online Journals (2008)	Three ISIs Kolkata, Delhi, Bangalore	51	1996 +	IPbased Unlimited
6	EconLit (American Economic Association)(2005)	Two ISIs Kolkata, Delhi	550	1969 +	IPbased User ID & Password

better service. Often product providers offer special pricing for consortia. In deals, expensive electronic products can become affordable for libraries because several libraries work together and share costs. In consortia deals, expensive electronic products can become affordable for small libraries because many libraries work together and share costs. Some expensive electronic databases or packages can be obtained directly from the publishers or by joining a larger consortium. Purchasing through a consortium results in significant financial savings to individual libraries.

OVERVIEW OF INDIAN STATISTICAL INSTITUTE LIBRARIES CONSORTIUM

The study by (Khatri, 2008) revealed that Indian Statistical Institute Libraries (Kolkata, Delhi and Bangalore) have initiated the following consortia based subscription to enhance the electronic collection and to cope with the increasing subscription cost and diminishing budget.

Under the scheme, the library has been providing full text articles (PDF files). Research scholars/visiting scientists desirous of consulting library resources were allowed to access these materials in the library through the library web page: http://www.isid.ac.in/~library/lib.htm

The study by (Khatri, 2010) reported that Consortia based subscription of electronic resources in the Indian Statistical Institute (ISI) library was first initiated in 1999. The initiative came into existence with a consortia-based subscription to MathSciNet database. The MathSciNet Consortia was formed by Indian Statistical Institute- Calcutta and members of the National Board for Higher Mathematics (NBHM-Eastern and Northern region) with a group of 20 members. These members were: Indian Statistical Institute libraries Kolkata, Delhi and Bangalore; University of Calcutta; Jadavapur university; Kalyani university; Burdwan university; University of North Bengal; Visva-Bharati; Sambalpur university; Utkal university; Gauhati university; Assam university; Institute of advanced study in science & technology; North-Eastern Hill university; Manipur university and Calcutta Mathematical society.

MathSciNet is a unique database of a scholarly nature of greater utility to faculty and students. It has an excellent coverage of current mathematics literature providing reviews of math articles, conference proceedings and books of mathematics research. It is a database which is useful not only to mathematicians but to science and engineering faculty also. Consortia subscription to MathSciNet are composed of two parts: Data Access Fee (DAF), which is the cost of maintaining and enhancing the database and MathSciNet (MSN) fee, which is the cost for the online delivery of the data. The consortium DAF is based on the number of subscribers to Mathematical Reviews (MR) in the consortium. MathSciNet consortia fees are calculated per site on "Mathematical Activity" (MA). MA is the number of items appearing in MR that have originated from that site in a three-year period. (www.ams.org/bookstor/mathsciprice)

Pricing Model of E-resources

The pricing models for subscription of e-resources and online databases varies from vendor to vendor, publishers to publishers. It is different in consortium subscription. Publishers offer different pricing slots for group of libraries from the universities, academic institutions, public and private colleges and corporations. Flexible subscription options at discounted rates allow libraries to spread the cost over one to three years consortium purchased bundles subscription, consortium partners get electronic access to all this subscribed therein is also beneficial to the group. So, there is need to keep a watch in the variation of pricing models. Price also varies with the number of users. Some publishers provide offer price based on strength of full-time students, faculty members and staff. Consortium Price may also be based on total number of subscribers for the particular e-product. Price may also be based on the number of simultaneous users or unlimited access including remote access. Publishers may charge more to large universities with multiple branches, sites and locations compared to small sized institutions/universities. The pricing model may also depend on the types of e-resources (e-books, e-journal packages, full-text databases etc.) and period of subscription such as yearly or one time purchase for archive products.

Some vendors offer bundled sets of titles in the electronic journal packages. Libraries may acquire the entire list of journals without any individual selection. In such deals, libraries may get relevant content at a lower price, but may have to pay for titles with less negligible or no relevance for the users; whereas, some providers or vendors of packages offer pay-per-view options. In such options, libraries are not required to have subscriptions to all journal titles in the package allowing users access to articles by paying the cost of an article from journals that are not subscribed to by the library. Sometimes, pricing models are based on a combination of print and electronic subscriptions. In such cases, publishers offer free electronic access or provide more discount for print plus electronic subscription.

License Agreement

Everything within a contract can be changed through negotiation. By its nature, a contract must be mutually acceptable before it is signed. Once the source of acquiring the product is confirmed, the license agreement becomes the key part of the acquisition process. Its agreement includes description of the product, responsible parties, that is licensor and licensee who are signing the agreement, authorized users of the product, use of the product, and rights of the license and the licensor. Inquiring into the license agreement with a representative of the product provider before ordering the product is recommended. Many content providers make available their licensing agreements with terms of use on their websites, while some license can be obtained through their representative. Sometimes, publishers have "click-on" or "click-through" licenses on their websites, where the library/user is required to click on a box to agree to the terms and agreements of the products. The librarian/Acquisition Librarian must review the agreement. If certain terms are not acceptable, they should be negotiated with the publishers. It is most critical to get the contract reviewed and signed by both parties before the invoice of the product is paid. Licensing has become a part of life and day-to-day duty the of acquisition librarian.

The challenges associated with the licensing agreement include understanding the content, determining the standard wording required by the institution, and identifying terms, which requires negotiation. Librarians who deal with licensing agreements should have negotiating skills and be required to work collaboratively with the institution's legal counsel. Librarians responsible for licenses should review each term and condition in the agreement very carefully. While reviewing the agreement, one should assure that each provision is clear. Librarians must work closely with content providers while reviewing the agreement and should make necessary changes to conform to the institution's policies. Almost all licenses are negotiable but require considerable time. Thus, librarians must be patient and persistent (Wilkinson & Lewis, 2003).

The license should clearly include the name of the product or the list of the titles that can be accessed. It is important to include names of the sites that have authorized access to the product. Definition of authorized users is an important clause in any license agreement. This clause defines authorized users such as students, faculty and staff of an academic institution. This clause should clearly include the cost of the subscription. Librarians should be very careful in reviewing the clause of cost and should be aware of their institution's policy. Perpetual access clause allows the library to retain access to the materials for which payment has been made after cancellation of the product. Libraries should ask for archival access if it is not included in the contract. Terms of payment and termination clause in the license agreement includes payment of invoices within certain timeframe as well as requirements for the renewal of the contract. Under the Usage statistics clause, the content provider agrees to provide usage statistics for e-resources. The content providers are becoming more familiar with libraries' needs it is important to have so consistent and transparent clauses. It is also important to keep copies of the signed agreement in the acquisition department for future reference. (Joshipura, 2008).

Ordering and Acquiring E-Resources

The ordering and acquisition process for electronic resources starts after the license is reviewed and signed. However, the process for acquiring electronic resources is more complex. The acquisition process for any e-journal is long, expensive and overly complex. Acquisitions personnel communicate with the content provider about the resource that is being requested and provide technical information, such as Internet protocol (IP) addresses. The acquisition department gets e-mail notification from the provider's technical support staff, once the access is set up. The content provider also provides URL details for the product through which the resource can be accessed. Acquisition librarian verify access of the product and inform the rest of the organization of the availability of the new resource.

The acquisition librarian should notify other library departments such as cataloguing, collection development, technology and public services, once access to an e-resource is activated. It is essential to communicate with the cataloguing department regarding access to the resource, because they maintain the online public access catalogue (OPAC). They also need all the details such as license restrictions, if any, content availability, mode of access, simultaneous use access, and so forth. The acquisition department informs the system or technology department, because they maintain the technical access and local tracking of the database. The acquisition department also informs the selector who requisitioned the product and the public services staff who publicize the new resource to users. It is also important to share details about contractual and legal terms such as acceptable and prohibited use of the resource and the number of authorized users.

Sometimes content providers offer training in the use of the resource once it is acquired by the library. In such a case, the acquisitions staff follows up with the provider's representative regarding training for public services staff. Periodically they also provide refresher training for the e-resources purchased by the library. The acquisition librarian should take advantage of such offers to set up training for staff members.

After access is confirmed, the provider sends an invoice to the acquisition department for review payment. Acquisition staff reviews the invoice to make sure that the charges are as per the agreement and then process it for payment. Now maintaining access to the resource also becomes a part of this department's task. Sometimes, access is disrupted owing to delay in the renewal of the resource. In such a case, acquisition personnel need to contact the content provider immediately to resolve the issue. Frequently access is effected due to technical problems such as a change in the URL. Under such circumstances, acquisitions or systems staff should follow up. It is important for acquisitions staff to communicate with the content provider whenever there is a change in the IP address so that records can be amended and access provided to additional sites. Another ongoing responsibility of acquisitions personnel is to receive usage statistics from the content provider and provide data to selectors so that they can review the usage and make informed decisions about reviewing or cancelling the resource (Joshipura, 2008).

Problems and Issues in E-Publishing

No doubt, electronic publishing has opened up new avenues for publishing industry but there are many issues that need to be addressed for the proper development of publishing industry to succeed.

Weber (1990) has identified some important problems that bother the information professionals about electronic resources. Some of the problems are:

- **Ownership:** With the emergence of e-publishing, the concept of ownership is no more in existence. For e-journals, publishers usually have their subscription policy for one year as in case of print journal with marginally less subscription cost as compared to the print copy. The publisher is not ready to provide the facility for retrospective searches. The problem for the librarian is what to do to meet the requirements of research scholars who need old issues or literature for their research. Many publishers provide access by taking extra charges on per access basis and this will cost extra charges either to library or to the research scholar.

- **Training of End Users for Access Requirements:** Electronic resources provides facility of access to large volume of data through hyperlinks, etc. But many times separate types of technological requirements are needed to access each publisher's titles. So it requires training of end users to handle the variety of technology. User education to handle the variety of hardware / software related technology is required to make the users competent to access different electronic publications.
- **Archiving:** Archiving the e-journals is a big question. Publishers are involving their commercial policy and exercising technical features and controls for delivering them to libraries for archiving. Some publishers offer choice to libraries to either use publisher's remote archive or to develop their own archives. Most of the e-journals, announced so far are available in image form, require a large disk space to store and archive. One can imagine the amount of disk space required for storing the issues of e-journals for several years with back volumes and providing access.
- **Copyright Issue:** Copyright seems to be the biggest problem for publishing trade as a whole. Presently, there is no system of security to keep check on unauthorized use of electronic publications. Downloading and redistribution of electronic information is very easy. Anybody can cut, copy, paste the complete document and distribute to any number of persons across the network. It is very difficult to track down such an action.

Challenges for Acquisition Librarian

Budgeting for e-resources presents several challenges. These include the high cost of some access agreements and increases in percentage of budget spent on e-resources; a variety of payment options that make comparisons difficult; supplemental costs not associated with print and other traditional formats. These are initial and continuing expenses in addition to the direct cost of the resource. They include costs to acquire, maintain, and upgrade expensive equipments; educate and assist users. It becomes difficult to add new resources. It is difficult to check access to the resources on a regular basis and inform to content provider in the case of loss of access, which requires special staff with technical skills. Providing access to electronic resources requires that a library reorganize its workflows and procedures. It will also have to hire or train staff with a new set of skills to negotiate the licenses for the electronic resources.

Complicated legal issues often require involvement with legal experts outside the library. The challenges associated with the licensing agreement include understanding the content, determining the standard wording required by the institution, and identifying terms, which requires negotiation. Acquisition librarian should understand the legal obligations and service consequences found in contracts and licenses.

The terms and conditions of the agreement and licensing policy pose serious problems at times especially after the expiry of the subscription. The license agreement requires reviewing various terms and conditions with legal/licensing personnel, and collaboration with different departments. In consortia purchase, libraries have to accept predefined package which of course seems to be quite affordable to libraries but may not be cost effective in terms of usability. It is difficult to decide pricing models. Bundle pricing for e-books is equally complex in which thousands of titles are put together under pricing model. It is not easy to make the exact assessment of the usage of the package and take right decision whether to go for bundle pricing or order selective titles. In the absence of standard pricing model, Acquisition librarians have to negotiate with the publishers or the vendors to arrive at mutually agreed subscription prices with terms and conditions. Managing the necessary record keeping for e-resources, such as license records, advance notification before cancellation or renewal, access follow-up, lists of various contacts is a major challenge. Another challenge concerns providing institutional details, such as data on full time equivalents, IP addresses, and proxy servers to the content provider. When processing an order for a new electronic subscription, acquisitions personnel should collaborate with technology staff in these matters (Joshipura, 2008).

Acquisition librarian should be unbiased when selecting content providers for a particular resource. Librarians should always consider their users and their institution's policies first.

Renewal/Cancellation of an Electronic Resource

Serials or journals or electronic resources are renewed every year. Renewal orders are placed usually after one year, much in advance. But sometimes contracts are signed for two or three years and are renewed accordingly. Generally, libraries go for renewal of subscription on the basis of performance of the agents in handling subscription in the previous year. Generally, Indian libraries subscribe periodical publications, through vendors or subscription agents. In case, a library subscribes to a large number of journals by the same publisher/society, it may be preferable to subscribe directly from the concerned publisher. In the emerging electronic environment, libraries have started using electronic ordering system. An acquisition librarian may use web-based file transfer. A librarian can order through online ordering forms that are linked to the web-based catalogues of the publishers, that allow placing of orders electronically.

Usually, publishers or subscription agents send a notice/reminder to the acquisition department for renewal in advance with price and a copy of contract. Standing order of e-journals and e-resources are most of the time automatically renewed unless there is increase in the price or some change in the licensing terms and agreement. Other electronic resources are reviewed by selectors based on evaluation criteria before the renewal invoice is processed. Selectors consider various criteria before renewing e-resources such as ranking based on access, usage statistics, breadth and audience, cost-effectiveness, currency, budget and uniqueness of the e-resources. Once a decision has been made, the acquisition department is informed to renew or cancel the subscription. The acquisition department process the invoice for payment. They also communicate with the product provider for cancellation.

CONCLUSION

Academic libraries are moving towards electronic access to full-text journals. With the increase in growth and demand by students and research scholars for e-resources, libraries need to purchase and maintain significant e-resources in their collection. The budget should be adjusted to provide higher funding for electronic resources. Purchasing through a consortium is significant financial savings to individual libraries. Nevertheless, in consortia, large electronic resources that are expensive for individual libraries, become affordable when several libraries work together and share the costs.

Comprehensive selection policy lays down guidelines to build up an adequate collection of e-resources. Selecting and adding e-resources for the collection becomes easier for the selectors when a collection development policy is in place. The role of a selection librarian is becoming increasingly complex owing to an exponential growth of multidisciplinary resources, increase in the number of formats and subscription charges. In such incidences, selectors must have clear understanding of the information needs of the users and sound knowledge about resources. This will result in building adequate resources to fulfill the mission and goals of the academic institutions. Both Selectors and Acquisition librarians are required to possess legal and technological knowledge and negotiation skills. It is important for them to keep up-to-date on various changes and developments taking place in the areas of collection development and acquisitions. Training for reference staff may be needed so that they become more knowledgeable about electronic resources. They should keep themselves updated by attending conferences, meetings, searching internet and reading relevant articles.

REFERENCES

American Library Association. (1987). *Guide for writing a bibliographer's manual: Collection Management and Development Guide No. 1*. Chicago, IL: ALA.

Balaram, P. (2000). Journals. *Current Science*, *79*(6), 685.

Boyle, P. (2000, August 24). What? Use a Book for Doing Research? College Students Forsake Library Shelves for Computers. *Washington Post*, p. M07.

Bradford, J. T., Costello, B., & Lenholt, R. (2005). Reference Service in the Digital Age: An Analysis of Sources Used to Answer Reference Questions. *Journal of Academic Librarianship*, *31*(3), 263–272. doi:10.1016/j.acalib.2005.03.001

Chapman, L. (2004). *Managing acquisitions in library and information services* (2nd ed.). London, UK: Facet Publishing.

Das, S. (2010). A three steps strategy for acquiring and promoting E-Resources at college libraries in Purulia District (West Bengal): A Case Study. In *7th Convention PLANNER*. Tezpur University.

Drury, F. K. W. (1930). *Book Selection*. Chicago, IL: American Library Association.

Gregory, V. L., & Hanson, A. (2006). *Selecting and managing electronic resources: A how-to-do- it manual for librarians* (Rev. ed). New York, NY: Neal-Schuman Publishers.

IFLA. (2012). *Key Issues for e-resources Collection Development: A Guide for Libraries*. IFLA.

Institute for the Future. (2001). *E-Journal Usage and Scholarly Practice: An Ethnographic Perspective on the Role and Impact of E-Journal Usage among Users of Biomedical Literature*. Palo Alto, CA: Stanford University, Institute for the Future.

Jindal, S., & Pant, A. (2013). Availability of E-books in Science: Case study of University of Delhi. *The Electronic Library*, *31*(3), 313–328. doi:10.1108/EL-12-2010-0159

Joshipura, S. (2008). Selecting, Acquiring And Renewing Electronic Resources. In H. Yu, & S. Breivod (Eds.), Electronic Resource Management in Libraries: Research and Practice. New York, NY: Information Science Reference. doi:10.4018/978-1-59904-891-8.ch004

Kaur, S., & Satija, M. P. (2007). Collection Development in Digital Environment: Trends and Problems. *SRELS Journal of Information Management*, *44*(2), 139–15.

Kennedy, M. R. (2004). Dreams of perfect programs: Managing the acquisition of electronic resources. *Library Collections, Acquisitions & Technical Services*, *28*(4), 449–458.

Khatri, N. K. (2008). Funding Opportunities for Mathematics Resources: A case study at I.S.I. Delhi Centre Library. In *Proceedings of the International Conference on Shaping the Future of Special Libraries: Beyond Boundaries*. Special Library Association.

Khatri, N. K. (2010, April). Enhancing Usage of E-Resources at Indian Statistical Institute Delhi Centre Library Through Consortia Based Subscription. In *Proceedings of the National Conference on Knowledge Management in the Globalization Era*. IASRI.

Kumbar, B. D., & Hadagali, G. S. (2007). Collection Development Policy in Academic Libraries in a changing Environment: Problems and Prospects. *PEARL: Journal of Library and Information Science*, *1*(1), 33–43.

Ranganathan, S. R. (1963). *The five laws of library science*. Bombay, India: Asia Publishing House.

Rao, N. K., Tripathi, M., & Kumar, S. (2016). Cost of Print and Digital Books: A Comparative Study. *Journal of Academic Librarianship*, *42*(4), 445–452. doi:10.1016/j.acalib.2016.04.003

Scammell, A. (Ed.). (2001). *Handbook of information management* (8th ed.). London, UK: Aslib-imi. doi:10.4324/9780203403914

Sottong, S. (2001). E-Book Technology: Waiting for the "False Pretender". *Information Technology and Libraries*, *20*(2), 72–80.

Spiller, D. (2001). *Book Selection: Principles and Practice*. London, UK: Clive Bingley.

Vashishth, C. P. (2011). Building Library Collection in e-environment: Challenges & Opportunities. *Library Herald*, *49*(1), 15–33. doi:10.5958/0976-2469.2015.00003.2

Weber, R. (1990). The Clouded Future of Electronic Publishing. *Publishers Weekly*, *237*(26), 76–80.

Welch, J. M. (2002). Hey! what about us?! Changing roles of subject specialists and reference librarians in the age of electronic resources. *Serials Review*, *28*(4), 283–286. doi:10.1080/00987913.2002.10764760

Wilkinson, F. C., & Lewis, L. K. (2003). *The complete guide to acquisitions management*. London, UK: Libraries Unlimited.

KEY TERMS AND DEFINITIONS

Consortium: A library consortium consists of a number of libraries, preferably with some common characteristics by subject. institutional affiliation or branches/ units of libraries, that come together with common interest and desire to do certain job collectively.

Impact Factor: It is a measure of the citations to science and social science journals which helps in evaluating the importance of the journal.

IP (Internet Protocol) Address: A unique identifier used by computers to communicate with each other over the internet.

License Agreement: A legal agreement between the library or institution and the content provider clearly stating the requirements and specifications of the agreement.

Packages: They are grouping or bundling of publication titles, generally all of the same format (i.e., either journals or books).

Perpetual Access: It is a permanent right to the library from the publisher to have access to paid licensed materials.

Trial: A request by the library to the content provider to supply free access to an e-resource for a limited time. The library uses such a trial to decide whether to add an e-resource to its collection.

Chapter 11 Digital Library and Distance Learning in Developing Countries: Benefits and Challenges

Jerome Idiegbeyan-ose
Landmark University, Nigeria

Okocha Foluke
Landmark University, Nigeria

Sola Emmanuel Owolabi
Landmark University, Nigeria

Eyiolorunshe Toluwani
Landmark University, Nigeria

Aregbesola Ayooluwa
Landmark University, Nigeria

Oguntayo Sunday
Landmark University, Nigeria

ABSTRACT

This chapter discussed the digital library and distance learning benefits and challenges in developing countries. It started with the general introduction of digital library and distance learning, and went further and discussed the nexus between the digital library and distance learning. The chapter further highlighted the benefits of digital library in distance learning. It also pointed out the challenges of distance learning in developing countries, such as finance, lack of conducive learning environment, poor policies on education, inadequate instructional materials, among others. The chapter further discussed the challenges of digital library in developing countries to include insufficient funding, high cost of instructional materials, insufficient and digital local content, and so on. The paper concluded that there is an urgent need for all stakeholders to take urgent attention in addressing the challenges of digital library in distance learning to create a full opportunity of what digital library provides in distance learning in developing countries.

DOI: 10.4018/978-1-5225-8437-7.ch011

INTRODUCTION

The journey to self-discovery, achievements and continuous relevance of man could be associated with the level of education, be it formal or informal. Science, politics, technology and other elements that relate to existence, survival, and relationship of humans with the environment are greatly influenced by the level of education and exposure to relevant information. It, therefore, suffices to note that national development may not be possible without quality education. Acemoglu and Autor (2012) identified the tangible contributions of education to economic growth, asserting that education is at the fulcrum of development. Educational activities that involve teaching, learning, research, and community development may, however, be hampered without relevant educational resources. This underscores the relevance of the library which focuses on selection, acquisition, processing, storage, preservation and dissemination of electronic and print education resources for meaningful educational activities.

The traditional approach to teaching and learning process has been predominant for several years in higher education. It focuses on face-to-face interaction between the teacher and the learner in a fixed location at a specific time. However, its limitation became conspicuous with the growth in the population of person seeking higher education. Other factors that revealed its weakness include but not limited to infrastructural challenges, incapability of educational stakeholders to maintain required workforce for traditional learning system, and the increasing number of potential learners that their work schedules would not permit to attend the traditional educational system.

To mitigate some of these challenges, reading by correspondence was instituted. The first university to commence studying by correspondence was the University of London in 1858 (Rothblatt, Muller, Ringer, Simon, Bryant, Roach, Harte, Smith & Symonds, 1988, Idiegbeyan-ose & Akpoghome 2009). Other western institutions also patterned after this form of higher education system. Distance learning in Africa could also be traced to the early 1950's (Leary & Berge, 2007) with majority concentrated in South Africa. Distance learning is an educational system in which learning takes place without physical contact between student and the lecturer. This is a direct opposite of the traditional education that insists on physical presence of students in the class. The principle behind distance learning focuses on ensuring that willing and qualified persons have uninhibited access to education within affordable cost. It also focuses on ensuring equality among persons.

Some social-demographic factors such as marriage, work status, financial status etc. has also been considered as one of the impetuses for distance learning.

The introduction and growth of Information and Communication Technologies in Africa has brought about a sudden boost in distance learning began. As reported by Adomi (2005), the unprecedented increase witnessed in the use of ICTs is monumental as the number of countries that had access to internet in 1996 moved from 11 to 53 by the year 2000. Acquiring degrees through distance education became easier and faster through the use of the internet and accompanying gadgets.

The internet has the capacity to project images, voices and texts gave it the superiority over phone conversation with students. Leaning can be personalized with the use of ICTs and students can replay lectures for as many periods as possible. This is unlike the traditional classroom which if students miss may not be repeated again. Internationally, distance learning witnessed high level of enrolment between the year 2000 and 2008 (Radford, 2011). The popularity of distance learning has also been boosted with social media that also allows for ease of advertisement of services and goods without having to pay exorbitant amount to advertising agencies.

It suffices to note that whether in Africa or in the western world, the efficiency and effectiveness of correspondence education did not become conspicuous until information and communication technologies (ICTs) were employed to facilitate the processes involved. From the point where ICTs were introduced into correspondence education, there has been unprecedented growth. The term such as distance learning, virtual education, online schooling and several nomenclatures have been used to represent education by correspondence.

The growth of ICTs which encouraged the rise in demand for distance learning consequently necessitated the provision of educational materials via the electronic platform. Traditional libraries have to give way to digital libraries as resources could be made available and accessed through the internet, hence the emergence of the digital library.

CONCEPT OF DIGITAL LIBRARY

The conventional library is entrenched in manual approach to acquisition, processing, storage, preservation, retrieval and dissemination of information resources. Manuscripts, books, maps and other records are presented in their original state and are usually limited in supply. These resources deteriorate easily through handling by library users, environmental influences and hazards. The traditional library is bound by time (opening hours and losing hours). It is referred to as the library within walls. The process of accessing information in the traditional library is rigid, stereotyped and limited. In order to allow for flexibility and ease of access to unlimited library users, library resources require conversion from the physical to electronic format. This paves the way for digitization.

Digitization entails conversion of physical materials to digital format. When resources are digitized, simultaneous access could be achieved as clients could use their electronic devices to access these resources. The digital library therefore is such that has been able to convert the physical resources to electronic format and provides access through either or both the Wide Area Network and the Local Area Network. (idiegbeyan-ose, Nduka, Adekunjo & koedion, 2015) However there are also library resources that are referred to as "born digital". This means that such resources have been acquired in digitized format.

The digital library is different from hybrid library. The hybrid library is such that possesses physical books and digitized collections, whereas the digital library contains collections that are fully digitized or acquired in digital format which are usually referred to as born digital. Operations in the digital libraries are usually in full automation. This makes information sharing very easy. It is a way of proffering solution to resource challenge in the traditional libraries. It is also the attestation to the fifth law of librarianship by Ranganathan which states that the library is a growing organism. The library has metamorphosed through several stages, from the medieval, renaissance through the digital age. Boundless opportunities abound for library users to access myriad of information sources through the digital library. The resources cut across all disciplines. This is a major high point for distance learning and the digital library.

Primarily, the digital library focuses on improving accessibility, ensuring effective and efficient utilization of library resources, thereby achieving user-satisfaction. Ifijeh, Idiegbeyan-ose, Ilogho & Isiakpona, 2015) Digitization of library materials could be an antidote to the lean budget of libraries. It may not be possible for the library to acquire required number of copies that could meet the need of all library users, but through digitization, a copy of book may be accessible to all library users, at the same time at different geographical locations and at relative low cost. Also, rare collections or books that may go into extinct could be preserved through digitization.

BUILDING DIGITAL COLLECTIONS

Building digital collections could constitute a herculean task; this may explain why majority of libraries maintain hybrid system in which physical and digital collections are maintained. To build a digital library, certain facilities are required. Some of them are:

Hardware: This includes scanners, computers and data storage
Software: This is necessary for capturing of images and editing of images captured.

Network: Stable internet connectivity to transmit data
Display and Printing Devices: These are necessary for effective services.

SOURCES OF DIGITAL LIBRARY COLLECTIONS

There are three main sources to derive digital collections. They are as presented below:

- **Digitization:** This involves the conversion of collections that are in print format to digital. It may be time-consuming and capital intensive but the gains outweigh the investment. Libraries usually opt for the hybrid approach considering the commitments in terms of personnel and other resources to be engaged in the digitization process. Some schools of thought believe that instead of doing the retrospective conversion of library holdings, it is preferable to begin digitization from the point of decision to digitize. This implies that previous resources would not be converted but the library would rather acquire materials in digital format henceforth or immediately convert new print resources to digital format
- **Pure Digital Materials:** These are electronic journals, books datasets, pictures and other information materials made available to users through electronic devices and the internet. These materials are sometimes referred to as 'born-digital'
- **Linkage with External Digital Contents:** A digital library may subscribe to electronic resources and databases of other organizations that provide access to these electronic resources at a specified cost. EBSCO, Elsevier, AGORA, AJOL amongst others are some of the online databases that offer such subscription packages. In the same vein, a library may have cooperation with other libraries for the purpose of resource sharing.

MERITS OF DIGITAL LIBRARIES

Digital libraries have significantly redefined the process of acquisition, processing, storage, preservation and dissemination of information in the 21st century. There are attestations that several benefits could be derived from the use of digital libraries. Some of those benefits are hereunder presented:

Speed of Information Transfer: The digital library ensures the swift movement of information via electronic devices connected through the internet in preferred versions: (video, audio, conferencing, graphics etc.)

Independence: Library users enjoy some levels of independence in accessing digitized collections through the internet. They do not need to see the librarian or library assistants to access most of information resources as long as they are registered with the library and have access passwords with internet connection and accompanying facilities.

Elimination of Physical Boundaries: Users do not have to physically come to the library to access required information. In the same vein, the stress of travelling from one geographical location to another is completely eliminated. No physical boundary. Library staff members are also granted some forms of rest as it may not be necessary for libraries to engage in round-the-clock physical library services.

Information Availability is Not Time-Bound: The "opening and closing hour rules" may not apply in the digital library. At any time of the day or night, users are at liberty to access information as machines are not like humans that are sensitive to time. As long as they are not faulty and there is internet with accompanying facilities, users are at liberty to access the available information resources.

Simultaneous Accesses: Several users have access to the same information resource at the same time without the access to one affecting that of others. This is unlike the traditional library where when the available copies are in use, other users are hindered from accessing them. Until one user returns the borrowed material, the next users are bound to wait.

Abolition of shelving and re-shelving of collections: digital resources are automatically organized as against the traditional libraries in which when a book is removed from the shelf, it will require the service of library assistants to put it back in the shelf. In some instances, traditional library users hoard information resources by removing them from the class they belong on the shelves to other classes where they may not be easily located, especially in libraries where shelve reading is not usually done.

Some of the merits of digital libraries discussed above, in brief, are affirmations of the fundamental role of digital libraries in facilitating distant learning.

RELATIONSHIP BETWEEN THE DIGITAL LIBRARY AND DISTANCE LEARNING

As information hubs of any higher educational institutions, academic libraries are generally established to support the tripartite objectives of teaching, learning, and research which are fundamental to academia. The library which is a hub of intellectual activities contributes significantly to accomplish and/ or support goals of their parent institutions by providing access to required information resources specifically designed for their users, to facilitate teaching, learning, and research across all disciplines offered by their host institutions - universities, polytechnics, and colleges. Apart from their primary focus, today's higher educational institutions actively engage in additional functions, including leadership, manpower development, knowledge dissemination, social and economic modernization (Ifidon & Okoli, 2002).

However, the increasing demands for flexible learning environments, more utilization of the Internet resources for learning activities and proliferation of distance education continue to expand educational opportunities and services (Simmons, 2002). These have now permitted the provision of core educational service delivery, such as library services, for distance education students that were previously unconceivable (Bates, 1995). Even though the library needs of distance learners are similar to students in traditional campus settings (Association of College and Research Libraries, 2016).

The growing proliferation of distance education facilitated by the use of information and communication technologies (ICTs) especially at colleges and universities has posed new challenges and tremendous implications for providing library services to distance learners. Library and information resources play much more relevant role in distance learning than in traditional education setting. Therefore, distance learners need specialised library services and there are concerns about their information access which are not experienced by on-campus students (Barron, 2002). Students in traditional campus settings, unlike distance learners, can visit traditional library, physically access library resources, seek face-to-face assistance and guidance from librarians.

In order to respond to this challenge as well as meet information needs of distance learners which is vital to learning and research, academic libraries are creating digital libraries where library resources and services are delivered to this special kind of students electronically. Faulhaber (1996) supported this assertion that it is impossible to have distance education without a digital library. Since libraries are primarily setup to meet the information needs of users including students irrespective of their physical location at any time (Barron, 2002).

In a variety of contexts, distance learners want to have access to digital information via the internet. This implies that this new means of education requires complementary information and communications technologies. There must be unhindered and continuous access to library resources and services remotely to support courses, degrees and other distance learning activities engaged by distance students. Therefore, libraries and librarians need to re-evaluate the development, management, and delivery of resources and services to meet the needs of geographically spaced students. The need for unhindered/round-the-clock remote access to information resources for higher productivity, pressurize academic libraries to find a lasting solution to these demands which led to the emergence of the digital library. In a digital library, distance learners who predominantly work away from their institution of learning can simultaneously access a wide range of library resources and services designed for/or useful to them remotely.

With remote access provided by the digital library to selected internet resources and online databases containing full-text materials such as journal articles, books, encyclopedias, and reference works, distance learners can make use of library materials remotely. Through computer-mediated communication such as email, instant messengers, social media, etc library users are enabled to contact and interact with librarians without coming to the library for research support. Hence, there is a need for libraries to be transformed not only in collections, as the majority of the resources of a digital library is expected to be in computer readable form, but also in meeting the changing nature of users' information needs. It is also important to note that the increasing expectation of users, changes in library usage patterns brought about by distance education system, information seeking strategy and more sophistication in the new interfaces of knowledge delivery underscore the need for digital library.

The major aim of digital library which is an essential component of distance learning system is to facilitate the organisation and provision of information and resources to its users. The library through its staff identifies, describes and provides access to wide range of quality online resources. Sharing information among researchers, faculty, students, and departments within an institution encourages teamwork, develop their skills, and leads to improved relationships. Collaboration between the library staff and its users (faculty and students) supports teaching, learning and research. This implies that the library is considered as an active entity of the learning environment (Peacock 2005).

Lee (2001) also formulated a number of ways digital libraries can support distance learning. This include improvement of student performance; increase the quantity, quality and comprehensiveness of internet-based educational resources; making resources easily discoverable and retrievable for users; and ensure availability of these resources over time.

Therefore, the function of the library is not limited to providing library resources but also meeting the continuous support of the needs of its clients. The library also sharpens the research skills of students by encouraging them to search, explore, discover, and take advantage of these rich online resources. The strength of digital libraries and its collections is the function of established relationships by libraries with authors, publishers, and aggregators of electronic resources, as well as with its users. The provision of continuous technical, reference and instructional support to distance students requires libraries to collaborated with these students and tailor services offered creatively towards the needs of their users.

BENEFITS OF DIGITAL LIBRARY IN DISTANCE LEARNING

Digital libraries play an indispensable role in distance learning. They offer convenient and immediate access to ever-increasing collections and information resources from a wide range of sources too numerous users simultaneously. These resources are provided via an internet connection from anywhere around the world at anytime. This implies that with digital libraries distance students can learn independently irrespective of their geographical location and spread (Abbasi & Zardary, 2012, Idiegbeyan-ose, & Akpoghome, 2009; Idiegbeyan-ose, Ilo, &Isiakpona, 2015). Digital libraries have capacity to store and manage large amounts of electronic resources such as full text journals, books, course materials, bibliographic databases, web-based library catalogues, multimedia etc. it creates conducive environment that permit bringing together of library collections, services and users which support creation, dissemination and preservation of data, information and resources.

With technological developments, educational changes have altered limitative assumptions about students affected as a result of their geographical location. However, digital library provides web-based library catalogues, electronic books and journals, bibliographic databases, and electronic tutorials for distance learners. Students reading online resources in the traditional library experiences the same interaction and engagement with the content of the resources as other students who access the same material remotely via the Internet.

Three roles are performed by any digital library in distance learning as observed by Marchionini and Maurer (1995). These are: sharing of expensive resources such as equipment, information and human resources – particularly librarians who permit sharing of such resources; organizing and preserving ideas and materials through library catalogues, indexes and other means to enable easy retrieval of relevant items to their needs; and playing social and intellectual roles by bringing people and ideas together with learning missions.

The ever-increasing availability of electronic resources in digital library enables educational institutions to provide distance learners more robust, more varied and more accessible information resources than what traditional library will provide (Tanner & Deegan, 2011). This allows the robust educational experience to be offered to students as new topics and programmes are studied

Pavani in Vrana (2017) while studying the suitability of digital library in learning found the following: that all kind of materials such as texts, animations, audio files, video, e-books, e-journals, interactive exercises, and online assessments can be described, managed and disseminated together through computer networks and internet; different access privileges can be assigned to various categorises of users of digital library; it allows authors to make their content available for others to use; contents of digital library can be used interactively; contents of digital library are flexible which allows it to be combined and usable by multiple programmes; the networked resources digital libraries have allows its contents to be used by different cooperating institutions; and allows learning to take place anywhere and anytime.

Pavani's assertion is supported by Dhiman (2010) who argued that digital library encourages knowledge sharing among key actors (the teachers, learners, and librarians) in the learning process. It encourages them "to work together, develop their skills, and form strong and unquestionable relationships". Furthermore, the researcher observed that digital library provides information resources and services driven by technology to enable the accessibility of relevant information resources and library services anywhere around the world anytime.

Observably, the digital library allows the provision of library services to distance education students which have helped to alleviate duplication of library resources at multiple remote locations as online access provides greater resources than traditional libraries are able to provide due to limiting factors such as cost and space. The digital library helps to bridge the gap between the distant learner and the library. It also enables libraries to serve distance learners better through networked access and Internet.

Another reason to use the digital library is that using various electronic tools, learners can search text materials and images easily and quickly, which can be applied broadly across all kinds of institutions. Innovative communication technologies, efficient search engines, the affordable deployment cost of a digital library, and large storage of digital content are the other reasons to implement a digital library in a flexible educational system.

While comparing print resources with electronic resources Brophy (1993) poised that electronic resources which form major collections in digital libraries permit more frequent updating, information retrieval is ease and quick, remote access to documents or/ resources - a particular advantage for the distance learner. Dadzie (2005) identified access to more current information, and provision of links to additional resources or related content as benefits of the digital library. Students do not have to physically visit the library to access its resources and services.

CHALLENGES OF DISTANCE LEARNING IN DEVELOPING COUNTRIES

Globally, distance learning has come of age in that many countries of the world both developed and developing countries are adopting it to solve the problems associated with acquiring education anywhere, anytime and at any age and more so to strengthen the concept of life-long learning. Distance Learning has become an integral part of the global educational structure in many parts of the world and prominent attention is being given to it in order to meet the educational needs of the teeming population of intending students. Adult citizens who intend to further their education or add to their knowledge, those restrained from conventional institutions for financial or other reasons, people with physical disabilities, employees who need to attain higher certifications to get a promotion or improve their salaries, etc. take advantage of this opportunity to fulfill their desires.

The establishment and acceptance of Distance learning in the developing countries has brought about laudable prospects and benefits to the educational sector and socio-economic aspect of developing countries of the world. Distance learning has created the possibility of increased access to tertiary education at more cost effective-level (Rena, 2007, Idiegbeyan-ose & Akpoghome, 2009) and it has the ability to cater for the peculiar needs of individual learner (Nnadi, 2015). However, as laudable as these benefits are, some short-comings and challenges have been identified with it, and these are more visible in Africa and other developing countries of the world. The challenges faced by these countries range from technology to socio-economics.

Studies have revealed that distance learning students in many of the developing countries have the problem of accessibility and utilization of technologies that can aid their mode of learning (Maxwell et al, 2015; Idowu, 2012; Traxler, 2018) while some countries are still battling with the implementation of Information Communication Technologies (ICT) in their educational sector and many others cannot cope with the evolving nature of ICT which depends heavily on electricity for operation (Lerra, 2014; Mpofu, 2016; Yusuf, 2006; Ajadi et al, 2008, Idiegbeyan-ose, Idahosa, & Adewole-Odeshi, 2014). According to Idowu (2012), no African country, including South Africa, is currently self-sufficient in electric supply, therefore, distance learning which is mostly dependent on the application of ICT may not meaningfully run without an adequate supply of electricity.

Other studies on the challenges of distance learning have also identified problems related to socio-economic. From the study conducted by Nnadi (2015) on students in a Nigerian distance learning center, he found out that students encountered several challenges in the course of acquiring this form of education. The challenges range from the expensive nature of the programme to lack of access to library and other facilities. Cloete (2017) observed that access to technology and technological literacy are a part of the challenges facing developing country like South Africa. From the observation by Rena (2007) on the challenges of introducing distance education in Eritrea, he identified two kinds of barriers which are faculty barriers and organizational barriers.

However, Pant (2014) highlighted seven problems arising from distance education which may be due to any of the factors above.

- Nature of study materials
- Lack of multi-media instructions
- Lack of feedback or contact with the teachers
- Lack of support and services
- Insecurities about learning.
- Lack of student training
- Lack of social interaction

Some other research works have also tried to classify the challenges of distance learning into related groups, some of which are: situational, attitudinal, psychological and pedagogical (Berge et al., 2002 cited in Maxwell, 2015), institutional and socio-cultural related challenges (Zirnkle, 2001 cited in Maxwell, 2015). For the sake of this study, the challenges of distance learning in developing countries will be classified under three main bodies which are: attitudinal, situational and instructional/institutional.

Attitudinal challenges emanate from the students' dispositions towards distance learning:

- **Technophobia:** Many students who enroll in distance learning do not have adequate ICT skills to cope with the demands of distance learning. In this 21st century, the main medium by which students get instructions from their tutors is through the medium of a computer with internet facility. However socio-economic factors such as financial constraint have affected many of the students as they could not afford to own technological tools that will aid their learning. For some that could afford the purchase of such tools, they exhibit fear when in contact with the tools because they lack information literacy skills to operate on them.
- **Individualism:** Since distance learning is student centered, the socio-demographics of the students such as age, gender, social status, cognitive skills, culture, academic preparedness, personal support systems, and expectations of the students have a lot to do with their attitude towards learning. Some students will complete their courses irrespective of deficiencies in the mode of learning while others will drop out in the first year. Also, many of the students assumed distance learning is an easier means of getting certifications compared to conventional school and so they exhibit a nonchalant attitude towards their studies which makes it harder to achieve their academic goal.

- **Low Level of Preparedness:** Many of the students in distance learning fail to prepare adequately for studies which may be due to its flexibility. Since students do not have contact with their tutors and peers and lack the conventional learning environment that can motivate and encourage them to study, they usually display complacent attitudes towards their studies. According to Kim and Shih (2003), the motivation of students is one of the key factors that will determine the success of a distance learning program.
- **Low Self-Esteem:** Due to the nature of distance learning, learners feel inadequate when they are in contact with their peers who attend conventional institutions. Some confessed they do not feel like a student because they combine work with studies. Also, the acceptability of certifications from distance education by would-be employers is low, this usually have an impact on the candidates' self-esteem as some of them feel like second class candidates.

Situational challenges encompass all the circumstances and conditions surrounding learning from a distance. Below are some of the challenges associated with it.

- **Work Obligations:** The combination of work and learning is one of the challenges distance learners face in the course of their studies. In the studies carried out by Mohanachandran and Ramalu (2013), on Malaysian distance learners, the first challenge identified was the hurdles of balancing the combination of work and education as most of them are older, have jobs and families. Some learners do not have the support of their employers to further their education, it is sometimes difficult to take permission to go for a test or an exam. The task of balancing all the above responsibility is truly challenging for most of them.
- **Finance:** Most of the distance learners face financial challenges in the course of their studies. A good number of them are self-sponsored, they have families and other financial obligations. In developing countries like Nigeria and many African countries, the income of an average citizen may not be sufficient to cater to financial demands of distance learning in addition to other needs calling for their attention. Government of many of the developing countries does not make funding allocation available to distance learning platforms unlike what obtains in a conventional system.
- **Lack of a Conducive Learning Environment:** Since learning takes place remotely, distance learners do not find it easy to concentrate on their studies. The home or work environment they find themselves may not allow them to

spent sufficient time on their studies. They can easily be distracted by the activities around them. Acquiring distance study habits by distance learning students is a herculean task as most of them are not supported by their learning community.

- **Isolation and Sense of Abandonment-** In distance learning, students are left to themselves, they seem to be studying independently. This makes them feel lonely and abandoned. Tutors do not monitor the progress of students in distance learning because there is no face to face contact with them. Moral supports and facilities like a library that can aid learning and self-evaluation which are found in the conventional system are absent in distance learning. Students sometimes lose the sense of belonging and this affects their self-perception.
- **Improper Communication Channels:** Distance learning system can only function properly if the right communication system is in place. In a face to face learning setting all barriers to effective communication are avoided for a proper understanding of the information being passed across to the students. Students are also able to interact with their tutors, feedback is quick and sometimes instant. This is not the case for distance learners in developing countries. Ndayambaje et al, (2012) quoting UNESCO (2002) stated that "Communication serves two purposes. One is the distribution of information, the second is the interaction between teachers and learners and where possible between learner-learner." In most cases in distance learning, the purpose of communication is mainly to pass information from teachers to learners.

Many distance learners do not have access to ICT devices which is supposed to alleviate the problem of communication and also help to complete their assignments. Some who have access to these devices do not always know how to make proper use of it for academic purposes.

Instructional/institutional challenges cover all problems relating to educational policies, logistics system, course facilitators, ICT penetration, economic factors, etc.

- **Lack of Proper Educational Policies:** Despite the proliferation of distance learning in the countries of the world, policies that engender good structure and platform is lacking in many of the developing countries there are no proper policies in place for distance learning to run with. Yusuf (2006) reported a situation in which a succeeding government truncated the attempt at Open University in the early'80s in Nigeria. Although another government has established it in early 2000, yet the onus lies in the successive government to keep supporting its existence through adequate funding. In some cases where there are defined policies, these policies may not be implementation.

- **Poor Economic Situation:** The unfavorable economic situation in many developing countries does not encourage learning. Distance education is not affordable by many distance learners as many of them fall into the category of low-income earners. Facilities such as uninterrupted electricity supply, sufficient internet bandwidth, and general citizenship empowerment found in developed countries are lacking in developing countries. This has made it difficult for students to get the best out of learning from a distance.
- **Poor Logistics System:** The administration of distance learning is usually poor compared to a conventional system. Rena (2015) stated that funding should be made available to create an administrative unit that is to be responsible for managing the system. Many students get lost and confused in the course of registering for their programmes. Since students are from different part of the country, study centers are not enough to meet the population of the students and in most cases, they are not well equipped. There is usually no regular visit to these centers by distance learning management; the attention and commitment given to this kind of education are very poor, this has a negative effect on the students.
- **Inadequate INSTRUCTIONAL MATERIALS:** Budgeting is a major challenge facing African institutions, and distance education is not left behind. Management of distance learning finds it hard to access funds to cater to sophisticated instructional materials to enhance the learning skills of their students. This has been the bane of the system as most of the ICT devices are obsolete. Sometimes the instructional modules to be used by the tutor do not get to them in good time.

CHALLENGES OF DIGITAL LIBRARIES IN DEVELOPING COUNTRIES

Digital Libraries has caused a change in the access of information sources and has bridged the knowledge gap between the developed and developing countries. Prior to the advent of digital libraries, researchers and institutions in developing countries had limited access to articles published in developed countries due to high cost and challenges encountered in the distribution of these materials However, despite the numerous benefits that digital libraries proffer, developing countries are still faced with challenges in building and using digital libraries (Arunachalam,2003, Idiegbeyan-ose, Okosun, Eruanga & Ojo-Igbinoba, 2005).The cost of building digital libraries is still very high as leaders of economies focus on more pressing needs in the economy, also knowledge has not fully been appreciated in the economy. These challenges involve the building, use and maintenance of these resources. Digital libraries in developing countries can be improved through a partnership between private institutions and funding agencies for sustainable funding, increasing the local content of digital publications, improving on infrastructural development in developing countries and investing in the training of library staff and users on digital libraries and literacy skills. Developing countries must leverage on their strengths so as to gain opportunities from the benefits of digital libraries.

SUSTAINABLE FUNDING

Libraries in developing countries are seeking an alternative means of funding to meet up with technological advancements. According to Ogundipe (2008), the National Universities Commission has recommended that 10% of the universities recurrent budget be allotted to the Library but this is hardly complied with because poor funding has been noted as the major hindrance to digital libraries in developing countries. This is because funds allotted to Libraries have a major influence in the provision of qualitative and quantitative information materials. Ahmed & Nwalo (2013). Swayaden (2003) states that fundraising must become an integral part of libraries budget and a close cooperation between local, national and international libraries must be encouraged. A study by Rosenberg and Raseraka (2000) showed that financing of institutions in Africa is still lower than developed countries, with international countries financing at six percent of the budget while Africa still finances at four percent. Afebende (2017) suggests that grants-in-aid and donations play a vital role in supporting Libraries and there is a need for Librarians to be trained on grant proposal writing. Libraries in Africa are heavily dependent on the national governments for most of their budgets. University of Zimbabwe and the University of Zambia suffered from budget cuts and were heavily dependent on gifts and donations in 2002. Also in the 2005 the University of Botswana suffered from budget cuts. It has become obvious that the challenge of budget cuts is recurrent in dwindling economies, also digital libraries are dependent on their parent organization, and inadequacy of funding is therefore linked to a depressed economy (Ofoegbu and Alonge, 2016). Emphasis has continually been made on decreased funding in developing countries since digital libraries exist within the parent organization, consequently funding is dependent on the amount is given by the institution.

HIGH COST OF INFRASTRUCTURE

In developing countries, a clear digital divide exists in access to information communication technology. These challenges include inadequate network infrastructures, bandwidth issues amongst others. Aluoch (2006), states that internet connectivity in Africa is still very poor, unreliable and very expensive. It has been noted from the African Tertiary Institution Connectivity survey that universities in Africa much higher fees for internet connectivity than the developed world. The high cost of internet connectivity has been in relation to the limited availability and capacity on the national fibre backbone Reliability and fast internet connection is required to access scholarly publications in the world. Christian (2008) observed that bandwidth allocation is too expensive and this makes it difficult to access academic resources in Nigeria. The findings from a survey by Echezona and Ugwanyi (2010) showed that African University have low-speed internet connection and the challenges with power supply in Africa has grossly endangered internet connectivity, and further noted that slow bandwidth is the main limitation to assessing digital libraries in developing countries.Omekwu and Echezona (2007) noted that the North-South divide is skewed against Africa making access to information faster and diverse in developed countries than in developing countries.In order to improve information access in spite of these challenges. Developing countries are encouraged to bridge this gap in the divide to ensure information and research exchange (Adekunle, Omaba and Tella, 2007, Idiegbeyan-ose, Nkiko, Idahosa & Nwokocha, 2016). Also, Information Technology policy makers must intensify effort in bridging this divide.

BUILDING DIGITAL COLLECTIONS

Developing countries should be empowered to produce digital collects not just being major consumers. In the developed world huge investments have been made in the establishment of digital libraries. For instance, the Library of Congress made an initial investment of sixty million dollars in the development of the American National Digital Library. Though building digital libraries are financially demanding. Developing countries can take advantage of partnerships and subscribe to open access software as tools in building their digital collections. Also, developing countries should subscribe to open access initiatives. Nwagwu (2016) noted that only three universities in Nigeria had subscribed to open access to digital libraries. Adebayo et al. (2018) highlighted challenges in digitizing to include increased expenditure, staffing issues and preservation challenges as major challenges encountered when building digital libraries in developing countries.

INSUFFICIENT DIGITAL LOCAL CONTENT

Local content in developing countries is still relatively low and this invariably affects digital libraries. In Africa, it has been noted that Africa produced content accounts for less than 0.05 percent of the global content (Taylor, 2002). Factors affecting the dearth of digital content include the high cost of building digital content, inappropriate training of content creators and being abreast with the latest technologies in content creation (Khan, 2007). Mutala (2008) noted that there is limited availability of information and knowledge systems that address African needs. Though local content is readily available in developing countries, these countries are still plagued with the challenge of capturing, repacking and disseminating this information. Most local contents in African countries are still in their traditional form and there is a need for African countries to make these contents more accessible by taking advantage of digital libraries and the latest advancements in computer applications development. Mutulu (2008) stated that factors such as poor policies, lack of electricity, low technology penetration, lack of content development, poor reading habits and brain drain still limited content development in Africa. In 2003, it was noted that 900,000 books are estimated to be published every year in the world of which the only 1.5percent is published in Africa (Sapova, 2003). A large amount of indigenous knowledge is currently available in African countries and there is a need for developing countries to wake up to this challenge and increase the local content available. Developing countries should focus more on building standard databases with local content. In Africa currently, an organization named African Journal Online provides access to African research, though AJOL is not open access. This is a welcome development to organizations in developing countries to focus on building digital libraries with local content.

LACK OF DIGITAL LITERACY

The information age demands the ability to identify, organize, understand and create information. Based on the enormous information available on the web, adequate skill is required. Several studies have shown that a lack of digital literacy is responsible for the underutilization of digital libraries. There is, therefore, a need for information literacy skill to be taught to all categories of users as general internet searches compete greatly with these resources. It is important for users to be taught the value of authoritative information. Digital libraries deliver library caliber knowledge and these enable users to be free from unauthoritative information. (Ekere, Omekwu, and Nwoha (2016). Library professionals should continue to intensify efforts on user education. Also as suggested by Igun (2006), 21st-century librarians should be trained on the relevant ICT skills. This is paramount because the capacity of use and access to digital libraries by users depends largely on literacy and mastery of these emerging technologies Ugwuanyi (2011).

COPYRIGHT CHALLENGES

Digital Libraries recognizes the protection of legal rights such as copyright, intellectual property rights, privacy amongst others. A copyright is the legal exclusive right granted by owners of intellectual property for economic reasons. However, there are legal issues that make management difficult in digital libraries. An example of this is the impact of social media on digital libraries. Academic social media websites request researchers to deposit their research output, without a proper understanding of these laws; this could pose a great challenge in digital libraries. Also in the building of institutional repositories, copyright laws must also be considered before research outputs are uploaded. Other Legal issues include issues defining the use of the intellectual property and how fair use applies to intellectual property. Managing intellectual property is one of the greatest challenges facing digital libraries in developing countries. Digital Librarian must protect digital content from unauthorized access, copying, and inappropriate use

EQUITY OF ACCESS

One of the challenges still facing digital libraries in developing countries is equity of access. Despite movements on open access initiatives in developing countries, researchers still find it difficult to access scholarly publications in digital libraries. Researchers are still required to pay a processing fee to access articles. Universities in developing countries periodically subscribe to electronic resources but researchers are still required to pay for access to some scholarly articles especially in sciences. This causes a digital divide making a clear gap between the developed and developing countries in research and development. Most countries in developing countries do not have an open access policy that guides the sharing of resources in their digital libraries. Only a few institutions in Nigeria have open access to institutional repositories. There is a need to promote effective access by making digital library collections easily accessible for use.

DIGITAL PRESERVATION

Digital preservation is the planning and application of preservation methods to ensure that digital content remains accessible and useable in the long-term. Preservation of digital materials has been in the forefront of research in the recent time. The preservation of digital resources aims at making local content accessible at a later time. Also, Jantz and Giarlo define digital preservation as managed activities for the long-term maintenance of a document and for continued accessibility in spite of changing technologies. Digital Libraries are still faced with numerous challenges in the preservation of digital content which includes inadequate funding, insufficient institutional support, lack of support from stakeholders and no clear policy on the preservation of digital content. In developing countries, preservation policies must be established to enable libraries to preserve digital collections effectively. Challenges in the preservation include the nature of digital materials, dependence on hardware and software technologies which are fragile and also the short life span of digital media, formats, and styles in digital preservation amongst others. In the preservation of digital libraries, library professionals should take advantage of advanced technologies and ensure that clear policy are put in place for seamless operations in the future.

CONCLUSION/RECOMMENDATIONS

Based on the failure of traditional distribution channels in the access to information, it has become obvious that digital libraries are not negotiable in developing countries. However, most leaders in developing countries still focus on meeting the basic needs of its people which lead to difficulties in building, use, and sustenance of digital libraries. Also, factors such as high cost of infrastructure, insufficient digital local content lack of digital literacy, copyright Issues, equity of access and digital preservation challenges still hamper digital libraries in developing countries. There is a need for stakeholders to address these challenges and take advantage of the freely available online digital libraries and open source software in the building of digital libraries in developing countries.

REFERENCES

Abbasi, F., & Zardary, S. (2012). Digital libraries and its role on supporting Learning. *AWERProcedia Information Technology & Computer Science*, *1*, 809–813.

Acemoglu, D., & Autor, D. (2012). What does human capital do? A review of Goldin and Katz's the race between education and technology. *Journal of Economic Literature*, *50*(2), 426–463. doi:10.1257/jel.50.2.426

Adekunle, P. A., Omoba, R. O., & Tella, A. (2007). Attitudes of librarians in selected Nigerian universities towards the use of ICT. *Library Philosophy and Practice*. Available at http://unllib.unl.edu/LPP/tella3.htm

Adomi, E. E. (2005). *Internet development and connectivity in Nigeria*. Department of Library and Information Science, Delta State University, Abraka, Nigeria. Retrieved from http://www.emeraldinsight.com/Insight/ViewContentServlet?Filename=Published/Em rldFullTextArticle/Articles/2800390306.html

African Tertiary institution connectivity survey. (2006). *ATICS 2006 Report*. Available at http://biotrade.aauorg/renul/docs/ATICS2006.pdf

Ahmed, A. O., & Nwalo, K., (2013). Fund Allocation as a Correlate of Sustainability of Departmental Libraries in Nigerian Universities. *Library Philosophy and Practice,* 936-951.

Ajadi, T. O., Salawu, I. O., & Adeoye, F. A. (2008). E-learning and distance education in Nigeria. *The Turkish Online Journal of Educational Technology*, 7(4), 1–10.

Aluoch, A. A. (2006). *The search for affordable quality Internet connectivity for African universities*. AAU.

Arunachalam, S. (2003). Information for research in developing countries: Information technology - friend or foe? *Bulletin of the American Society for Information Science and Technology*.

Association of College and Research Libraries. (2016). *Standards for Distance Learning Library Services*. Retrieved from http://www.ala.org/acrl/standards/guidelinesdistancelearning

Barron, B. B. (2002). Distant and distributed learners are two sides of the same coin. *Computers in Libraries*, *22*(1), 24–28.

Bates, A. W. (1995). *Technology, Open Learning, and Distance Education*. New York, NY: Routledge.

Brophy, P. (1993). Networking in British academic libraries. *British Journal of Academic Librarianship, 8*(1), 49-60.

Chowdhury, G. G. (2002) Digital Divide: How Can Digital Libraries Bridge the Gap? *Proceedings of the 5th International Conference on Asian Digital Libraries: Digital Libraries: People, Knowledge, and Technology*. 10.1007/3-540-36227-4_43

Cloete, A. L. (2017). Technology and education: Challenges and opportunities. *Hervormde Teologiese Studies, 73*(4), a4589. doi:10.4102/hts.v73i4.4589

Dadzie, P. S. (2005). Electronic resources: Access and usage at Ashesi University College. *Campus-Wide Information Systems, 22*(5), 290–297. doi:10.1108/10650740510632208

Dhiman, A. K. (2010, August). Evolving roles of library & information centres in e-learning environment. In *World Library and information Congress: 76th IFLA General Conference and Assembly. Gothenberg, IFLA* (p. 12). Academic Press.

Ekere, Omekwu, & Nwoha (2016). Users' Perception of the Facilities, Resources and Services of the MTN Digital Library at the University of Nigeria, Nsukka. *Library Philosophy and Practice*, 1390. Available at http://digitalcommons.unl.edu/libphilprac/1390

Eyitayo, O. T. (2008). Internet facilities and the status of Africa's connectivity. In L. O. Aina, S. M. Mutuala, & M. A. Tiamiyu (Eds.), *Information and knowledge management in the digital age: Concept, technologies and African perspectives*. Ibadan, Nigeria: Third World Information Services.

Faulhaber, C. B. (1996). Distance learning and digital libraries: Two sides of a single coin. *Journal of the American Society for Information Science, 47*(11), 854–856. doi:10.1002/(SICI)1097-4571(199611)47:11<854::AID-ASI9>3.0.CO;2-1

Idiegbeyan-ose, J., & Akpoghome, T. U. (2009). Distance Learning in Nigeria and the Role of Virtual Library. Gateway. *Library Journal, 12*(2), 75–85.

Idiegbeyan-ose, J., Ilo, P., & Isiakpona, C. (2015). The 21st Century Library and Information Services for the Enhancement of Teacher Education. In P. O. Nwachukwu (Ed.), *Handbook of Research on Enhancing Teacher Education with Advanced Instructional Technologies*. Hershey, PA: IGI Global. Available at https://www.igi-global.com/chapter/the- 21st-century-library-and-information-services-for-the-enhancement-of-teacher- education/133804

Idiegbeyan-Ose, J., Idahosa, M., & Adewole-Odeshi, E. (2014). Adoption and Use of Information and Communication Technologies (ICTs) in Library and Information Centres: Implications on Teaching and Learning Process. In B. F. Adeoye (Ed.), *Effects of Information Capitalism and Globalization on Teaching and Learning*. Hershey, PA: IGI Global. Available at https://www.igi- global.com/chapter/adoption-and- use-of-information-and -communication- technologies-icts-in-library-and-information-centres/1132422

Idiegbeyan-Ose, J., Okosun, H., Eruanca, C., & Ojo-Igbinoba, M. E. (2005, June). Benson ldahosa University Virtual Library: A case study. *A Compendium of Papers Presented at the 43rd National Annual Conference & AGM of the Nigerian Library Association at Cultural Centre*. Available at http://eprints.covenantuniversity.edu.ng/4914/1/Mr%20Jerome.pdf

Idiegbeyan-ose, J., Nduka, S., Adekunjo, O. A., & Okoedion, I. (2015). An Assessment of Digital Library Functions and Services in Nigerian Academic Libraries. In S. Thanuskodi (Ed.), *Handbook of Research on Inventive Digital Tools for Collection Management and Development in Modern Libraries*. Hershey, PA: IGI Global. Available at https://www.igi-global.com/chapter/an-assessment-of-digital-library-functions-and-services-in-nigerian- academic-libraries/133967

Idiegbeyan-Ose, J., Nkiko, C., Idahosa, M., & Nwokocha, N. (2016). Digital Divide: Issues and Strategies for Intervention in Nigerian Libraries. *Journal of Cases on Information Technology, 18*(3), 29-39. Available at https://www.igi-global.com/article/digital- divide/172153

Idowu, B. (2012). Open and Distance Learning: Achievements and challenges in a developing sub-educational sector in Africa. In O. M. Modise (Ed.), Cases on Leadership in Adult Education (pp. 27-62). Hershey, PA: IGI Global.

Ifidon, S. E., & Okoli, G. N. (2002, June). *40 Years of academic and research library services in Nigeria: Past, present, and future*. A paper presented at the 40th anniversary National Conference and Annual General Meeting of the NLA held at the Administrative Staff College of Nigeria, Togo-Badagry.

Ifijeh, G., Idiegbeyan-ose, J., Ilogho, J., & Isiakpona, C. (2015). Disaster and Digital Libraries in Developing Countries: Issues and Challenges. In E. N. Decker (Ed.), *Handbook of Research on Disaster Management and Contingency Planning in Modern Libraries*. Hershey, PA: IGI Global. Available at https://www.igi-global.com/chapter/disaster-and-digital- libraries-in-developing-countries/135207

Igun, I. E. (2006). Human Capital for Nigerians Libraries in the 21st century. *Library Philosophy and Practice, 8*(2).

Leary, J. & Berge, Z. (2007). Successful distance education programs in sub-Saharan Africa. *Turkish Online Journal of Distance Education, 8*(2), 136-145.

Lee, L. Z. (2001). Growing a national learning environments and resources network for science, mathematics, engineering, and technology education. *First Monday, 6*(4).

Lerra, M. D. (2014). The Dynamics and challenges of distance education at private higher institutions in South Ethiopia. *Asian Business Consortium, 1*(3), 137–150.

Marchionini, G., & Maurer, H. (1995). The roles of digital libraries in teaching and learning. *Communications of the ACM, 38*(4), 67–75. doi:10.1145/205323.205345

Maxwell, C. C. (2015). Challenges for open and distance learning (ODL) students: Experiences from students of the Zimbabwe Open University. *Journal of Education and Practice*, *6*(18), 55–69.

Mohanachandran, D. K., & Ramalu, S. S. (2013). Work and schooling challenges of open distance learning: Case study. *Research Journal of Social Sciences and Management*, *2*(10), 198–207.

Mpofu, S. (2016). The Challenges facing distance education in Southern Africa. In S. J. Levine (Ed.), Making distance education work: Understanding learning and learners at a distance (pp. 221-229). LearnersAssociates.net.

Ndayambaje, I., & … . (2012). A study on the practices and challenges of Distance Training Programme (DTP) under Kigali Institute of Education (KIE). *Rwandan Journal of Education, 1*(2), 69–76.

Nnadi, E. J. (2014). Challenges and strategies for improvement in distance education of students in Abagana Study Centre, Anambra state, Nigeria. *Ind. J. Sci. Res. and Tech*, *3*(2), 34–37.

Nwalo, K. I. N. (2003). *Fundamentals of library practice: A manual on library routines*. Ibadan, Nigeria: Sterling-Horden Publishers

Ofoegbu, F. I., & Alonge, H. O. (2016). Internally generated revenue and effectiveness of University Administration in Nigeria. *Journal of Education and Learning*, *5*(2), 1–8.

Ogundipe, O. O. (2005). *The Librarianship of Developing Countries: the librarianship of diminished resources*. Lagos, Nigeria: Ikofa Press Limited.

Omekwu, C. O., & Echezona, R. I. (2008). *Emerging challenges and opportunities for Nigerian libraries in global information environment*. Paper presented at the 46th annual NLA conference in Kaduna, Nigeria.

Pant, A. (2014). Distance Learning: History, Problems and Solutions. *Advances in Computer Science and Information Technology*, *1*(2), 65–70.

Peacock, J. (2005). Information literacy education in practice. In P. Levy & S. Roberts (Eds.), *Developing the New Learning Environment: The Changing Role of the Academic Librarian* (pp. 153–180). London, UK: Facet Publishing. Available at http://eprints.qut.edu.au/archive/ 00000706/01/Peacock_Levy2.PDF

Radford, W. (2011). Learning at a Distance: Undergraduate Enrollment in Distance Education Professional approach. *INFOLIB*, *7*(1-4), 19–23.

Rashid, N., & Rashid, M. (2012). Issues and problems in distance education. *Turkish Online Journal of Distance Education*, *13*(1), 20–26.

Rena, R. (2007). Challenges in introducing distance education programme in Eritrea: Some observations and implications. *Turkish Online Journal of Distance Education*, *8*(1), 191–205.

Rosenberg, D. (2005). *Towards the digital library: Findings of an investigation to establish the current status of university libraries in Africa*. Oxford, UK: INASP.

Rothblatt, S., Muller, D. K., Ringer, F., Simon, B., Bryant, M., Roach, J., ... Simmons, D. E. (2002). The forum report: e-learning adoption rates and barriers. In A. Rossett (Ed.), *The ASTD E-Learning Handbook* (pp. 19–23). New York, NY: McGraw-Hill.

Rothblatt, S. (1988). Supply and demand: The "two histories" of English education. *History Education Quarterly, 28*(4), 627-644.

Tanner, S., & Deegan, M. (2011). Inspiring research, inspiring scholarship. In *The Value and Benefits of Digitised Resources for Learning, Teaching, Research and Enjoyment*. London, UK: JISC. Retrieved from http://www.kdcs.kcl.ac.uk/fileadmin/ documents/Inspiring_Research_Inspiring_Scholarsh ip_2011_SimonTanner.pdf

Traxler, J. (2018). Distance Learning—Predictions and Possibilities. *Turkish Online Journal of Distance Education, 8*(2), 136-145.

Ugwuanyi, C. F. (2011). Influence of ICT literacy skills on its application for library use among academic librarians in south east Nigeria. *Journal of Education and Learning, 5*(2).

Verma, M. K., & Verma, N. K. (2014). Concept of hybrid, digital and virtual library: A professional approach. *InfoLib*, *7*(14), 19–23.

Vrana, R. (2017). The perspective of use of digital libraries in era of e-learning. In 40th jubilee international convention-MIPRO 2017. Croatian Society for Information and Communication Technology, Electronics and Microelectronics-MIPRO. doi:10.23919/MIPRO.2017.7973555

Yusuf, M. O. (2006). Problems and prospects of open and distance education in Nigeria. *Turkish Online Journal of Distance Education*, *7*(1), 22–29.

Chapter 12
Metaliteracy in Academic Libraries:
Learning in Research Environment

Shiva Kanaujia Sukula
Jawaharlal Nehru University, India

ABSTRACT

Metaliteracy is very significant as it recognizes the conventional information skills. The framework of metaliteracy is staged on information literacy including new facets. The relevance of metaliteracy for the students is crucial in developing metaliterate learners. Discerning the goals and various learning objectives are concrete competencies and metaliteracy for the learning are the basic components. The elements of information literacy have been associated with social media in recent times. Digital literacy is accompanied with visual literacy as well as cyberliteracy in developing the metaliteracy resources and environment. In this current age, where the information has its own value in all the known and unknown contexts, the research is based on retrospective and the latest information. The discussion on the application of metaliteracy in learning and stake-holders considers as a reflective space with the analytical and observational thinking for the learning. The role of the librarian is instrumental while the creation of content takes place keeping the metaliteracy aspects in planning. The experiences of networked information, as well as engagement of students, are the stepping stones for the creation of learning spaces. The role of the learner as participants, contributor and metaliteracy and learner-centered design is associated with metaliteracy and course-design. In this context, the metaliteracy assignments are significant, the metaliteracy assignments are kind of a method to motivate the learners and find out hidden knowledge. The chapter provides an example of the Case of Jawaharlal Nehru University, New Delhi.

DOI: 10.4018/978-1-5225-8437-7.ch012

It discusses the methods applied at Dr. B. R. Ambedkar Central Library, Jawaharlal Nehru University, New Delhi for inducing information literacy and metaliteracy among the scholars to include various training programs, workshops, etc. The details of various activities are discussed as various training programs which are focused on educating the users about library resources, accessing them, etc.

INTRODUCTION

The scholars are using various media such as blogging, digital devices, MOOCs etc. for creating and sharing of information. In this context the concept and term of 'metaliteracy' coined by experts Mackey and Jacobson understands the recognition of complex information literacy scenario. The metaliteracy recognizes the conventional information skills, given as following:

1. Determination
2. Access to information
3. Location of information
4. Understanding the process and information
5. Production of information output
6. Usage of information by the users.

The metaliteracy concentrates upon the role of participatory digital environments. The participation is established through collaboration among users, production of information and finally sharing of information for repeat of collaboration as well as generating information products. This collaboration and sharing of information involves:

1. Significance of media and visual literacy, digital literacy
2. Engagement of contributors in the technological niche
3. Understanding of technology spaces.

The framework of metaliteracy is staged on information literacy including new facets. The explanation of Metaliteracy reflects "learners to engage in the information environment as active, self-reflective, and critical contributors to the collaborative spaces" relate to the current virtual world (Mackey, & Jacobson, 2014, p.14). It is observed that metaliteracy has a significant component in the form of 'metacognition'. The concept of metacognition makes us understanding and having the knowledge "about one's own thinking."

Relevance of Metaliteracy for the Students: Developing Metaliterate Learners

The metaliteracy confirms the roles of users as learners as well as creators of information. The information environment of current days supports the metaliteracy in the participative and collaborative scenarios. The information users also alter their status from information literate to meta-literate. Conversing about the connected world gives few glimpses about the empowerment of users; including the following attributes:

1. Critical thinking
2. Augmented nature to consume information
3. Creation and sharing of information
4. Navigation among the vast resources
5. Evaluation and reviewing the information output in various settings.

The users in connected information scenario collaborate and access the Massive Open Online Courses (MOOCs), including online resources. The activeness among the users is differentiable from conventional users; as they become self-reflective and self-reliant. The informed consumer turns into an active contributor due to metaliteracy. This depends upon continuous improvement in abilities such as:

1. Searching through the plethora of information,
2. Evaluation of process as well as retrieved information.
3. Expansion and further application of critical thinking capabilities are instrumental for research.

The scholars go for lifelong learning and in such areas, the metaliteracy and related course-works are significant for them. Such programs are useful for learners who are interested in seeking knowledge in a changed niche, to develop various competencies. The learners begin to understand the kind of strategies useful for metaliteracy among them.

Discerning the Goals and various Learning Objectives

Various aspects are related to metaliteracy and its relation with learners. Various goals, aims, and objectives are based upon information literacy. The various facets related to metaliteracy are as following:

1. Behavioral

2. Cognitive
3. Affective
4. Metacognitive

The status of meta-literate users is achieved due to continuous exposure and enhanced learning in the information environment which is highly evolving in nature. The information landscape is unevenly altering; demanding the attention in all the concerned areas. The choice of goals and framed objectives provide the guidelines to the instructors also. The importance of methods, learning goals and contexts is related to scales as well as flexibility in the system. Various aims and objectives are as following:

1. Evaluation of content as well as user's perception
2. Providing an interactive platform and engaging the users with information
3. Creation of information and collaboration among the users.
4. Devising the tools and techniques for learning

Concrete Competencies and Metaliteracy for the Learning

The competencies among learners are must for becoming meta-literate or metaliteracy-savvy. Kinds of competence in a user reflect the combination of possessed knowledge and willingness to learn the innovative techniques. Various competencies in the form of literacies are as following:

1. ICT Literacy
2. Digital and Cyberliteracy
3. Mobile Literacy
4. Media / New Media Literacy including Visual Literacy
5. Transliteracy

Information Literacy

The elements of information literacy have been associated with social media in recent times. The times have witnessed the role of collaborative communities in the online medium. The learners participate in a highly interactive and collaborative environment, which are networked in nature. This pervasive online nature of the information world is providing various forms (i.e. fluidic in nature) of information. The inclusion of web 2.0 and social media with the information literacy has emerged as metaliteracy; compelling information users and service providers to rethink the previous practices of information literacy. The inherent characteristics and connections of various interrelated components of information literacy have been instrumental for the development of a metaliteracy model. The redevelopment of information literacy into metaliteracy has brought out the suitability for interactive and collaborative electronic environments. The usage of technology and information skills has been persuasive in adapting the metaliteracy among the learners.

Digital Literacy

Digital literacy is the skill and ability to judge the online results a user finds, in general. In this context, Paul Gilster defines digital literacy as "the ability to access networked computer resources and use them," which encompasses both the "access" and "use" characteristics of information literacy. Further (Barbara R. Jones-Kavalier and Suzanne L. Flannigan) "the ability to read and interpret media (text, sound, images), to reproduce data and images through digital manipulation, and to evaluate and apply new knowledge gained from digital environments" is a comprehensive definition and explanation on digital literacy. The users apply the analytical way of thinking and evaluation in a digital environment. But digital literacy is needed to be understood in different contexts. If compared with information literacy, it is associated with digital environments only. While discussing the Information Communication and Technology (ICT), it is assumed as "using digital technology, communications tools, and/or networks to access, manage, integrate, evaluate, and create information in order to function in a knowledge society" (by the International ICT Literacy Panel). The ICT Literacy is more concerned with the technical aspects such as the efficiency of technology usage etc.

Visual Literacy

The visual literacy and competency are related to visual and design issues. As defined, "a visually literate person can communicate information in a variety of forms and appreciate the masterworks of visual communication" (JonesKavalier and Flannigan), relate to the sense of design reflecting the participation in the digital niche. Visual literacy has also been defined as a lifelong learning competency (Peter Felton) related to images, pictures, and objects. The visual literacy helps in understanding like visual designers. This competency equips the learners with the confidence to explore further.

Cyberliteracy

The term cyberliteracy was introduced by Laura J. Gurak. According to her, "cyberliteracy means voicing an opinion about what these technologies should become and being an active, not passive participant." It is clear that this literacy is related to the World Wide Web and Internet-based environments. The active participation from the user is one of the main characteristics of this literacy, along with the critical consumption of web-based content available through various media (Evelyn Stiller and Cathie LeBlanc). The cyberliteracy is comprised of issues such as privacy issues, kinds of communications and accessibility.

Transliteracy

The new media has compelled to the emergence and development "transliteracy", which is "the ability to read, write and interact across a range of platforms, tools, and media from signing through handwriting, print, TV, radio, and film, to digital social networks" (Thomas et al.) Transliteracy expresses about the inclusion of multiple methodologies. In this context, the new media literacy has been identified as the "key unifying principles" (Renee Hobbs) as the "representations of the world." The metaliteracy has taken approaches to include the 'collaborative media production.' So the modern times are considering that the metaliteracy has strengthened the relations and connections among various kinds of literacies.

DEVELOPING METALITERACY RESOURCES AND ENVIRONMENT

In this current age, where the information has its own value in all the known and unknown contexts, the research is based on retrospective and the latest information. The role of research is found as an inquisitive entity. The inquiry through research involves the knowledge and skills to bring out the best suitable information from myriad sources. The users turn towards the digital information world with the research-oriented mind. The creation of information in this context paves way for the constructed as well as contextual authority. The further roles of scholarly communication are surfaced as the conversation among academic users or intellectuals in a setting. Here the information searching becomes a task and demands an appropriate strategy. The libraries play a vital responsibility in facilitating the search by becoming a key partner with the faculty. The library collaborates with faculty members, specialized instructors, etc. This partnership and collaborative relationship create a platform for designing the coursework as well as methods of instructions covering the wide range of concepts along with and techniques. The development of metaliteracy sources and activities involves a number of components. These

1. Assigning the responsibility to the learners in order to understand their roles according to meta-literate Learner Model.
2. Creation of audio-visual material for the inter-related concepts.
3. Spreading the collaborative ideas and nurture them.
4. Development of assignment for learners as roles of instructors to be played by them.

Such components invite attention towards few aspects; bringing together various projects involving creativity; assessing the learners' aspirations as well as the depth of knowledge, and evaluating the role and significance of open educational resources in the context of metaliteracy.

METALITERACY AND MOOCS

The "Massive Open Online Course" (MOOC) appeared to revolutionize the academic scenario. The learning experiences due to MOOCs have changed the students' perceptions; the breaking of geographical barriers and connecting with global learning sources has happened. The instructors are finding a wide range of resources and platforms along with opportunities. The classroom is global-size big and the extension is beyond the boundaries. The MOOCs are not only technological solutions but also provides pedagogy a different way of earning. The availability of network-based learning platforms, resources, and student-oriented approach are the basic infrastructure as well as futuristic needs.

To leverage and get benefited from the various 'attributes' of MOOC platforms, the understanding of transformation is needed. The following examples express the roles and responsibilities played:

- **cMOOCs:** The 'connectivist theory' is: relating to the "network-based pedagogy". (Downes, 2007), the connectivist or "cMOOCs" are an example.
- **xMOOC:** In this context, "xMOOC" platforms, which include Coursera, are different from cMOOCs due to scalable content delivery.

- **Hybrid and blended MOOCs:** Since The cMOOCs provide collaborative opportunity and xMOOC platforms are providing presentations centrally. The time has witnessed the arrival of hybrid and blended MOOCs. The emerging times have forced to review the cMOOCs and xMOOC platforms. Thus blending the characteristics of previous one into the later emergent platform.

The decentralized models have the following attributes:

1. Evaluative capacity for decision-making,
2. Adaptability to the learning niche

The learners are required to play of roles of contributors as well as users in the decentralized learning model. The utility of metaliteracy is functional to overcome the challenges of MOOC which have user-centric structures. According to Mackey & Jacobson (2011), "Metaliteracy expands the scope of information literacy as more than a set of discrete skills, challenging us to rethink information literacy as active knowledge production and distribution in collaborative online communities".

The Applications and Answers Needed!

1. Utilization of MOOC platforms within metaliteracy substructure.
2. Application of metaliteracy for pedagogy related functions in the learning scenario.
3. Approaches in MOOCs and outcomes for self-regulated learner's activity
4. The design and implementation of Metaliteracy MOOCs in various technological contexts.
5. Social media, participatory environments, and metaliteracy; in the context of redefining the practices of information literacy.
6. Networked environment and metaliteracy finding roles for teaching practices.

BRIDGING THE MOOCS AND PEDAGOGY THROUGH METALITERACY

The MOOCs have been associated with the 'self-regulated learning' along with few psychological challenges such as flexibility of the structure and nature, responsibility of the learner, less-deviating features, and autonomy of learning. The diversity and variety of various MOOCs platforms and learners make is nearly difficult to provide the individual attention. The learners are required and motivated as well for self-learning. The pedagogy is different when compared between the routine online learning environment and the MOOCs platforms.

The self-regulatory skills are not only essential but also guide the learning in such metaliteracy based environment. The self-regulating attributes of learners have variations due to their psychosocial and cognitive abilities. Such attributes and abilities are associated with motivation and involvement within the metaliteracy framework based learning scenario. The student-centered MOOCs are both 'boon and bane' if not found in relation to student's psychological abilities. The metaliteracy provides a connection between learners and MOOCs along with a focus on active learning. The networked environment requires some sociological features associated with pedagogy while the learners interact and share information; these features are as follows:

1. Navigation in the vast learning materials.
2. Evaluating the various forms of information,
3. Augmenting the analytical thinking

APPLICATION OF METALITERACY IN LEARNING AND STAKE-HOLDERS

The metaliteracy provides a platform for an interactive pedagogy involving the inquisitive minds of learners. The students find metaliteracy and such pedagogy as a reflective space with the analytical and observational thinking for the learning. The metaliteracy is quite pervasive, especially in academic and special libraries. In this context, the academic librarians, information service providers from various backgrounds in mutual understanding with scholars and users of the library are practicing the metaliteracy. The perception for the networked knowledge and navigating within is also affected in an increasing manner. Here the metaliteracy acts as a promotional tool with an in-depth approach involving the thorough teamwork in the form of participation, collaboration, and further mind-application. The role of metaliteracy has 'metacognition' as an intrinsic learning characteristic. In this way, "a metacognitive approach to information literacy allows us to move beyond rudimentary skills development and prepares students to dig deeper and assess their own learning" (Mackey & Jacobson; 2014). The metacognitive learning is extended towards the various arena such as open technological and learning spaces, virtual environments; related to that MOOCs are providing learning strategies. The emerging literacy along with the established ones, the metaliteracy has become umbrella literacy for the faculty members and students. The educational initiatives and ventures including metaliteracy are inviting interests and transferring the knowledge. The ideas are becoming easily exchanged due to the inclusion of learner's metacognition. The relationship is well understood what is established between metaliteracy and various newer technologies, the efforts and steps towards digital learning are supporting the inclusion of social networking and media. The neo-structuring and discovery of information literary within has been reframed as metaliteracy at the College & Research Libraries, way back during 2011. This gave the development of a connectivist MOOC and a Coursera MOOC, later on. The instructional and organizational design settings are created in order to fulfill the informational requirements of library professionals and the concerned learning facilitators. These professionals consider and evaluate the wide range of practices and endeavors for the learners' enthusiasm and success.

ROLE OF LIBRARIAN BOTH AS INSTRUCTIONAL AND COLLECTION DEVELOPMENT LIBRARIAN

The role of the librarian is instrumental while the creation of content takes place keeping the metaliteracy aspects in planning. At various libraries, there may be similarity in framework, goals, course-works, and evaluation, etc. The libraries focus on strengthening the skills among students contextual of metaliteracy; by pragmatic and experience-based practices. The kinds of interaction and content define the learning outcome along with the encouragement received from the library. The examples are comprised of activities related to libguides, Wikipedia, including several social media platforms.

The two intrinsic components such as self-awareness and self-reflective activities are crucial while the assessment takes place. The assessment includes 'written reflection' as well as the learners' surveys. The evaluation of the process for completing the assignment is also significant. In this context, (Mackey and Jacobson), the metaliteracy framework include various skills such as" behavioral, cognitive, affective, and metacognitive". Various 'practitioners' such as Donna Witek and Teresa Grettano; Barbara J. D'Angelo and Barry M. Maid; Sandra K. Cimbricz and Logan Rath; and Paul Prinsloo have found the metaliteracy having a dynamic role as well as contributing in the usage of library resources. According to Prinsloo, "literacy-as-agency is a prerequisite to living a fully human, dignified life" provides an examination. The librarians understand the broader framework of human needs and their impact on the niche in which they habitat. The role of libraries as agencies to encourage the application of metaliteracy has been found impressive as well as demanding. Practicing metaliteracy for those who have teaching roles in organizations are the platforms for interaction with the students. Such interactions provide guidelines while planning some course since the beginning or redefining the modules in between related with the metaliteracy.

DESIGNING FOR STUDENT-CENTERED LEARNING

The students are a pivotal component in the design of MOOCs when we talk about the metaliteracy. The experiences of networked information, as well as the engagement of students, are the stepping stones for the creation of learning spaces. The challenge of the ownership of the received learning is one of the significant features of metaliteracy. The learning and translating that learning into actions is a constant component of metaliteracy. The students reflect the practices being done by them in the online environments playing roles as consumers and producers (Mackey & Jacobson, 2014). In a decentralized learning environment, the learners function as an agency themselves as the learning meant for their own. The "personal learning networks" (Dunaway, 2011, p.682), create the position of students at the center of learning related with the processes of information (Mackey & Jacobson, 2014) along with the various roles. These roles may be categorized as "participants, contributors, and teachers" in the learning arena.

LEARNER AS PARTICIPANTS

The early MOOCs were considered as "community of practitioners" by Downes (2011) due to their methods of completing tasks. The learning of metaliteracy and practicing the same is related to practicing and being self-directed students as well as self-reflective consumers of information. The environment of metaliteracy provides an opportunity to bring together learners and instructors and engaging them for collaborative learning. The collaborative learning environment gives ample opportunities for participation due to active engagement, intricate interpretation and receiving responses. There has been a shift from the teacher-centric information environment to the learner-centric due to the integration of learner-generated components. The organization of content has been found in topics, including the overview as well as a few key readings. Such arrangements provided the platform for broader discussions and in-depth interaction with the content.

The definitions and interpretations of the students are pivotal components in the metaliteracy. Keeping personal blogs, using the readings, finding spaces for own understanding depend upon certain activities such as remixing as well as repurposing the metaliteracy concepts and definitions along with the meanings. These platforms provide a facility for conversations, engagement, and webinars, etc. The learners get in touch not only with the course content but also the recordings of themed talks to explore various concepts such as "metacognition, visual literacy, open learning, global perspectives related to literacy, media, and news literacy, digital storytelling, and technobiophilia" (Thomas, 2013). The 'real time' and 'real world' routines make the metaliteracy worthwhile (Mackey et al., 2015, p. 34–40). The active engagement of students with guest instructors or speaker is significant. The in-house, as well as guest instructors, intend to cover various issues and a wide range of components of metaliteracy.

METALITERACY AND LEARNER-CENTERED DESIGN

Various components complete the metaliteracy for the students; these components are animations, lectures, narrations, videos, interviews. These components are useful for engaging the students in types of documents such as open source information material and instructor-created materials. The variation in content, style, and presentation facilitate the fun in learning. The fluidity in the structure, of course, is significant for the learners. The opportunity to contribute and interrogate for the learners and helps in the assignment completion. The participation in open discussion forums involves initiating threads; discussing queries make the learner engaged in metaliteracy concepts. The direction of learning is based on content and defined the scope in the course modules. The open source materials also support the metaliteracy learning. The "flexible pedagogy" principle is based on 'gaming' style, creation of the videos with the software, periodical quests, digital badge, and digital portfolios including students' active participation. The students utilize discussion forums for course navigation and solving queries with proper dialogue.

LEARNER AS CONTRIBUTOR

The creative aspect of metaliteracy is that it allows the learners to play the roles of consumer as well as creator in the information niche. In this context, Siemens (2012) stated about the "learners need to create and share stuff." The learner's 'personal learning networks' support the creation of new knowledge (Downes, 2011, section 4). The observations inform about the facility provided by the learner-centered course designing to students in functioning as a contributor in the networked environment along with other participants. The engagement, either in a focus group or wider learners' community, provides interaction as well as opportunities for sharing the content while going through the course.

METALITERACY AND COURSE-DESIGN

The course designing in the perspectives of metaliteracy is related to pedagogy and focus on learning the outcome. According to Terras and Ramsay (2015), "Meta-cognition captures the ability to reflect on how we think and learn, and students who apply metacognitive reflection, especially those who are highly self-regulated and accept responsibility for directing their own learning are more effective learners". In this context, metaliteracy is supposed to function as a tool of motivation for the students to participate actively in the learning process and reflect the different pedagogy skills. The following components are significant in metaliteracy course designing:

1. The goals and aims of course
2. The structure and contents of assignments
3. The framing of schedule for the learners

The above components are built and considered keeping the learners and instructors, both in mind. There may be few or more instances of including social media or other interactive platforms. The classroom learning becomes more than instructor-focused; the learner-centric. The course designing allows the students to analyze and investigate the contents and methods to develop information literacy as well as practicing vehicles of learning. The revisions in the courses are must steps; the pedagogical rationale involves various aspects such as contents and outcomes of revisions with the aim to know the results of those revisions. This task reflects the relation between the method of revising and impact on the metaliteracy on the learners as well as trainers. The metaliteracy approach is taken into consideration for designing the course which involves the analysis of units and consisting elements of the course-syllabus across the curriculum.

METALITERACY ASSIGNMENTS

The metaliteracy assignments are kind of a method to motivate the learners and find out hidden knowledge. This is more than skills-having activity. The encouragement received from the metaliteracy assignments allows self-regulatory learning among the students. The assignments induce smartness in the learner by providing a wide range of sources, choices of learning methods, and relevancy of the practices for the future. A number of audio-visual inclusions can be utilized for the learners. Since the class include learners from across the world, the involvement of different kinds of tools is possible. The learning environment relates to the use of metaliteracy-related elements. The metaliteracy in the classroom is about experimenting with the aims and objectives of learning along with the various methods classroom. The innovative and interactive 'metaliteracy' has characterized the students as capable learners with active participation. They are consuming as well as creating content due to being continuously motivated the metaliteracy-based information niche. This is the outcome of analytical thinking and knowledge of various competencies and literacies. The instructor's role augments courage to learn new technologies, methods to solve information related requirements and become self-aware of needs and purposes. Such instructors create learners as information producers. Sometimes the students in the classroom are in need of general education; few may require the research related learning. The class may be a mix of different backgrounds yet common goals. The classroom activity may range from reading a piece to the discussion; blogging and its use for the students for the learners' views. The learning activities include quizzes, the formation of annotated bibliography on a particular subject, sharing of information, creation of a Twitter account, tag cloud, and multimedia presentations.

THE CASE OF JAWAHARLAL NEHRU UNIVERSITY, NEW DELHI

The methods applied at Dr. B. R. Ambedkar Central Library, Jawaharlal Nehru University, New Delhi for inducing information literacy and metaliteracy among the scholars include various training programs, workshops, etc. The details of various activities are discussed as follows:

Training Program

The training programs are focused on educating the users about library resources, accessing them etc. The training programs are meant not only for the common students but also the visually impaired students. The inclusion of lessons on assistive technologies is an example of comprehensive learning. The various aspects are expressed in Tables 1 and 2.

Table 1. Training programs organized for the scholars during 2015-2017

Sl. No.	Training Programs	Date
1.	"Access and Use of e-Book"	31 March 2017
2.	"SciFinder for Academic Research"	8 October 2015
3	"URKUND Plagiarism detection tool provided by INFLIBNET"	21 September 2015
4.	"Assistive Technologies for Visually Challenged Research Scholars & Students"	15 September 2015
5.	"Orientation Program on Library Resources and Research Support Services"	27 August 2015

Table 2. Training Programs organized for the scholars during 2012-2014

Sl. No.	Training Programs	Year
1.	"Orientation program on Library E-Resources and Services"	2014
2.	"Discovery services"	2014
3.	"How to use EBSCO E-Books Library"	2014
4.	"Hands-on Training and Practices for offering Library Services"	2013
5.	"Assistive Technologies for Visually Challenged Research Scholars & Students"	2013
6.	"Orientation program on Library E-Resources and Services"	2013
7.	"Creation of JNU ETD Archive using Dspace"	2013
8.	"DIGITAL RESOURCES"	2012
9.	"Training of Master Trainers in use of ASSISTIVE TECHNOLOGIES"	2012
10.	"USER EDUCATION-CUM-ORIENTATION- DIGITAL RESOURCES"	2012
11.	"EDS (EBSCO Discovery Service) of JNU Library"	2012

Lecture Series:

The lecture series provides extensive learning and understanding among the students. The topics and durations are given in Tables 3 through 6.

Workshops Organized by the Library

The library organized workshops on various topics such as using similarity detection tools, reference management tools, searching for information from an institutional repository, etc.

Table 3. Lecture Series Programs organized for the scholars during 2015-2017

Sl. No.	Lecture Series	Year
1.	"28th Library Lecture Series and Outreach Programme"	2017
2.	"Ashok Jambhekar Memorial Lecture"	2017
3.	"Research Evaluation"	2017
4.	"Research Support Services at Academic Libraries in the USA… Thinking Out of the Box"	2016
5.	"Are we silent victims of plagiarism?"	2015
6.	"World Bank and Knowledge sharing session on Plagiarism and How to get it published in Academic Journals"	2015
7.	"Addressing Inequality in South Asia"	2015
8.	"Libraries and Development: On the Agenda"	2015
9.	"Information/digital literacy initiatives at Rice-Aron Library at Marlboro College, USA and JNU Library"	2015

Table 4. Lecture series programs organized for the scholars during 2014

Sl. No.	Lectures	Year
1.	"North Carolina State University Libraries: Trends and Challenges"	2014
2.	"Enabling Open Scholarship: Open Access Policies, Issues, and Resources for Higher Education Institutions"	2014
3.	"EXPANDING INNER HORIZONS!"	2014
4.	"Developments at the UK Open University Library"	2014
5.	"Library Science and Librarianship in Swaziland: An overview"	2014
6.	"Rock your paper: An open access repository"	2014
7.	"Common heritage of Indian and Turkic people, lexical elements"	2014

Table 5. Lecture series programs organized for the scholars during 2013

Sl. No.	Lecture Series	Year
1.	"Large-Scale Multimedia Digital Library Collections: Challenges and Research Opportunities"	29 November 2013
2.	"Quality Assessment and Open Access at the Faculty of Fine, Applied and Performing Arts, University of Gothenburg, Sweden"	2013
3.	"Art and Science of Online Search Strategies for Research Scholars"	2013
4.	"Launching chat reference, Facebook, Twitter & other social media initiatives in a University Library"	2013
5.	"Building a Print Fanzine Collection in a Digital Era"	2013
6.	"Databib: Cataloging the World's Data Repositories"	2013
7.	Laptop Distribution among Visually Impaired Research Scholars of JNU	2013
8.	"Keeping it Glocal: Best Practices for International Outreach in an Academic Library"	2013

Table 6. Lecture series programs organized for the scholars during 2012

Sl. No.	Lecture Series	Year
1.	"Knowledge Management in Academic Libraries Southern African perspectives"	2012
2.	"Depleting Archives and Disintegrating Histories"	2012
3.	"Creating Socio-economic Value through Open Public Data"	2012
4.	"E-books: Choices and Challenges"	2012
5.	"Embedded Librarianship New ways of building a relationship with Faculty"	2012
6.	"Documentation of Oral History: Experiences at South Asian Oral History project at the University of Washington Libraries"	2012

Table 7. Workshops organized to equip the students with latest technologies during 2014-2017

Sl. No.	Workshop topics	Year
1.	Plagiarism and Reference Management Tools	2017
2.	Plagiarism and Reference Management	2017
3.	Institutional Digital Repository and Metadata Engineering	2016
4.	Turnitin and Reference Management Tool	2016
5.	"Plagiarism and how to publish in Academic Journals"	2015
6.	"Plagiarism and Reference Management"	2015
7.	"Digitization, Digitization Project Management and Digital Archiving: A Workshop for Librarians"	2014
8.	"Book Care, Repair and Restoration"	2014
9.	"Plagiarism and Reference Management using Mendeley"	2014
10.	"SWATCHHA BHARAT ABHIYAN"	2014
11.	"Mendeley Workshop"	2014

Various other topics such as data curation, creative writing, scholarly writing, digital archiving, digital information preservation have been taught to students. The following table expresses the organization of such workshops and the areas of learning.

CONCLUSION

The metaliterary empowers the learners to collect, understand, evaluate, construct and generate the information. The development of dynamic environment happens for the creation and enhancement of the data. The students learn evaluation and management of information along with the understanding the impact of metaliteracy

Table 8. Workshops organized to equip the students with the latest technologies during 2012-2013

Sl. No.	Workshop topics	Year
1.	"Data Curation in the University: Libraries, Research, and Learning"	2013
2.	How to Write for and Get Published in the Best Journals	2013
3.	"Capacity Building on Digitization, Digital Archiving and Digital Preservation in Media Libraries and Archives"	2013
4.	"Author Workshop"	2013
5.	"Wiley Author Workshop "	2012
6.	"Elsevier Science Author Workshop"	2012
7.	"How to Write for and Get Published in Scientific Journals"	2012
8.	"Development of Institutional Repository using Dspace with special reference to the creation of ETD Archive"	2012

in their learning. The engagement with the information is strengthened and the users of information reach towards the achievement of their academic or other intellectual goals. The active applications of methods and learning occur in various contexts. The metaliteracy is instrumental in creating reliance upon the diverse learning environments. In this current age of IT governed aspects of the learning environment, the awareness and practices of metaliteracy should be extended, collaborated and made available to a larger number of people. The domains such as behavioral, cognitive, affective and metacognitive should be taken into consideration for the broader interests in learning communities.

REFERENCES

Downes, S. (2007). What connectivism is [Web log post]. Available at http://halfanhour. blogspot.com/2007/02/what-connectivism-is.html

Downes, S. (2011, Jan. 5). "Connectivism" and connective knowledge. *The Huffington Post.*

Dunaway, M. K. (2011). Connectivism: Learning theory and pedagogical practice for networked information landscapes. *RSR. Reference Services Review*, *39*(4), 675–685. doi:10.1108/00907321111186686

Mackey, T. P., Forte, M., Allain, N., Jacobson, T. E., & Pitera, J. (2015). MOOC talk: A connectivist dialogue about our metaliteracy MOOC experience. *All About Mentoring, 46*, 34–40. Retrieved from https://www.esc.edu/news/magazines-journal/all-about-mentoring

Mackey, T. P., & Jacobson, T. E. (2011). Reframing information literacy as a metaliteracy. *College & Research Libraries, 72*(1), 62–78. doi:10.5860/crl-76r1

Mackey, T. P., & Jacobson, T. E. (2014). *Metaliteracy: Reinventing information literacy to empower learners*. Chicago, IL: ALA Neal-Schuman.

Metaliteracy Learning Collaborative. (2014, Sept. 11). Goals and learning objectives: Developing meta-literate learners [Web log post]. Retrieved from https://metaliteracy.org/learning-objectives

Prinsloo, P. (2016). Metaliteracy, networks, agency, and praxis. In T. E. Jacobson & T. P. Mackey (Eds.), *Metaliteracy in practice* (pp. 183–201). Chicago, IL: ALA Neal-Schuman.

Siemens, G. (2012, June 3). *What is the theory that underpins our MOOCs?* Retrieved from http://www.elearnspace.org/blog/2012/06/03/what-is-the-theory-that-underpins-our-moocs/

Terras, M., & Ramsay, J. (2015). Massive open online courses (MOOCs): Insights and challenges from a psychological perspective. *British Journal of Educational Technology, 46*(3), 472–487. doi:10.1111/bjet.12274

Thomas, S. (2013). *Technobiophilia: Nature and cyberspace*. London, UK: Bloomsbury Academic.

Chapter 13
Technological Innovation in Academic Libraries Among Universities:
Librarians' Perceptions and Perspectives

Champeswar Mishra
Tripura University, India

Surendra Kumar Pal
Tripura University, India

Amitabh Kumar Manglam
Tripura University, India

ABSTRACT

Innovation is no longer an option but a necessity for an organization to survive during a crisis. Innovations in terms of products, process, technologies, and services, can effectively be used to resolve the crisis of the current educational system to survive and thrive in the 21st century. Academic libraries should re-think and re-invent the existing technologies, services, and facilities to fulfill the demands of users. Management, organization, and dissemination of information can be done quickly and effectively with the application of information and communication technology (ICT) in an innovative way. Technological innovation (TI) can be considered as an innovative solution for the sustenance of libraries during a crisis. This chapter attempts to describe the essence of TI in academic libraries and highlights the perceptions of librarians on TI in the university libraries system in India. Therefore, this chapter will explore individual innovative behavior and its influencing factors on technological innovation in academic libraries in Indian universities.

DOI: 10.4018/978-1-5225-8437-7.ch013

BACKGROUND

Innovative behavior is considered as a crucial element for effective functioning and survival of the organization, as it leads to the implementation of new and useful methods for performance (Grant, 2000). Such behavior in employees has great importance for organizational outcomes; and in many organizations, different actions are taken to stimulate innovativeness within employees (Martins &Terblanche, 2003). Thanks to a rapidly changing environment, the realization of the importance of innovation towards organizational survival and success has been increasing significantly with every passing day. However, much literature has been developed pertaining to the domain of organizational innovation, while little has been studied on the construction at the individual level (Martin, Salanova & Peiro, 2007; Parker, Williams & Turner, 2006). During the last decade, there have been numerous innovations in terms of technologies, services, and tools developed, which have a significant impact on the higher education system. Innovation is no longer an option but a necessity for the organization to survive during a crisis. Innovative technologies, services, and tools can be potentially exploited to resolve the crisis of the current educational system to survive and thrive in the 21st century.

It may not be wrong to say that most of the academic libraries are dazed and confused in current times. They are trying hard to rework on their mission and relevance for technology, which anchored their knowledge over the past half millennium is being usurped, thanks to the rapid revolution of information technology. The development of print in the 15th century and the 19th-century industrialization of print has made libraries what they are, or to be precise, what they were. However, with the beginning of the Web era in 1993, the libraries had to decide with surety toward going beyond authority, control, and classification of information. They ought to redefine their roles in the current and future information ecology, lest they are content with being transformed to a little-used museum of the book (Lewis, 2007). Thus, the academic librarians must innovate to reinforce their utility.

Defining Technological Innovation

Innovation is discussed very frequently in the literature of academic libraries, but it remains an ambiguous and narrowly defined concept. Hence, it is important to analyze and argue the importance of innovation in the context of this study. Innovation is nothing but the newness in service, product, process, techniques, and methods applicable to an organization. Damanpour defined innovation as "the introduction into the organization of a new product, a new service, a new technology, or a new administrative practice; or a significant improvement to an existing product, service, technology, or administrative practice" (Damanpour, 1996). Baregheh, Rowley, and Sambrook(2009) categorically defined innovation as a multiple-stage process whereby "organizations transform ideas into new/improved products, service or processes, in order to advance, compete and differentiate themselves successfully in their marketplace". Based on the above concept and innovation frameworks, innovation can be of many types having the number of attributes and multiple stages on which organizations have to ultimately adapt and follow for survival and success. Draft differentiated the theory of innovation into three categories i.e administrative or technical, incremental or radical, and ambidexterity i.e the initiation and implementation stages of innovation (Daft 1978). Technological innovation is one of the important types of innovation, which is much essential in the digital era.

Technological Innovation (TI) is the combination of new products and processes having significant technological changes in products and processes in an organization. Technological innovation is the new invention and application of innovative technologies in products, processes, tools and value-added services in an organization. Specifically, technological innovation refers to the transformation of ideas in new and useful products and/or processes by the application of technologies for the improvement of an existing product, process, services, etc. Technological innovation has a positive impact on academic libraries due to the continuous emergence of new means of technological products, services, and tools, and its application ultimately helps the blended librarians to attract more users.

STATEMENT OF THE PROBLEM

In view of the growing uncertainty over the sustenance of the academic library, it becomes increasingly important to understand the effectiveness of technological innovation. Since the application of innovative technologies, services, and tools is highly anticipated in academic libraries, it has become a necessity among the librarians to be blended and innovative by displacing technological management skills in workplaces. Currently, stakeholders are unaware of the effectiveness and importance of technological innovation in the library in general, academic libraries in particular. Therefore, an empirical investigation was undertaken to explore the perceptions, perspectives, and effectiveness of technological innovation among the academic librarians in term of process, products, services, resources and facilities in organizational success. Also, this study will investigate the current evidenced-based innovative practices being followed in academic libraries, especially in the university library.

REVIEW OF LITERATURE

Information and Communication Technology (ICT) has influenced hugely library activities, services, and resources. ICT is no more an option but has become a necessity among academic libraries to thrive and survive in the 21st century. Academic libraries have to re-evaluate and re-think their traditional approach and services of libraries to overcome inadequacies and deficiencies by adopting innovative ICT technologies and tools for the larger benefit of the users. Recent trends in technological innovations such as Library automation and digitization; digital library; open access; virtual library; cloud computing; web-scale discovery; e-publishing; MOOC; M-Library; social media; remote library; digital literacy; 3-D technologies and virtual reference have emerged as innovative ideas that have influenced academic libraries. A paradigm change has been noticed in the 1990s in the application of ICT in academic libraries such as the internet, World Wide Web protocols, information retrieval standards, integrated library systems, virtual reference, online databases. In the 2000s, library noticed some kind of revolutionary changes in the form of digital libraries, virtual library, digital and virtual collections, paperless library, virtual representation, 24/7 instant remote access to unlimited resources due to rapid advancements and transformations in digital development such as computers and telecommunications. In the past two decades, globalization in libraries in the form of services and networking has been witnessed, which is very vital for the users. Thus, Prentice discussed that academic librarians as managers "must understand, anticipate and adapt rapidly changing factors influencing the libraries and advised library leaders react positively during the crisis by taking timely decisions to integrate changes in the information provision into library operations" (Prentice, 2005). The historical perspectives of technological innovation such as electric lighting, radio, television, ventilation, and telephones are important in the initial stage of technological innovation in libraries (Musmann, 1993). Rogers' (2003) diffusion of innovation theory can be adopted in libraries to understand the importance of technological innovation as a part of the technological integration and Roger's theory outlining technological innovation usually has at least some extent of benefit for adopting it by adopters. Lavoie, Henry, and Dempsey (2006) noticed that innovative technologies have brought out greater changes in libraries, where library expert systems, virtual library, digital collections, innovative web interfaces, library blogs, informative library portals, and personal web portals are the prominent adopters. Lukasiewicz (2007) highlights that changing demands of students in the academic environment need evidence-based innovative approaches by embracing digital technologies to fulfill demands through the application of technologies such as instant messaging (IM), podcasting and blogging. Her study further reveals that the use of social networking tools is widespread among the newest generation of students. Dunlap

(2008) urges librarians to adopt information technologies for the larger benefit of the academic community by adopting innovative technologies namely discovery tool, cloud computing, social media, WebOpac, online databases, open access in order to meet the challenges of new technologies as well as to provide innovative services to their patrons. Further, the study proposed library professionals to be innovative by enhancing skills and expertise on new information and communication technologies by participating in conferences, workshops, seminars for the implementation of innovative ideas in the library. The study conducted by Lietzau (2009) reveals that the web 2.0 technologies are truly innovative technologies that can be used to encourage patron's participation in the virtual environment. Vaughan (2007) has studied the perceptions and influences of technological innovation among the directors of the Association of Research Libraries (ARL). The study reveals that the application of innovative technologies such as web-scale discovery, makerspace, cloud hosting, and patron-driven acquisition is most significant among patrons where librarians as the leaders should quickly adopt to an academic library. Jantz (2012) study on innovation performance in academic research libraries is one of the significant studies which can be treated as a directive in adopting innovation in academic libraries. The study finds that five key variables, i.e organizational size, behavioral integration, decision awareness, structural differentiation, and ambidextrous orientation were very prominent and considered as significant predictors of the level of innovation in research libraries. Chen, Yao, and Jiang (2017) study on the application of new technologies in the context of technological innovation is to promote development and innovation in academic libraries in China. The study reveals that academic libraries are progressing and have shown a positive development in adopting technological innovation to meet user demands in the new information environment. Adopting rate of technological innovation among top ranking Universities in China is found positive, where reader-oriented strategies such as integration of OPAC, discovery systems, database, journal, and book navigation, and other searching functions in the most conspicuous location on the homepage are very prominent. Social media has a significant impact on academic librarians in providing necessary information to users. Social media are considered one of the fastest means to provide information. Social Networking Sites (SNSs) are becoming more and more popular among librarians in disseminating information and promoting services for users. Academic libraries are increasingly using social media to promote service and resource among faculty and students. Maness (2006) highlights the application of web 2.0 in academic libraries, including synchronous messaging and streaming media, blogs, wikis, social networks, tagging, RSS feeds, and Mashups have great influence in libraries in providing access to their collections and significant impact on technological innovation and it has been proposed that those libraries as forerunners must adapt to it in order to sustain during the crisis and must adapt for the foreseeable future. Farkas (2007) reveals that Facebook is one of the most popular social media tools that promote library services among faculty, students and staff in academic libraries, and librarians should adopt Facebook and Myspace to promote and market library services and resources among patrons. Chu and Du (2013) study are on the use of social media tools among 140 University libraries in Asia, North America and Europe. The study reveals that the adoption rate of social media is very significant; and Facebook, followed by Twitter, was the most used tools for users. Further, though the participation of library professionals is found positive, the negative attitude of library staff and the limited participation of users are the main barriers in adopting it. Web-scale discovery platform had been widely adopted among academic libraries across the world as "it is highly available, reliable, transparent, high performance, scalable, accessible, secure, usable, and inexpensive" (Teets, 2009). Among the open source platforms, VuFind is the very common innovative tool which is widely being used in libraries as noted by Emanuel (Emanuel, 2007). Similarly, Mehrjerdi (2009) study reveals that using Radio Frequency Identification (RFID) as a key innovative and emerging platform to reduce the time and speed in delivery of service in academic libraries. Wei (2015) highlights that Library Apps have seen as one of the innovative and emerging tools that are widely being used in library services to provide new services to patrons, and it has been predicted that in the future, smartphones are likely to become crucial for delivering contents and library services with the extensive use of the Mobile Library (M-Library) system.

Dynamic leadership, positive attitude and digital literacy skill are essential for librarians to use appropriate technologies in libraries for the benefit of patrons. Youngman (2009) assumed that technological innovation would continue to impact libraries that ultimately affect patrons. Klein, Conn, and Sorra (2001) observed that application of innovative technologies and tools more about an attitudinal concern than technical issue among librarians "as attitudes of librarians is of significance because if people responsible for implementing change respond poorly to it". Further, the study emphasizes that librarians need to have an understanding about complex and varied attitudes towards emerging technological innovations in libraries to effectively use the library's human resources and technologies. Librarians are the early and key adopters of technological innovation in their libraries as studied by Johnson and Magusin (2005). Sommers (2005) urges librarians to adopt the pro-active vision and blended approach while adopting technological innovation, thereby taking library services to a new height and expanding the role of libraries in the community.

There has been plenty of literature available on innovation in higher education and learning in developed countries, but limited research has been conducted on this topic in the developing country like India, particularly among the library professionals at the university level in India. This motivated the researchers to undertake a study, which will be helpful for decision makers, and Library and Information Science (LIS) professionals to adopt an evidence-based innovative approach in adopting technological innovation for facilitating and promoting services and resources in academic libraries in the digital era.

RESEARCH QUESTIONS

To fulfill the purposes of the study, the following research questions will be addressed in this study.

RQ 1: What is the scope, characteristics, and significance of innovation as understood by the academic librarians in university?

RQ 2: What are the stimulating factors that exhibit technological innovation or, alternatively act as barriers in adopting technological innovation in libraries?

RQ 3: How do they rate the adoption of technological evidence-based innovative approaches on technological innovation that will add value to users in the Library?

RQ 4: What are the innovative methods as perceived by the University librarians in stimulating skills and competencies on technological innovation in libraries?

RQ 5: How do the University librarians feel about technological innovations in academic libraries? Do they wish to adopt innovative technologies of the future to add value in your library?

RQ 6: What are the evidence-based innovative methods adopted by the academic librarians to manage electronic resources in academic libraries? What are the innovative strategies being adopted for the marketing of library services and resources?

SIGNIFICANCE OF THE STUDY

The main purpose of this study is to explore and investigate the perceptions of academic librarians on adoption of technological innovation in universities and its significance on organizational success amid changes due to the trends and challenges faced by today's libraries. The present research seeks to provide a theoretical framework for the understanding of factors facilitating and inhibiting the adoption of technological innovation in academic libraries. The insight and outcomes gained from this study may serve as a guide and foundation for future work to investigate more determinants on adoption and practices of technological innovation in different sectors of libraries in the turbulent environment. The magnitude of innovation varies by library and institution; in this context, it becomes more important to access whether "innovation and creativity" facilitate the transition to a new library paradigm. This study will underpin the importance of developing organizational capacity to generate and integrate cognitive diversity for the success of innovation. This study is significantly important due to the changing landscape of librarianship to sustain and thrive in the turbulent environment. The outcome of the study will help the policy makers, administrators, decision makers, etc. adopt innovative strategies and approaches, which could lead to improving libraries in terms of services, products, process, facilities, and resources that are vital to retaining the users of the organizations. This study is also significant, as there are currently no specific studies within the scholarly library literature that deals with the significance of technological innovation in academic libraries in the context of India and their possible influences on academic libraries in university. Thus, this study attempts to create literature that can help understand the characteristics and significance of technological innovation in the context of libraries in general, academic libraries in particular.

RESEARCH METHODOLOGY

In the present study, in order to collect relevant data from the respondents, a quantitative research methodology based on structured questionnaire within a naturalistic framework has been adopted to gather research data in the form of a survey method. Research questions were asked on background, demographic information, generational characteristics, and perceptions of technological innovation of academic librarians. As described by Westbrook, naturalistic design helps the researcher undertake basic research to add to the general knowledge of the respective field as well as helps determine new knowledge to aid in solving a particular problem (Westbrook, 1994). The questionnaires were distributed among the respondents through both emails and hardcopy. The questionnaires were collected via an online and personal meeting with the respondents. A total number of 52 questionnaires were distributed among librarians (n=52) of all disciplines, of which n=38 (73%) responses were received from the respondents for the study. The Likert scale was used to measure the perception and attitude of respondents, which they were agreed or disagreed with particular questions in this study. The survey data from questionnaires were exported to Excel and SPSS for analysis. The quantitative data were analyzed predominately by means of descriptive statistics.

FINDINGS

The findings of the study reveal the following answers to the research questions about the perceptions of librarians on technological innovation in academic libraries in university.

RQ 1: What is the scope, characteristics, and significance of innovation as perceived by the academic librarians?

The findings of the study from Table 1, perceptions of innovation among respondents were asked in the scale of "yes" and "no". The table very much depicted that a large number of respondents showed positivity towards organizational innovation in terms of feeling of doing something new (100%); pro-active involvement and showing dynamic in work for sustaining (100%); awareness in the term innovation (100%); innovation as one the critical factors to sustain and survive of Library (100%); application of ICT as stimulating factor with special emphasis on Technological Innovation (TI) (100%) and significance of TI for organizational direction and goal (100%). Thus, the study reveals that the perception of librarians on innovation in the digital era was positive and considered as one of the significant factors for providing services and resources to academic libraries.

RQ 2: What are the factors that you feel stimulating innovation in the context of technological innovation in your Library?

In Table 2, factors that stimulate technological innovation in academic libraries were asked in the range between 'very undesirable' and 'strongly desirable'. A very large number of respondents expressed that competitive threats from external

Table 1. Scope and significance of innovation among academic librarians

Perceptions on Technological Innovation	Yes	No
Motivate to do something new due to new trends and challenges	100%	0
Proactive involvement and work dynamically for Library sustainability	100%	0
Awareness about the term "Innovation" and its importance in library	100%	0
Innovation as critical factors for Library sustainability and survival	100%	0
Feel application of ICT as one of the stimulating factors on innovation	100%	0
Technological Innovation (TI) as one of the sustaining factors for survival	100%	0
Technological Innovation (TI) has positive and significant impact on organizational innovation	100%	0

Table 2. Factors that stimulate the adoption technological Innovation in academic libraries

Factors that stimulate Technological Innovation	1 %	2 %	3 %	4 %	5 %
Competitive threats from external environment	0	0	2.6	10.5	86.9
Financial crisis, new trends and challenges in Libraries	0	0	10.5	7.9	81.6
Availability of innovative ICT tools	0	0	7.9	15.8	76.3
Aligning with organizational direction and goal	0	2.6	10.5	21.1	65.9
Encouragement from authority to provide new services and implement ideas	0	0	10.5	31.6	57.9
Team involvement & dedicated team available for new test	0	0	5.3	34.2	60.5
Open-minded exploration of market drivers of innovation	0	0	13.2	18.4	68.4
Library visibility & brand building	0	0	7.9	36.8	55.3
Availability of resources and facilities for testing of new ideas	0	0	7.9	28.9	63.2
Addition value and reputation to organizations	0	2.6	7.9	23.7	65.8
Changing perceptions of users on library usability	0	0	13.1	34.2	52.7

[1=Very undesirable 2= Undesirable 3=Moderately Desirable 4= Desirable 5=Strongly Desirable]

environment 33 (86.85%), followed by financial crisis and new challenges 31 (81.6%); availability of innovative ICT tools 29 (76.3%); addition of value and reputation to organizations 25 (65.8%) and open-minded exploration of marketplace drivers of innovation 26 (68.4%) in Libraries were some of the strong motivating factors and very significant in adopting technological innovation. The other factors such as aligning with organizational direction and goal 25 (65.8%), library visibility & brand building 24 (63.2%) etc., were also found significant among the respondents.

RQ 3: How do you rate the adoption of the following technological evidence-based innovative approaches that will add value to users in your Library?

Influences of ICT tools and services in academic libraries are much reflective since the last two decades. The value and visibility of libraries have been improved by applying innovative ideas in terms of process, products and services as well as of the engagement of users. Respondents have noted that technology has added value to users in their Libraries. From Table 3 of this study, it is seen that value-added services based on technology, including how do I feature in Library portal 34 (89.5%); providing online instruction via Library portal 32 (84.2%); adding library subject guide 31 (81.6%); implementation of single sign-on solution/VPN 31(81.6%);providing online library instruction sessions 30 (79%); adding citation

Table 3. Perceptions in adopting evidence-based approaches on Technological Innovation

Value added Library Services	1 %	2 %	3 %	4 %	5 %
Adding How Do I features in Library Portal	0	0	0	10.5	89.5
Online Instruction via Library Portal	0	0	0	15.8	84.2
Creating Library Subject Guide	0	0	2.6	15.8	81.6
Implementation of Single Sign-on Solution/VPN	0	0	7.9	10.5	81.6
Provide Online Library Instruction Sessions	0	0	2.6	18.4	79
Adding Citation Support in Library Portal	0	0	7.9	13.1	79
Online Reservation of Books via OPAC	0	0	2.6	21.1	76.3
Library Marketing and outreach via Social Media	0	0	0	26.3	73.7
Use of APIs to Enhance Library Service	0	0	13.1	15.8	71
Document Delivery through Email	0	2.6	5.3	31.6	60.5
Payment of fine through e-payment Device	0	2.6	5.3	57.9	34.2
Mobile Library Services	0	7.9	7.9	57.9	26.3
Adding QR Code for Patron Activities	0	5.3	10.5	65.8	18.4
Use of Web Analytics for User Tracking	2.6	10.5	26.3	44.8	15.8

[1=Not at all valuable 2=Least valuable 3=Moderately Valuable 4=Valuable 5=Most valuable]

support in Library portal 30 (79%);online reservation of books via OPAC 29 (76.3%) and Library marketing through social media 28 (73.7%)were very prominent and most valuable among respondents. However, respondents expressed that pay fine through e-payment device 22(57.9%); adding QR code for patron activities 25 (65.8%) and mobile Library (M-Library) services 22 (57.9%) found valuable in adding value to libraries.

RQ 4: How do the academic librarians feel about library innovativeness on technological innovations in academic libraries? Do you wish to adopt innovative technologies in future that will add value to your Library?

In terms of library innovativeness of adopting technological innovation among respondents in the range between 'Not at all valuable' and 'most valuable' were asked as shown in Table 4. Respondents expressed that application of innovative tools/technologies in providing evidence-based innovative services and facilitating resources in innovative ways is very significant, innovative and vital for academic libraries. Respondents have noted that technological innovation has largely benefitted in archiving research publications by hosting Institutional Repository 36 (94.7%) in

Table 4. Perceptions of library innovativeness on technological innovation

Innovativeness of Technological Innovation	1 %	2 %	3 %	4 %	5 %
Library representation within a virtual environment (e.g. Second Life)	0	2.6	2.6	23.7	71
Design of web-based multimedia tools (e.g., Audio, video instruction sessions, How to do I features etc.)	0	0	5.3	10.5	84.2
Use of QR code in Library Operation (e.g., to link physical collections with online)	0	2.6	5.3	18.4	73.7
Creative use of mobile app (e.g. iOS or Android app) in Library	0	0	0	13.1	86.9
Web scale discovery services (e.g. Serials Solutions-Summon, EBSCO 360, VuFund)	0	0	0	10.5	89.5
Application of APIs to enhance visibility and access to research articles	0	0	0	18.4	81.6
Use of open source content management system (e.g. Drupal, Joomla)	0	10.5	0	21.1	68.4
Library services platforms (e.g., Worldshare Management, KualiOLE, Alma Services)	0	5.3	5.3	65.8	23.7
Implementation of responsive Mobile Library Portal	0	0	0	13.1	86.9
Data migrating related applications in Library (e.g. Amazon Web Services)	0	0	0	21.1	79
Social media integration (e.g., Facebook, Twitter)	0	0	2.6	76.3	21
Library gaming/gamification (e.g., game to help patrons to locate call number of books)	0	0	36.8	52.7	10.5
Use of devices such as laptops/tablets/Kindles etc to enhance library circulation services	0	2.6	2.6	28.9	65.8
Installation of self check-out & drop box in libraries	0	0	0	7.9	92.1
Archiving of scholarly publications (e.g. Institutional Repository)	0	0	0	5.3	94.7

[1= Not at all innovative 2=Least innovative 3= Marginally innovative 4= innovative 5=Most innovative]

their University. The result of the study revealed that technological innovations in academic libraries, including installation of self-check-out &dropbox for circulation activities 35 (92.1%);web-scale discovery services such as serials Solutions-Summon, EBSCO 360, VuFund etc. 34 (89.5%) as information retrieval solution for libraries for quickly connect users were very prime.

Interestingly perceptions on adopting promising innovative technologies such as implementation responsive mobile library portal and mobile apps (e.g. iOS or Android app) 33 (86.9%) were invariably the same and very significant among respondents. Adoption rate of Application Programming Interfaces (APIs) to improve library services and access to research articles and enhance visibility 31(81.6%); creation of web-based multimedia value-added features such as audio, video instruction sessions, how do I features etc. for engaging library users 32 (84.2%); data migrating related applications in Library such as Amazon Web Services 30 (78.9%); use of QR codes to link physical collections with online activities in Library 28 (73.7%); using of e-reading devices such as laptops/tablets/Kindles etc to enhance library circulation services 25 (65.8%); using of open source content management system (e.g. Drupal, Joomla) 27 (71.1%) and Library representation within a virtual environment such as Second Life 26 (68.4%) were also significant and found most innovative technologies among respondents that can be used for improving library services. Application social media i.e Facebook, Twitter, etc. 29 (76.3%) in marketing library resources and services were also found innovative among respondents. There was mixed response observed among respondents on acceptance of other innovative technologies/tools i.e platforms of library services through Worldshare Management, Kuali OLE, Alma Services 25 (65.8%) and library Gaming/gamification 20 (52.7%) in libraries which might be due to the lack of awareness and appropriate skills and competencies to use such emerging technologies in library.

Innovative technology will continue to evolve and shape the future of libraries in the impending future. For example, smart appliances and voice-controlled assistants are just two prominent examples of how technology is evolving to make people's lives easier. Library has to accommodate new applications of technologies for teaching, learning and research. Respondents were asked on innovative technology they wish to adopt in future in a range of 'definitely would not consider' and 'definitely would consider' that will add value to their libraries in terms of services as shown in Table 5. Respondents expressed that innovative technologies such as Augmented Reality Apps 31 (81.6%); Hackerspaces/Makerspace 27 (71%); Self-service printing, copying and scanning 21(55.3%) and Digital Interface for Printed Books 20 (52.7%) might consider for facilitating library services in future. Though usability of Robotic library 23 (60.5%); Book delivery drone 27 (71%) and electronic outposts 17 (44.8%)

Table 5. Innovative technologies of the future library

Innovative Technologies	1 %	2 %	3 %	4 %	5 %
Digital interface for printed books	0	5.3	28.9	52.6	13.1
Self-service printing, copying and scanning	0	0	26.3	55.3	18.4
Electronic outposts	0	7.9	44.8	26.3	21.1
Augmented Reality Apps	0	0	10.5	81.6	7.9
Robotic library	0	5.3	60.5	18.4	15.8
Hackerspaces/Makerspace (e.g 3D Printer)	0	0	5.3	71	23.7
Book delivery drone	0	0	71	23.7	5.3

[1=Definitely would not consider 2= Might not consider 3= Can't say now 4= Might consider 5= Definitely would consider] have emerged as valuable technologies for library services. However, on the other hand, most of the repondents stated that it was very difficult them to predict the innovativeness and usability of future innovative technologies in the present situation.

RQ 5: What are the evidence-based innovative methods adopted by the academic librarians in managing electronic resources in academic libraries?

A large number of respondents showed a positive perception towards application of technologies in collecting, managing and disseminating information resources 38 (100%) in their Library as shown in Table 6. The finding of the study from Table 7, revealed that managing and organizing of online resources in term of A-Z listing 35 (92.1%), followed by organizing resources in subject wise 32 (84.2%) was very innovative and popular in academic libraries. Other innovative techniques such as organizing online resources in discipline wise 19 (50%) and content type 12 (31.6%) were just found innovative among respondents which might be due to popularity. Respondents were asked about library innovativeness in terms of evidence-based approaches as showed in Table 8. Most respondents expressed that popular innovative techniques i.e organizing resources and providing information about e-resources through informative library interface/portal 36 (94.7%) was most innovative, followed by adding of how do I link to online resources 35 (92.1%) and facilitating resources through web-scale discovery tools 35 (92.1%) and adding library subject guide through digital interface 34 (89.5%) were most innovative. Other innovative techniques such as using link resolver to provide access to electronic resources 25(65.8%); remote access/single sign facility for 24X7 access of resources 23 (60.5%) and provide IP based authentication to online resources 22 (57.9%) were also most innovative methods adopted by libraries. Integration of social media with online resources 27 (71%) and making alert through text message 18 (47.4%) was less innovative through these platforms are very prominent in the present scenario which might be due to publishers restrictions and data privacy. Thus, the findings of the study reveal that the application of technological innovation in managing and organizing electronic resources and services among respondents were very significant and impact positively on libraries.

RQ 6: What are the innovative marketing strategies and approaches adopted by the academic librarians in marketing library resources and services?

Role of ICTs in marketing library information resources and services have remarkable influence among libraries in the changing landscape of digital era. Respondents were asked in term of innovative approaches adopted in marketing library resources and services in the context of technological innovation, as shown

Table 6. Adoption of technological innovation in managing e-resources

Measure of Perceptions	Yes (%)	No (%)
Accordance and impact of adopting technological innovation in managing and organizing electronic resources and services	100	0
Accordance of Library automation	100	0
Web discovery services as an innovative approach to managing and facilitating e-resources/services	100	0

Table 7. Innovative techniques in managing resources in library

Innovative Techniques	1 %	2 %	3 %	4 %	5 %
Organizing Online Resources by A-Z Listing	0	0	0	7.9	92.1
Organizing Online Resources by Subject Wise	0	10.5	0	5.3	84.2
Organizing Online Resources by Discipline Wise	7.9	15.8	0	50	26.3
Organizing Online Resources by Content Type	7.9	47.4	0	31.6	13.1

[1= Not at all innovative 2=Least innovative 3=No opinion 4= innovative 5=Most innovative]

Table 8. Library innovativeness in managing, organizing and disseminating e-resource and services

Innovative Approaches	1 %	2 %	3 %	4 %	5 %
Informative Library Portal	0	0	0	5.3	94.7
Creating of Subject Guide of Online Resources	0	0	0	10.5	89.5
Provide How Do I link to online resources	0	0	0	7.9	92.1
Web Scale Discovery Service	0	0	0	7.9	92.1
Remote Access/Single Sign-On Solution	0	0	21	18.4	60.5
Providing information alert through Text Messaging	5.3	7.9	10.5	47.4	28.9
Use of Link Resolver to access e-resources	0	0	2.6	31.6	65.8
Integration of Social Media for providing information on Online Resources	0	0	7.9	71.1	21.1
Providing IP Authenticity	0	0	10.5	31.6	57.9

[1= Not at all innovative 2=Least innovative 3=Marginally innovative 4= Innovative 5=Most innovative]

in Table 9. The result highlights that technological innovation through innovative library portal based on usability interface 35 (92.1%) was one of the most innovative methods to provide informationamong users, as expressed by respondents. Library

Table 9. Strategies adopted for innovative marketing of library services and resources

Strategies for Innovative Library Marketing	1 %	2 %	3 %	4 %	5 %
Innovative Library Portal	0	0	0	7.9	92.1
Social Media Integration (e.g. Facebook)	0	0	15.8	57.9	26.3
Email Marketing	0	0	7.9	18.4	73.7
Uploading and Posting Online Videos	0	0	0	15.8	84.2
Digital Signage and way findings	0	0	7.9	13.1	79
Widgets (eg, BookJetty, Shelfari)	0	0	13.1	26.3	60.5
Posting through RSS Feeds	0	0	7.9	71	21.1
Library Tagging (e.g. Library Thing)	0	5.3	47.4	31.6	15.8
Instant Messaging and Alerts	0	5.3	5.3	68.4	21.1
Search Engine Optimization (SEO)	0	0	0	73.7	26.3
Online Library Instruction	0	0	0	5.3	94.7
Library Blogging	0	2.6	39.5	42.1	15.8
Invasive Marketing (e.g. pop-ups)	0	0	7.9	60.5	31.6

[1= Not at all innovative 2=Least innovative 3=Marginally innovative 4= Innovative 5=Most innovative]

marketing techniques that were found most innovative among respondents such as uploading and posting online videos about collections, services, resources and their usability 32 (84.2%) ; providing online Library Instruction via Library portal required by users 36 (94.8%); promoting library through social media platform i.e Facebook 22 (57.9%) and applying library Widgets such as BookJetty, Shelfari23 (60.5%) for effective utilization of resources. Similarly, innovative library marketing techniques, including Search Engine Optimization 28 (73.7%); adding RSS feeds 27 (71%); providing information about instant messaging 26(68.4%) and invasive marketing (e.g. pop-ups)23 (60.5%) were found innovative by respondents. Library blogging 16 (42.1%) and Library tagging via Library Thing12 (31.6%) were found marginally innovative and low usage by respondents which might be due to newness and low popularity.

In the present digital landscape, integration of social media with library has emerged as innovative and popular platform and considered as one of the fastest media to disseminate information among users. A very large number of respondents consider that application of social media will help users get updated information about value-added services of library, as showed in Table 10. Respondents were noted that use of Facebook 37 (97.4%), followed by WhatsApp35 (92.1%); Twitter32 (84.2%); and Library blogger 27 (71%) was found most innovative, which can be used as a medium to disseminate information among library users. Respondents have agreed

Table 10. Impact of social media tools in marketing of library services and resources

InnovativePlatforms	1 %	2 %	3 %	4 %	5 %
Facebook	0	0	0	2.6	97.4
Twitter	0	0	0	15.8	84.2
WhatsApp	0	0	0	7.9	92.1
Snapchat	0	21.1	31.6	21.1	26.3
Instagram	0	63.2	18.4	13.1	5.3
Slideshare	0	2.6	23.7	44.8	28.9
Library Blogger	0	0	10.5	26.3	63.2
Delicious	7.9	31.6	21.1	36.8	2.6
Second Life	0	26.3	15.8	47.4	10.5

[1= Not at all innovative 2=Least innovative 3=Marginally innovative 4= Innovative 5=Most innovative]

that social media platforms such as Second Life 18 (47.4%); Slideshare 17 (44.8%) and Delicious 14 (36.9%) were found innovative. Other innovative mediums i.e Instagram 24 (63.2%) and snapchat 12(31.6%) were found marginally innovative, not so significant and less popular among respondents in promoting library services.

RQ 7: What are the innovative methods as perceived by the academic librarians used for honing skills and competencies on technological innovation in libraries?

In Question-7, the use of innovative methods for honing skills and competencies on technological innovation was asked among respondents, as shown in Table 11. The majority of respondents revealed that Peer-to-Peer (P2P) activity on technological innovation was very effective and most innovative 35 (92.1%), followed by leading Library discussion of ideas on technological innovation 34 (89.5);Library collaborations, networks & joint projects34 (89.5%);attending capacity building programme on technological innovation 33 (86.8%) and hand on training on implementation of innovative technologies 33 (86.8%) were found most innovative and important in stimulating skills and competencies on technological innovation in Library. The perception of respondents on the other type of methods in stimulating technological innovation, such as motivating to attend online webinars on technological innovation 27 (71%); sharing experiences with staff on technological innovation 22 (57.9%) and joining online forums/ attending webinars 22 (57.9%), were stated as extremely innovative strategies to develop innovative skill and competencies in libraries.

Table 11. Innovative strategies for stimulating skills and competencies on technological innovation

Enablers of Innovation	1 %	2 %	3 %	4 %	5 %
Attending conference/seminar/workshop	0	0	7.9	21	71
Hands on training on the implementation of innovative technologies	0	0	2.6	10.5	86.9
Library talk on technological innovation	0	0	5.3	21.1	73.7
Motivating to attend online webinars on technological innovation	0	0	13.1	71	15.8
Hold library discussion on ideas about technological innovation	0	0	0	10.5	89.5
Award/reorganization on innovative work	0	0	5.3	26.3	68.4
Peer-to-Peer (P2P) activities on technological innovation	0	0	0	7.9	92.1
Attending capacity building programme on technological innovation	0	0	0	13.1	86.9
Sharing experiences with staff on technological innovation	0	2.6	18.4	57.9	21.1
Joining of online forums/ webinars	0	0	13.1	52.7	34.2
Library collaborations, networks and joint projects	0	0	2.6	7.9	89.5
Visiting other library websites	0	5.3	28.9	39.5	26.3

[1= Not at all innovative 2=Less innovative 3 =Marginally innovative 4=Innovative 5=Most innovative]

RQ 8: What are factors that discourage the academic librarians from adopting Technological Innovation?

Regarding discouraging factors that act as a barrier in stimulating technological innovation, the respondents were asked to state their perception in five-point Likert scale that ranges between 'strongly disagree' and 'strongly agree' as shown in Table 12 The result of the study revealed that a very large number of respondents were expressed that lack of visionary leadership in adopting technologies 34 (89.5%), followed by lack of right strategy or vision 33 (86.9%), non-availability ICT support 31 (81.6%); negative attitude of management in adopting technologies 32 (84.2%); lack of skilled and competent library staff and their negative attitude 31(81.6%);lack of budget and financial crisis in Library 30 (78.9%); un-conducive workplace & culture to adopt new technology and tools 28 (73.7%) and lack of infrastructure and outdated 20 (52.7%) were found as most discouraging factors in stimulating and adopting technological innovation in academic library. Other discouraging factor such as lack of time to do innovative work was not at all consider as a factor that inhibits to be innovative to adopt technological innovation in the library.

Table 12. Barriers in adopting technological innovation in academic library

Discouraging Factors	1 %	2 %	3 %	4 %	5 %
Lack of budget	0	0	5.3	15.8	78.9
Negative attitude of management	0	0	0	15.8	84.2
Lack of discussion on technological innovation	0	15.8	18.4	44.8	21.1
Lack of right strategy	0	0	0	13.1	86.9
Lack of infrastructure	5.3	21.1	15.8	5.3	52.7
Lack of skilled and competent staff and their negative attitude	0	0	2.6	15.8	81.6
Lack of visionary leadership	0	0	2.6	7.9	89.5
Lack of time to do innovative work	68.5	21.1	0	10.5	0
Un-conducive workplace & learning culture	0	10.5	2.6	13.1	73.7
Lack of availability of ICT support	0	0	0	18.4	81.6
Low library reputation	0	10.5	5.3	60.5	23.7

[1= Strongly disagree 2= Disagree 3=Marginally agree No opinion 4=Agree 5=Strongly agree]

Lastly, the respondents were asked about their perceptions on adopting and applying technological innovation in libraries in terms of radical (complete) changes and incremental (gradual) changes. All most all respondents expressed for adopting incremental innovation 35(92.1%) as opposed to radical innovation in the context of technological innovation, anticipating the fear of failure in adopting drastic and complete changes on process, products, services and resources in the context of applying technologies in academic libraries.

DISCUSSION

Innovation is one of the essential factors for the survival and sustain in the 21st century. Academic libraries being the key service providers should implement new and innovative ideas to provide services and resources for the larger benefit of users. As discussed in the findings of this study, scores of innovative ideas have already been implemented in the majority of academic libraries across India. However, some of them are still under consideration and some are in experimental stage, and the library professionals think that immediate implementation of new products, processes, ideas etc., would be a risk for them.

Library Pro-Activeness

From the findings, all the respondents agreed that academic libraries must change and tune themselves in order to cope up with the latest challenges for sustainability in the Library. Most of the respondents are on theview that academic libraries must change now and should not be static. These findings are highly consistent with Stoffle, Renaud, and Veldof (1996) who urged that "academic libraries must change fundamentally and irreversibly, what and how they do it with the immediate and quick way". The findings revealed that innovation as one of the critical factors for the success of the organization, where technological innovation is one of key type innovation which should be given due emphasis for the survival and sustenance of academic libraries in the digital era. The pro-activeness and dynamic role of library professionals is highly essential for adopting technological innovation in academic libraries.

Innovation as an Opportunity During Crisis

As regards to factors that stimulate innovation, especially in the context of technological innovation, this study showed that financial crisis; latest trends and new challenges, followed by availability of innovative ICT tools, competitive threats from external environment were very significant among the respondents. As a consequence, the study urged the university librarians' to use current financial crisis as an opportunity for exploring and experimenting implementing innovative ideas to maintain the vitality of academic library through fundamental changes that have long been a necessity, which ultimately allow them to survive and thrive in terms of facilitating resources and services in institutions.

Adding Library Value

The respondents were asked to note their responses on evidence-based innovative services through technological innovation in the range between 'not at all innovative' and 'most innovative'. This study showed that adoption of technological innovation in terms of services and resources has added value and visibility to their library among users. A majority of respondents revealed that value-added services such as adding how do I features about what, how and why of online resources, orient users through online instruction via Library portal, creating library subject guide and adding citation support link to Library portal for researchers have improved the visibility of the library. Though innovative features like pay fine through e-payment device, adopting of QR code for library services and M-Library services were a very promising concept, their acceptance among the university librarians are not significant which might be due to the experimental stage and lower confidence.

Technological Innovation as Library Sustainability

In terms of library innovativeness on adopting technological innovation among respondents in the range between 'Not at all valuable' and 'Most valuable' was asked in academic libraries, the study revealed that technological innovation in terms of providing evidence-based innovative services and resources in innovative ways was very significant, innovative and highly essential for libraries. The study explored that Institutional Repository (IR) for archiving scholarly publications, Web-scale discovery services/tools, Hackerspaces/Makerspaces (e.g. 3D printer); responsive Library portal and mobile Library App (e.g. iOS or Android app) were very significant to them for developing library services. Technological innovations in terms of Application Programming Interfaces (APIs), creation and uploading of online videos about the library, adding How to do I features, etc. for engaging library users; using of QR codes to link physical collections, Open source content management system (e.g. Drupal, Joomla) and social media integration in library services were also significant and found innovative. Though the adoption of technological innovation was very significant and essential in the sustainability of the library, most of them preferred to adopt the ideas in an incremental way as opposed to radical.This finding has strongly supported the argument of Jantz (2012) who proposed in the context of research libraries that "the activity of technical innovation in research libraries will be predominantly incremental as opposed to radical". Latest technologies will be going to shape the Library of the future. Though promising technologies such as Augmented Reality Apps; Hackerspaces/Makerspace; Library Mobile Apps; Self-service printing, copying and scanning and Digital Interface for Printed Books, etc. were very vital for library survival, however, respondents expressed to implement in the future subject to finical and administrative support.

Information Management

Regarding evidence-based innovative approaches adopted by University librarians' in terms of collecting, organizing and disseminating electronic resources in academic libraries were asked to respondents, the study revealed that organizing and disseminating information sources and services through innovative library portal/interface was considered as most innovative and ideal method. This study confirmed the study of Letha (2006), who emphasized that the library portal as a platform enable and enhance web information and services among users in the digital environment. Similarly, Web Scale Discovery (WSD) service/tool was one of the most innovative and popular media among respondents for quick retrieval of e-resources. The result showed that an increase in the use of WSD as a platform of knowledge management is due to decrease of the traditional form of information resources and a dramatic increase in the access of online resources and collections. These findings have confirmed the observation made by Doug Way (2010) who noticed that observed that increasing use of online full-text and decreasing of traditional abstracting and indexing databases among users in academic institutions is linked to the implementation of a web-scale discovery tool.

Strategic Innovative Library Marketing

The respondents were asked to state the innovative strategies being adopted to market library services and resources in the range between 'not at all innovative and 'most innovative'. The study revealed that the most frequently used strategies by librarians in university libraries in India are marketing library resources through innovative library portal by adding innovative features, uploading and posting online videos about library resources and services, online library instruction, digital Signage and way findings and marketing use of social media platforms were predominantly used to promote library services. The study also revealed that by using social media among libraries have emerged as an emerging marketing platform, still level usage of social media are very low in marketing library resources and services among academic libraries. The study is in accord with Lwoga (2011), who specifically focused on the potential side of social media in marketing library services.The popularity of other promising media such as RSS Feeds, instant messaging, search engine optimization (SEO) and invasive marketing (e.g. pop-ups) were innovative or marginally innovative. The reason low usage may be connected to the unwarranted fear among the librarians to adjust in the paradigm shift of marketing library services to users as observed by Rogers (2009), traditionalist values as well as unsubstantiated fear of possible security breaches to libraries online and integrated systems.

Innovative Skills and Competencies

Adoption of technological innovation required competent skills and capability among library professionals to effectively implement ideas, products, processes and services in order to serve users having several choices in this digital era. Librarians as a forerunner of technological innovation, have to follow the suitable strategic plan and adopt an effective approach in order to stimulate innovation and enhance skills and competencies to cope up with the latest technologies. Respondents in this study reported that stimulating activities such as Peer-to-Peer (P2P) activities based on technological innovation,collaborations, networks & joint projects on innovation, participating in technological innovation, attending capacity building related application of innovative technologies/tools, sharing experiences with staff on about why and how of technological innovation and reward and recognition of accomplishing innovative works were the most innovative and effective way to enhance technological skills and competencies among library professionals. On the contrary, respondents were asked regarding factors that inhibit technological innovation, the findings of the study revealed that lack of visionary leadership in adopting innovative technologies, financial crisis, financial crisis from idea generation to implementation requires adequate funding to succeed TI, incompetent and unskilled staff with negative attitude to adopt technological innovation and un-conducive environment to test and generate innovative ideas are main discouraging factors to adopt TI among academic libraries. The finding of the study supported the argument of Zhio (2005), who argued that organizational culture and conducive working environment are crucial in stimulating innovation and entrepreneurship attitude among employees in an organization.

Visionary Leadership

Adoption of innovative technologies in a turbulent environment required a strong leadership with a strategic and logical bend of mind to cope up with changes. Librarians as a leader must understand the challenges and evaluate the situation, accordingly problems should be addressed. As library leader, skills and competencies of staff engaged in technological innovation process must be assessed and suitable measures required to be taken to enhance their capacity to know about new technologies and services that are essential for users in an academic library. Resistance is evident in technological innovation, but library leaders have to articulate how differing cultures, conflicting goals, and immediate challenges can be address and covert crisis as an opportunity for benefit of the organization. As recommended by Hamel (2006), innovation is an integral part and sustained a process for organizations to thrive in the 21st century, where the role of visionary leadership is vital to uphold the sustainability by identifying innovative as survival strategic, and promulgating this sustainable strategy among institutions for the larger benefit of stockholders.

FURTHER RESEARCH

The purpose of this research is to investigate the perceptions of librarians' on technological innovation and strategies used in adopting technological innovation among academic librarians in India. The results of the study revealed that technological innovation has a positive and significant impact on academic libraries in terms of resources and services. Hence, individual perceptions on other kind of innovation in terms of administrative vs technical; product vs processor incremental or radical can be studied from either a qualitative or quantitative perspective. In the ambit of this study, the researcher has studied technological innovation in academic libraries perspective, where other categories of libraries are not in the scope of the study. Thus, further research can be conducted on these aspects. Researchers can conduct the study in the context of technological innovation among other higher institutions in the discipline of engineering, management, legal education, medical, etc.,. The library sustainability requires strong leadership to survive in the crisis. Innovative skills and competencies are critical factors for success in leadership. Thus, technological innovation in the form of transformational or transactional leadership in the context of skills and competencies might be an interesting study for further research. It would also be a very interesting study to investigate the application of technological innovation in different sections of the library and the adoption of different benchmarking techniques for the larger benefit of the users.

CONCLUSION

Influences of technological innovation in academic libraries found significant and very relevance in turbulent atmosphere. Much emphasis must be given to adopt and implement promising technologies and tools for providing effective services in libraries. Library professionals should have confidence and competent enough to put innovative ideas into practice. A pro-active and visionary leadership is highly essential to support technological innovation in academic libraries in order to sustain and thrive in the digital era. Not only able leadership but the innovative method and strategy action also requires for effectively implement innovative products, process, services and resources in libraries. Continued changes are evident in the libraries. Library professionals must be ready to accept challenges though pro-activeness and dynamism. The inhibiting factors on technological innovation must be addressed with appropriate solutions. Technological innovation is an opportunity, which should be utilized for the benefit of users in the digital landscape by enhancing technological skills and competencies.

REFERENCES

Baregheh, A., Rowley, J., & Sambrook, S. (2009). Towards a multidisciplinary definition of innovation. *Management Decision*, *47*(8), 1323–1339. doi:10.1108/00251740910984578

Chen, W., Yao, F., & Jiang, A. (2018). Technology Innovations in Academic Libraries in China. In Library Science and Administration: Concepts, Methodologies, Tools, and Applications, (pp. 144-164). Hershey, PA: IGI Global. doi:10.4018/978-1-5225-3914-8.ch007

Chu, S. K. W., & Du, H. S. (2013). Social networking tools for academic libraries. *Journal of Librarianship and Information Science*, *45*(1), 64–75. doi:10.1177/0961000611434361

Crant, J. M. (2000). Proactive behaviour in organizations. *Journal of Management*, *26*(3), 435–462. doi:10.1177/014920630002600304

Lewis, D. W. (2007). *A strategy for academic libraries in the first quarter of the 21st century*. Academic Press.

Daft, R. L. (1978). A dual-core model of organizational innovation. *Academy of Management Journal*, *21*(2), 193–210.

Damanpour, F. (1996). Organizational complexity and innovation: Developing and testing multiple contingency models. *Management Science*, *42*(5), 693–716. doi:10.1287/mnsc.42.5.693

Dunlap, I. H. (2008). Going digital: The transformation of scholarly communication and academic libraries. *Policy Futures in Education*, *6*(1), 132–141. doi:10.2304/pfie.2008.6.1.132

Farkas, M. (2012). Participatory technologies, pedagogy 2.0 and information literacy. *Library Hi Tech*, *30*(1), 82–94. doi:10.1108/07378831211213229

Hamel, G. (2006). The why what, and how of management innovation. *Harvard Business Review*, *84*(2), 72. PMID:16485806

Jantz, R. C. (2012). Innovation in academic libraries: An analysis of university librarians' perspectives. *Library & Information Science Research*, *34*(1), 3–12. doi:10.1016/j.lisr.2011.07.008

Jantz, R. C. (2013). *Incremental and radical innovations in research libraries: An exploratory examination regarding the effects of ambidexterity, organizational structure, leadership and contextual factors* (Doctoral dissertation). Retrieved from ProQuest Dissertations and Theses. (3597757)

Johnson, K., & Magusin, E. (2005). *Digital libraries: a cultural understanding*. Academic Press.

Klein, K. J., Conn, A. B., & Sorra, J. S. (2001). Implementing computerized technology: An organizational analysis. *The Journal of Applied Psychology*, *86*(5), 811–824. doi:10.1037/0021-9010.86.5.811 PMID:11596799

Lavoie, B., Henry, G., & Dempsey, L. (2006). A service framework for libraries. *D-Lib Magazine*, *12*(7/8), 1082–9873. doi:10.1045/july2006-lavoie

Letha, M. M. (2006). Library portal: A tool for web-enabled information services. *DESIDOC Journal of Library and Information Technology*, *26*(5).

Lietzau, Z. (2009). US Public Libraries and Web 2.0: What's Really Happening? *Computers in Libraries*, *29*(9), 6–10.

Lukasiewicz, A. (2007). Exploring the role of digital academic libraries: Changing student needs demand innovative service approach. *Library Review*, *56*(9), 821–827. doi:10.1108/00242530710831275

Lewis, D. W. (2007). A strategy for academic libraries in the first quarter of the 21st century. *College & Research Libraries*, *68*(5), 418–434. doi:10.5860/crl.68.5.418

Lwoga, E. T. (2011). Making Web 2.0 technologies work for higher learning institutions in Africa. *Campus-Wide Information Systems*, *29*(2), 90–107. doi:10.1108/10650741211212359

Maness, J. M. (2006). Library 2.0 theory: Web 2.0 and its implications for libraries. *Webology*, *3*(2), 2006.

Martín Hernández, P., Salanova, M., & Peiró, J. M. (2007). Job demands, job resources and individual innovation at work: Going beyond Karasek's model? *Psicothema*, *19*(4). PMID:17959117

Martins, E. C., & Terblanche, F. (2003). Building an organisational culture that stimulates creativity and innovation. *European Journal of Innovation Management*, *6*(1), 64–74. doi:10.1108/14601060310456337

Musmann, K. (1993). *Technological innovations in libraries, 1860 – 1960: An anecdotal history*. Westport, CT: Greenwood Press.

Parker, S. K., Williams, H. M., & Turner, N. (2006). Modelling the antecedents of proactive behavior at work. *The Journal of Applied Psychology*, *91*(3), 636–652. doi:10.1037/0021-9010.91.3.636 PMID:16737360

Sommers, P. C. (2005). The role of the library in a wired society–compete or withdraw: A business perspective. *The Electronic Library*, *23*(2), 157–167. doi:10.1108/02640470510592915

Stoffle, C. J., Renaud, R., & Veldof, J. R. (1996). Choosing our futures. *College & Research Libraries*, *57*(3), 213–225. doi:10.5860/crl_57_03_213

Teets, M. (2009). What is Web-Scale? *Designing the future blog, 7.*

Westbrook, L. (1994). Qualitative research methods: A review of major stages, data analysis techniques, and quality controls. *Library & Information Science Research*, *16*(3), 241–254.

Rogers, E. (2003). *Diffusion of innovations*. New York, NY: Free Press.

Vaughan, D. S. (2007). *Planning for information technology: A comparative case study of the factors affecting the alignment of institutional strategic plans and information technology plans* (Doctoral dissertation). University of Michigan.

Way, D. (2010). The impact of web-scale discovery on the use of a library collection. *Serials Review*, *36*(4), 214–220. doi:10.1080/00987913.2010.10765320

Wei, Q., Chang, Z., & Cheng, Q. (2015). Usability study of the mobile library App: An example from Chongqing University. *Library Hi Tech*, *33*(3), 340–355. doi:10.1108/LHT-05-2015-0047

Youngman, P. (2009). Procyclicality and value at risk. *Bank of Canada Financial System Review*.

Zare Mehrjerdi, Y. (2009). RFID-enabled supply chain systems with computer simulation. *Assembly Automation*, *29*(2), 174–183. doi:10.1108/01445150910945624

Zhao, F. (2005). Technological and organizational innovations: A Case study of Siemens (Australia). *International Journal of Innovation and Learning, 3*(1), 95-109.

Chapter 14
Research Data Analysis Using EViews:
An Empirical Example of Modeling Volatility

Erginbay Uğurlu
Istanbul Aydın University, Turkey

ABSTRACT

The aim of this chapter is to provide a detailed empirical example of autoregressive conditional heteroskedasticity (ARCH) model and selected generalized ARCH models. Before the ARCH/GARCH models are estimated, several calculations and tests should be done. The mean model is determined using the autocorrelation function and partial autocorrelation function and also the unit root test. The existence of ARCH effect is tested using ARCH-LM test. After these steps are done, then ARCH/GARCH models can be estimated. All these theoretical aspects are applied to Sofia Stock Indexes (SOFIX) using EViews 9 software package. The windows and output of EViews are presented. To show the output's academic writing format researchers' outputs are presented in a table.

INTRODUCTION

Modeling volatility is an important issue in the finance literature. Over the last decades many models have developed in the literature for modeling volatility. Financial data show the conditional distribution of high-frequency returns this conditional distribution produce some features. The most challenging features are excess of

DOI: 10.4018/978-1-5225-8437-7.ch014

kurtosis, negative skewness, and temporal persistence in conditional movements. To cope with these problems many tools have developed not only to model volatility but also forecasting volatility, namely ARCH/GARCH (Auto-Regressive Conditionally Heteroscedastic/Generalized Auto-Regressive Conditionally Heteroscedastic) models. After the GARCH model, many different GARCH-type models are developed such as EGARCH, IGARCH, TARCH so on.

This chapter serves as an overview of important members of the ARCH family, which are an ARCH, GARCH, and EGARCH models. Also, the empirical example is presented using EViews 9 software package. Daily observations of Bulgarian Stock Exchange (SOFIX) data covering the period between 04.01.2010 and 26.01.2017 will be used as an example.

This chapter is organized as follows. The first part is an introduction and the second part covers the history y of the ARCH, GARCH, and EGARCH models. The third part is the core of the paper and provides a guide to the estimation procedure of three models in EViews 9. In the last part, the chapter is, summarized.

BACKGROUND OF GARCH MODELS

Whereas heteroskedasticity is associated with models for cross-section data in textbooks, autoregressive conditional heteroskedasticity (ARCH) can be found in time-series models. Volatility is a vital concept for financial series. It is used in portfolio optimization, risk management, and asset pricing. The main problem of this kind of data is the impossibility of modeling using a linear model because this kind of data includes leptokurtosis, volatility clustering, long memory, volatility smile, and leverage effects. Also, one of the assumptions of linear models, which is homoscedasticity is not appropriate when using financial data (Floros 2008:35). In order to model volatility, Engle (1982) developed the Autoregressive Conditional Heteroscedastic (ARCH) models. Engle observed that large and small errors tend to occur in clusters, and then formulated it as follows: information from the recent past might influence the conditional disturbance variance. After Engle, Bollerslev (1986) extended ARCH to Generalized Autoregressive Conditional Heteroscedastic (GARCH) model. Bollerslev's improvement is to add the forecasted variance from the last period (the GARCH term) to the volatility of the past (ARCH term). Nelson (1991) proposed the Exponential GARCH (EGARCH) model an EGARCH model that is often employed to capture the asymmetric effect of innovations on volatility. It is not the last GARCH type model, but in this chapter, we investigate only these three models.

ARCH Model

ARCH models based on the variance of the error term at time t depend on the realized values of the squared error terms in previous time periods. The model is specified as:

$$y_t = u_t \tag{1}$$

$$u_t \sim N\left(0, \sigma_t^2\right)$$

$$\sigma_t^2 = \alpha_0 + \sum_{t=1}^{q} \alpha_j u_{t-i}^2 \tag{2}$$

This model is referred to as ARCH(q), where q refers to the order of the lagged squared returns included in the model. If we use the ARCH(1) model it becomes

$$\sigma_t^2 = \alpha_0 + \alpha_1 u_{t-1}^2 \tag{3}$$

Conditional variance is presented by σ_t^2 in the equation. Conditional variance must always be strictly positive to have meaningful variance at any point in time. To ensure that the conditional variance is a strictly positive coefficient in the equation must be $\alpha_0 > 0$ and $\alpha_1 \geq 0$.

GARCH Model

After the ARCH model, it is extended by Bollerslev (1986), and Taylor (1986) proposed a GARCH(p,q) model. In this model, the conditional variance of the variable dependent upon its previous lags and also the lagged squared returns which were in the ARCH model too. The GARCH model is as follows:

$$\sigma_t^2 = \alpha_0 + \sum_{i=1}^{q} \alpha_i u_{t-i}^2 + \sum_{i=1}^{p} \beta_i \sigma_{t-i}^2 \tag{4}$$

GARCH models have some restrictions. All parameters in the variance equation must be positive and $\sum_{i=1}^{q} \alpha_i + \sum_{i=1}^{p} \beta_i$ are expected to be less than one.

Exponential GARCH (EGARCH) Model

Exponential GARCH (EGARCH) proposed by Nelson (1991) has a form of leverage effects in its equation. In the EGARCH model the specification for the conditional covariance is given by the following form:

$$\log\left(\sigma_t^2\right) = \alpha_0 + \sum_{j=1}^{q} \beta_j \log\left(\sigma_{t-j}^2\right) + \sum_{i=1}^{p} \alpha_i \left|\frac{u_{t=i}}{\sigma_{t=i}}\right| + \sum_{k=1}^{r} \gamma_k \frac{u_{t-k}}{\sigma_{t-k}} \tag{5}$$

In the equation γ_k represents leverage effects which account for the asymmetry of the model. While the basic GARCH model requires the restrictions, the EGARCH model allows unrestricted estimation of the variance (Thomas and Mitchell 2005:16). If $\gamma_k < 0$ it indicates the presence of leverage effect and means that bad news increases volatility if $\gamma_k > 0$ it indicates positive innovations are more destabilizing than negative innovations. In addition, γ_k gives information about the asymmetry of the series. If $\gamma_k \neq 0$ the impact is asymmetric, if it equals to zero impact is symmetric.

EMPIRICAL EXAMPLE USING EVIEWS

This paper employs daily observations of Bulgarian Stock Exchange (SOFIX) covering the period between 04.01.2010 and 26.01.2017. Data was collected from Reuters and was named as SOFIX in EViews File.

Before the empirical application starts; generally, the return series are calculated to apply a GARCH model. Return (r) is defined as the natural logarithm of prize relatives. Before the GARCH model is estimated, descriptive statistics of the variables must be calculated at first. As it stated above skewness, kurtosis and Jarque Bera statistics of the series are very important to understand volatility. Linear structural (and time series) models are unable to explain some important features which are leptokurtosis, volatility clustering or volatility pooling and leverage effects mostly exist in financial data. To determine the existence of a long right tail skewness of the series must be calculated. If the skewness is positive, it means that the series have a long right tail. To determine whether the series is leptokurtic kurtosis of the series must be calculated. If the kurtosis exceeds 3, the distribution is peaked (leptokurtic) relative to the normal distribution. After these statistics are checked ARCH effect must be investigated in the data using ARCH test, the first step of the test is estimating the residual from the model then take a square of estimated residuals and regress those on q own lags to test ARCH of order. If the value of the test statistic is higher than the critical value from the residual squared distribution, the null hypothesis is rejected. This ARCH order test is done using ARCH-LM test. Finally, ARCH and GARCH models are estimated and interpreted.

If the ARCH test concludes with the existence of ARCH effect in the series, the ARCH model can be estimated.

Note that by using EViews 9 to create a workfile, click File/ New. Because we have data in Excel, we will use click File/Open/Foreign Data as Workfile (Figure 1) and click the all files option which is presented in Figure 2.

EViews can be read the data from the Excel file, after clicking OK in Figure 2 Eviews opens the 'Text read' dialog window. In the first step there is a 'Column specification' option and the other three window lots of options (Figure 3) are available. Generally, default options are used therefore click on the "Next" button and EViews will correctly guess it. Note that EViews has figured out that the first line holds variable names rather than data. Only clicking on the next button EViews generates the work file.

When a workfile is first created, the sample includes all observations in the workfile. In Figure 4, there are two data periods which are entitled 'Range' and 'Sample.' In the window they are equal, but if we are interested in the different period of the data we can to adjust the sample. The sample can be changed by clicking the 'Sample' button. In this empirical application, we start from the first day of 2000

Figure 1. The complete options of the open file

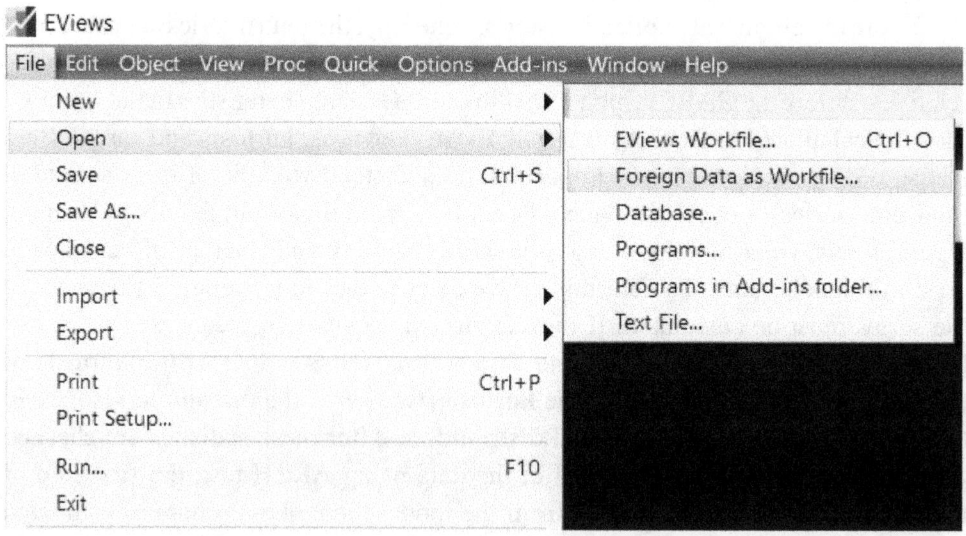

Figure 2. Importing data from sheet1 from an Excel file

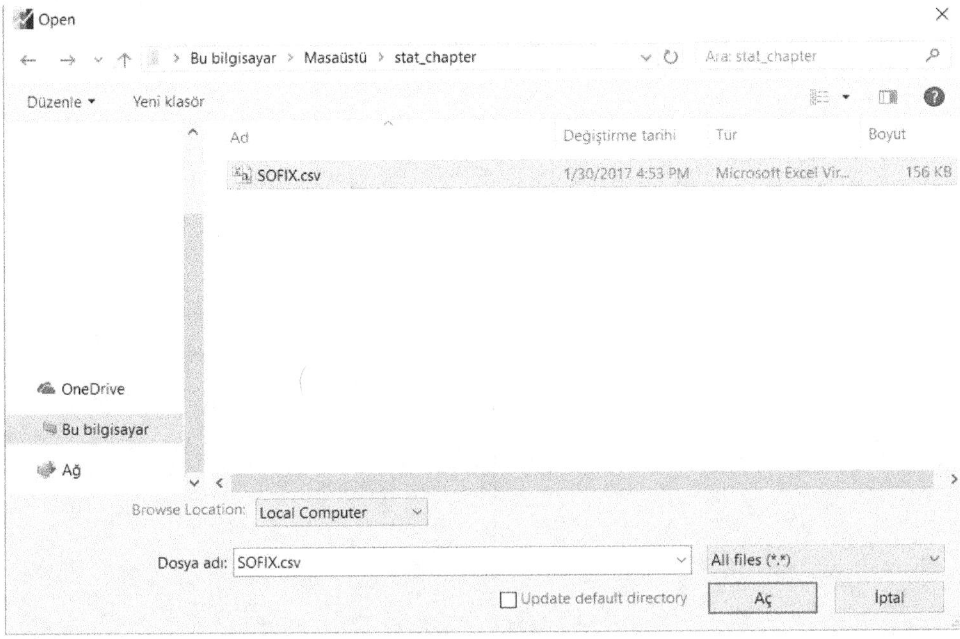

and the last observation of the data. Thus the sample period starts at 1/04/2010 and ends on 1/26/2017 (Figure 5).

Another way to change sample is to use a command pane. To set the sample, the format of the command is “simply start date finish date” which is below for our sample.

```
simply 1/04/2010 1/26/2017
```

We use returns to denote proportionate price change over a stock exchange indices interval. Return (r) is defined as the natural logarithm of prize relatives as follows:

$$r = \log\left(\frac{X_t}{X_{t-1}}\right) \tag{6}$$

where X_t is capital index

The return variables must be generated before modeling variance. We decided to name it RSOFIX. To generate RSOFIX click Quick/Generate Series.

Figure 3. Importing data from sheet2 from an Excel file Spreadsheet read dialogs

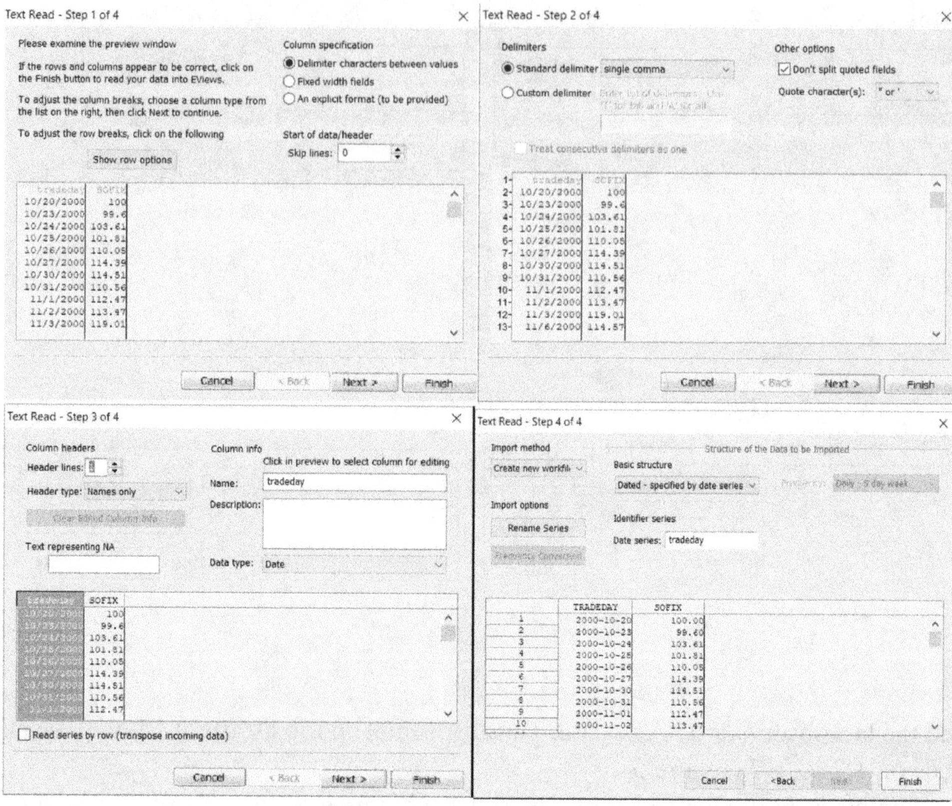

We can use functions and operations in 'Generate Series' and the most common ones are as follows,

= Equal
^ Raise to the Power
log(X) Natural Log Transformation
exp(X) Exponential Function
D(X) First Difference of X, X(t)-X(t-1)
X(-1) One Lagged Value of X

Then next the window 'Generate Series by Equation' opens. In that window formula of the return has to be specified

```
RSOFIX = log((SOFIX/SOFIX(-1)))
```

Figure 4. The workfile with the imported data

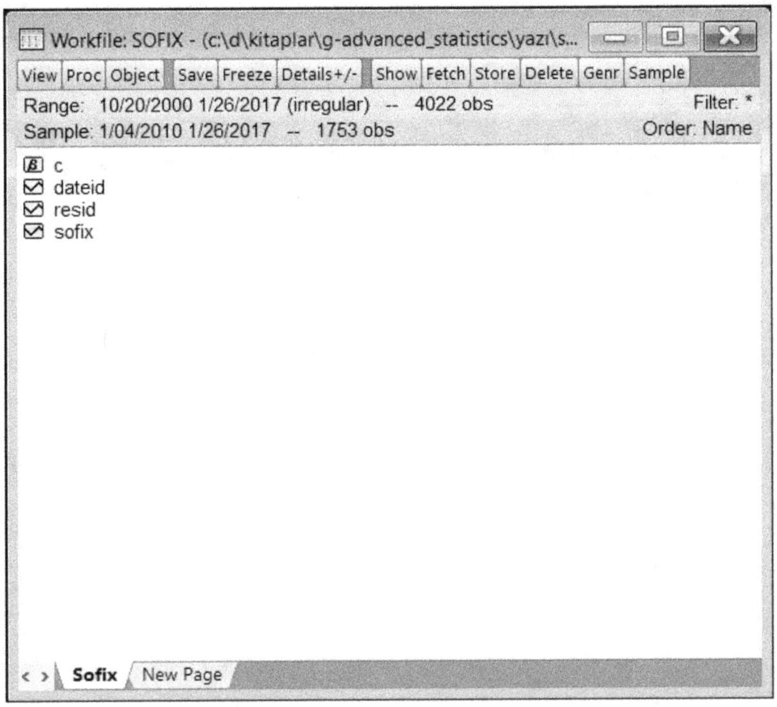

Figure 5. Changing Sample

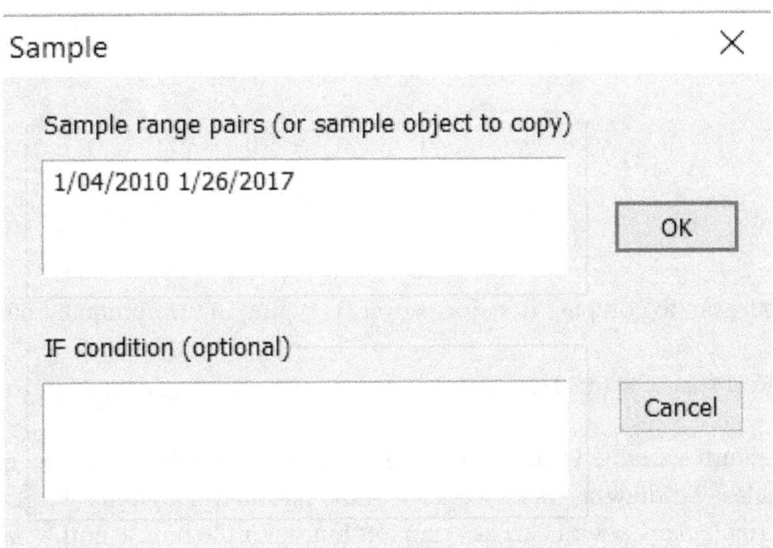

Figure 6. Command pane to change the sample

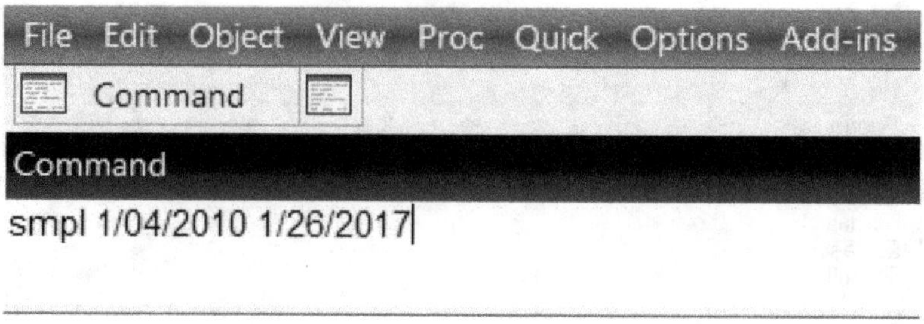

Figure 7. The window to generate series by equation

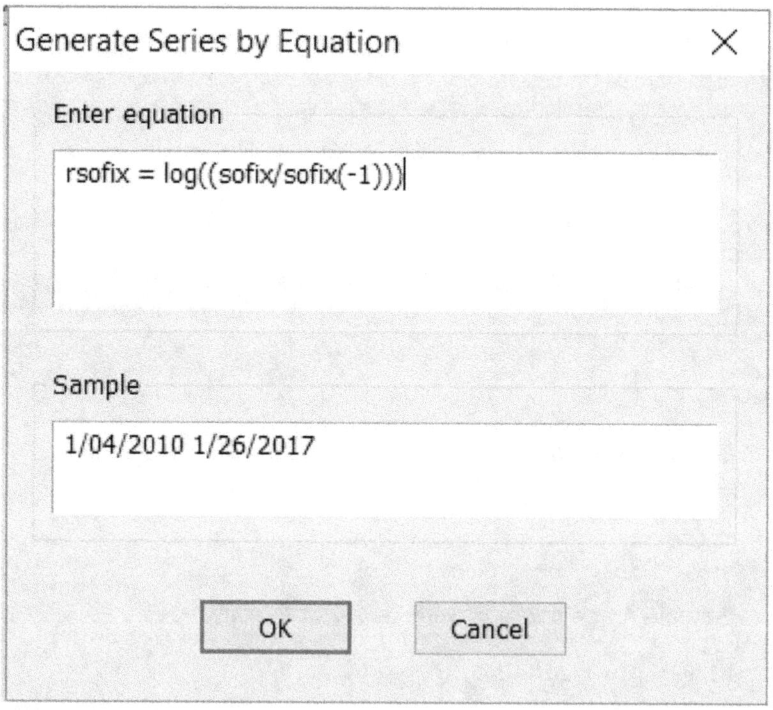

Another way to compute transformations is typing in the command pane

```
genr RSOFIX = log((SOFIX/SOFIX(-1)))
```

Thus return variable is defined RSOFIX. It is always better to see graphs of the variables. To draw a graph we have some alternative options. First, clicking on the variable names with Ctrl key and left button of the mouse at the same time,

Figure 8. Command pane to generate series by equation

this makes the variables shaded. At the next step click Open/Group (Figure 8) thus EViews opens the variables as a grouped data.

In the grouped data window (Figure 9) click View/Graph. After these choices, we see that the 'Graph Options" window will appear.

In that window (Figure 11), some dialog boxes and drop down menus appear corresponding to create a wide variety of graph types. Also, this window allows changing axes, scaling legends, and many other features. Because we have two graphs; we chose 'Multiple graphs' from the drop-down menu and because of using continuous/financial data we have chosen line and symbol.

To produce a simple line graphs click on 'OK' then we will get the two graphs below in Figure 12.

We can easily 'copy and paste' or 'cut and paste' the graphs into Word from EViews. The graphs of the index and daily returns are presented in Figure 12.

Another way to compute transformations is typing in the command pane as follows:

```
graph line sofix
```

If we use this command EViews create the object (line) therefore to see the graph we have to click on the line and the graph will be open (Figure 15).

Additionally, we can draw two graphs together with one command which is below.

```
graph gr2.line sofix rsofix
```

As it is necessary for the line graph, after this command, again we have to click on the object (gr2) to open the graph too. In Figure 17, 'gr2' shows the grouped data of SOFIX and RSOFIX.

One of the conditions to say the series have a volatility effect; the series must contain leptokurtosis and positive skewness. To check these features, we have to calculate descriptive statistics of the variables.

After opening series with a double-click; click View/ Descriptive Statistics & Tests/Stats Table (Figure 18)

Figure 9. Preparing a graph

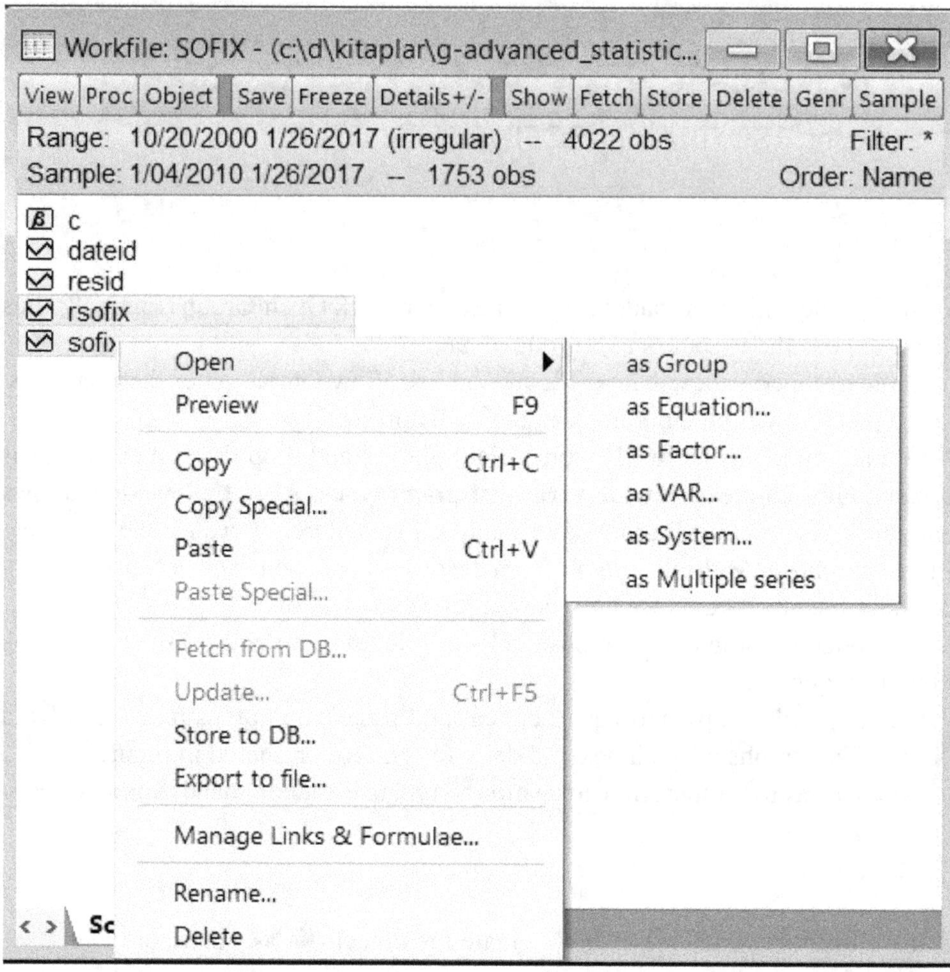

Figure 19 shows the output of the EViews for descriptive statistics of the return series and Table 1 shows how it is represented in the research paper. Jarque Bera test is used to test the normality of the data. The null hypothesis is the series has a normal distribution, and the test is distributed as Chi with two df (degrees of freedom).

The descriptive statistics of the return series show that RSOFIX has negative skewness and high positive kurtosis. These values signify that the distributions of the series have a long left tail and leptokurtic. Jarque-Bera (JB) statistics reject the null hypothesis of normal distribution at the 1% level of significance.

Figure 10. Grouped Data

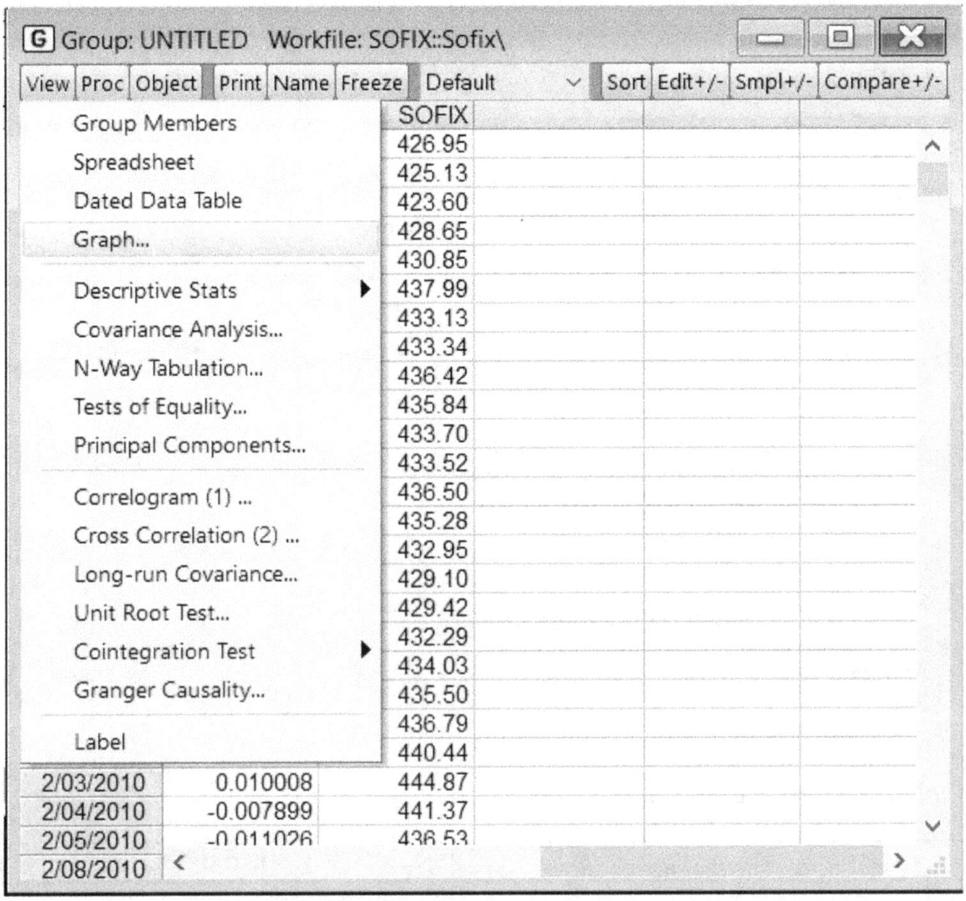

Time series have a stochastic process; therefore, firstly the mean model must be defined, using its AR(p), MA(q) and integration level, namely autoregressive integrated moving average models (ARIMA models).

Before the ARIMA model is estimated, the stationarity of the series must be tested. Unit root tests are used to do this investigation. Unit root tests show a d component of ARIMA(p,d,q). Since a model is an ARIMA(p,d,q) model, then the GARCH model will be named the ARIMA(p,d,q)_GARCH(a,b) model. For example, if our mean model is ARIMA(1,1,2) and GARCH model is GARCH(1,1) the model named ARIMA(1,1,2)_GARCH(1,1).

If we apply this to RSOFIX in EViews; the RSOFIX must be selected by double-clicking on its name, and the window opens, in the new window click View/Unit Root Test (Figure 20) then Unit Root test window (Figure 21) opens.

Figure 11. The window to adjusting the graph

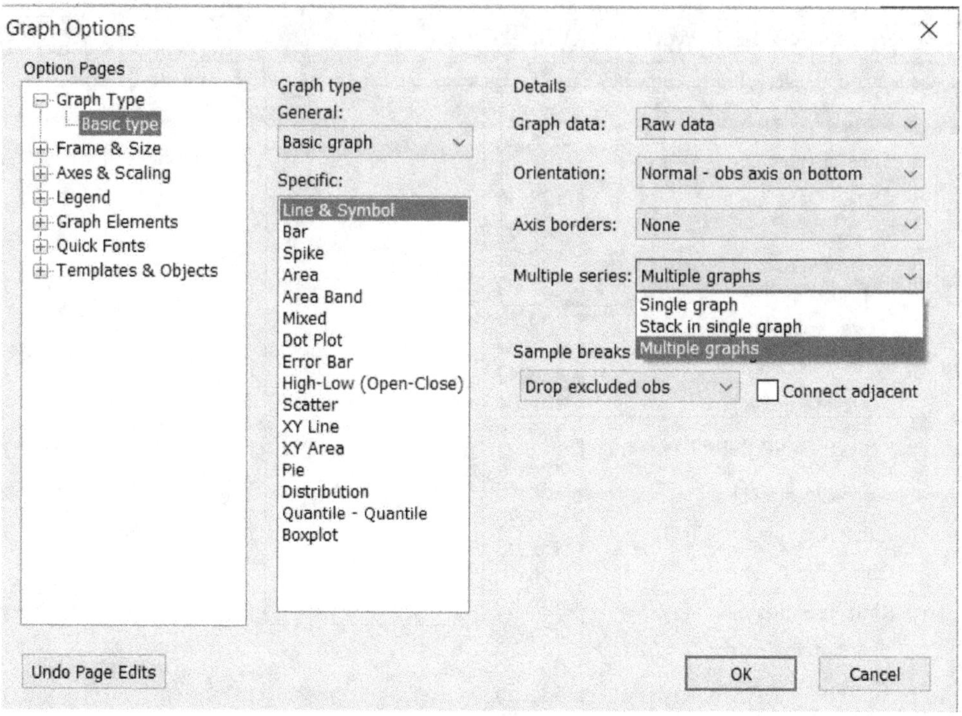

Table 1. Descriptive statistics

	RSOFIX
Mean	0.000205
Median	0.000239
Maximum	0.056383
Minimum	-0.047372
Std. Dev.	0.008611
Skewness	-0.107471
Kurtosis	7.435402
Jarque-Bera	1440.308
Probability	0.000
Sum	0.35876
Sum Sq. Dev.	0.129897
Observations	1753

Figure 12. The graphs of the raw series and return series

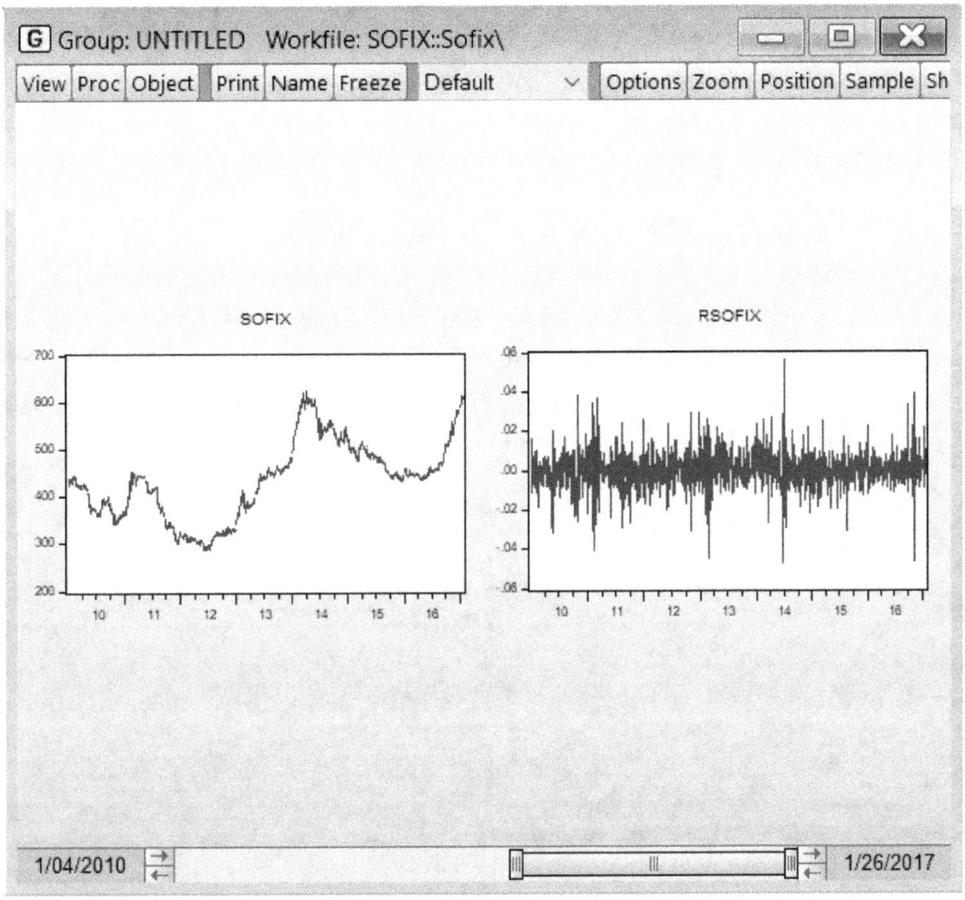

Figure 13. Bulgaria, SOFIX daily prices and returns

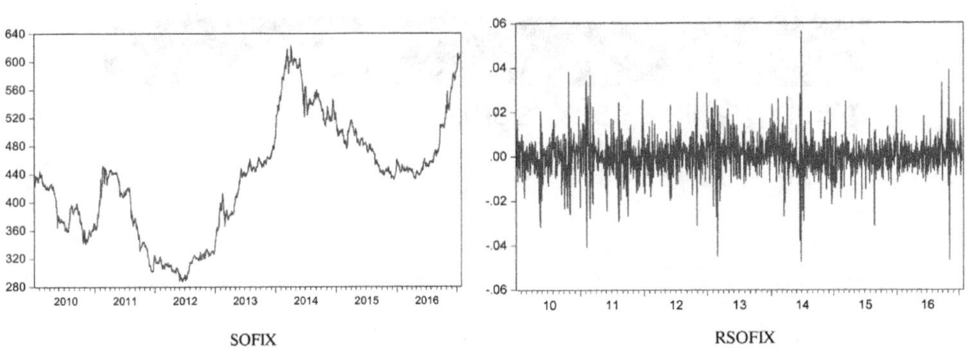

Figure 14. Command pane to generate the graph

Figure15. The window to open the line with the line graph

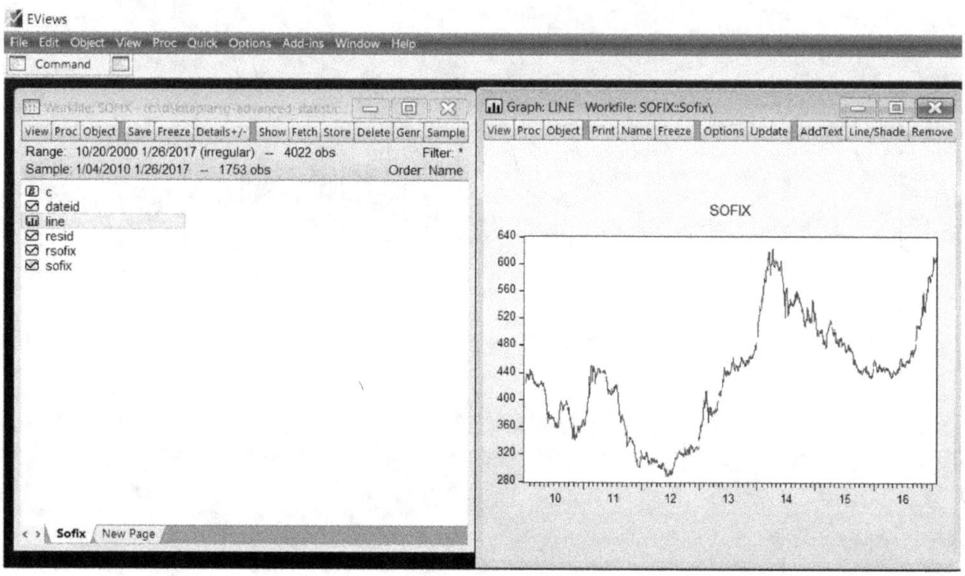

Figure 16. Command pane to generate the group of graphs

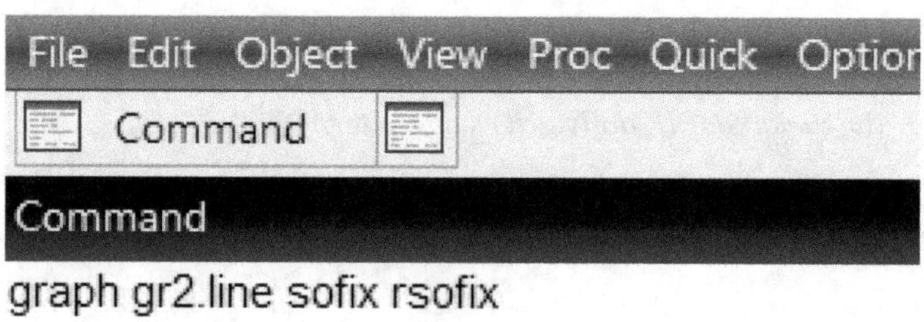

Figure 17. A grouped data object (gr2)

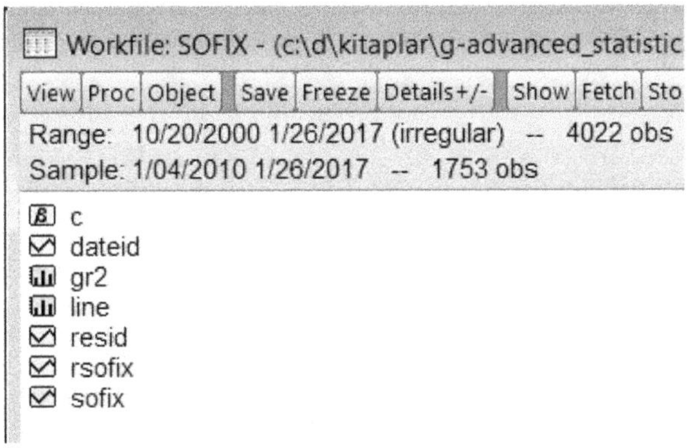

Figure 18. The window to open descriptive statistics of the variable

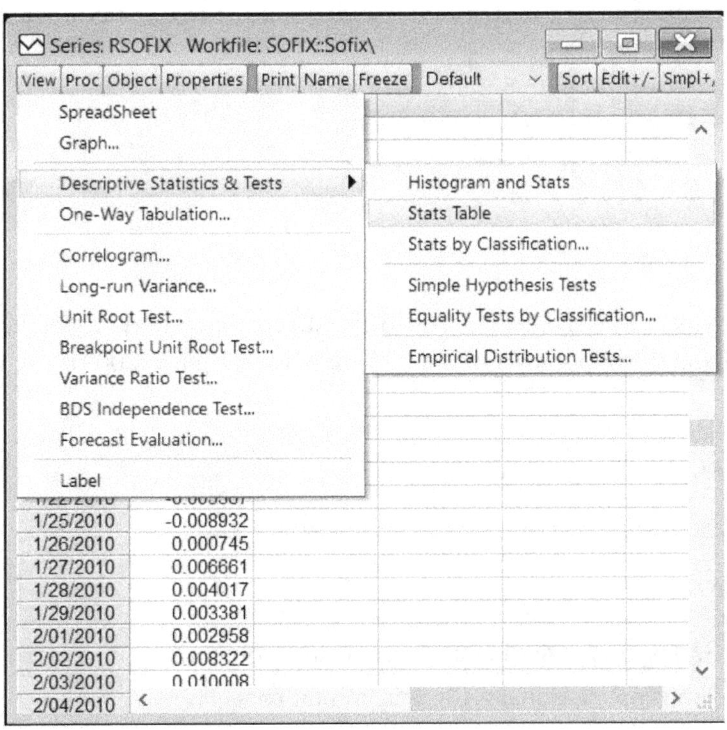

In 'Unit Root Test' window; on the left, there is a drop-down menu to determine the type of the unit root tests which are Augmented Dickey-Fuller (ADF), Dickey-Fuller GLS (ERS), Phillips- Perron, Kwiatkowski-Phillips-Schmidt-Shin (KPSS). Elliott, Rothenberg, and Stock Point Optimal (ERS, 1996), and Ng and Perron (Figure 22).

Figure 19. Descriptive statistics output

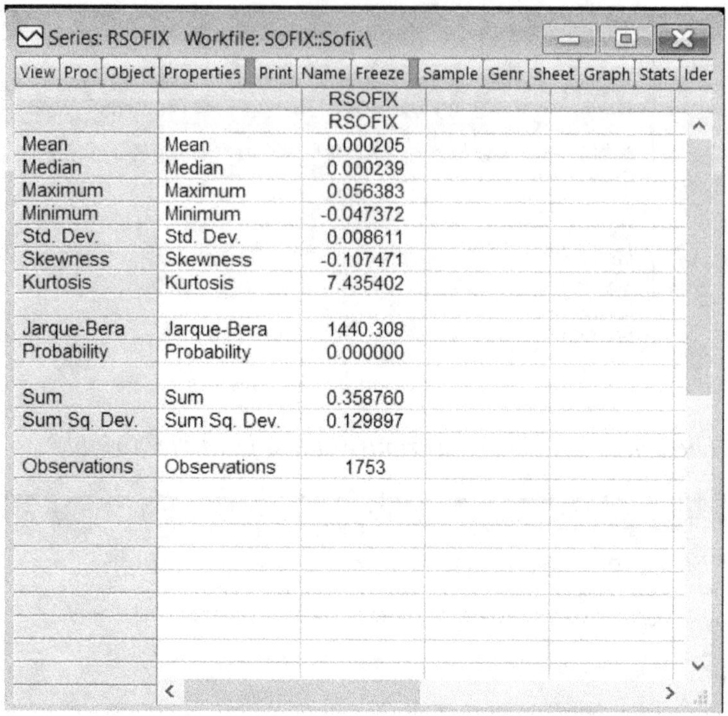
Series: RSOFIX Workfile: SOFIX::Sofix\

View | Proc | Object | Properties | Print | Name | Freeze | Sample | Genr | Sheet | Graph | Stats | Ider

		RSOFIX
		RSOFIX
Mean	Mean	0.000205
Median	Median	0.000239
Maximum	Maximum	0.056383
Minimum	Minimum	-0.047372
Std. Dev.	Std. Dev.	0.008611
Skewness	Skewness	-0.107471
Kurtosis	Kurtosis	7.435402
Jarque-Bera	Jarque-Bera	1440.308
Probability	Probability	0.000000
Sum	Sum	0.358760
Sum Sq. Dev.	Sum Sq. Dev.	0.129897
Observations	Observations	1753

In this chapter, the ADF test is used to investigate the stationarity of the variables. The model and the hypothesis of the test are below (Ugurlu,2009):

$$\Delta Y_t = \alpha_0 + \delta Y_{t-1} + \sum_{i=1}^{k} \Delta Y_{t-1} + \varepsilon_t \tag{7}$$

Test Hypothesis

$H_0: \delta = 0$ Series are not stationary, there is unit root
$H_1: \delta < 0$ Series are stationary, there is no unit root

After test type is chosen the level of the series must be chosen from 'Test for unit root' dialog box, hen model type Include in test equation'.'

$\Delta Y_t = \delta Y_{t-1} + \varepsilon_t$ None

Figure 20. The window to select unit root tests

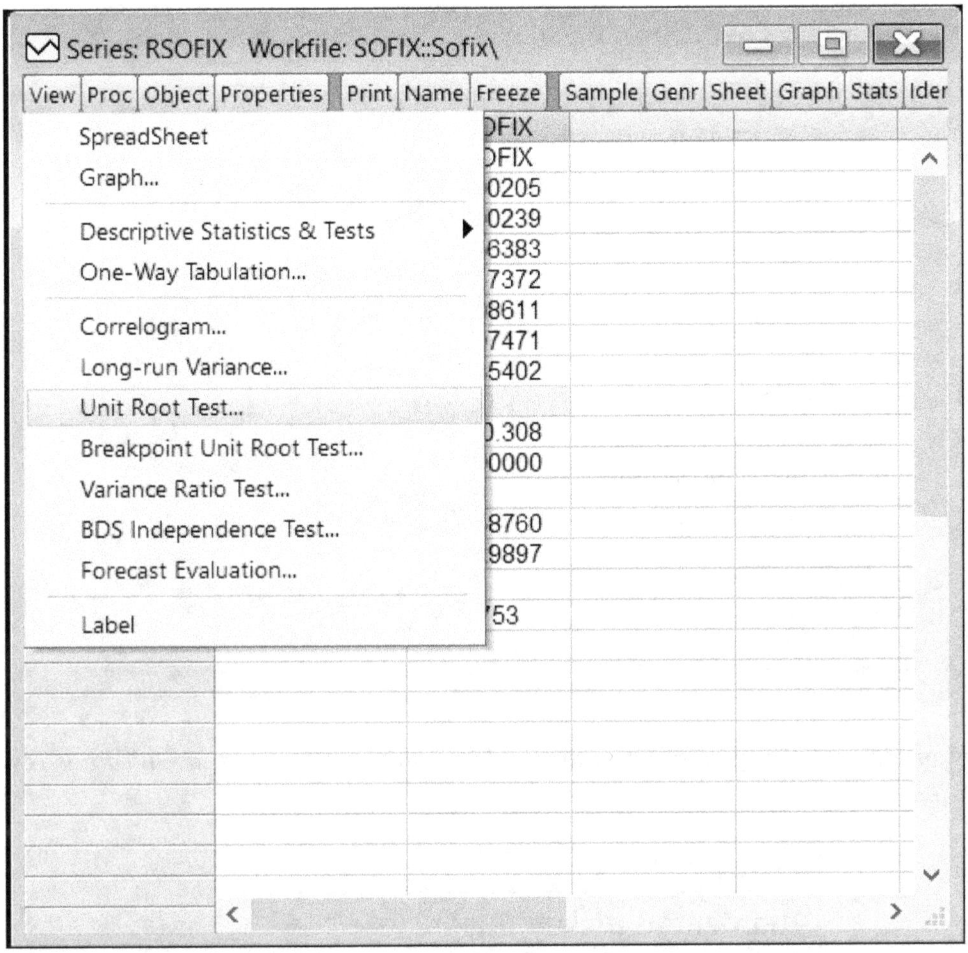

$$\Delta Y_t = \alpha_0 + \sum_{i=1}^{k} \Delta Y_{t-1} + \varepsilon_t \text{ Intercept}$$

$$\Delta Y_t = \alpha_0 + \delta Y_{t-1} + \sum_{i=1}^{k} \Delta Y_{t-1} + \varepsilon_t \text{ Trend and Intercept}$$

In the first step stationarity of level, series are tested. If the process of level series (RSOFIX in this application) is non-stationary and the process of differenced series (Δ RSOFIX in this application) is stationary, then the level of the series has a unit root, and the variable is known to be integrated of the first order. In conclusion, it is said that RSOFIX is I(1). In Figure 23 the output of unit root test can be seen. In this output selected options are as follows:

Figure 21. Selection and specification of a unit-root test

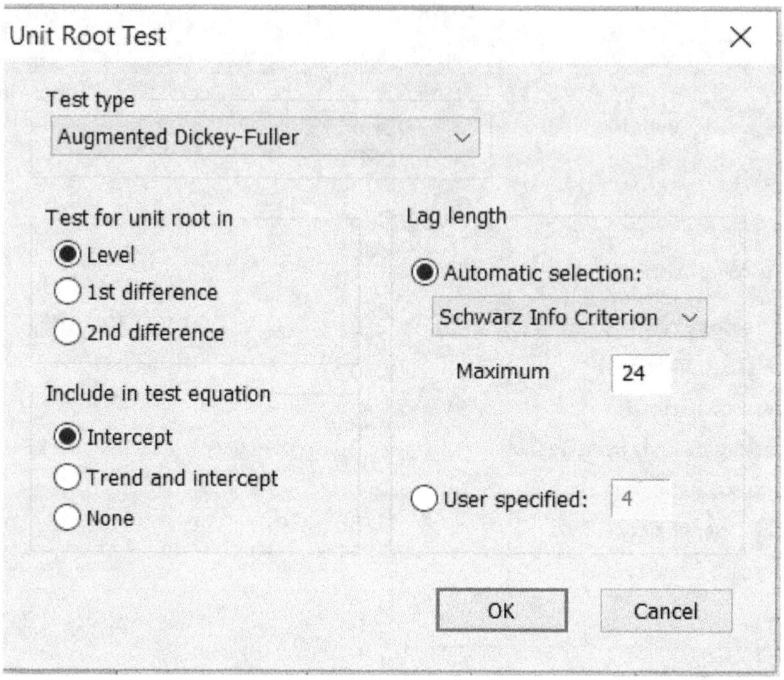

Figure 22. Some different types available for the unit root test in Unit Root Test Window

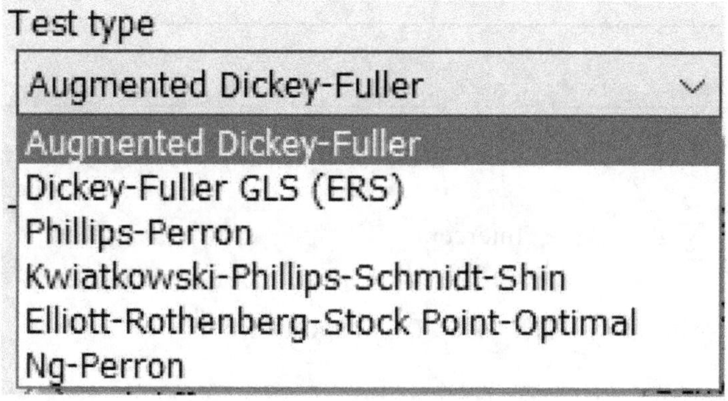

Test type Augmented Dickey-Fuller Test
Test for a unit root in Level
Include in test equation Intercept
Lag Length Schwarz Information Criterion (Automatic selection)

Figure 23. A unit root test output for SOFIX

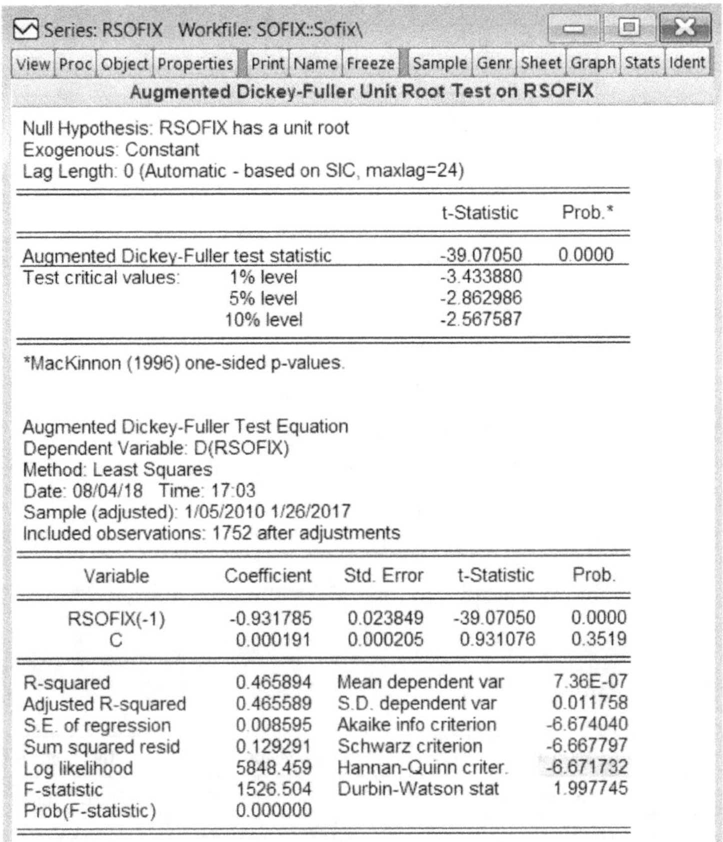

Series: RSOFIX Workfile: SOFIX::Sofix\

View | Proc | Object | Properties | Print | Name | Freeze | Sample | Genr | Sheet | Graph | Stats | Ident

Augmented Dickey-Fuller Unit Root Test on RSOFIX

Null Hypothesis: RSOFIX has a unit root
Exogenous: Constant
Lag Length: 0 (Automatic - based on SIC, maxlag=24)

		t-Statistic	Prob.*
Augmented Dickey-Fuller test statistic		-39.07050	0.0000
Test critical values:	1% level	-3.433880	
	5% level	-2.862986	
	10% level	-2.567587	

*MacKinnon (1996) one-sided p-values.

Augmented Dickey-Fuller Test Equation
Dependent Variable: D(RSOFIX)
Method: Least Squares
Date: 08/04/18 Time: 17:03
Sample (adjusted): 1/05/2010 1/26/2017
Included observations: 1752 after adjustments

Variable	Coefficient	Std. Error	t-Statistic	Prob.
RSOFIX(-1)	-0.931785	0.023849	-39.07050	0.0000
C	0.000191	0.000205	0.931076	0.3519

R-squared	0.465894	Mean dependent var	7.36E-07
Adjusted R-squared	0.465589	S.D. dependent var	0.011758
S.E. of regression	0.008595	Akaike info criterion	-6.674040
Sum squared resid	0.129291	Schwarz criterion	-6.667797
Log likelihood	5848.459	Hannan-Quinn criter.	-6.671732
F-statistic	1526.504	Durbin-Watson stat	1.997745
Prob(F-statistic)	0.000000		

The model output can be represented below

$$\Delta RSOFIX_t = \alpha_0 + \delta RSOFIX_{t-1} + \varepsilon_t \tag{8}$$

$$\Delta RSOFIX_t = 0.000191 \pm 0.931785 RSOFIX_{t-1} + \varepsilon_t$$

This test is used for 'Trend and intercept' and 'None' options, therefore in Table 2 all test results are summarized, and the results show that Augmented Dickey-Fuller (ADF) statistics reject the null hypothesis of a Unit Root at the 1% level of significance. Table 2 presents the representation of the results in a format or a research paper.

Figure 24. The window to draw correlograms of series

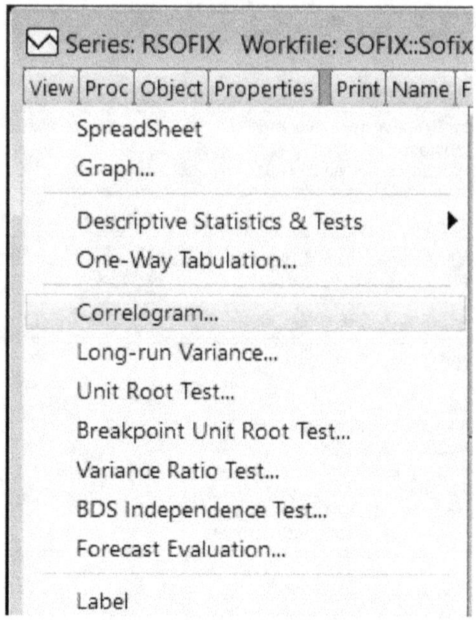

Table 2: ADF test results

	None		Intercept		Intercept and Trend	
Variable	ADF stat	p	ADF stat	P	ADF stat	P
RSOFIX	-39.06089***	0.0000	-39,08148***	0.0000	-39,1339***	0.0000
Note: *** denotes significance at the 1% level						

To continue to estimate ARIMA, we must plot the correlograms of the series; these measures help to determine the order of AR and MA terms. Correlogram plots the ACF (Autocorrelation Function) and PACF (Partial Autocorrelation Function) jointly with two-standard error bands around zero, and the correlogram can be interpreted as follows. If the PACF displays a sharp cutoff at lag p while the ACF decays more slowly, we say that the series has an AR(p) component, and vice versa.

To identify an AR and MA components of the model by using EViews, double-click on the variable name, EViews opens the series then click on ' View' and select 'Correlogram.' The new dialog window opens, and the lag selection of correlogram appears. We chose ten lags.

When we were estimating them we checked the correlograms to see if there were any significant Q-Stat values; then we estimated the exact models. In Figure 25, all p-values are lower than 0,01 observed in all cases except second and third lags. According to the ACF and PACF values both two values relatively high and decline slowly, therefore it is concluded that the RSOFIX has an AR(1) component. We estimate the mean model by clicking Quick/Estimate Equation.

Equations are written in the 'Equation Estimation' window using the format below:

Dependent variable constant independent variables

or

Dependent variable=c(1)+c(2)*independent variable1 + c(2)*independent variable2

For example, if our dependent variable is Y and independents are X, Z, and T; the equation will be

Y c X Z T

or

Y= c(1) +c(2)*X +C(3)*Z+ c(4)*T

In our example, we conclude that the suggested as an appropriate specification is ARIMA(1,0,0) model is shown in Figure 27 "RSOFIX" as a dependent variable, "c" intercept and AR(1) as an independent variable.

In the 'Estimation settings' options, the method selected is the least squares (LS) estimation method (NLS and ARMA), as well as the sample used in this analysis.

Figure 25. The output of the correlogram of SOFIX

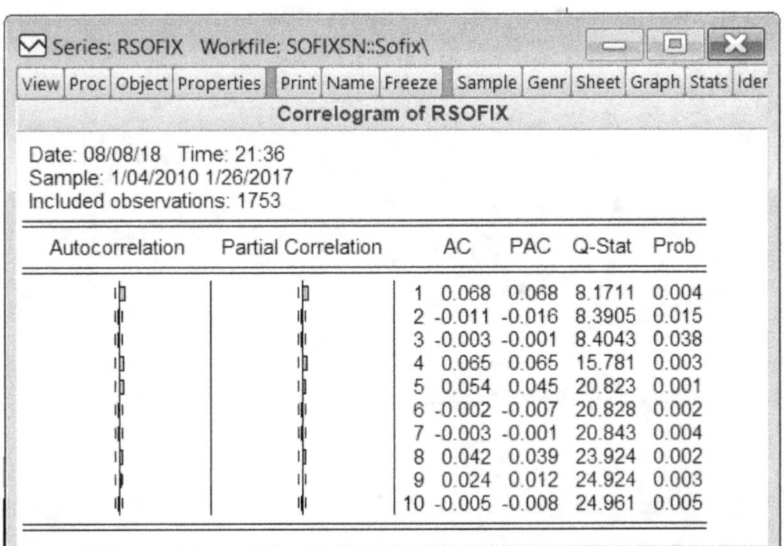

Series: RSOFIX Workfile: SOFIXSN::Sofix\

View | Proc | Object | Properties | Print | Name | Freeze | Sample | Genr | Sheet | Graph | Stats | Ider

Correlogram of RSOFIX

Date: 08/08/18 Time: 21:36
Sample: 1/04/2010 1/26/2017
Included observations: 1753

Autocorrelation	Partial Correlation		AC	PAC	Q-Stat	Prob
		1	0.068	0.068	8.1711	0.004
		2	-0.011	-0.016	8.3905	0.015
		3	-0.003	-0.001	8.4043	0.038
		4	0.065	0.065	15.781	0.003
		5	0.054	0.045	20.823	0.001
		6	-0.002	-0.007	20.828	0.002
		7	-0.003	-0.001	20.843	0.004
		8	0.042	0.039	23.924	0.002
		9	0.024	0.012	24.924	0.003
		10	-0.005	-0.008	24.961	0.005

Figure 26. The window to estimate an equation

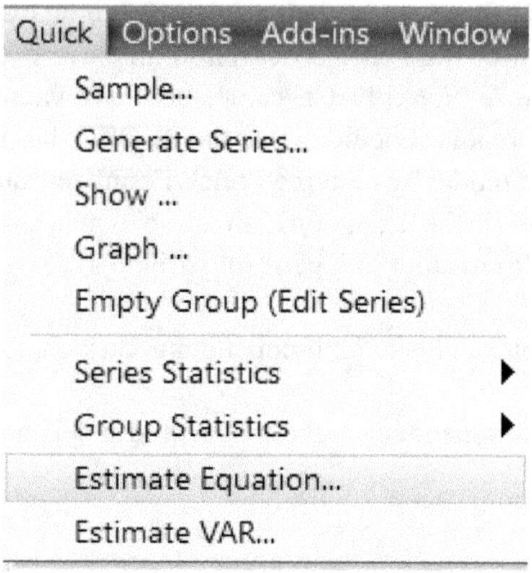

Figure 27. Equation specification, estimation settings, and options

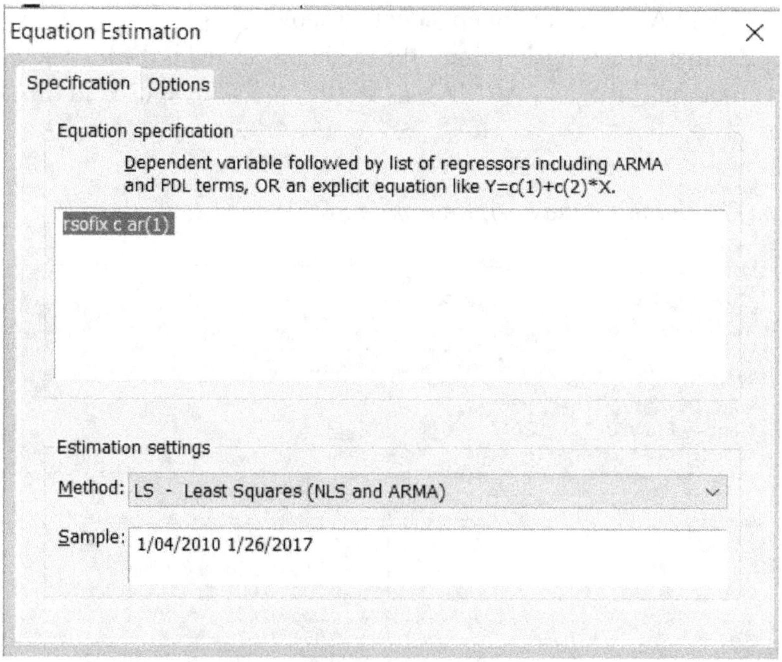

Figure 28 shows the output of the ARIMA(1,0,0) model, in the model AR (1) coefficient is significantly different from zero (p<0,01). This means that AR(1) component is right to use in the man model. If it were not significant, we would try other AR and MA components to find significant model.

Although we use ARIMA (1,0,0) model, alternative models can be estimated, and the performance of the alternative models can be compared based on some criteria such as AIC and BIC. In this chapter, we use another procedure which is based on residual. We check the residuals if the residuals have no AR and MA component in its correlogram, it means that the model is true. In this procedure, we have to pay attention to the statistical significance of AR and MA coefficients before checking residuals.

To apply this procedure click on residual after the model estimation output obtained and drew its correlogram Figure 29 shows the correlogram of the residuals and the results show that all Q-Stat p values are reasonably high, and no ACF and PACF values are out of the dashed line.

Before the ARCH/GARCH model estimated, we need to test whether the residual of the model includes ARCH effects. If residuals have no ARCH effect, then it makes no sense to estimate the model with ARCH disturbances. This test is very important in time series analysis to assure that the model ARCH is appropriate for data that will be the case in the analysis.

Figure 28. The output of the model

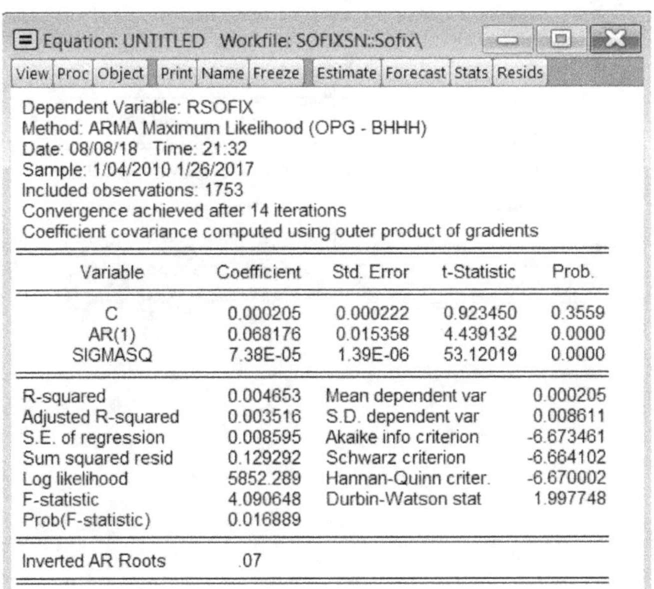

Equation: UNTITLED Workfile: SOFIXSN::Sofix\

View | Proc | Object | Print | Name | Freeze | Estimate | Forecast | Stats | Resids

Dependent Variable: RSOFIX
Method: ARMA Maximum Likelihood (OPG - BHHH)
Date: 08/08/18 Time: 21:32
Sample: 1/04/2010 1/26/2017
Included observations: 1753
Convergence achieved after 14 iterations
Coefficient covariance computed using outer product of gradients

Variable	Coefficient	Std. Error	t-Statistic	Prob.
C	0.000205	0.000222	0.923450	0.3559
AR(1)	0.068176	0.015358	4.439132	0.0000
SIGMASQ	7.38E-05	1.39E-06	53.12019	0.0000

R-squared	0.004653	Mean dependent var	0.000205
Adjusted R-squared	0.003516	S.D. dependent var	0.008611
S.E. of regression	0.008595	Akaike info criterion	-6.673461
Sum squared resid	0.129292	Schwarz criterion	-6.664102
Log likelihood	5852.289	Hannan-Quinn criter.	-6.670002
F-statistic	4.090648	Durbin-Watson stat	1.997748
Prob(F-statistic)	0.016889		

Inverted AR Roots	.07

Figure 29. The output of the correlograms of the residuals of the ARIMA model

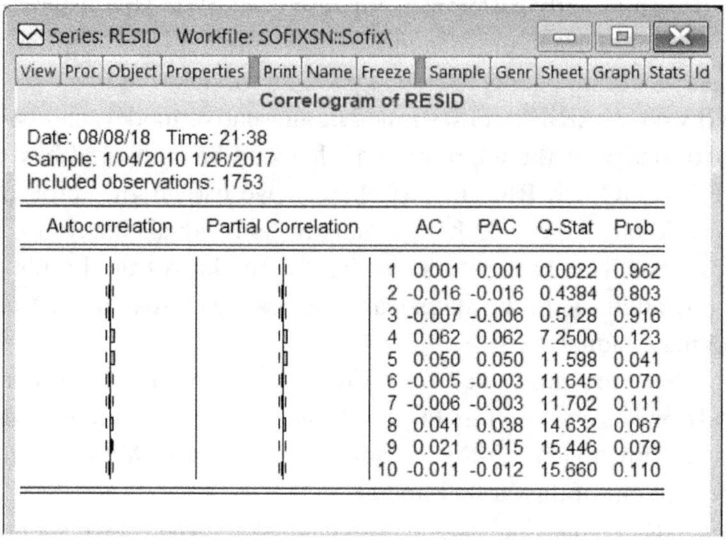

Figure 30. The window to select Heteroscedasticity Tests

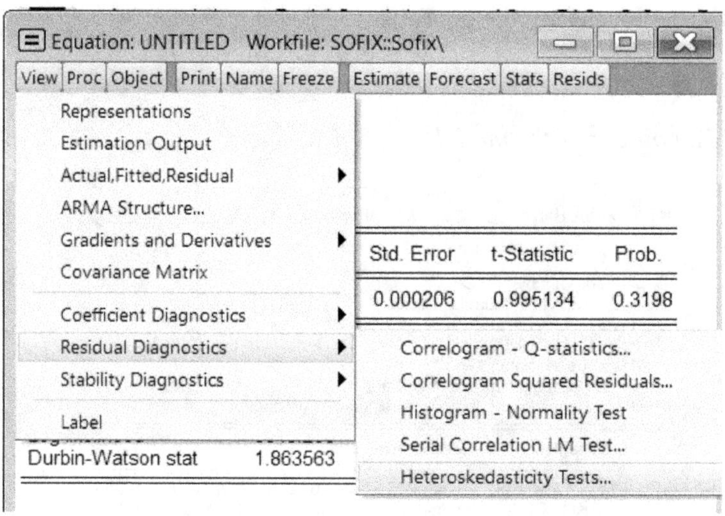

The ARCH test null hypothesis is one of a joint hypothesis that assumes all q lags of the squared residuals have coefficient values that are not significantly different from zero.

The first step of the ARCH test is estimating the residual $\left(\hat{u}_t\right)$ from the model, then take a square of estimated residuals and regress them on q own lags to test ARCH of order:

$$\hat{u}_t^2 = \alpha_0 + \alpha_1 \hat{u}_{t-1}^2 + \alpha_2 \hat{u}_{t-2}^2 + \ldots + \alpha_q \hat{u}_{t-q}^2 + v_t \tag{8}$$

where v_t is an error term. From the regression R^2 is obtained to calculate test statistics. The test statistics is defined as n(number of observation) x R^2.

$H_0 : \alpha_1 = 0$ and $\alpha_2 = 0$ and $\alpha_3 = 0 \ldots$. and $\alpha_q = 0$ No ARCH effect.

The statistic n*R^2 is asymptotically Chi distributed under the null hypothesis. If the value of the test statistic is greater than the critical value from the Chi distribution, the null hypothesis is rejected. We test all models for the ARCH effect by ARCH-LM test. To test the existence of ARCH effect click 'Residual Diagnostics/ Heteroskedasticity Tests' then 'Heteroscedasticity Tests' window opens.

In the 'Heteroskedasticity Tests' window (Figure 31), 'Number of lags' option shows the ARCH order. If the number of lag is 1 the result shows the ARCH(1) test result.

The null hypothesis is tested with the statistic n*R^2, n is the number of observation and R^2 from the regression. In the output (Figure 32) Obs*R-squared shows calculated test statistics. Prop. Chi-Square(1) presents the critical value of the Chi-Square table. Thus the output shows that the null hypothesis of no heteroscedasticity is rejected. Furthermore, the existence of heteroscedasticity in the residuals are tested for ARCH(2), ARCH(3), ARCH(4), ARCH(8), ARCH(12) and ARCH(24) then summarized in Table 4.

Table 4 presents the representation of ARCH test results for the research paper.

Table 4 shows the result of ARCH tests for different lags from first to twenty-fourth. All the ARCH-LM test results show that the series has an ARCH effect on their residuals. Therefore, the residual terms of return series which are investigated can be modeled by GARCH models.

Figure 33 there are so many dialog boxes and drop down menus. We specify ARCH type model which will be used from the 'Model' drop-down menu. Also, a variety of error distributions can be specified from 'Error distribution' drop-down menu. We use Generalized Error Distribution (GED) to capture the fat tails.

Figure 31. The window to select ARCH Heteroscedasticity Tests

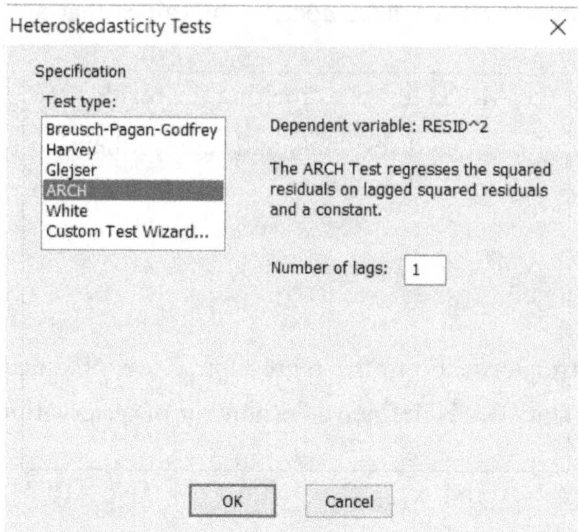

Figure 32. The output of White's heteroskedasticity test

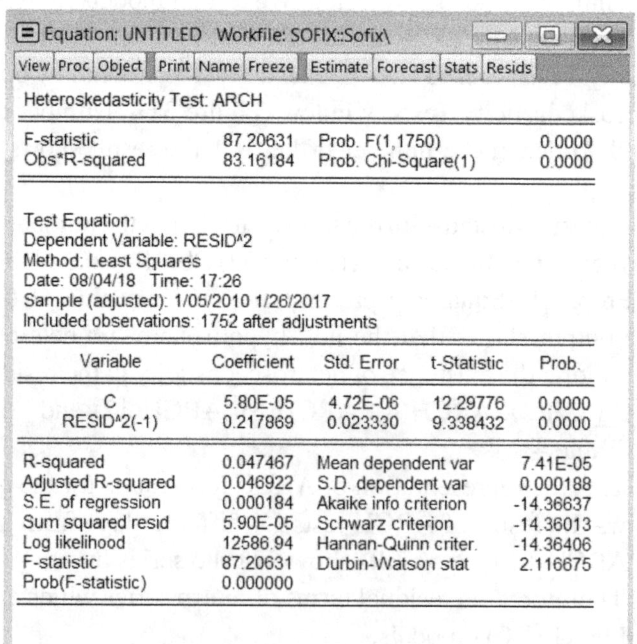
Equation: UNTITLED Workfile: SOFIX::Sofix\

View | Proc | Object | Print | Name | Freeze | Estimate | Forecast | Stats | Resids

Heteroskedasticity Test: ARCH

F-statistic	87.20631	Prob. F(1,1750)	0.0000
Obs*R-squared	83.16184	Prob. Chi-Square(1)	0.0000

Test Equation:
Dependent Variable: RESID^2
Method: Least Squares
Date: 08/04/18 Time: 17:26
Sample (adjusted): 1/05/2010 1/26/2017
Included observations: 1752 after adjustments

Variable	Coefficient	Std. Error	t-Statistic	Prob.
C	5.80E-05	4.72E-06	12.29776	0.0000
RESID^2(-1)	0.217869	0.023330	9.338432	0.0000

R-squared	0.047467	Mean dependent var	7.41E-05
Adjusted R-squared	0.046922	S.D. dependent var	0.000188
S.E. of regression	0.000184	Akaike info criterion	-14.36637
Sum squared resid	5.90E-05	Schwarz criterion	-14.36013
Log likelihood	12586.94	Hannan-Quinn criter.	-14.36406
F-statistic	87.20631	Durbin-Watson stat	2.116675
Prob(F-statistic)	0.000000		

Table 4. ARCH test results

	RSOFIX
ARCH(1)LM Stat	87.20631***
ARCH(2)LM Stat	203.3906***
ARCH(3)LM Stat	205.3573***
ARCH(4)LM Stat	205.6046***
ARCH(8)LM Stat	231.7501***
ARCH(12)LM Stat	237.9849***
ARCH(24)LM Stat	241.3814***
Note: *** denotes rejection of null hypothesis at the 1% level	

Figure 33. The window to estimate an ARCH model

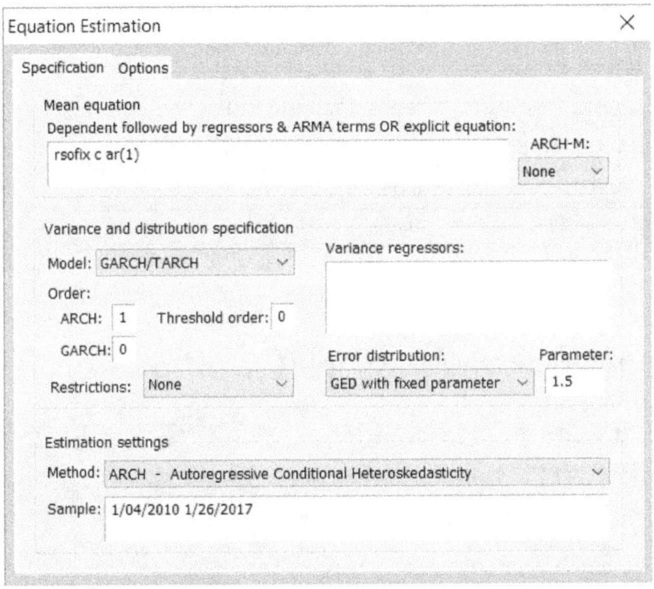

The window is shown in Figure 33 an ARCH(l) model is estimated by clicking "0" to 'GARCH order' and "0" to 'Threshold order' and "1" to 'ARCH order' options. To estimate the ARCH(2) model write a "2" to 'ARCH order' option and so on.

Figure 34 shows the output of the ARCH(1) model which is estimated in Figure 33.

To estimate the GARCH model, 'Model' drop down menu is chosen as a GARCH/ TARCH. 'Threshold order 'must be specified as a 0 and ARCH and GARCH order can be chosen based on user demand. We use GARCH(1,1), model.

Figure 36 shows the output of the GARCH model which is estimated Figure 35.

Figure 34. The output of the ARCH estimation

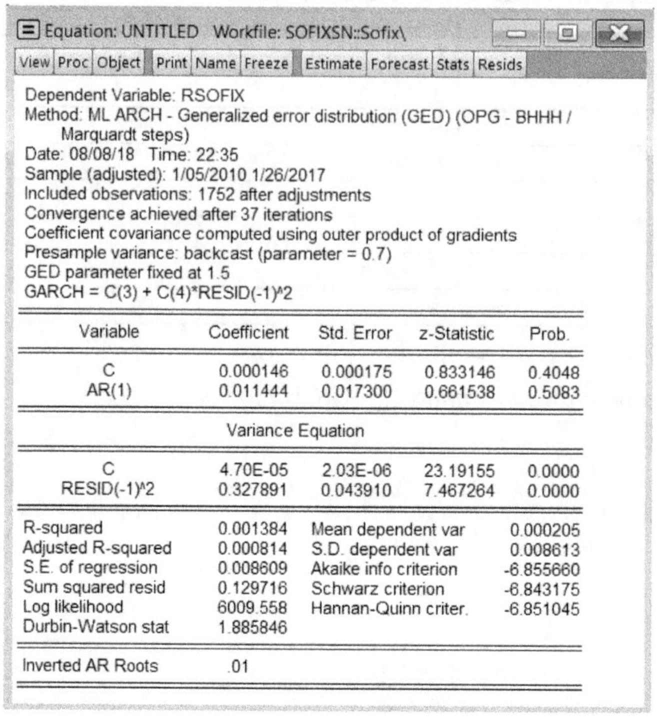

Equation: UNTITLED Workfile: SOFIXSN::Sofix\

View | Proc | Object | Print | Name | Freeze | Estimate | Forecast | Stats | Resids

Dependent Variable: RSOFIX
Method: ML ARCH - Generalized error distribution (GED) (OPG - BHHH / Marquardt steps)
Date: 08/08/18 Time: 22:35
Sample (adjusted): 1/05/2010 1/26/2017
Included observations: 1752 after adjustments
Convergence achieved after 37 iterations
Coefficient covariance computed using outer product of gradients
Presample variance: backcast (parameter = 0.7)
GED parameter fixed at 1.5
GARCH = C(3) + C(4)*RESID(-1)^2

Variable	Coefficient	Std. Error	z-Statistic	Prob.
C	0.000146	0.000175	0.833146	0.4048
AR(1)	0.011444	0.017300	0.661538	0.5083
		Variance Equation		
C	4.70E-05	2.03E-06	23.19155	0.0000
RESID(-1)^2	0.327891	0.043910	7.467264	0.0000

R-squared	0.001384	Mean dependent var	0.000205
Adjusted R-squared	0.000814	S.D. dependent var	0.008613
S.E. of regression	0.008609	Akaike info criterion	-6.855660
Sum squared resid	0.129716	Schwarz criterion	-6.843175
Log likelihood	6009.558	Hannan-Quinn criter.	-6.851045
Durbin-Watson stat	1.885846		

Inverted AR Roots	.01

Figure 35. The window to estimate a GARCH

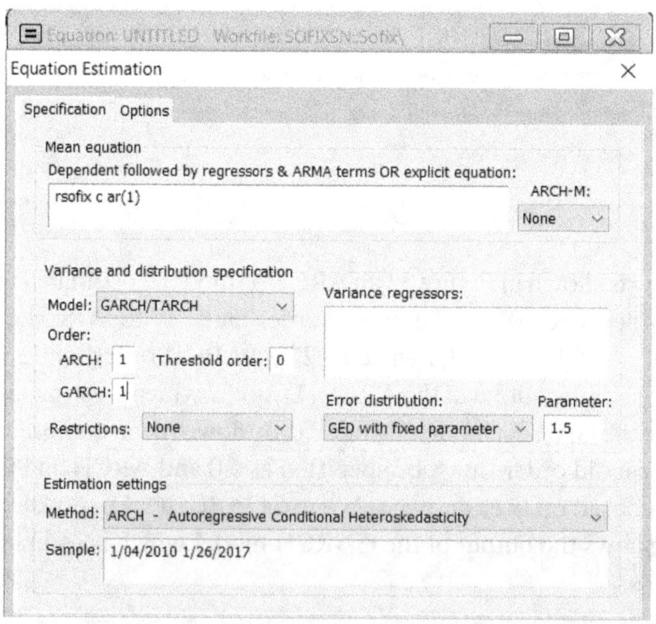

Figure 36. The output of the GARCH estimation

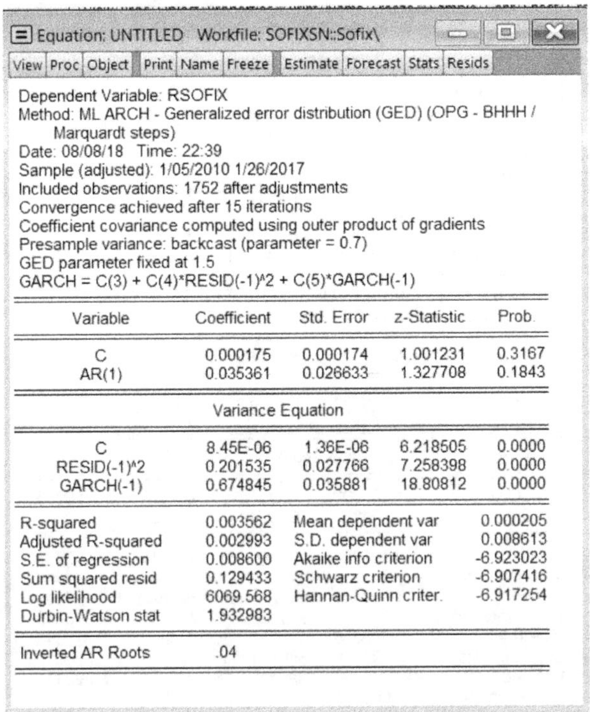

Equation: UNTITLED Workfile: SOFIXSN::Sofix\

View | Proc | Object | Print | Name | Freeze | Estimate | Forecast | Stats | Resids

Dependent Variable: RSOFIX
Method: ML ARCH - Generalized error distribution (GED) (OPG - BHHH / Marquardt steps)
Date: 08/08/18 Time: 22:39
Sample (adjusted): 1/05/2010 1/26/2017
Included observations: 1752 after adjustments
Convergence achieved after 15 iterations
Coefficient covariance computed using outer product of gradients
Presample variance: backcast (parameter = 0.7)
GED parameter fixed at 1.5
GARCH = C(3) + C(4)*RESID(-1)^2 + C(5)*GARCH(-1)

Variable	Coefficient	Std. Error	z-Statistic	Prob.
C	0.000175	0.000174	1.001231	0.3167
AR(1)	0.035361	0.026633	1.327708	0.1843
		Variance Equation		
C	8.45E-06	1.36E-06	6.218505	0.0000
RESID(-1)^2	0.201535	0.027766	7.258398	0.0000
GARCH(-1)	0.674845	0.035881	18.80812	0.0000

R-squared	0.003562	Mean dependent var	0.000205
Adjusted R-squared	0.002993	S.D. dependent var	0.008613
S.E. of regression	0.008600	Akaike info criterion	-6.923023
Sum squared resid	0.129433	Schwarz criterion	-6.907416
Log likelihood	6069.568	Hannan-Quinn criter.	-6.917254
Durbin-Watson stat	1.932983		

Inverted AR Roots .04

Figure 37. The window to estimate an EGARCH

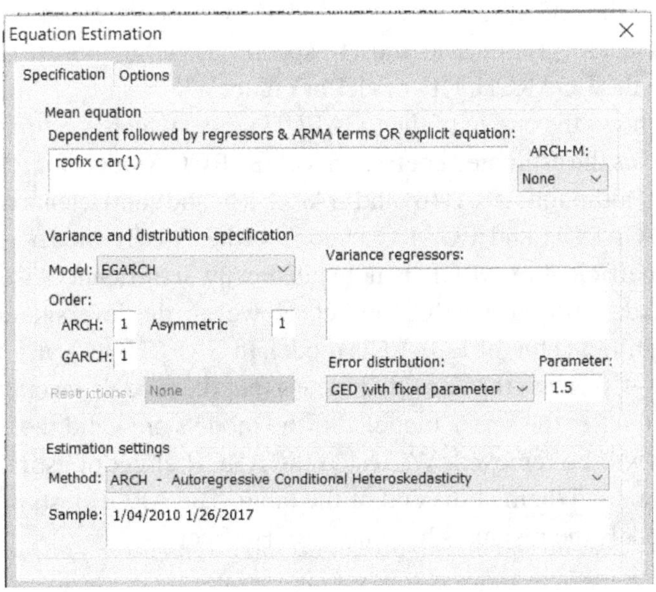

Figure 38. The output of the EGARCH estimation

Equation: UNTITLED Workfile: SOFIXSN::Sofix\

View | Proc | Object | Print | Name | Freeze | Estimate | Forecast | Stats | Resids

Dependent Variable: RSOFIX
Method: ML ARCH - Generalized error distribution (GED) (OPG - BHHH / Marquardt steps)
Date: 08/08/18 Time: 22:41
Sample (adjusted): 1/05/2010 1/26/2017
Included observations: 1752 after adjustments
Convergence achieved after 24 iterations
Coefficient covariance computed using outer product of gradients
Presample variance: backcast (parameter = 0.7)
GED parameter fixed at 1.5
LOG(GARCH) = C(3) + C(4)*ABS(RESID(-1)/@SQRT(GARCH(-1))) + C(5)*RESID(-1)/@SQRT(GARCH(-1)) + C(6)*LOG(GARCH(-1))

Variable	Coefficient	Std. Error	z-Statistic	Prob.
C	0.000184	0.000171	1.074693	0.2825
AR(1)	0.021254	0.025518	0.832911	0.4049
	Variance Equation			
C(3)	-1.426693	0.211310	-6.751651	0.0000
C(4)	0.354202	0.035114	10.08726	0.0000
C(5)	-0.004510	0.019477	-0.231578	0.8169
C(6)	0.881003	0.020185	43.64643	0.0000

R-squared	0.002442	Mean dependent var	0.000205
Adjusted R-squared	0.001872	S.D. dependent var	0.008613
S.E. of regression	0.008605	Akaike info criterion	-6.915340
Sum squared resid	0.129579	Schwarz criterion	-6.896612
Log likelihood	6063.838	Hannan-Quinn criter.	-6.908418
Durbin-Watson stat	1.905211		

Inverted AR Roots	.02

To estimate the EGARCH model, 'Model' drop down menu is chosen as an EGARCH/TARCH. 'Asymmetric' must be specified as a 1 or more to have a leverage effect. We use the EGARCH(1,1) model in Figure 37.

Figure 38 shows the output of the EGARCH model which is estimated Figure 38

Table 5 shows the estimated coefficients of GARCH Models for RSOFIX series. In these results, although ARCH (α) and GARCH(β) and coefficients are statistically significant in GARCH and EGARCH models, the ARCH model is not relevant because the coefficient of ARCH is not statistically significant. Also, residuals of the ARCH model still have ARCH effect. However, the leverage effects are not statistically significant for the EGARCH model. In GARCH(1,1), all coefficients are positive, and $\alpha + \beta$ is less than one that means that the models meet the restrictions (Uğurlu,2014). After the series modeled if the models are valid the ARCH effects of the models will be removed. We tested the ARCH effect of estimated GARCH model and presented them at the end of the table. The ARCH tests show that after the ARCH models the residuals have no ARCH effect.

Table 5 presents the representation format of GARCH-type models for a research paper. Although in this application we only estimate ARCH(1), GARCH(1,1) and EGARCH(1,1) model, different ARCH, GARCH or EGARHC model can be estimated such as ARCH(2), ARCH(3), GARC(1,2), EGARCH(2,21) and so on. After different types of the model estimated they could be compared using some statistical criteria and the best model can be chosen based on them.

CONCLUSION

ARCH and GARCH type models have been applied in time series analyses especially on financial time series data. Because it is more successful in financial data because those have some features which need non-linear modeling. This chapter has presented an overview of the ARCH model and two principal members belonging to the GARCH-type models that are ARCH, GARCH, and EGARCH models. Furthermore, the estimation procedure of them has been examined in detail using EViews 9 software

Table 5. Estimated coefficients of GARCH models for RSOFIX

	ARCH		GARCH(1,1)		EGARCH	
	Coefficient	**p**	**Coefficient**	**p**	**Coefficient**	**p**
Mean Equation						
AR(1)	0.059040***	0.0006	0.035361	0.1843	0.021254	0.4049
α_0	3.50E-05	0.9666	8.48E-06 ***	0.0000	-1.426693***	0.0000
α	0.480934	0.6990	0.201535***	0.0000	0.354202***	0.0000
γ	-	-	-		-0.004510	0.8169
β	-	-	0.674845***	0.0000	0.881003***	0.0000
AIC	-6.781446		-6.923023		-6.915340	
SIC	-6.768961		-6.907416		-6.896612	
DW-stat	1.885846		1.932983		1.905211	
ARCH(1)LM Stat	82.88639	0.0000	0.300760	0.5834	0.012264	0.9118
ARCH(2)LM Stat	203.1080	0.0000	0.940801	0.6248	1.432841	0.4885
ARCH(3)LM Stat	205.1988	0.0000	2.251945	0.5218	2.441195	0.4860
ARCH(4)LM Stat	205.3870	0.0000	2.286820	0.6832	2.440887	0.6553
ARCH(8)LM Stat	231.1710	0.0000	6.635872	0.5764	6.696002	0.5698
ARCH(12)LM Stat	237.4293	0.0000	9.036179	0.6998	8.622250	0.7348
ARCH(24)LM Stat	240.5435	0.0000	14.77923	0.9271	14.22562	0.9414

package, and the representations of the outputs are demonstrated with examples. The data ranges from January 1st, 2010 to January 26th, 2017.

The ARIMA model in the chapter was chosen using ACF and PACF. The results indicate that the ARIMA(1,0,0) model is convenient. Since the ARCH test evidenced heteroskedasticity in the data, the ARCH(1), GARCH(1,1) and EGARCH(1,1) models are used to model volatility. In conclusion, we formulate and estimate selected volatility models and show their representation and interpretation.

REFERENCES

Bollerslev, T. (1986). Generalized Autoregressive Conditional Heteroskedasticity. *Journal of Econometrics*, *31*(3), 307–327. doi:10.1016/0304-4076(86)90063-1

Engle, R.-F. (1982). Autoregressive Conditional Heteroskedasticity with Estimates of The Variance of UK Inflation. *Econometrica*, *50*(4), 987–1008. doi:10.2307/1912773

Floros, C. (2008). Modelling Volatility Using GARCH Models, Evidence From Egypt and Israel. *Middle Eastern Finance and Economics*, (2), 31-41

Nelson, D.-B. (1991). Conditional Heteroscedasticity In Asset Returns, A New Approach. *Econometrica*, *59*(2), 347–370. doi:10.2307/2938260

Taylor, S.-J. (1986). *Modelling Financial Time Series*. Chichester, UK: John Wiley & Sons.

Thomas, S., & Mitchell, H. (2005). *GARCH Modeling of High-Frequency Volatility in Australia's National Electricity Market* (Discussion Paper). Melbourne Centre for Financial Studies.

Ugurlu, E. (2009). Real exchange rate and economic growth: Turkey. *Manas University Journal of Social Sciences*, *22*, 191–212.

Uğurlu E. (2014). Modelling Volatility: Evidence from The Bucharest Stock Exchange. Journal of Applied Economic Sciences, 9(4-30), 718-727.

Chapter 15
Access to Research Online:
Technology, Trends, and the Future

Kristina Symes
OpenAthens, UK

ABSTRACT

The world is hungry for knowledge and quickly-producing researchers of varying caliber who are less dependent on the physical space than ever before. This presents a number of challenges to librarians, out of which issues related to technology stand out prominently. How can the library pave roads to curated digital content and make it easily accessible from any location? How does it remain relevant in the age of Google, sophisticated piracy and the open access movement? The chapter begins with an overview of IP-based and federated access technologies, touching on less-used methods as well. Personally-conducted interviews with library industry experts aim to determine current trends in order to provide a collective insight into future developments. These include the widespread migration towards cloud-based services, the global RA21 initiative, the open access movement, the need for better statistics, and new ways of content delivery, all of which affect libraries' demands for remote access in different ways.

INTRODUCTION

Society's need to access information has increased massively in the last decade. Why? Many reasons. For one, the technology is there. Google has made it easy to get excited about learning. On the other hand, due to technological advances, nobody can predict what the future will look like. The ability to adapt has long been considered one of the top survival skills and it is now taking a digital form. Universities now

DOI: 10.4018/978-1-5225-8437-7.ch015

offer more student exchange, work experience and distance learning programmes than ever before, remote working is becoming more popular and field research is no longer a privilege reserved for post-graduate academics but a requirement for most professionals regardless of their qualification level. Library director Dr. Katherine O. Quinnell illustrated this trend by telling the author that 60% of Athens State University students are accessing resources online and the distance learning programme is expected to grow to 75% remote student population within the next 2 years (personal interview, June 24, 2018). Remote access is now an inseparable part of any library's offering, however, despite technological advances that gave the world Artificial Intelligence, biometric authentication, the Internet of Things and Blockchain, librarians still have a limited choice of products when looking to enable remote access to online resources for their patrons.

At the same time, the internet users are starting to realise their data has value (Fontana, 2018). Long-established access methods, such as username and password authentication, are no longer good enough. Sharing credentials, in particular, is receiving a lot of criticism and is now considered a big no-no. IP-based access, although still widely prevalent, is also considered unsafe. While security is a very important aspect of users' daily interactions with the World Wide Web, the user experience is often the deciding factor, determining what services are going to be used more. Personalisation – the ability to tailor each website to one's needs – is a significant part of that while Single Sign-On is another highly desirable feature. Initiatives like RA21 (Resource Access for the Twenty-First Century) are striving to eradicate both user experience and security compromises each researcher has to deal with when older access methods are at play, also marking a step towards the end of the IP-based access to content.

The chapter begins with a brief but comprehensive overview of IP-based and federated access technologies, touching on less used (and occasionally misused) SIP/NCIP, OpenID Connect, and OAuth. Drawing on daily interactions with information professionals from all over the world and personally conducted interviews with other library industry experts, including software vendors and publishers, the author aims to identify and discuss current trends in order to provide a collective insight of what may be around the corner. Some of the trends discussed in this chapter include the widespread migration towards cloud-based services and infrastructures, the global RA21 initiative, the open access movement, the need for better statistics and new ways of content delivery, all of which affect libraries' demands for remote access products in different ways. Participants in the conversation demonstrate progressive thinking without resistance to new technology. On the contrary, they embrace the multitude of possibilities these advancements will bring. The library is ready to transform.

BACKGROUND

The days when research was conducted exclusively in the library with a select few academics sitting amongst admirable piles of books, are gone. The world is hungry for knowledge and quickly producing researchers of varying calibre who are less dependent on the physical space than ever before. This presents a number of challenges to librarians, out of which issues related to technology stand out prominently. How can the library pave roads to curated digital content and make it easily accessible from any location? How does it remain relevant in the age of Google, Wikipedia, and sophisticated piracy as well as the open access movement? To find answers to these questions, one must courageously indulge in the understanding of existing and upcoming technologies. Why so? A wide sample of librarians the author had the privilege to speak to believe that in the world of technological revolution and the generation of the digital native users, this is what the future of the library will depend on, its ability to continuously innovate itself in ways of knowledge delivery to those who seek it.

As written in 'Access to Online Resources: A Guide for the Modern Librarian', the sheer number of technologies librarians deal with on a daily basis is astonishing (Botyriute, 2018). What is even more surprising is that helpful literature is scarce and often limited to an article or an overview of the implementation of a certain product. Only a limited amount of material exists to help library professionals make sense of all the options available to them and encourage technological progress within the library. While various national and regional communities exist to support collaboration and knowledge-sharing, a lot of the librarians the author has spoken to indicated they are not sure how their library's remote access strategy compares to the global picture – are they behind the curve or ahead of it? Compelled to investigate this further, the author was fascinated to determine how the thoughts of librarians from different parts of the world seem to form similar trends. Furthermore, the daily struggles and concerns related to remote access are common to the industry, irrespective of librarians' geographical location. This reaffirmed the author's belief that the world's libraries are all in the same boat, unified by their struggles and aspirations.

This chapter explores the most popular remote access technologies used in the libraries around the world, providing a side-by-side comparison of each as well as the views of those who utilise these methods. A collection of personal interviews with industry experts forms the basis of the author's aim to identify trends as the community sees them and predict how the library is going to change in the near future.

TECHNOLOGY

In a digital library context, remote access refers to the patron's ability to enter protected websites and read content subscribed to by their institution, from a geographical location other than the site itself. There are several methods to achieve this and the main technologies digital libraries utilise to help researchers access online resources remotely are Virtual Private Network (VPN), proxy, and federated access. VPN and proxy are IP-based methods while federated access is based on SAML. New protocols, such as OAuth and OpenID Connect are starting to get attention as well, although their use is not yet widespread as far as the library is concerned.

Before continuing, it is important to cover two technologies that are in the 'grey area' as far as the remits of remote access go.

LTI – Learning Tools Interoperability, is a standard that 'prescribes a way to easily and securely connect learning applications and tools with platforms like learning management systems (LMS), portals and learning object repositories<…>without the need for expensive custom programming' ('Learning Tools Interoperability | IMS Global Learning Consortium', 2018). This standard can greatly contribute to a better user experience when using one of the 359 certified products, for example, to surface Cengage Learning content on Blackboard Learn or link to BrainPOP directly from the Google Classroom. The remote login to the user portal or LMS will be achieved by other means – usually a username and password, facilitated by an integration with the institutional accounts directory. Based on the OAuth2.0 authorisation framework, LTI is a way for applications to communicate with each other on the user's behalf.

SIP – Standard Interchange Protocol, better known by the name of its second version SIP2, is a proprietary protocol, initially developed for communication between a library's computer systems and the 3M™SelfCheck™ system in 2006 (3M™ Standard Interchange Protocol, 2006), soon to be widely adopted by many other library automation vendors and some integrated library systems, such as Koha. Donated to the National Information Standards Organization (NISO) in 2012 (Enis & Schwartz, 2012), it has since formed the basis for the NISO Circulation Interchange Protocol – NCIP (Needleman, Bodfish, O'Brien, Rush & Stevens, 2001), an XML-based standard able to communicate with other systems over the Internet. Both the SIP and the NCIP enjoy a widespread adoption for interlibrary loan purposes. For example, the Reaching Across Illinois Library System RAILS, is currently implementing an Auto-Graphics' SHAREit product for its new 'Find More Illinois' resource sharing system (PR Newswire, 2018). The same product is used for Pennsylvania's ACCESS (Asia News Monitor, 2018). In his overview of the NCIP Basic Patron Authentication Profile, Steve Gregory remarks that 'an excellent trust relationship must be in place' prior to initiating communication between the patron and any NCIP-enabled system (2005). In the NCIP, the patron's credentials are transferred over the web in plain text and, unless HTTPS is used, the access method is very vulnerable to abuse in comparison to other standards, such as SAML. While some vendors choose to ignore the lack of security, others, such as Ex Libris Alma, address the issue by writing their own code to mediate it. Until SIP3 (drafted in 2011 but not adopted yet) enters the industry, Alma developers support SIP2 connections by means of a lightweight, installable component, called Stunnel – communication channel between Alma cloud environment and the library, secured by SSL/TLS and certificate. Moreover, this workflow is only supported for interactions between physical self-check stations and Alma, nothing else (Developer Network, 2018).

The author recommends to take Ex Libris' approach and use SIP2/NCIP thoughtfully. With new user data protection legislations coming into effect and piracy actors such as Sci-Hub continuously taking advantage of weak security measures (why bother guessing a user's password when you can fetch it straight from the plain text traffic?), it is more important than ever to consider security over convenience.

IP-BASED ACCESS METHODS

Virtual Private Network (VPN)

A VPN or a Virtual Private Network is a network where data is transferred over the Internet using security features preventing unauthorised access (Downing, 2013). In other words, this technology provides a tunnel access to the organisation's internal network when the user is off-site. Accessing the library's online subscriptions, in this case, is based on the publisher believing the user is within the registered IP range of a known geographical location, such as a university or hospital. Other well-known use cases for this technology are anonymised web surfing and bypassing geographical restrictions to access digital services, such as Netflix, Spotify, BBC iPlayer or adult content, as detailed on the SecureThoughts website (2018) which evaluates the best VPN software products alongside instructions on how to achieve the two aforementioned goals. VPN tunnelling requires software installation on each user's machine. Most VPN clients are endpoint security dedicated applications, sold as stand-alone products or as a module to a bigger offering, for example, the Microsoft Azure, F5 or Cisco suite of products. Xhu, Zong and He (2012) wrote that the VPN will inevitably become the main development direction of library internetwork in the future with the increasing maturity of the VPN technology. In the past decade, the world has actively engaged in a movement towards cloud computing, resulting in the birth of the VPNaaS (VPN-as-a-Service), among many other concepts. Whilst

VPNaaS may not require the user to install any software locally thus resolving the small inconvenience this presented before, digital libraries using this access method are now facing a different challenge: dynamic IP ranges in the cloud, which is forcing them to look for alternatives to IP-based access or mixed solutions, where the user gains entry using something else than a pre-approved IP address.

Web Proxy

There may not be a practicing librarian who has not heard of proxy access or not worked with EZProxy or the Innovative Interfaces' Web Access Management (III WAM) proxy at some point in their careers (or some less known solutions such as CC Proxy, Squid Proxy, and RHN Proxy). While web proxying is used for a wide variety of purposes, such as security, load balancing or cache (faster static content delivery), digital libraries are only concerned with a network proxy – a mechanism to access content protected by IP restrictions. The proxy, in this case, is a bridge between two networks and its only task is to redirect requests and responses (Durieux, Hamadi & Monperrus, 2018), as illustrated in Figure 1.

Since Chris Zagar developed EZProxy in 1999 (Bunton, 2017), this product has become nearly synonymous with remote access to digital resources, especially in the academic sector. 'When Harvard and MIT were among the first to sign up for EZproxy, I knew I had underestimated the problem of authentication and access to these licensed materials,' Zagar said (Hadro, 2008). 'EZproxy was <…> designed to simplify access to IP-authenticated databases. Its role was to keep itself between the remote user and the remote database, retrieving content on behalf of the remote user and rearranging all of the links to point them back to EZproxy instead of toward the database' (Zagar, 2007). This is how Innovative's Millennium rewriting proxy works as well, as illustrated by an excerpt from the Innovative Interfaces documentation website (2018):

```
http://<port>-<target server>.<Innovative server>/<rest of URL>
```

Figure 1. Fundamentals of proxy access

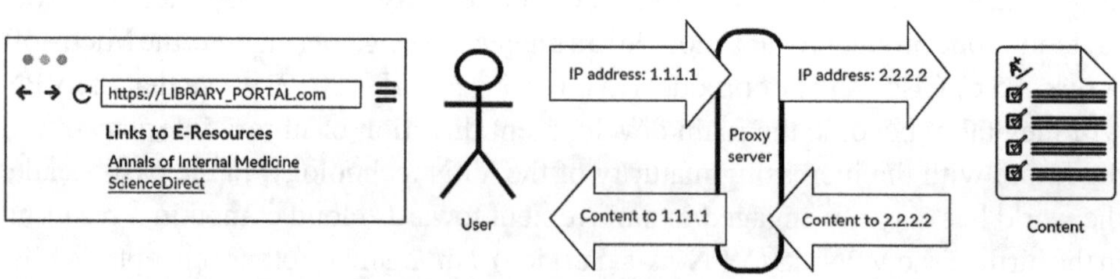

For example, if your current link is:

`http://galenet.gale.com/a/acp/name/db/bgmi/`

Change the link to:

`http://0-galenet.gale.com.web.library.edu/a/acp/name/db/bgmi/`

It is worth pointing out that the above example of rewriting URLs is somewhat different from EZProxy which no longer requires specification of the port in the prefix. Due to its popularity, this solution has been enhanced to interact with many other authentication systems, such as LDAP, Shibboleth, and CAS. Since OCLC's acquisition of the EZProxy software (Hadro, 2008), EZProxy is now available as a locally installable or hosted version and the latter is an attractive offer for libraries in the cloud computing era. In addition to this, new cloud-based services have shown up on the market – RemoteXS and LibLynx (Shibbolized proxy) that are also starting to draw the attention of those who do not fancy managing their own proxy stanzas.

The proxy access method may be well understood due to its age, however, it is not without drawbacks. It is interesting that the following was written in 2001 when proxy access in the library environment was rapidly taking over the world: 'Remote resource access is the most popular use of proxies in libraries today, but it represents a cumbersome and inefficient way to solve the remote resource access problem. These proxies can be complicated to set up, both for the user and the library, and cause content for the remote resource user to cross an institution's Internet connection twice' (Murray, 2001).

Fast forward 17 years, one of the most prominent drawbacks in a user-centred digital era is no longer the technically challenging set-up but a poor user experience: first, the inability to access resources directly from the vendor's website (anyone wishing to gain access must first start at the library portal or become adept at configuring their institution's proxy URLs) and second, no direct access to personalisation features such as bookmarks, saved searches, etc., unless a vendor-specific account is manually created and logged into upon every visit. Browser extension tools such as LibX, Zotero, Kopernio and LeanLibrary help alleviate the problem by reloading web pages via a user's organisational authentication mechanism, usually by simply adding a prefix to each web address the user navigates to.

Another headache, known to librarians as the 'https issue', is the global migration to the TLS 1.2 cryptographic standard, which is causing older proxy software versions to fail and deny access to secure websites. This is one of the problems new open source initiatives such as the self-healing BikiniProxy (Durieux, Hamadi & Monperrus, 2018) seek to mitigate.

Finally, as a result of IPv4 addresses' exhaustion anticipated since the 80s, the future of IPv6 is on the doorstep. Vint Cerf, who invented the Internet Protocol together with Bob Kahn, said: 'I thought it was an experiment and I thought that 4.3 billion would be enough to do an experiment. Who the hell knew how much address space we needed?' (Agence France-Presse, 2011) For the benefit of clarity, below is a quick visual comparison of IPv4, the IP address as we know it, and IPv6 addresses (Table 1).

AFRINIC, the regional Internet registry for Africa, is the last one standing with few IPv4 addresses left and due to become depleted by April 2019 (Geoff Huston, 2018). When presenting at the 2018 MLA Annual Meeting and Exhibition in Atlanta, USA, the author asked the attendees how they felt about dealing with IPv6 addresses to ensure that IP-based access to library subscriptions is maintained. Many have not heard about it yet and the reactions to the visual display of an example address were that of horror and disbelief. When asked who would be comfortable to work with this address type on a daily basis, no hands were raised.

Federated Access (SAML)

Overall, 72 countries in the world maintain their own research and education identity federations ('Federations – REFEDS', 2018). These are collectives of institutions and content providers that have met the technical, financial, geographical and category requirements of joining the 'club' and have been listed in a publicly shared list of trusted entities, otherwise known as the metadata file. The membership, in most cases, is limited to educational or research bodies, preventing commercial organisations from joining the group as Identity Providers - organisations looking to access content but rarely restrictive to Service Providers – websites or applications with valuable content. There are two global federations at the moment of writing: eduGAIN, an international interfederation service, connecting the participating national federations mentioned earlier, and OpenAthens. The latter does not restrict access to commercial institutions on either side but ensures that each participant's implementation adheres to the highest quality standards prior to making them visible to other members.

Table 1. IPv4 And IPv6 comparison

IPv4	**185.222.219.127**
IPv6	**2001:0db8:85a3:0000:0000:8a2e:0370:7334**

When talking about identity and access management federations, one must think of SAML, which is the protocol this access method is based on. SAML, Security Assertion Markup Language, is an open standard, first adopted as an OASIS (Organization for the Advancement of Structured Information Standards) standard in November 2002. Its latest version, widely adopted today, was released in March 2005 and is still making headlines when technology giants such as Amazon Web Services start supporting it (Asia News Monitor, 2018). SAML was designed to aid secure but seamless access between web services or applications. Theoretically, a username and password are not necessary in order to use this protocol - if the institution's system is configured to use something else, such as biometrics, this should be sufficient. Consider the following scenario:

James is a doctor working at Hospital A. He has just come across an interesting article about stem cells on the Science Direct website and opted to login via his institution as he knows his hospital subscribes to this resource. Science Direct (Service Provider) immediately sends a request to Hospital A (Identity Provider), asking to respond with details confirming James' affiliation with this institution. Hospital A, in turn, prompts James to log in as it seeks to verify his identity against its local directory. James logs in and Hospital A sends Science Direct an affirmative response along with the encrypted attributes statement about James. This statement contains the value of 'member@hospitalA.com' as well as James' unique identifier, specific to this vendor. The identifier is arrived by means of a complex calculation that bears no personal information, however, it allows Science Direct to bind this identifier to James' personal profile on the platform, allowing him to unlock bookmarks, saved searches, etc. as soon as he logs in. In comparison, IP-based access offers no such luxury, the user would always have to log in twice if personalisation features are to be utilised.

There are many vendors that offer Single Sign-On, especially for the purpose of connecting on-premise applications within the organisational network. Some of the examples include ADFS (Active Directory Federation Services), Azure AD, CAS, Ping Identity, OKTA, OneLogin, My1Login, and many others. As far as the library is concerned, these are not helpful when it comes to managing remote access to online resources unless one is prepared to make a bunch of one-to-one connections with each content provider. Up until 2008, organisations seeking to implement federated access have been required to install Shibboleth – an open-source software application, developed specifically for accessing web services in a seamless fashion. Since 2008, OpenAthens has entered the market as a proprietary solution and until today, these two remain the only two choices to achieve Single Sign-On to a global network of federated online resources. The publishing industry is in no hurry to adopt new (or in this case, a decade old) technologies. Because of this, libraries find that their Shibboleth service has to be supplemented by a proxy solution to ensure full coverage of resources. OpenAthens provides a managed proxy built into the service alongside the federated access management facilities to address this. Here is a quick side-by-side comparison of these two products (Table 2).

To sum up the section, below is a summary table of the technologies discussed so far (Table 3):

None of the access methods discussed are perfect as far as the user experience goes. Federated access, although advanced by design, suffers from human short sight, such as non-standardised Shibboleth implementations on publishers' websites where users could face anything from a single login button to extensive lists of hundreds of institutions to choose from before they can proceed to establish a session. On the other hand, proxy users would not be able to log in at all if they were unlucky enough to start from the search engine or publisher's website itself. Browser extensions such as LibX, Zotero, Kopernio, and LeanLibrary are powerful tools that can greatly assist in resolving user journey issues. The author spoke to LeanLibrary's founder and CEO Johan Tilstra, who said that developing the Library Access browser extension was a very natural, logical step. 'Forcing users to access content through the library portal is unreasonable, especially in the mobile era', he said. 'Libraries will have to step up to provide a better user experience, otherwise patrons will simply walk away.' Users of LeanLibrary are not concerned with where their research starts – at the portal, search engine or the vendor's website itself, the extension makes sure only one login is required. (personal communication, July 2, 2018).

Table 2. Shibboleth – OpenAthens comparison

Shibboleth	OpenAthens
Software for Service and Identity Providers	Software for Service and Identity Providers
Open-source	Proprietary
Compatible with any SAML-enabled app	Compatible with any SAML-enabled app
Connects to AD and relational databases	Connects to any user directory
Supports DuoSecurity MFA	Supports any delegated MFA
Supports CAS 2 protocol	Supports SirsiDynix proprietary API
User permissions managed in the XML file	User permissions managed in the admin portal
Attribute release managed in the XML file	Attribute release managed in the admin portal
Allows for development of reporting facility	Granular reports available in the admin portal
Locally installed	Cloud based

Table 3. Remote access technologies at a glance

Technology	VPN (Virtual Private Network)
Popular vendors	Microsoft, F5, CheckPoint, Cisco, Pulse Secure, etc
Use case for the library	Routes user via organisational network to meet geographical/IP criteria for accessing subscriptions
Librarian's comments	"<…>campus Virtual Private Network (VPN) or an integrated library system (ILS) proxy module suffer from the same problems that existed in the past. They either require actions on the part of the end-user, involve somewhat complicated hardware and networking, or are more complex to administer than EZproxy" (Bunton, 2017)
Technology	**Proxy**
Popular vendors	OCLC, Innovative, OpenAthens, RemoteX, LibLynx
Use case for the library	Enables remote access via a dedicated proxy IP address when a proxy link is used
Librarian's comments	"The implementation of EZproxy remote login access program at the KMC Health Sciences Library, Manipal is a working model for providing the users the convenient and efficient interfaces to access e-resources" (Baikady, Jessy, 2014) "It is not correct to say that EZProxy cannot distinguish between user types, but its capabilities in this regard are limited." (Lodwick, 2015)
Technology	**Federated access**
Popular vendors	Shibboleth, OpenAthens
Librarian's comments	"The federated access model separates the authentication function—accomplished via an "identity provider"—from access to the resource itself. This division of labour yields benefits in efficiency and privacy, and also in the greater degree of granularity of access that can be achieved. <…> Depending upon the "attributes" associated with a particular user, a FAM product such as Shibboleth can fine tune the user's access to specific resources with considerable specificity" (Lodwick, 2015)

OAuth 2.0 and OpenID Connect

The automated exchange of data between systems on behalf of the user is something that is desirable and will become more prevalent in the future (M. Efron, personal communication, June 28, 2018). OAuth 2.0, although flawed security-wise when implemented on its own, provides a great way to achieve this. This relatively young authorisation protocol forms the basis for LTI and OpenID Connect – the new authentication standard that has the potential to replace SAML. Designed for Single Sign-On, OpenID Connect uses a much more lightweight approach to data transfer, using JSON instead of the old and clunky XML. Since its 'release to the wild' in 2014, this protocol has enjoyed an enthusiastic reception, first by its founders

Google, Microsoft and Ping Identity but soon by other well-known companies such as Amazon, ForgeRock, IBM and PayPal (Botyriute, 2018). A number of library applications have adopted and encourage the use of OpenID Connect, including providers such as Moodle, OpenAthens, TalentLMS, MyDay by Collabco, Open edX, Canvas, Absorb LMS, Blackboard Learn, Lynda.com, Litmos and many others. There is more to come from the OpenID Foundation, who has already drafted the federated framework based on OpenID Connect (Hedberg, Gulliksson, Jones & Bradley, 2018). Once reviewed and approved, this might transform federated access, making it the tool of preference for many vendors.

TRENDS AND THE FUTURE

Library in the Cloud

'With the emergence of cloud computing, a new Library era has started, where new features, services, platforms, and solutions are invading the old library's approaches.' (Shawish & Salama, 2018) While some may perceive it as a challenge or a steep learning curve, others find relief entrusting Software-as-as-Service providers with their systems. 'There is a growing relationship between academic libraries and cloud computing', claim Robert Iles and Emre Erturk from the Eastern Institute of Technology, New Zealand in their 'Case Study on Cloud Based Library Software as a Service: Evaluating EZProxy'. Many libraries are facing cost-cutting measures (2015) and therefore part of the attraction is cost savings, not just on hardware but also human resources and expertise required to maintain high service availability and ensure data security. For example, Texas Tech University has migrated their EZProxy to the cloud quoting the main attraction as service's management and maintenance transfer to OCLC 'while the Libraries could focus on managing the purchasing and licensing of the resources to be proxied' (Edgar, 2015). The University of Leeds decommissioned their locally managed Shibboleth in favour of the OpenAthens Identity hosted solution. In the author's opinion, an increased uptake of this service confirms the global migration to the cloud is of interest to the libraries as much as it is to anyone else. Naturally, along with services in the cloud come requirements for stronger security. Jon Agland, principal UK federation technical support specialist observed 'increased requirements for Multi-Factor Authentication both from institutions (probably unilaterally applied to their IdP for authentication to all services) and from publishers and other SPs for access to high value resources' (personal communication, July 2018).

New Ways of Content Delivery

The migration from print to electronic resources has been ongoing for a while now so this trend will not surprise anyone. Some organisations, such as the Pacific Health Organisation's Medical Library, made the decision to go digital as early as 2005 (and certainly, there are even earlier adopters out there), managing to fully transition its holdings to the digital sphere in an impressive timescale of six months (Glusker & Hoelscher, 2018). Talking to librarians on a daily basis, the author has observed a widespread belief that e-resources will soon gain more prevalence over printed books and although the physical library space may not go away as it is essential for communities, it may be eventually repurposed (R. Wilson, personal interview, June 24, 2018). Chris Chiancone, CIO for the City of Plano went one step further and emphasised the economies of just-in-time educational content in a video format, which may eventually take precedence over written information. His sons have managed to fix broken wooden shutters in a day by looking up instructions on YouTube. It would have taken them more time to find and read a relevant book and it would have cost more money to hire a contractor to fix the shutters. In his opinion, libraries who embrace new technologies may become innovation hubs, crucial to the future of advanced society (personal interview, June 23, 2018). With more and more librarians opting to acquire technical skills, this should not be a problem. 'We see a new generation of librarians enter the space – they can code, they can tweak their own systems and I hope this will become more prevalent in the future', says Christine Peterson, Amigos eShelf Service Manager for Amigos Library Services (personal interview, June 23, 2018).

Focus on the User

'I hope that in the future we will see more focus on user experience and access to resources will become much more streamlined. We make them jump through too many loops at the moment', says Nancy Noe, the Interim Dean at the Auburn University in Alabama, US. This is also the hope of the RA21 – Resource Access for the 21st Century movement, too, whose goal is to facilitate more seamless – and secure - user experience across the scientific content provider platforms ('What is RA21 – RA21: Resource Access for the 21st Century', 2018). With two pilots on the way, RA21 is gaining momentum and a following. Gone are the days when the users of the systems were to blame if something was not working. The increasingly competitive marketplace had a positive impact on users' thinking and poorly designed systems or products are now to blame. The attention is coming back to the user and some libraries are going to great lengths to make sure their community gets the best service there is. Russell Palmer, Assistant Director for GALILEO Support Services shares GALILEO's plans to improve user experience across the state of Georgia:

'In the last year, GALILEO has put forth a strategic plan with goals that will sustain innovation, prepare us for the future, and serve the evolving lifelong learning needs of the residents of Georgia effectively. The strategic planning process helped us by identifying and prioritising areas for future development, and the areas below will be a focus for GALILEO in the next 5 years:

- **Authentication and Access:** Make authentication as easy as possible
- **User Experience:** Solicit user feedback in order to create interfaces that are easy to access and designed and customised to meet the needs of GALILEO libraries and the learners they serve
- **Content:** Provide a robust set of electronic resources (open and licensed) that meet the lifelong learning needs of all Georgians, leveraging local and statewide purchasing power.

There are many interdependencies in the three areas I have identified above. Authentication and access were identified by GALILEO constituents as the most important planning priority. Barriers to access put users off, and send them off to seek information in less reliable (but more accessible) environments. Authentication and access is a huge part of the user experience as well; users are extremely dissatisfied when they are unable to authenticate successfully.

A quality authentication system designed to pass many attributes/metadata also offers developers and systems a means to customise content and discovery for the user and provides more options for interactivity with content. Users thrive in a portal environment which gives them not only access to quality content but the ability to interact with it in meaningful ways that will enrich it for the user or the user's audience - sharing, commenting, annotating, remixing...' (personal communication, June 25, 2018).

Lucy Harrison, Assistant Vice Chancellor for Academic Library Services and Executive Director of GALILEO emphasises the importance of delivering seamless user experience regardless of the machine used to access the library content. 'Users want to be able to modify their own interface, just like they're used to on their mobile devices. I think UX design will become more user-centric in the future'. Lucy is tirelessly working to ensure the delivery of the service that opens doors to discovery and exploration. The mission is to enable lifelong, self-paced learning for all citizens of Georgia (personal communication, June 29, 2018).

Striving for Better Statistics

Inconsistent usage logs are well-known culprits for making electronic resource specialists work long hours. Whilst introducing COUNTER in 2003 helped a lot, the list of compliant content providers at the time of writing is limited to 58 audited entities in the registry ('Register | Project Counter', 2018) and librarians are still forced to manipulate large spreadsheets of varying data to measure the return on investment or value to the community based on usage. Another consideration is whether the data provided by the publishers can be fully trusted. The author's personal experience indicates that facilities dedicated to statistics can often malfunction even for the largest of publishers. At the dawn of the user-centric era, libraries are recognising the importance of understanding their patrons and tracking resource usage internally as well as externally (Yeager, 2017). The author spoke to the SirsiDynix director of product strategy, Ranny Lacanienta, who shared his observations on how academic libraries are keen to improve their services by seeking better understanding on what contributes to their users' success: 'Learning Analytics (LA) is a trend that has emerged in the past few years to measure students' success in their educational careers. This helps students and researchers become more efficient in their learning by taking the paths that are proven to be successful which may include the activities happening in the libraries, such as the collection, services, study carrels and rooms, tools, databases that it offers, time in the library and all the way across campus to academic advisement, Learning Management Systems such as Blackboard, computer, math science or writing labs and talking to one's professors and teaching assistants. All of these learning points across university departments are measured and extrapolated to ensure student success and better learning outcomes' (personal communication, June 27, 2018). A more thorough understanding of the library's patrons may not be the only reason to seek better data. Russell Palmer, Assistant Director for GALILEO support services, says that 'in the next five years, libraries will be working harder to curate content as both the open and licensed content options and environments grow increasingly more complex. Careful assessment, good reporting and statistics, and user feedback will be essential to successful curation, but also open mindedness, as the traditional content models will be shifting-big data sets, treasure troves of metadata, tools for data evaluation, and video content are already in play, and this landscape will only evolve more' (personal communication, June 25, 2018).

Various remote access vendors are responding to libraries' need for more meaningful data in different ways. SaaS products such as OpenAthens offer granular, Google Analytics powered reports counting every authentication instance. OpenAthens product manager Adam Snook says that 'with decreasing budgets for libraries and changing subscription models the need for metrics will continue to increase which is why it is essential to continuously improve this aspect of the service' (personal communication, June 27, 2018). An open-source software application, Shibboleth, also lends itself to customisation, should anyone wish to write their own reporting scripts against its server logs. For EZproxy users, server logs provide a lot of raw data, however, similar to Shibboleth, working with this sort of output requires some technical expertise. Elon University's Carol Grotnes Belk Library (North Carolina, USA), for example, is tackling this challenge by using ezPAARSE and Google Analytics combination, employing a wide range of tools to achieve meaningful statistics every month (2017).

Open Access

'Our library is working a lot with open access resources at the moment' (N. Noe, personal communication, June 24, 2018). Today, this phrase is as popular in libraries as they are 'migrating to the hosted version of [insert the name of your software].' For the purposes of this chapter, the author has spoken to librarians from a wide geographical area - the USA extending to Norway and New Zealand - and all of them mentioned open access as one of the key elements of the digital library's future. One of the reasons for this could be the 10-15% increase in yearly subscription prices, which is an unsustainable trend library may increasingly struggle to cope with, as pointed out by the Head of Emerging Technologies & Systems, Robert Wilson from Bridgewater State University. Actors such as Sci-Hub will probably remain if this does not change, he says, not until someone develops the libraries' equivalent of Spotify (personal communication, June 24, 2018). Robert's perspective is echoed by Sørlandet Sykehus librarian Jørn Hjørungnes, who feels that academic libraries have failed the society by locking publicly funded information behind paywalls (personal communication, June 29, 2018) and frustration is justified as a recent study on Sci-Hub suggests paywalls on the web limit access to three-quarters of scholarly literature (Himmelstein, D. S., Romero, A. R., Levernier, J. G., et al., 2018). Uri Blackman, founder and CEO of GIDEON Informatics adds the vendor's point of view to this discussion. 'Publishers have to focus on providing more value beyond what you can get for free on Google. Users demand more accountability for how the dollar is being spent.' He believes that the vendor's ability to integrate their content into the day-to-day workflow on users' systems so it is there at the point of need is very important, especially as libraries are becoming more digital (personal communication, June 26, 2018). Going back to Spotify, the idea of a similar subscription model for digital libraries has been around for a while. It is becoming a true credit to Spotify's success as new library suppliers start referencing this service as a means to promote their product, calling it, for example, 'Spotify of the textbook world' ('The Spotify of the textbook world takes off as Bibliotech is go', 2018). OpenAthens' Kieran Prince and Robert Scaysbrook concur that the industry is ripe for disruption and actors such as Sci-Hub are starting to change the landscape in a similar manner of Spotify changing the music industry (personal communication, June 24, 2018). According to Jude Sheeran, the CEO of Eduserv, the well-known double-pay issue where the research is conducted for tax payers' money and then locked behind a paywall to be paid for again, is a real threat to the publishing industry (personal communication, July 5, 2018). Open access initiatives are gaining momentum, nearly every event now includes a presentation on this. Germany's and Sweden's recent actions against major publishers (Yeager, 2018; Else, 2018) are helping to reinforce the idea that educational materials should be accessible to everyone (K. Prince, personal communication, June 24, 2018).

Talking of education for everyone, SirsiDynix's Ranny Lacanienta notes that the Open Educational Resources, also known as the OER movement, is getting a lot of attention within academia (personal communication, June 27, 2018). The OER has its roots in 2002 when the Hewlett Foundation introduced a major component into the strategic plan of its Education Programme, called 'Using Information Technology to Increase Access to High-Quality Educational Content'. The original goal was 'to use information technology to help equalize the distribution of high quality knowledge and educational opportunities for individuals, faculty, and institutions within the United States and throughout the world' (Atkins, Seely Brown & Hammond, 2007, pp. 5-6).

John Seguin, MLS, President, COO & Chief Librarian at Third Iron (creators of journal engagement platform BrowZine) offers a realistic scenario on how open access may influence current subscription models to content online in the future:

'Whereas in the past you could count on library collections to be made up principally of subscribed journals, the libraries of the near future will place a greater emphasis on open access materials alongside subscribed and, critically, pay-per-view (PPV) services of subscribed titles rather than always subscribing to low-use titles. PPV and document delivery has made significant technical advances in recent years in delivering full text to users in a nearly instant fashion for a large amount of content which finally provides libraries with additional flexibility in how they shape their collection. With the decline of print journals, this also means that libraries can afford to move from a "just in case" to a "just in time" model where immediate access is more important than archival access for their patrons. Tools and services in use by libraries would be wise to prepare to accommodate these new hybrid models of collection development to ensure they do not become the bottleneck in the library delivering content in this fashion' (personal communication, June 2018).

Artificial Intelligence

Artificial Intelligence is exciting. It is one of those ground-breaking general-purpose technologies that are going to change the world in a similar way TCP/IP and the World Wide Web did. Technology giants such as Google and Microsoft are investing heavily into transforming their businesses with AI and in turn, everyone's lives (Brynjolfsson, Rock & Syverson, 2017). What has it got to do with the library? The publishing and library industries have historically been slow to adopt technological advancements. Not anymore. During the 2018 ALA Annual conference in New Orleans, the author attended a live presentation on Voice Search powered by AI and IBM Watson integration into OCLC's WorldCat discovery service 'Ask Watson', delivered by OCLC's executive director for management services, Scott Livingston. The demonstration of a bot, assisting the end-user in finding the relevant material on Shakespeare was greeted with applause. 'These are the types of technologies you can expect to see from companies like OCLC in the next few years', Scott said (2018). OCLC is not the only vendor experimenting with AI. Elsevier is currently running a pilot on hypotheses generation using the Euretos AI platform ('Elsevier and Euretos start an innovative pilot to bring AI-derived hypotheses into the scholarly dialog', 2018). Mike Shamel, application support analyst for the City of Plano is feeling positive about what the emergence of AI might bring to the library: 'Libraries will be able to automate most processes, thanks to AI. For example, it currently takes three people to process book returns and donations but soon users will be able to scan the book barcode and the system will take care of the rest. The technology is already there, all it takes is few good developers.' Mike is convinced libraries will recognise the value of automation very soon. Chris Chiancone agreed with him that once that happens, '3D printers for kids won't be the only exciting technology people will find in there' (personal interview, June 23, 2018).

While some librarians may fear losing their jobs in the wake of AI adoption, not everyone believes this is a plausible scenario. 'I don't believe the AI can ever replace the librarian', says Jon Bentley, commercial director for OpenAthens. 'The librarian may no longer be a gatekeeper to information, however, absolutely critical as a curator to aid research. What if the user does not know what they're looking for or how to ask? AI bots are not built for that' (personal interview, June 27, 2018). Rob Scayscbrook, Head of Sales for Identity at OpenAthens feels there are no conflicting interests between technological advancement and librarianship, or certainly do not have to be. This is an opportunity to 'become more about the user and less about the institution. AI may have a big part to play in that, improving the user journey and enabling libraries to automate a lot of their current processes, allowing librarians to concentrate on content curation tasks and less on systems maintenance' (personal interview, June 24, 2018).

CONCLUSION

Artificial Intelligence, unsurprisingly, is on everyone's mind when it comes to subjects related to the future. While some interviewees remain skeptical whether AI is not just another passing fad, the author is led to believe that the sheer amount of thought put into it is an indication that this technology's entrance to the library space may occur sooner than expected. This presents a wonderful potential for the role of the librarian to be transfigured. Liberated from repetitive admin tasks, knowledge experts may finally be able to focus on more meaningful endeavours, such as guiding researchers to the best sources of information so someday, they can change the world. TDNet Vice President for Sales & Business Development Moshe Efron agrees on that point. He believes that as technology advances, librarians may rebrand themselves as information professionals. Admin, content acquisition and repetitive tasks may be outsourced to third-party providers, others may be taken care of by automation. The role of the librarian will be different and focused on tasks that require a certain level of expertise: research projects, content curation and knowledge management (personal interview, June 28, 2018). But how does this relate to remote access to online resources? In author's experience, remote access technology vendors tend to operate reactive development cycles, continuously adjusting their products in response to the demands of their user base. The trends observed in this chapter are, therefore, already beginning to affect various vendors' product roadmaps. In the last few years Shibboleth has integrated with Multi-Factor Authentication provider DuoSecurity, OpenAthens has developed an OpenID Connect-based federated access product for publishers, OCLC have implemented IPv6 support and new players, such as RemoteXS and LibLynx have emerged. This is a clear indicator of the increasing demand for libraries to support their mobile user base while adapting to the new standards and ways of working introduced by the IT industry. As Russel Palmer said, open-mindedness will serve well in the all-digital era (personal communication, June 25, 2018). Courage and relentless effort to improve the lives of communities will be the key to overcoming any learning curves new technology may create. That said, most contributors to this chapter cannot wait to get started.

ACKNOWLEDGMENT

Sincere thanks to everyone who shared their thoughts on the library future for this chapter.

Adam Snook, Product Manager, OpenAthens (United Kingdom)

Andrew Anderson, President & CEO, Library and Information Resources Network (FL, USA)

Chris Chiancone, CIO, City of Plano (TX, USA)

Christine Peterson, Amigos eShelf Service Manager, Amigos Library Services (TX, USA)

Johan Tilstra, Founder and CEO, Lean Library (Netherlands)

John Seguin, President, COO & Chief Librarian, Third Iron (MN, USA)

Jon Agland, Principal UK federation technical support specialist (United Kingdom)

Jon Bentley, Commercial Director at OpenAthens (United Kingdom)

Jørn Hjørungnes, Librarian at Sørlandet Sykehus (Norway)

Jude Sheeran, CEO, Eduserv (United Kingdom)

Dr. Katherine O. Quinnell, Library Director, Athens State University (AL, USA)

Kieran Prince, International Sales Manager, OpenAthens (United Kingdom)

Lucy Harrison, Assistant Vice Chancellor for Academic Library Services and Executive Director of GALILEO (GA, USA)

Mike Shamel, Application Support Analyst, City of Plano (TX, USA)

Moshe Efron, Vice President for Sales & Business Development, TDNet (Israel)

Nancy Noe, Interim Dean, Auburn University Libraries (AL, USA)

Ranny Lacanienta, Director of Product Strategy, SirsiDynix (UT, USA)

Robert Scaysbrook, Head of Sales – Identity, OpenAthens (United Kingdom)

Robert Wilson, Head of Emerging Technologies & Systems, Bridgewater State University (MA, USA)

Russell Palmer, Assistant Director, GALILEO Support Services (GA, USA)

Uri Blackman, Founder and CEO, GIDEON Informatics (CA, USA)

REFERENCES

Agence France-Presse. (2011). World 'running out of Internet addresses' - INQUIRER.net, *Philippine News for Filipinos*. Retrieved from https://web.archive.org/web/20110125195711/http://technology.inquirer.net/infotech/infotech/view/20110121-315808/World-running-out-of-Internet-addresses

Atkins, D., Seely Brown, J., & Hammond, A. (2007). *A Review of the Open Educational Resources (OER) Movement: Achievements, Challenges, and New Opportunities*. William and Flora Hewlett Foundation. Retrieved from https://hewlett.org/wp-content/uploads/2016/08/ReviewoftheOERMovement.pdf

Auto-graphics SHAREit upgrades ACCESS Pennsylvania's resource sharing, saving 1,500 libraries across the state time and money. (2018, March 20). *Asia News Monitor*. Retrieved from https://search.proquest.com/docview/2015024298

Baikady, M. R., & Jessy, A. (2014). Off Campus Access to Licensed E-resources of Library: A Case Study. *DESIDOC Journal of Library and Information Technology*, *34*(6), 486–490. doi:10.14429/djlit.34.6.7509

Brynjolfsson, E., Rock, D., & Syverson, C. (2017). *Artificial Intelligence and the Modern Productivity Paradox: A Clash of Expectations and Statistics*. The National Bureau of Economic Research. doi:10.3386/w24001

Bunton, G. A. (2017). EZproxy: The Key to Remote Access. *The Serials Librarian*, *73*(2), 119–126. doi:10.1080/0361526X.2017.1338635

CloudGate UNO announces federated access support for amazon web services. (2018, May 28). *Asia News Monitor*. Retrieved from https://search.proquest.com/docview/2044803283

Developer Network. (2018). *Self Check*. Retrieved from https://developers.exlibrisgroup.com/alma/integrations/selfcheck

Durieux, T., Hamadi, Y., & Monperrus, M. (2018). *Fully Automated HTML and JavaScript Rewriting for Constructing a Self-healing Web Proxy*. Cornell University Library. doi:10.1109/ISSRE.2018.00012

Edgar, L. E. (2015). EZproxy: Migrating From a Local Server to a Hosted Environment. *Journal of Electronic Resources Librarianship*, *27*(3), 194–199. doi:10.1080/1941126X.2015.1059655

eduGAIN. (2018). *eduGAIN model* [Image]. Retrieved from https://edugain.org/about-edugain/key-concepts/

Else, H. (2018). *Europe's open-access drive escalates as university stand-offs spread*. Retrieved from https://www.nature.com/articles/d41586-018-05191-0

Elsevier and Euretos start innovative pilot to bring AI-derived hypotheses into the scholarly dialog. (2018). Retrieved from https://www.elsevier.com/about/press-releases/science-and-technology/elsevier-and-euretos-start-innovative-pilot-to-bring-ai-derived-hypotheses-into-the-scholarly-dialog

Enis, M., & Schwartz, M. (2012). InfoTech. *Library Journal*, *137*(12), 15. Retrieved from https://search.proquest.com/docview/1022969639

Erturk, E., & Iles, H.R. (2015). *Case Study on Cloud Based Library Software as a Service: Evaluating EZproxy.* CoRR, abs/1511.07578

Federations – REFEDS. (2018). Retrieved from https://refeds.org/federations

Fontana, J. (2018). *Hacks battered IT optimism in 2016; can 2017 enrich defenses.* ZDNet. Retrieved from http://www.zdnet.com/article/hacks-battered-it-optimism-in-2016-can-2017-enrich-defenses

Glusker, A., & Hoelscher, E. (2018). Transitioning from Print to Online-Only Resources. In Library Science and Administration (pp. 175–187). Hershey, PA: IGI Global. doi:10.4018/978-1-5225-3914-8.ch009

Gregory, S. (2005). *NCIP Basic Patron Authentication Profile*. Colorado State Library. Retrieved from http://www.ncip.info/uploads/7/1/4/6/7146749/ncip_basicauthenticationprofile_20050317.pdf

Hadro, J. (2008). OCLC acquires EZproxy. *Library Journal, 133*(3), 23. Retrieved from https://search.proquest.com/docview/196880015

Hedberg, R., Gulliksson, S., Jones, M., & Bradley, J. (2018). *OpenID Connect Federation 1.0 - draft 04.* Retrieved from http://openid.net/specs/openid-connect-federation-1_0.html

Himmelstein, D. S., Romero, A. R., Levernier, J. G., Munro, T. A., McLaughlin, S. R., Tzovaras, B. G., & Greene, C. S. (2018). Sci-Hub provides access to nearly all scholarly literature. *eLife*, *7*, e32822. doi:10.7554/eLife.32822 PMID:29424689

Huston, G. (2018). *IPv4 Address Report.* Retrieved from http://www.potaroo.net/tools/ipv4/

Interfaces, I. (2018). *Proxy Rewrite Method*. Retrieved from https://csdirect.iii.com/tutorials/wam/setup2_2_2.html

Learning Tools Interoperability. (2018). Retrieved from http://www.imsglobal.org/activity/learning-tools-interoperability#LTIpublic

Livingston, S. (2018). *Exploring new technologies to better serve users*. Presentation, ALA Annual Conference and Exhibition 2018.

Lodwick, D. (2015). Access and Identity Management for Libraries: Controlling Access to Online Information. *Technical Services Quarterly*, *32*(1), 112–113. doi:10.1080/07317131.2015.972909

Murray, P. E. (2001). Library web proxy use survey results. *Information Technology and Libraries*, *20*(4), 172–178. Retrieved from https://search.proquest.com/docview/215832929

Needleman, M., Bodfish, J., O'Brien, T., Rush, J., & Stevens, P. (2001). The NISO circulation interchange protocol (NCIP) – an XML based standard. *Library Hi Tech*, *19*(3), 223–230. doi:10.1108/07378830110405526

Open, O. (2005). *SAML Executive Overview*. Retrieved from https://www.oasis-open.org/committees/download.php/11785/sstc-saml-exec-overview-2.0-draft-06.pdf

Reaching across Illinois library system (RAILS) selects auto-graphics SHAREit® for resource sharing. (2018, April 5). *PR Newswire*. Retrieved from https://search.proquest.com/docview/2021790309

Register | Project Counter. (2018). Retrieved from https://www.projectcounter.org/about/register/

Rodriguez, M. (2017). Upgrading EZproxy from Local to Hosted Solution. In *Reframing Librarianship in the 21st Century*. Burlington, VT: University of Massachusetts Amherst Libraries. Retrieved from https://scholarworks.umass.edu/acrl_nec_conf/2017/posters/20/

SecureThoughts. (2018). *Best VPN | List of The TOP VPN services with full VPN reviews*. Retrieved from https://securethoughts.com/best-vpn/

Shawish, A., & Salama, M. (2018). Cloud-Based Digital Library Era. In Library Science and Administration (pp. 1276–1293). Hershey, PA: IGI Global. doi:10.4018/978-1-5225-3914-8.ch061

3M. Standard Interchange Protocol. (2018). Retrieved from http://multimedia.3m.com/mws/media/355361O/sip2-protocol.pdf

The Spotify of the textbook world takes off as Bibliotech is go. (2018). Retrieved from https://www.jisc.ac.uk/news/the-spotify-of-the-textbook-world-takes-off-as-bibliotech-is-go-01-aug-2017

Virtual Private Network (VPN). (2013). In D. Downing (Ed.), *Barron's business guides: Dictionary of computer and internet terms* (11th ed.). Hauppauge, NY: Barron's Educational Series. Retrieved from https://search.credoreference.com/content/entry/barronscai/virtual_private_network_vpn/0?institutionId=292

What is RA21 – RA21: Resource Access for the 21st Century. (2018). Retrieved from https://ra21.org/index.php/what-is-ra21/

Yeager, A. (2018). *Sweden Cancels Agreement With Elsevier Over Open Access.* Retrieved from https://www.the-scientist.com/?articles.view/articleNo/54593/title/Sweden-Cancels-Agreement-With-Elsevier-Over-Open-Access/

Yeager, H. J. (2017). Using EZproxy and Google Analytics to Evaluate Electronic Serials Usage. *Serials Review*, *43*(3-4), 208–215. doi:10.1080/00987913.2017.1350312

Zhu, Z., Zong, J., & He, N. (2012, June). Discussion on application of VPN technology in library management system. In *Proceedings of 2012 IEEE Symposium on Robotics and Applications (ISRA)* (pp. 809–812). IEEE. 10.1109/ISRA.2012.6219314

KEY TERMS AND DEFINITIONS

EZProxy: A popular proxy solution, known to most librarians around the world.

Federation: A collective of Service Providers and Identity Providers that trust each other.

Identity Provider (IdP): Creates and manages virtual identities for users. Examples of IdP systems: ADFS, Shibboleth, OpenAthens, Ping Identity, OKTA, etc.

IPv4 Address: An identifier assigned to each device connected to a computer network. Looks like this: 185.222.219.127.

IPv6: A new version of connected device identifier, intended to replace IPv4. Looks like this: 2001:0db8:85a3:0000:0000:8a2e:0370:7334.

OpenAthens: A popular cloud based single sign on solution for content providers and institutions. Aids access management using both federated and proxy access methods.

RA21: Resource Access for the 21st Century, a joint STM and NISO initiative looking to improve user experience when accessing scientific online resources.

Rewriting Proxy Server: A server that dynamically changes web URLs to point back to itself and acts as an intermediary between the user and the content provider, processing all traffic.

SAML: Security Assertion Markup Language, designed to facilitate secure password-less access and SSO between individual applications and on the web.

Service Provider (SP): Makes authorization decisions to grant or deny access to content based on the attributes about the user, received from the Identity Provider.

Shibboleth: An open-source federated access management system, used to facilitate single sign on and secure access to online resources.

SSO (Single Sign-On): A set of technologies allowing user login once and access to all permissible applications.

TLS 1.2: The latest version of TLS, formerly known as SSL and often used interchangeably. Encrypts data in transit to ensure secure transmission, used on most https websites.

VPN: Virtual private network. Facilitates secure access to private networks over the internet.

Chapter 16
Research Outcome of Faculty Members of Library and Information Science in North Indian Universities: A Study

Jyoti Sharma
Panjab University, India

ABSTRACT

The chapter aims to ascertain the ranks of 10 universities on the basis of participative index (PAI), average publications per faculty member (APPFM), and combined arithmetic mean (CAM). The data used for the present study was obtained by an online questionnaire. However, detailed information regarding their research output was collected directly from them. A total of 971 publications were published by LIS faculty till 31st December 2014. The results found that the position of some universities goes up and the position of some universities fall down when evaluated on different parameters. PU has the 2nd rank as per PAI but on the basis of other two parameters (i.e., on the basis of APPFM and CAM, it has 1st rank whereas BHU has the 1st rank as per PAI, but on the basis of APPFM it has 4th rank, and on the basis of CAM, it has the 3rd rank).

DOI: 10.4018/978-1-5225-8437-7.ch016

INTRODUCTION

Research plays a vital role as a source of latest information in the educational process. The research helps to reveal the truth which is hidden. It is done on the basis of some specific objectives. In short, research can be conceptualized as diligent, protracted investigations using adequate methods to discover latest knowledge, to develop unique applications of existing knowledge or to explain relationships between ideas or events (Mestri, 2008). The research reports, dissertations, theses, proceedings, books, and articles etc are the results of the research carried out by scholars and scientists which is published. Publication is a formal means of communication. It is the most appropriate way to share and disseminate one's knowledge. Publications can be defined as "Communication of a message, statement, or text through any means: audio, video, print, electronically as an e-book or on the web ("What is publication? definition and meaning - BusinessDictionary.com," n.d.). Reputation, Ranking and recognition of the academic institutions globally depend on research and publications. This is quite evident from the rankings of educational institutions released or published by several reputed agencies. The research performance of the Universities can be measured by different parameters i.e. Participative Index (PAI), Average Publication Per Faculty Member (APPFM) and Combined Arithmetic Mean (CAM). In the present study PAI, APPFM and CAM are different parameters to assign the rank to the 10 North Indian Universities. The PAI is expressed as ratio of the number of publications generated in an institution and the total number of publications by institution considered together. APPFM is the ratio of total publications of University and number of faculty members in University. CAM is calculated on the basis of individual mean of faculty members. Subsequently, university wise combined arithmetic mean is calculated. There are some studies in which authors tried to find out research output on the basis of these parameters. Kannappanavar, Swamy & Kumar found that in 1998, the average number of authors per paper was maximum i.e. 13.97 and Sharma & Chakravarty revealed that BBAU has 2nd rank as per PAI but on the basis of other two parameters it has 1st rank whereas DU has 1st rank as per PAI but on the basis of APPFM, it has 2nd rank and on the basis of CAM, it has 3th rank. The objectives of the study are as follows:

- To calculate Participative Index of select Universities under study
- To know Average Publications per Faculty Member
- To find out Combined Arithmetic Mean

METHODOLOGY

The data used for the present study was obtained by online questionnaire. However, detailed information regarding their research output was collected directly from them. To collect the publication information, the researcher made use of emails, telephonic conversation and personal visits wherever required. In some cases data was also obtained from the website of respective universities, personal blogs, databases, letters, and SMS. To complete the data collection process the researcher also used social media like Facebook, WhatsApp etc. A total of 971 publications were published by LIS faculty till 31st December 2014. The study covered ten select universities of north India, which has the department of Library and Information Science and only presently working permanent employees are considered for gathering publication details.

The study is restricted to the LIS departments in selected ten universities of North India. The publications of permanent (regular) faculty members (Assistant Professor, Associate Professor, and Professor) having at least one-year service length has been considered. The researcher has considered the total research output of faculty members irrespective of their present job/position. The study included only presently (during the time of data collection) working faculty members in the selected ten universities of North India. The faculty members retired during 2013-2016 is included in the study. The universities conducting LIS program through distance education mode has not been included in this study. The date of establishment of the departments of Library and Information Science has been ignored).

LITERATURE REVIEW

Several studies have been identified relating to the topic. However, select studies have been included in the literature review.

Kannappanavar, Swamy & Kumar (2004) highlighted productivity of information generators in the field of Chemistry. The study undertook Indian Science abstract (ISA) as the database for collecting data from 1996 to 2000.There were 13587 total numbers of papers. The authors revealed that majority of papers were multi-authored. The degree of collaboration and team work in the discipline was maximum i.e. 0.83. The average number of authors per paper had increased from 7.52 in 1996 to 8.39 in 2000. In 1998, the average number of authors per paper was maximum i.e. 13.97. The researchers concluded that the trend towards collaborative research was increasing in the Chemical Science.

Kademani, Kumar, Kumar, Sagar, Mohan, Surwase, & Gaderao (2005) analyzed the 475 papers published by the Bio-Organic Division of Bhabha Atomic Research Centre (BARC) during 1972-2002 in various domains. The source of data collected was BARC Annual Progress Reports. The highest number of publications in a year 2001 was 38. The average number of publications per year was 15.3 and the highest collaboration coefficient 1.0 was found in the years 1972, 1976-1977, 1980-1985, 1987, 1989-1990 and 1993. A. Banerji (125) was the most prolific author. Indian Journal of Chemistry (56) was the highly preferred journal.

Sevukan, Nagarajan, & Sharma (2007) analyzed research output in Plant Sciences of the faculties in central universities of India. There is the total of 348 bibliographic records of Plant Sciences retrieved from ISI Science Citation Index Extended (SCIE) for a period of 10 years from 1997-2006. The results of the study revealed that the Plant Science literature had grown steadily during the study period except for 1997-2002.The study revealed that the journal articles occupy the highest percentage of output i.e. 95.34%.The Participative Index (PAI) of Jawaharlal Nehru University (JNU) was 23% of total research output of specified universities during the period of study. The productivity of authors was found to be fitted Lotka's distribution and scattering of journal articles did not fit into Bradford's distribution. The study concluded that there was no upward sight of collaboration at national and international level. Major individual contributions were from Banaras Hindu University. Faculties preferred to publish their papers in international journals from foreign countries.

Jahan (2009) analyzed the Scientific Research (Life Sciences, Physical Sciences and Health Sciences) in central universities of Northern India during the period 2000-2008.The data for the present study was retrieved form SCOPUS database. There were total 16317 articles in Science Literature under the period of study. The research output of the universities under study in scientific literature was increasing every year in an average of 303 papers per year. University of Delhi (DU) (7,031) is the most productive university. Jawaharlal Nehru University (JNU) and DU had highest inter-university collaboration. The study indicated that out of the top ten most preferred periodicals authors from Aligarh Muslim University (AMU), Allahabad University (AU) and Banaras Hindu University (BHU) preferred to contribute articles both nationally and internationally, whereas authors from DU, Jamia Millia Islamia (JMI) and JNU preferred periodicals of foreign origin. The most prolific author in all six central universities was Anil Kumar Singh (144), Dept. of Chemistry, DU. The study concluded that the exception of BHU, none of the universities in this study was currently accredited by National Assessment and Accreditation Council (NAAC).

Suryani, Yaacob, Hashima, Rashid & Desa (2013) highlighted Research Publication Output by Academicians in Public and Private Universities in Malaysia. The data for the present study was retrieved form SCOPUS database. Comparison was made between the average number of publications by the private and the public universities. Findings show that the spur on publishing among Malaysian universities has taken effect. The study found that the Malaysian private universities published a distinctively smaller number of documents in Scopus compared to the public universities. The percentage for publication of journal article from the overall Scopus publication type journal articles published by the private universities was also smaller compared to the public universities. In other words, compared to the public universities, the authors in the Malaysian private universities had lower inclination to publish journal articles and were more likely to publish in conference proceedings, reviews and articles in press. The discussion section explores the reasons for these differences and presents the possible trending on the issue of publication in Malaysia.

Sharma & Chakravarty (2017) depicts Usage of Multi-Parameters on Research Output of Library and Information Science Faculty for Ranking of Select North Indian Universities. The data for the study was collected by questionnaire and from the websites of universities. A total of 1449 publications were published by LIS faculty during till 31st December 2014. The study covered five select universities of north India, which has the department of library and information science and only presently working permanent employees are considered for gathering publication details. The authors revealed that the position of some universities goes up and position of some universities fall down. BBAU has 2nd rank as per PAI but on the basis of other two parameters it has 1st rank whereas DU has 1st rank as per PAI but on the basis of APPFM, it has 2nd rank and on the basis of CAM, it has 3th rank.

PARTICIPATIVE INDEX (PAI)

Table 1 depicts total number of publications by faculty members of select North Indian Universities and Participative Index (PAI) of Universities under study. The table indicates PAI which assesses the research publications based on performance level of institutions. It is expressed as ratio of the number of publications generated in an institution and the total number of publications by institution considered together.

The table also depicts the PAI value of the 10 Universities under study, arranged in descending order reveals that BHU has highest PAI (0.188) whereas BRAU has lowest PAI (0.026). According to Table 1, the PAI value of BHU (0.188) followed by PU (0.157), KUK (0.150), CUHP (0.139), GNDU (0.114), BU (0.0830, MDU (0.064), JU (0.046), UOL (0.032) and BRAU (0.026) respectively.

Further, it can be observed that 5 Universities have more than 100 publications, fall between 111 publications to 183 publications and 5 Universities have less than 100 publications, fall between 31 publications to 81 publications.

Table 1. List of universities along with number of publications and PAI

SN/ Rank	Name of Universities	Abbreviations	Publications	PAI
1	Banaras Hindu University, Varanasi	BHU	183	0.188
2	Panjab University, Chandigarh	PU	152	0.157
3	Kurukshetra University, Kurukshetra	KUK	146	0.150
4	Central University of Himachal Pradesh, Dharamshala	CUHP	135	0.139
5	Guru Nanak Dev University, Amritsar	GNDU	111	0.114
6	Bundelkhand University, Jhansi	BU	81	0.083
7	Maharishi Dayanand University, Rohtak	MDU	62	0.064
8	University of Jammu, Tawi	JU	45	0.046
9	University of Lucknow, Lucknow	UOL	31	0.032
10	Dr. B.R. Ambedkar University, Agra	BRAU	25	0.026
Total			971	

Figure 1 reveals that out of the 10 Universities, BHU has highest number of publications (183, 18.85%) followed by PU (152,15.65%), KUK (146,15.04%), CUHP (135,13.90%), GNDU (111,11.43%), BU (81, 8.34%), MDU (62,6.39%), JU (45, 4.63%), UOL (31, 3.19%) and BRAU (25, 2.57%). There are 5 Universities having less than 5% contribution in total publications.

UNIVERSITY WISE FACULTY STRENGTH AND THEIR AVERAGE PUBLICATIONS PER FACULTY MEMBER

Table 2 depicts numbers of Faculty Members (FM) presently working with the department of Library and Information Science and their average publication per faculty member. The following table indicates that 10 Universities covered under study have produced 971 publications till December 2014. The Average Publications per

Figure 1. University wise total research output

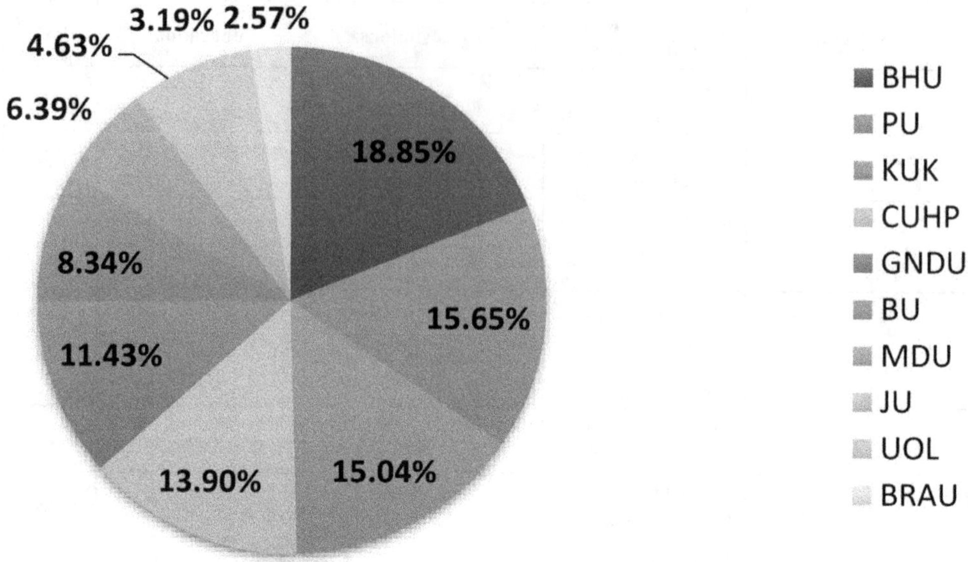

University (APPU) was found to be 97.1 publications. Out of these 10 universities, 5 universities contributing higher than above APPU, while rest i.e., 5 universities contribute lower than APPU. The Average Publication per Faculty Member (APPFM) is 29.42 publications. The table also indicates that out of 10 universities considered for the study, there are 5 universities which have contributed higher than the APPFM.

Table 2 depicts that strength of faculty varies across the select universities (1 to 6). KUK has maximum faculty members i.e., 6 followed by BHU i.e. 5, BU and MDU have 4 faculty members. PU, CUHP, GNDU and JU comprise of 3 faculty members followed by UOL and BRAU with only one faculty member.

Table 2 reveals the rank of the universities on the basis of their total number of publications and Average Publication Per Faculty Member (APPFM). There is noticeable variation in the ranks of the universities, when calculated through these two criteria i.e. total number of publications and APPFM. When total numbers of publications are considered then BHU is at 1st position with 183 publications. However, when APPFM is considered then BHU obtains 4th rank while PU holds the 1st rank. The 2nd and 3rd position according to total number of publications is maintained by PU and KUK. Thus, according to total number of publications, the top 5 universities are BHU (183), PU (152), KUK (146), CUHP (135) and GNDU (111) respectively. However according to APPFM the top positions are maintained by PU (50.67), CUHP (45.00), GNDU (37.00), BHU (36.60) and UOL (31.00). BRAU (25) has lowest number of publications, while JU (15.00) has lowest APPFM.

Table 2. University wise faculty strength and their average publications per faculty members

SN/ Rank	Abbreviations	Publications	No. of FM	Average = Publications/ No. of FM
1	Panjab University, Chandigarh	152	3	50.67
2	Central University of Himachal Pradesh, Dharamshala	135	3	45.00
3	Guru Nanak Dev University, Amritsar	111	3	37.00
4	Banaras Hindu University, Varanasi	183	5	36.60
5	University of Lucknow, Lucknow	31	1	31.00
6	Dr. B.R. Ambedkar University, Agra	25	1	25.00
7	Kurukshetra University, Kurukshetra	146	6	24.33
8	Bundelkhand University, Jhansi	81	4	20.25
9	Maharishi Dayanand University, Rohtak	62	4	15.50
10	University of Jammu, Tawi	45	3	15.00
Total		971	33	29.42

Thus, the rank of universities based on total number of publications changes when APPFM is considered.

Combined Arithmetic Mean of Select North Indian Universities

Table 3 depicts combined arithmetic mean of research output in Library and Information Science of select universities. The combined arithmetic mean is calculated on the basis of individual mean of faculty members. Subsequently, university wise combined arithmetic mean is calculated. For calculating combined arithmetic mean following formula is used:

$$\bar{X} = \frac{n_1\bar{x}_1 + n_2\bar{x}_2 + \ldots\ldots\ldots n_n\bar{x}_n}{n_1 + n_2 + \ldots\ldots\ldots\ldots n_n} = \bar{X} = \frac{\sum n_i\bar{x}_i}{\sum n_i}$$

Table 3. Number of faculty members along with their combined arithmetic mean

SN/ Rank	Name of Universities	Combined Arithmetic Mean
1	Panjab University, Chandigarh	3.62
2	Central University of Himachal Pradesh, Dharamshala	2.55
3	Banaras Hindu University, Varanasi	2.21
4	Maharishi Dayanand University, Rohtak	1.77
5	University of Lucknow, Lucknow	1.72
6	Kurukshetra University, Kurukshetra	1.32
7	Dr. B.R. Ambedkar University, Agra	1.25
8	Jammu University, Tawi	1.22
9	Bundelkhand University, Jhansi	1.03
10	Guru Nanak Dev University, Amritsar	0.76

Where,

n_i = Total no. of active years as author
$\bar{x}_i$ = Mean publications of individual faculty member (per year)
i= Number of faculty members (Minimum=1; Maximum=9)

The study reveals that PU holds highest position in the 10 universities under study followed by CUHP. GNDU has lowest value of combined arithmetic mean. There are 7 universities having combined arithmetic mean less than 2, 2 universities having combined arithmetic mean between 2-3 and only 1 universities having combined arithmetic mean higher than 3. It can be concluded that combined arithmetic mean gives the status of research productivity in actual sense as it is based upon the publications of faculty members during their active years as author. So, BHU has 4th rank in research productivity when it is seen as Average Publication Per Faculty Member (APPFM) member whereas according to combined arithmetic mean, BHU ranks 3rd. In the same pattern, KUK, MDU and JU have rise in their positions i.e 7th to 6th, 9th to 4th and 10th to 8th respectively whereas GNDU, BRAU and BU have declined from 3rd to 10th, 6th to 7th and 8th to 9th respectively. PU, CUHP and UOL remain on the same position i.e 1, 2 and 5 respectively based on the combined arithmetic mean as well as APPFM.

Figure 2 depicts positions of universities on the basis of Participative Index, APPFM and combined arithmetic mean. The figure reveals change in the position of universities under study in term of different parameters. The position of some universities goes up and position of some universities fall down. PU has 2nd rank as

Figure 2. Rank of universities according to participative index, average (APPFM) and combined arithmetic mean

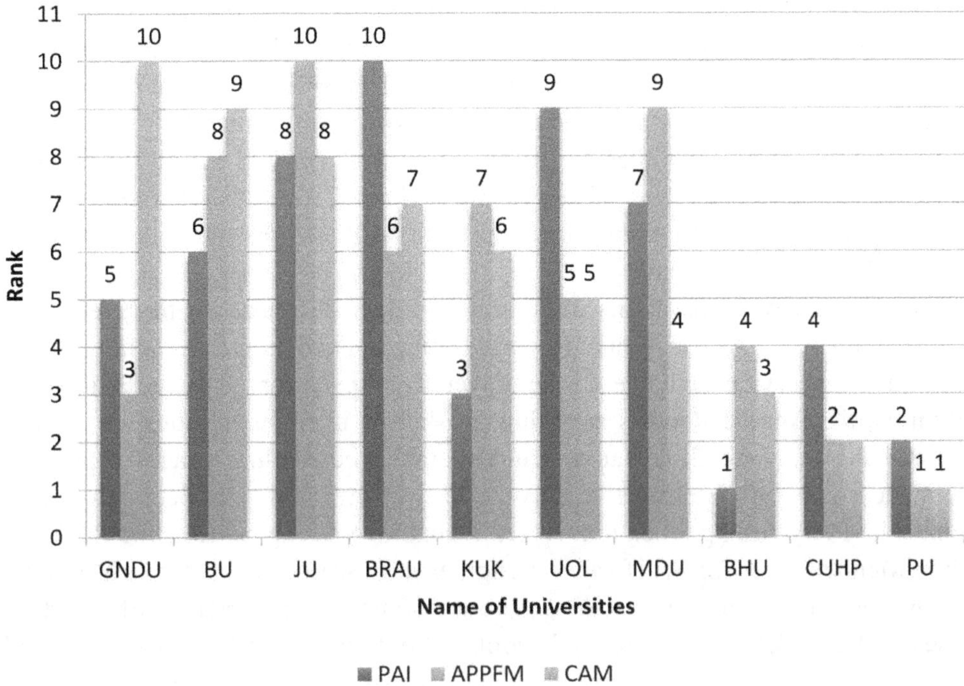

per PAI but on the basis of other two parameters it has 1st rank whereas BHU has 1st rank as per PAI but on the basis of Average (APPFM), it has 4th rank and on the basis of combined arithmetic mean, it has 3rd rank. KUK has 3rd rank as per PAI but on the basis of Average, it has 7th rank and on the basis of combined arithmetic mean, it has 6th rank. CUHP has 4th rank as per PAI but on the basis of Average and combined arithmetic mean, it has 2nd rank. GNDU has 5th rank as per PAI but on the basis of Average, it has 3rd rang and on the basis of combined arithmetic mean, it has 10th rank. BU has 6th rank as per PAI but on the basis of Average, it has 8th rank and on the basis of combined arithmetic mean, it has 9th rank. MDU has 7th rank as per PAI but on the basis of Average, it has 9th rank and on the basis of combined arithmetic mean, it has 4th rank. JU has 8th rank as per PAI and CAM, but on the basis of Average, it has 10th rank. UOL has 9th rank as per PAI but on the basis of Average and CAM, it has 5th rank. BRAU has 10th rank as per PAI but on the basis of Average, it has 6th rank and on the basis of combined arithmetic mean, it has 7th rank. It reveals universities under study have obtained different ranks on the basis of different parameters.

DISCUSSION

In this study author tried to cover all the parameters for finding the research productivity of select 10 North Indian Universities. The results revealed that different parameters change the ranking of Universities under study. The results found that the position of some universities goes up and position of some universities fall down when evaluated on different parameters. PU has 2nd rank as per PAI but on the basis of other two parameters i.e. on the basis of APPFM and CAM, it has 1st rank whereas BHU has 1st rank as per PAI but on the basis of APPFM it has 4th rank and on the basis of CAM, it has 3rd rank.

On the basis of observations and findings of the research study, there are some suggestions like 1. As the Annual Report is compiled and prepared in digital form, they should be made available on the university website for easy access. In some libraries, the Annual Reports are lying on shelves in libraries, but they are not maintained year-wise. 2. Updated faculty members curriculum vitae (CV) should be made online on the respective universities websites with complete publication details. 3. For getting publications freely available tools can be used like Research Gate, Mendeley etc. This will further strengthen the research impact of the discipline.

In view of the present research, there are some recommendations for further research like 1. The present study is confined only to department of Library and Information science of select North Indian Universities. This study can be extended to various Library and Information Science departments of universities situated in other regions of India as well. 2. The same can be replicated to other disciplines of Arts, Humanities and Social Sciences (AHSS) as well as Science, Technology, Engineering, Math, and Medicine (STEMM) also. This will facilitate comparative analysis and deeper insight. 3.Further studies covering other disciplines and other universities should be based on primary data collected from the faculty members directly as databases do not cover publications in all formats (Journals, Conference Proceedings and Book/book Chapters) (specially Indian) adequately.

CONCLUSION

The author concludes that in the Table 1, the PAI value of the 10 Universities under study, BHU has highest PAI (0.188) whereas BRAU has lowest PAI (0.026). The Average Publications per University (APPU) was found to be 97.1 publications. Out of these 10 Universities, 5 Universities contributing higher than above APPU, while rest i.e., 5 Universities contribute lower than APPU. The Average Publication per Faculty Member (APPFM) is 29.42 publications. The Table 2 also indicates that out of 10 Universities considered for the study, there are 5 Universities which have contributed higher than the APPFM. The strength of faculty varies across the select Universities (1 to 6). The study reveals that PU holds highest position in the 10 Universities under study followed by CUHP. GNDU has lowest value of combined arithmetic mean. PU has 2nd rank as per PAI but on the basis of other two parameters it has 1st rank whereas BHU has 1st rank as per PAI but on the basis of Average (APPFM), it has 4th rank and on the basis of combined arithmetic mean, it has 3rd rank. The study reveals that universities under study have obtained different ranks on the basis of different parameters. The present study is limited to the quantity of research output instead of the quality of publications (citations). The study does not include deemed and private universities only central and state universities are included in the study.

REFERENCES

Banaras Hindu University Varanasi. (2016). Retrieved from http://www.bhu.ac.in/aboutus/history.php

Bundelkhand University Bundelkhand. (n.d.). Retrieved from https://www.bujhansi.org/index.aspx

Central University of Himachal Pradesh Dharamshala. (2013). Retrieved from http://cuhimachal.ac.in/cuhp_about_genesis.aspx

Department of Library & Information Science, Central University of Himachal Pradesh, Dharamshala. (2013). Retrieved from http://cuhimachal.ac.in/math_vision_mission.aspx

Department of Library & Information Science, Panjab University Chandigarh. (2016). Retrieved from http://libraryscience.puchd.ac.in/ index.php

Department of Library and Information Science, Dr. B. R. Ambedkar University, Agra. (2014). Retrieved from http://www.dbrau.ac.in/department_%20of_Library_and_Information_science.html

Department of Library and Information Science, Banaras Hindu University. (2014). Retrieved from http://www.bhu.ac.in/arts/lis/history.html

Department of Library and Information Science, Bundelkhand University, Bundelkhand. (n.d.). Retrieved from https://www.bujhansi.org/frmViewcampusFaculty.aspx

Department of Library and Information Science, Guru Nanak Dev University, Amritsar. (n.d.). Retrieved from http://www.gndu.ac.in/gndu2014/ShowFacultyDetailProforma.asp?D=20

Department of Library and Information Science, Kurukshetra University, Kurukshetra. (2010). Retrieved from http://www.kuk.ac.in/information.php?action=showContent&L01_id=OA==&L01_direction=H&L03_id=Mzk=&L02_id=MjE=&sublevel=y

Department of Library and Information Science, Maharshi Dayanand University, Rohtak. (2011). Retrieved from http://www.mdurohtak.ac.in/info/acad_fac_socscie_libraryinformscience.html

Department of Library and Information Science, University of Lucknow, Lucknow. (2016). Retrieved from http://www.lkouniv.ac.in/ arts_libais.html

Departments: Library Science, Jammu University, Tawi. (2010). Retrieved from http://www.jammuuniversity.in/ departments/lib%20 science/intro.asp

Dr. B. R. Ambedkar University, Agra. (2014). Retrieved from http://www.dbrau.ac.in/about_university.html

Guru Nanak Dev University Amritsar. (n.d.). Retrieved from http://www.gndu.ac.in/gndu2014/aboutus.html

Jammu University Tawi. (2009). Retrieved from http://www.jammuuniversity.in/uni_profile.asp

Kurukshetra University Kurukshetra. (2010). Retrieved from http://www.kuk.ac.in/

Maharshi Dayanand University Rohtak. (2011). Retrieved from http://www.mdurohtak.ac.in/

Mestri, D. D. (2008). Doctoral Theses in Library and Information Science Completed in Indian Universities, 2001–2007. *Education for Information*, *26*(3), 213–234. doi:10.3233/EFI-2008-263-405

Panjab University Chandigarh. (2016). Retrieved from http://puchd.ac.in/

Sharma, J., & Chakravarty, R. (2017). Usage of Multi-Parameters on Research Output of Library and Information Science Faculty for Ranking of Select North Indian Universities. *Diviner: A Research Journal of the Humanities and Social Sciences*, *14*(1), 239–244.

Suryani, I., Yaacob, A., Hashima, N., Rashid, S. A., & Desa, H. (2013). Research publication output by academicians in public and private universities in Malaysia. *International Journal of Higher Education*, *2*(1), 84–90. doi:10.5430/ijhe.v2n1p84

University of Lucknow. (2016). Retrieved from http://www.lkouniv.ac.in/history.html

What is publication? definition and meaning. (n.d.). Retrieved from http://www.businessdictionary.com/definition/publication.html

KEY TERMS AND REFERENCES

Average Publication per Faculty Member (APPFM): It means average number of publications of each faculty member.

Average Publications per University (APPU): It means average number of publications of each university (i.e., 10 universities).

Combined Arithmetic Mean (CAM): CAM is calculated on the basis of individual mean of faculty members. Subsequently, university wise combined arithmetic mean is calculated.

Participative Index (PAI): PAI assesses the research publications based on performance level of institutions.

Compilation of References

3M. Standard Interchange Protocol. (2018). Retrieved from http://multimedia.3m.com/mws/media/355361O/sip2-protocol.pdf

Abbasi, F., & Zardary, S. (2012). Digital libraries and its role on supporting Learning. *AWERProcedia Information Technology & Computer Science*, *1*, 809–813.

Abel, F., Celik, I., Hauff, C., Hollink, L., & Houben, G.-J. (2011). *U-sem: Semantic enrichment, user modeling, and mining of usage data on the social web.* arXiv preprint arXiv:1104.0126

Abubakar, B. M. (2010). Digital libraries in Nigeria in the Era of Global change: A Perspective of the major Challenges. *TRIM*, *6*(2), 125–131.

Access, O. (2018). What is open access? *Open Access.nl.* Retrieved from http://www.openaccess.nl/en/what-is-open-access

Acemoglu, D., & Autor, D. (2012). What does human capital do? A review of Goldin and Katz's the race between education and technology. *Journal of Economic Literature*, *50*(2), 426–463. doi:10.1257/jel.50.2.426

Achakulvisut, T., Acuna, D. E., Ruangrong, T., & Kording, K. (2016). Science Concierge: A fast content-based recommendation system for scientific publications. *PLoS One*, *11*(7), e0158423. doi:10.1371/journal.pone.0158423 PMID:27383424

Adam, L. (2016). *Riding the National Research and Education Networking Train in Africa.* Retrieved from http://africanopenscience.org.za/wp-content/uploads/2018/01/AAURiding-the-NREN-Train-final-draft-.pdf

Adekunle, P. A., Omoba, R. O., & Tella, A. (2007). Attitudes of librarians in selected Nigerian universities towards the use of ICT. *Library Philosophy and Practice*. Available at http://unllib.unl.edu/LPP/tella3.htm

Adomi, E. E. (2005). *Internet development and connectivity in Nigeria.* Department of Library and Information Science, Delta State University, Abraka, Nigeria. Retrieved from http://www.emeraldinsight.com/Insight/ViewContentServlet?Filename=Published/Em rldFullTextArticle/Articles/2800390306.html

African Tertiary institution connectivity survey. (2006). *ATICS 2006 Report*. Available at http://biotrade.aauorg/renul/docs/ATICS2006.pdf

Agence France-Presse. (2011). World 'running out of Internet addresses' - INQUIRER.net, *Philippine News for Filipinos*. Retrieved from https://web.archive.org/web/20110125195711/http://technology.inquirer.net/infotech/infotech/view/20110121-315808/World-running-out-of-Internet-addresses

Ahmed, A. O., & Nwalo, K., (2013). Fund Allocation as a Correlate of Sustainability of Departmental Libraries in Nigerian Universities. *Library Philosophy and Practice,* 936-951.

Ajadi, T. O., Salawu, I. O., & Adeoye, F. A. (2008). E-learning and distance education in Nigeria. *The Turkish Online Journal of Educational Technology*, 7(4), 1–10.

Akintunde, S. A., & Anjo, R. (2012). *Digitizing Resources in Nigeria: An Overview*. Retrieved from www.netlibrarynigeria.net/downloads/Akintunde.doc/pdf

Alemayehu, M. W. (2010). *Researcher's attitude to using Institutional Repositories: A case study of the Oslo University Institutional Repository.* Retrieved from http://hdl.handle.net

Alotaibi, S., & Vassileva, J. (2015). *Multi-dimensional Ratings for Research Paper Recommender Systems: A Qualitative Study.* Paper presented at the International Symposium on Web AlGorithms, Deauville, France.

Alpha Network Babel Library. (2007). *Guidelines for the creation of Institutional Repositories at Universities and Higher Education Institutions*. Columbus, OH: Europe Aid Co-operation Office.

Aluoch, A. A. (2006). *The search for affordable quality Internet connectivity for African universities*. AAU.

Alzoghbi, A., Ayala, V. A. A., Fischer, P. M., & Lausen, G. (2016). *Learning-to-Rank in Research Paper CBF recommendation: Leveraging Irrelevant Papers.* Paper presented at the CBRecSys@RecSys, Boston, MA.

Amatriain, X., Jaimes, A., Oliver, N., & Pujol, J. M. (2011). Data mining methods for recommender systems. In Recommender systems handbook (pp. 39–71). Boston, MA: Springer. doi:10.1007/978-0-387-85820-3_2

American Library Association. (1987). *Guide for writing a bibliographer's manual: Collection Management and Development Guide No. 1*. Chicago, IL: ALA.

Amorim, R. C. (2016). *A Comparison of research data management platforms: architecture, flexible metadata and interoperability*. Univ Access Inf Soc.

Anderson, M., Gallinger, M., & Potter, A. (2009). *The National Digital Stewardship Alliance Charter: Enabling Collaboration to Achieve National Digital Preservation.* In iPRES 2009: the Sixth International Conference on Preservation of Digital Objects, San Francisco, CA.

Antelman, K. (2004). Do open-access articles have a greater research impact? *College & Research Libraries*, *65*(5), 372–382. doi:10.5860/crl.65.5.372

Arlitsch, K., & Grant, C. (2018). Why So Many Repositories? Examining the Limitations and Possibilities of the Institutional Repositories Landscape. *Journal of Library Administration*, *58*(3), 264–281. doi:10.1080/01930826.2018.1436778

Arning, U. (2015). GMS publishes your research findings and makes the related research data available through Dryad. *GMS Zeitschrift für Medizinische Ausbildung*, *32*(3), Doc34. PMID:26413172

Arnold, A., & Cohen, W. W. (2009). *Information extraction as link prediction: Using curated citation networks to improve gene detection.* Paper presented at the International Conference on Wireless Algorithms, Systems, and Applications. 10.1007/978-3-642-03417-6_53

Arunachalam, S. (2003). Information for research in developing countries: Information technology - friend or foe? *Bulletin of the American Society for Information Science and Technology.*

Association of College and Research Libraries. (2016). *Standards for Distance Learning Library Services.* Retrieved from http://www.ala.org/acrl/standards/guidelinesdistancelearning

Atkins, D., Seely Brown, J., & Hammond, A. (2007). *A Review of the Open Educational Resources (OER) Movement: Achievements, Challenges, and New Opportunities*. William and Flora Hewlett Foundation. Retrieved from https://hewlett.org/wp-content/uploads/2016/08/ReviewoftheOERMovement.pdf

Auer, S., Kovtun, V., Prinz, M., Kasprzik, A., Stocker, M., & Vidal, M. E. (2018). Towards a knowledge graph for science. In *WIMS'18 Proceedings of the 8th International Conference on Web Intelligence, Mining and Semantics.* New York, NY: ACM. 10.1145/3227609.3227689

Austin, C. E. (2015). Research Data Repositories: A review of current features, gap analysis, and recommendations for minimum requirements. *IASSIST Quarterly.*

Auto-graphics SHAREit upgrades ACCESS Pennsylvania's resource sharing, saving 1,500 libraries across the state time and money. (2018, March 20). *Asia News Monitor.* Retrieved from https://search.proquest.com/docview/2015024298

Avancini, H., Candela, L., & Straccia, U. (2007). Recommenders in a personalized, collaborative digital library environment. *Journal of Intelligent Information Systems*, *28*(3), 253–283. doi:10.100710844-006-0010-3

Avedas. (2017). *CONVERIS. Managing the Research Life Cycle.* Karlsruhe, Germany: Avedas AG. Retrieved from https://www.campus-innovation.de/fileadmin/dokumente/Loesungen_und_Praxis/CONVERIS_Produktbeschreibung_Details.pdf

Awre, C. (2003). Open access and the impact on publishing and purchasing. *Serials, 16*(2), 205-208. Retrieved from https://www.researchgate.net/profile/Chris_Awre/publication/276594507_Open_access_and_the_impact_on_publishing_and_purchasing/links/5603709d08ae460e2704de31.pdf

Ayris, P., Achard, P., Fdida, S., Gradmann, S., Horstmann, W., Labastida, I., & Smit, A. (2013). *LERU Roadmap for Research Data. LERU Advice Paper* (Vol. 14). Leuven, Belgium: LERU.

Baez, M., Mirylenka, D., & Parra, C. (2011). Understanding and supporting the search for scholarly knowledge. *Proceeding of the 7th European Computer Science Summit*, 1-8.

Baikady, M. R., & Jessy, A. (2014). Off Campus Access to Licensed E-resources of Library: A Case Study. *DESIDOC Journal of Library and Information Technology, 34*(6), 486–490. doi:10.14429/djlit.34.6.7509

Bailey, C. W. Jr. (2005). The Role of Reference Librarians in Institutional Repositories. *RSR. Reference Services Review, 33*(3), 259–26. doi:10.1108/00907320510611294

Balaram, P. (2000). Journals. *Current Science, 79*(6), 685.

Banaras Hindu University Varanasi. (2016). Retrieved from http://www.bhu.ac.in/aboutus/history.php

Bancu, C., Dagadita, M., Dascalu, M., Dobre, C., Trausan-Matu, S., & Florea, A. M. (2012). ARSYS--Article Recommender System. In *2012 14th International Symposium on Symbolic and Numeric Algorithms for Scientific Computing*(pp. 349-355). IEEE.

Bankier, J. G., Gleason, K., & UNESCO. (2014). *Institutional Repository Software Comparison.* Retrieved from http://www.unesco.org/new/en/ communication-and-information/resources/publications-and-communication-materials/publications/full-list/institutional-repository-software-comparison/

Baregheh, A., Rowley, J., & Sambrook, S. (2009). Towards a multidisciplinary definition of innovation. *Management Decision, 47*(8), 1323–1339. doi:10.1108/00251740910984578

Barga, R. S., Andrews, S., & Parastatidis, S. (2007). A Virtual Research Environment (VRE) for Bioscience Researchers. In *Proceedings of the International Conference on Advanced Engineering Computing and Applications in Sciences*, (pp. 31-38). IEEE. 10.1109/ADVCOMP.2007.14

Barron, B. B. (2002). Distant and distributed learners are two sides of the same coin. *Computers in Libraries, 22*(1), 24–28.

Bates, A. W. (1995). *Technology, Open Learning, and Distance Education.* New York, NY: Routledge.

Beel, J. (2017). *Towards effective research-paper recommender systems and user modeling based on mind maps.* arXiv preprint arXiv:1703.09109

Beel, J., & Gipp, B. (2009). Google Scholar's ranking algorithm: the impact of citation counts (an empirical study). In *2009 Third International Conference on Research Challenges in Information Science* (pp. 439-446). IEEE.

Beel, J., & Langer, S. (2015). *A comparison of offline evaluations, online evaluations, and user studies in the context of research-paper recommender systems.* Paper presented at the International Conference on Theory and Practice of Digital Libraries. 10.1007/978-3-319-24592-8_12

Beel, J., Langer, S., Genzmehr, M., Gipp, B., Breitinger, C., & Nürnberger, A. (2013). Research paper recommender system evaluation: a quantitative literature survey. *Proceedings of the International Workshop on Reproducibility and Replication in Recommender Systems Evaluation.*

Beel, J., Langer, S., Genzmehr, M., Gipp, B., Breitinger, C., & Nürnberger, A. (2013, October). Research paper recommender system evaluation: a quantitative literature survey. In *Proceedings of the International Workshop on Reproducibility and Replication in Recommender Systems Evaluation* (pp. 15-22). ACM.

Beel, J., Genzmehr, M., Langer, S., Nürnberger, A., & Gipp, B. (2013). A comparative analysis of offline and online evaluations and discussion of research paper recommender system evaluation. *Proceedings of the international workshop on reproducibility and replication in recommender systems evaluation.* 10.1145/2532508.2532511

Beel, J., Gipp, B., Langer, S., & Breitinger, C. (2015). Research-paper recommender systems: A literature survey. *International Journal on Digital Libraries*, 1–34.

Beel, J., Langer, S., Genzmehr, M., & Nürnberger, A. (2013). Introducing Docear's research paper recommender system. *Proceedings of the 13th ACM/IEEE-CS joint conference on Digital libraries.* 10.1145/2467696.2467786

Berlin Declaration on Open Access to Knowledge in the Sciences and Humanities. (2003). Retrieved from http://www.redalyc.org/pdf/782/78241008.pdf

Berman, J. (2003). A tool for sharing annotated research data: The "Category 0" UMLS (Unified Medical Language System) vocabularies. *BMC Medical Informatics and Decision Making, 3*(6). PMID:12809560

Bernius, S., & Hanauske, M. (2009, January). Open access to scientific literature-increasing citations as an incentive for authors to make their publications freely accessible. In *Proceedings of 42nd Hawaii International Conference on System Sciences, 2009. HICSS'09.* (pp. 1-9). IEEE. Retrieved from http://www.is-frankfurt.de/publikationenNeu/OpenAccesstoScientificLiteratu3032.pdf

Bernius, S. (2010). The impact of open access on the management of scientific knowledge. *Online Information Review, 34*(4), 583–603. doi:10.1108/14684521011072990

Bethard, S., & Jurafsky, D. (2010). Who should I cite: learning literature search models from citation behavior. *Proceedings of the 19th ACM international conference on Information and knowledge management.* 10.1145/1871437.1871517

BioMed Central. (2018). About BMC: Open Access. *BMC Part of Springer Nature*. Retrieved from https://www.biomedcentral.com/about/open-access

Björk, B. C. (2017). Open access to scientific articles: a review of benefits and challenges. *Internal and Emergency Medicine, 12*(2), 247-253. Retrieved from https://link.springer.com/article/10.1007/s11739-017-1603-2

Björk, B. C., & Solomon, D. (2012). Open access versus subscription journals: A comparison of scientific impact. *BMC Medicine, 10*(1), 73. doi:10.1186/1741-7015-10-73 PMID:22805105

Björk, B. C., Welling, P., Laakso, M., Majlender, P., Hedlund, T., & Guðnason, G. (2010). Open access to the scientific journal literature: Situation 2009. *PLoS One, 5*(6), e11273. doi:10.1371/journal.pone.0011273 PMID:20585653

Bodenreider, O. (2004). The unified medical language system (UMLS): Integrating biomedical terminology. *Nucleic Acids Research, 32*(90001), 267–270. doi:10.1093/nar/gkh061 PMID:14681409

Bogers, T., & Van den Bosch, A. (2008). Recommending scientific articles using CiteULike. *Proceedings of the 2008 ACM conference on Recommender systems*. 10.1145/1454008.1454053

Bollacker, K. D., Lawrence, S., & Giles, C. L. (1998). CiteSeer: An autonomous web agent for automatic retrieval and identification of interesting publications. *Proceedings of the second international conference on Autonomous agents*. 10.1145/280765.280786

Bollacker, K. D., Lawrence, S., & Giles, C. L. (2000). Discovering relevant scientific literature on the web. *IEEE Intelligent Systems & their Applications, 15*(2), 42–47. doi:10.1109/5254.850826

Bollen, J., & Van de Sompel, H. (2006). An architecture for the aggregation and analysis of scholarly usage data. *Proceedings of the 6th ACM/IEEE-CS joint conference on Digital libraries*. 10.1145/1141753.1141821

Bollerslev, T. (1986). Generalized Autoregressive Conditional Heteroskedasticity. *Journal of Econometrics, 31*(3), 307–327. doi:10.1016/0304-4076(86)90063-1

Boyle, P. (2000, August 24). What? Use a Book for Doing Research? College Students Forsake Library Shelves for Computers. *Washington Post*, p. M07.

Bradford, J. T., Costello, B., & Lenholt, R. (2005). Reference Service in the Digital Age: An Analysis of Sources Used to Answer Reference Questions. *Journal of Academic Librarianship, 31*(3), 263–272. doi:10.1016/j.acalib.2005.03.001

Brase, J., & Schindler, U. (2006). The publication of scientific data by the world data centers and the national library of science and technology in Germany. *Data Science Journal, 5*, 205–208. doi:10.2481/dsj.5.205

Brin, S., & Page, L. (1998). The anatomy of a large-scale hypertextual web search engine. *Computer Networks and ISDN Systems*, *30*(1), 107–117. doi:10.1016/S0169-7552(98)00110-X

British Library. (2015). *Living Knowledge: The British Library 2015-2023*. London, UK: British Library.

Brophy, P. (1993). Networking in British academic libraries. *British Journal of Academic Librarianship, 8*(1), 49-60.

Brown, E. (2010). "I know what you researched last summer": How academic librarians are supporting researchers in the management of data curation. *The New Zealand Library & Information Management Journal, 52*(1), 55–69. Retrieved from http://www.lianza.org.nz/sites/lianza.org.nz/files/nzlimj_vol_52_issue_no_1_oct_2010.pdf

Brusilovski, P., Kobsa, A., & Nejdl, W. (2007). The adaptive web: methods and strategies of web personalization (Vol. 4321). Berlin, Germany: Springer Science & Business Media. doi:10.1007/978-3-540-72079-9

Bryant, R., Oxnam, M., & Mangiafico, P. (2017). *The Emergence of Research Information Management (RIM) within US libraries.* CNI Spring Meeting, Albuquerque, NM.

Brynjolfsson, E., Rock, D., & Syverson, C. (2017). *Artificial Intelligence and the Modern Productivity Paradox: A Clash of Expectations and Statistics*. The National Bureau of Economic Research. doi:10.3386/w24001

Buchhorn, M., & McNamara, P. (2006). *Sustainability Issues for Australian Research Data. The Report of the Australian e-Research Sustainability Survey Project.* Retrieved from http://www.apsr.edu.au

Bundelkhand University Bundelkhand. (n.d.). Retrieved from https://www.bujhansi.org/index.aspx

Bunton, G. A. (2017). EZproxy: The Key to Remote Access. *The Serials Librarian, 73*(2), 119–126. doi:10.1080/0361526X.2017.1338635

Burke, R. (2002). Hybrid recommender systems: Survey and experiments. *User Modeling and User-Adapted Interaction, 12*(4), 331–370. doi:10.1023/A:1021240730564

Burton, M., Lyon, L., Erdmann, C., & Tijerina, B. (2018). *Shifting to Data Savvy: The Future of Data Science in Libraries*. Pittsburgh, PA: University of Pittsburgh.

Cambridge University Press. (2018). *Benefits of open access.* Cambridge University Press. Retrieved from https://www.cambridge.org/core/services/open-access-policies/open-access-resources/benefits-of-open-access

Canadian Association of Research Libraries (CARL). (2014). A Guide to Setting-Up an Institutional Repository. *CARL.* Retrieved from http://www.carl-abrc.ca/en/scholarly communications/carl-institutional-repository-program/a-guide-to-setting-up-an institutional-repository.html

Capocci, A., & Caldarelli, G. (2008). Folksonomies and clustering in the collaborative system CiteULike. *Journal of Physics. A, Mathematical and Theoretical*, *41*(22), 224016. doi:10.1088/1751-8113/41/22/224016

Caragea, C., Silvescu, A., Kataria, S., Caragea, D., & Mitra, P. (2011, December). *Classifying scientific publications using abstract features*. In Ninth Symposium of Abstraction, Reformulation, and Approximation, Catalonia, Spain.

Caragea, C., Silvescu, A., Mitra, P., & Giles, C. L. (2013). Can't see the forest for the trees?: a citation recommendation system. *Proceedings of the 13th ACM/IEEE-CS joint conference on Digital libraries.* 10.1145/2467696.2467743

Central University of Himachal Pradesh Dharamshala. (2013). Retrieved from http://cuhimachal.ac.in/cuhp_about_genesis.aspx

Chakraborty, T., Krishna, A., Singh, M., Ganguly, N., Goyal, P., & Mukherjee, A. (2016). *Ferosa: A faceted recommendation system for scientific articles.* Paper presented at the Pacific-Asia Conference on Knowledge Discovery and Data Mining. 10.1007/978-3-319-31750-2_42

Chakraborty, T., Modani, N., Narayanam, R., & Nagar, S. (2015, April). *Discern: a diversified citation recommendation system for scientific queries.* Paper presented at the 2015 IEEE 31st International Conference on Data Engineering (ICDE). 10.1109/ICDE.2015.7113314

Chandrasekaran, K., Gauch, S., Lakkaraju, P., & Luong, H. P. (2008). Concept-based document recommendations for citeseer authors. *Proceedings of the Adaptive hypermedia and adaptive web-based systems.* 10.1007/978-3-540-70987-9_11

Chapman, L. (2004). *Managing acquisitions in library and information services* (2nd ed.). London, UK: Facet Publishing.

Chapman, J. W., Reynolds, D., & Shreeves, A. (2009). Repository metadata: Approaches and challenges. *Cataloging & Classification Quarterly*, *47*(3-4), 309–325. doi:10.1080/01639370902735020

Chen, W., Yao, F., & Jiang, A. (2018). Technology Innovations in Academic Libraries in China. In Library Science and Administration: Concepts, Methodologies, Tools, and Applications, (pp. 144-164). Hershey, PA: IGI Global. doi:10.4018/978-1-5225-3914-8.ch007

Chen, L.-C., Kuo, P.-J., & Liao, I.-E. (2015). An ontology-based library recommender system using MapReduce. *Cluster Computing*, *18*(1), 113–121. doi:10.100710586-013-0342-z

Chigwada, J., Chiparausha, B., & Kasiroori, J. (2017). Research Data Management in research institutions in Zimbabwe. *Data Science Journal*, *16*(0), 31. doi:10.5334/dsj-2017-031

Chisenga, J. (2006). *The development and use of digital libraries, institutional digital repositories and open access archives for research and national development in Africa: Opportunities and challenges.* WSIS Follow-up Conference on Access to Information and Knowledge for Development. Retrieved from http://www.uneca.org/disd/events/2006/wsislibrary/presentations/Development%20and20Use%20of%20Institutional%20Repositories%20-%20Justin%20Chisenga%20 %20EN.pdf

Chiware, E., & Becker, D. A. (2018). Research Data Management services in Southern Africa: A readiness survey of academic and research Libraries. *African Journal of Library Archives and Information Science*, *28*(1), 1–16.

Choochaiwattana, W. (2010). *Usage of tagging for research paper recommendation.* Paper presented at the 2010 3rd International Conference on Advanced Computer Theory and Engineering (ICACTE). 10.1109/ICACTE.2010.5579321

Chowdhury, G. G. (2002) Digital Divide: How Can Digital Libraries Bridge the Gap? *Proceedings of the 5th International Conference on Asian Digital Libraries: Digital Libraries: People, Knowledge, and Technology.* 10.1007/3-540-36227-4_43

Christian, G.M. (2008). *Issues and Challenges to the Development of Open Access Institutional Repositories in Academic and Research Institutions in Nigeria.* Academic Press.

Chudnov, D., & Gallinger, M. (2016). Library of Congress Lab: Library of Congress Digital Scholars Lab Pilot Project Report. Washington, DC: Academic Press.

Chu, S. K. W., & Du, H. S. (2013). Social networking tools for academic libraries. *Journal of Librarianship and Information Science*, *45*(1), 64–75. doi:10.1177/0961000611434361

Clements, A., & McCutcheon, V. (2014). Research data meets research information management: Two case studies using (a) Pure CERIF-CRIS and (b) EPrints repository platform with CERIF extensions. *Procedia Computer Science*, *33*, 199–206. doi:10.1016/j.procs.2014.06.033

Cloete, A. L. (2017). Technology and education: Challenges and opportunities. *Hervormde Teologiese Studies*, *73*(4), a4589. doi:10.4102/hts.v73i4.4589

CloudGate UNO announces federated access support for amazon web services. (2018, May 28). *Asia News Monitor.* Retrieved from https://search.proquest.com/docview/2044803283

Collins, E. (2012). The National Data Centres. In G. Pryor (Ed.), *Managing Research Data* (pp. 151–172). Facet. doi:10.29085/9781856048910.009

Conrad, S., Shorish, Y., Whitmire, A. L., & Hswe, P. (2017). Building professional development opportunities in data services for academic librarians. *IFLA Journal*, *43*(1), 65–80. doi:10.1177/0340035216678237

Corrall, S. (2012). Roles and responsibilities: libraries, librarians and data. In G. Pryor (Ed.), *Managing Research Data* (pp. 105–134). London, UK: Facet Publishing. doi:10.29085/9781856048910.007

Corrall, S., Keenan, M. A., & Afzal, W. (2013). Bibliometrics and research data management services: Emerging trends in library support for research. *Library Trends*, *61*(3), 636–674. doi:10.1353/lib.2013.0005

Cox, A. M., & Pinfield, S. (2014). Research Data Management and libraries: current activities and future priorities. *Journal of Librarianship and Information Science*. Retrieved from http://lis.sagepub.com/cgi/doi/10.1177/0961000613492542

Cox, A. N., & Verbaan, E. (2016). How academic librarians, IT staff and research administrators perceive and relate to research. *Library & Information Science Research*, *38*(4), 319–326. doi:10.1016/j.lisr.2016.11.004

Crant, J. M. (2000). Proactive behaviour in organizations. *Journal of Management*, *26*(3), 435–462. doi:10.1177/014920630002600304

Creamer, A., Morales, M. E., Crespo, J., Kafel, D., & Martin, E. R. (2012). An assessment of needed competencies to promote the data curation and management librarianship of health sciences and science and technology librarians in New England. *Journal of Escience Librarianship*, *1*(1), 18–26. doi:10.7191/jeslib.2012.1006

Crow, R. (2002). Open access and scholarly communications. *SPARC/Science Commons*. Available at http://surf.nl/download/countryupdate2005.pdf

Crow, R. (2002). *The case of Institutional Repositories: A SPARC Position Paper.* Retrieved from http://www.arl.org/sparc/bm~doc/ir_final_release_102.pdf

Dadzie, P. S. (2005). Electronic resources: Access and usage at Ashesi University College. *Campus-Wide Information Systems*, *22*(5), 290–297. doi:10.1108/10650740510632208

Daft, R. L. (1978). A dual-core model of organizational innovation. *Academy of Management Journal*, *21*(2), 193–210.

Damanpour, F. (1996). Organizational complexity and innovation: Developing and testing multiple contingency models. *Management Science*, *42*(5), 693–716. doi:10.1287/mnsc.42.5.693

Danesh, S., Sumner, T., & Martin, J. H. (2015). SGRank: Combining Statistical and Graphical Methods to Improve the State of the Art in Unsupervised Keyphrase Extraction. In *Proceedings of the fourth joint conference on Lexical and Computational Semantics (SEM 2015),* (pp. 117-126). Academic Press.

Danesh, S., Sumner, T., & Martin, J. H. (2015). SGRank: Combining Statistical and Graphical Methods to Improve the State of the Art in Unsupervised Keyphrase Extraction. *Lexical and Computational Semantics (* SEM 2015)*, 117.

Das, S. (2010). A three steps strategy for acquiring and promoting E-Resources at college libraries in Purulia District (West Bengal): A Case Study. In *7th Convention PLANNER*. Tezpur University.

Dattolo, A., Ferrara, F., & Tasso, C. (2009). *Supporting personalized user concept spaces and recommendations for a publication sharing system.* Paper presented at the International Conference on User Modeling, Adaptation, and Personalization. 10.1007/978-3-642-02247-0_31

Daud, A., Shaikh, A. M. A. R., & Rajpar, A. H. (2009). Scientific reference mining using semantic information through topic modeling. *Research Journal of Engineering & Technology*, *28*(2), 253–262.

Davenport, E., & Cronin, B. (1994). Competitive intelligence and social advantage. *Library Trends*, *43*(2), 239–252.

Davidson, J. (2015). *Developing an organisational profile for research data management services - a guide for HEIs*. Edinburgh, UK: Digital Curation Centre. Retrieved from http://www.dcc.ac.uk/projects/opd-for-rdm

Davidson, J., Jones, S., Molloy, L., & Kejser, U. B. (2014). Emerging good practice in managing research data and research information within UK Universities. *Procedia Computer Science*, *33*, 215–222. doi:10.1016/j.procs.2014.06.035

Davis, P. M., & Connolly, M. J. L. (2007). Institutional Repositories: Evaluating the Reasons for non-use of Cornell University's Installation of DSpace. *D-Lib Magazine*, *13*(3&4). Retrieved from http://www.dlib.org/dlib/march07/davis/03davis.html

DeoghuriaS.PaulG. (2018). *Open Access journals.* Retrieved from http://arxiv.iacs.res.in:8080/jspui/bitstream/10821/4052/1/Open-Access-Impact.docx

Department of Library & Information Science, Central University of Himachal Pradesh, Dharamshala. (2013). Retrieved from http://cuhimachal.ac.in/math_vision_mission.aspx

Department of Library & Information Science, Panjab University Chandigarh. (2016). Retrieved from http://libraryscience.puchd.ac.in/ index.php

Department of Library and Information Science, Banaras Hindu University. (2014). Retrieved from http://www.bhu.ac.in/arts/lis/history.html

Department of Library and Information Science, Bundelkhand University, Bundelkhand. (n.d.). Retrieved from https://www.bujhansi.org/frmViewcampusFaculty.aspx

Department of Library and Information Science, Dr. B. R. Ambedkar University, Agra. (2014). Retrieved from http://www.dbrau.ac.in/department_%20of_Library_and_Information_science.html

Department of Library and Information Science, Guru Nanak Dev University, Amritsar. (n.d.). Retrieved from http://www.gndu.ac.in/gndu2014/ ShowFacultyDetailProforma.asp?D=20

Department of Library and Information Science, Kurukshetra University, Kurukshetra. (2010). Retrieved from http://www.kuk.ac.in/information.php?action=showContent&L01_id=OA==&L01_direction=H&L03_id=Mzk=&L02_id=MjE=&sublevel=y

Department of Library and Information Science, Maharshi Dayanand University, Rohtak. (2011). Retrieved from http://www.mdurohtak.ac.in/info/acad_fac_socscie_libraryinformscience.html

Department of Library and Information Science, University of Lucknow, Lucknow. (2016). Retrieved from http://www.lkouniv.ac.in/ arts_libais.html

Departments: Library Science, Jammu University, Tawi. (2010). Retrieved from http://www.jammuuniversity.in/ departments/lib%20 science/intro.asp

DePaul University Library. (2018). *Research Data Management (A How-To Guide): Research Data Management Definition*. Retrieved from https://libguides.depaul.edu/c.php?g=620925&p=4324498

Developer Network. (2018). *Self Check*. Retrieved from https://developers.exlibrisgroup.com/alma/integrations/selfcheck

Dhiman, A. K. (2010, August). Evolving roles of library & information centres in e-learning environment. In *World Library and information Congress: 76th IFLA General Conference and Assembly. Gothenberg, IFLA* (p. 12). Academic Press.

Digital Curation Centre. (2016). *Data lifecycle model*. Retrieved from http://www.dcc.ac.uk/resources/curation-lifecycle-model

Dong, R., Tokarchuk, L., & Ma, A. (2009). Digging friendship: paper recommendation in the social network. *Proceedings of Networking & Electronic Commerce Research Conference (NAEC 2009)*, 21-28.

Dong, R., Tokarchuk, L., & Ma, A. (2009). Digging friendship: paper recommendation in the social network. *Proceedings of Networking & Electronic Commerce Research Conference (NAEC 2009)*.

Downes, S. (2007). What connectivism is [Web log post]. Available at http://halfanhour. blogspot.com/2007/02/what-connectivism-is.html

Downes, S. (2011, Jan. 5). "Connectivism" and connective knowledge. *The Huffington Post*.

Dr. B. R. Ambedkar University, Agra. (2014). Retrieved from http://www.dbrau.ac.in/about_university.html

Drury, F. K. W. (1930). *Book Selection*. Chicago, IL: American Library Association.

Dunaway, M. K. (2011). Connectivism: Learning theory and pedagogical practice for networked information landscapes. *RSR. Reference Services Review*, *39*(4), 675–685. doi:10.1108/00907321111186686

Dunlap, I. H. (2008). Going digital: The transformation of scholarly communication and academic libraries. *Policy Futures in Education*, *6*(1), 132–141. doi:10.2304/pfie.2008.6.1.132

Durieux, T., Hamadi, Y., & Monperrus, M. (2018). *Fully Automated HTML and JavaScript Rewriting for Constructing a Self-healing Web Proxy*. Cornell University Library. doi:10.1109/ISSRE.2018.00012

Edgar, L. E. (2015). EZproxy: Migrating From a Local Server to a Hosted Environment. *Journal of Electronic Resources Librarianship*, *27*(3), 194–199. doi:10.1080/1941126X.2015.1059655

eduGAIN. (2018). *eduGAIN model* [Image]. Retrieved from https://edugain.org/about-edugain/key-concepts/

Eke, H. N. (2011). *Digitizing resources for University of Nigeria Repository: Process and Challenges.* Retrieved from http://www.webology.org/2011/v8n1/a85.html

Ekere, Omekwu, & Nwoha (2016). Users' Perception of the Facilities, Resources and Services of the MTN Digital Library at the University of Nigeria, Nsukka. *Library Philosophy and Practice*, 1390. Available at http://digitalcommons.unl.edu/libphilprac/1390

Ekstrand, M. D., Kannan, P., Stemper, J. A., Butler, J. T., Konstan, J. A., & Riedl, J. T. (2010). Automatically building research reading lists. *Proceedings of the fourth ACM conference on Recommender systems*. 10.1145/1864708.1864740

Ell, B. (2015). *User Interfaces to the Web of Data based on Natural Language Generation.* Karlsruhe, Germany: Scientific Publishing.

Elliot. (2014). Access to knowledge: a basic human right. *Creative Commons.* Retrieved from https://creativecommons.org/2014/01/07/access-to-knowledge-a-basic-human-right/

Else, H. (2018). *Europe's open-access drive escalates as university stand-offs spread.* Retrieved from https://www.nature.com/articles/d41586-018-05191-0

Elsevier and Euretos start innovative pilot to bring AI-derived hypotheses into the scholarly dialog. (2018). Retrieved from https://www.elsevier.com/about/press-releases/science-and-technology/elsevier-and-euretos-start-innovative-pilot-to-bring-ai-derived-hypotheses-into-the-scholarly-dialog

Elsevier. (2014). *Pure Hosted Edition.* Retrieved from https://www.elsevier.com/__data/assets/pdf_file/0004/53437/pure-hosted-edition-brochure-version2.01August2014.pdf

Elsevier. (2017). *Responses to NLM Strategic Vision and Plan-Related Requests for Information (RFIs).* Retrieved from https://www.nitrd.gov/nitrdgroups/images/a/ad/ElsevierResponseNLM.pdf

Elsevier. (2018). *Elsevier PURE-Features*. Retrieved from https://www.elsevier.com/solutions/pure/features

Engle, R.-F. (1982). Autoregressive Conditional Heteroskedasticity with Estimates of The Variance of UK Inflation. *Econometrica*, *50*(4), 987–1008. doi:10.2307/1912773

Enis, M., & Schwartz, M. (2012). InfoTech. *Library Journal*, *137*(12), 15. Retrieved from https://search.proquest.com/docview/1022969639

Erturk, E., & Iles, H.R. (2015). *Case Study on Cloud Based Library Software as a Service: Evaluating EZproxy.* CoRR, abs/1511.07578

European Union. (2016). *H2020 Programme: Guidelines on FAIR Data Management in Horizon 2020.* Version 3.0. Author.

Eyitayo, O. T. (2008). Internet facilities and the status of Africa's connectivity. In L. O. Aina, S. M. Mutuala, & M. A. Tiamiyu (Eds.), *Information and knowledge management in the digital age: Concept, technologies and African perspectives*. Ibadan, Nigeria: Third World Information Services.

Ezeani, C. N., & Ezema, I. J. (2011). Digitizing Institutional Research Output of University of Nigeria, Nsukka. *Library Philosophy and Practice.* Retrieved from http://unllib.unl.edu/LPP

Farkas, M. (2012). Participatory technologies, pedagogy 2.0 and information literacy. *Library Hi Tech*, *30*(1), 82–94. doi:10.1108/07378831211213229

Faulhaber, C. B. (1996). Distance learning and digital libraries: Two sides of a single coin. *Journal of the American Society for Information Science*, *47*(11), 854–856. doi:10.1002/(SICI)1097-4571(199611)47:11<854::AID-ASI9>3.0.CO;2-1

Federations – REFEDS. (2018). Retrieved from https://refeds.org/federations

Feldman, C., & Meyer, D. (2015). *IR to RIMS: Transforming an institutional repository into a Research Information Management System.* IFLA.

Ferrara, F., Pudota, N., & Tasso, C. (2011). *A keyphrase-based paper recommender system. Digital Libraries and Archives* (pp. 14–25). Springer. doi:10.1007/978-3-642-27302-5_2

Figueiredo, A. S. (2017). Data sharing: Convert challenges into opportunities. *Frontiers in Public Health*, *5*, 327. doi:10.3389/fpubh.2017.00327 PMID:29270401

Fitzgerald, A., & Pappalardo, K. (2007). *Building the infrastructure for data access and reuse in collaborative research: an analysis of the legal context.* Retrieved from http://eprints.qut.edu.au/8865/1/8865.pdf

Flores, J. R., Brodeur, J. J., Daniels, M. G., Nicholls, N., & Turnator, E. (2007). *Libraries and the Research Data Management landscape.* Retrieved from https://www.clir.org/wp-content/uploads/sites/9/RDM.pdf

Floros, C. (2008). Modelling Volatility Using GARCH Models, Evidence From Egypt and Israel. *Middle Eastern Finance and Economics*, (2), 31-41

Fontana, J. (2018). *Hacks battered IT optimism in 2016; can 2017 enrich defenses.* ZDNet. Retrieved from http://www.zdnet.com/article/hacks-battered-it-optimism-in-2016-can-2017-enrich-defenses

Ford, H. (2005). *Why the Lack of Open Content in Africa?* Retrieved from http://www.culturalivre.org.br/english/index.php?option=com_content

Fujii, A. (2007). Enhancing patent retrieval by citation analysis. In *Proceedings of the 30th annual international ACM SIGIR conference on Research and development in information retrieval* (pp. 793-794). New York, NY: ACM.

Fujii, A. (2007). Enhancing patent retrieval by citation analysis. *Proceedings of the 30th annual international ACM SIGIR conference on Research and development in information retrieval, 793-794.*

Gargouri, Y., Hajjem, C., Larivière, V., Gingras, Y., Carr, L., Brody, T., & Harnad, S. (2010). Self-selected or mandated, open access increases citation impact for higher quality research. *PLoS One*, *5*(10), e13636. doi:10.1371/journal.pone.0013636 PMID:20976155

Geyer-Schulz, A., Hahsler, M., Neumann, A., & Thede, A. (2003). Behavior-based recommender systems as value-added services for scientific libraries. *Statistical Data Mining & Knowledge Discovery*, 433-454.

Geyer-Schulz, A., Hahsler, M., & Jahn, M. (2001). Educational and scientific recommender systems: Designing the information channels of the virtual university. *International Journal of Engineering Education, 17*(2), 153–163.

Ghosh, S. B., & Kumar Das, A. (2007). Open access and institutional repositories—a developing country perspective: a case study of India. *IFLA Journal, 33*(3), 229-250. doi:10.1177/0340035207083304

Giesecke, J. (2011). *Institutional Repositories: Keys to Success.* Retrieved from http://digitalcommons.unl.edu/cgi/viewcontent.cgi?a

Giles, C. L., Bollacker, K. D., & Lawrence, S. (1998). CiteSeer: An automatic citation indexing system. *Proceedings of the third ACM conference on Digital libraries.* 10.1145/276675.276685

Gillitzer, B. (2010). Der Empfehlungsdienst BibTip—Ein flächendeckendes Angebot im Bibliotheksverbund Bayern. *BIT Online, 13*(1), 47.

Gipp, B., & Beel, J. (2009). Citation Proximity Analysis (CPA)-A new approach for identifying related work based on Co-Citation Analysis. *Proceedings of the 12th International Conference on Scientometrics and Informetrics (ISSI'09),* 571-575.

Gipp, B., & Beel, J. (2009). Citation Proximity Analysis (CPA)-A new approach for identifying related work based on Co-Citation Analysis. *Proceedings of the 12th International Conference on Scientometrics and Informetrics (ISSI'09).*

Gipp, B., Beel, J., & Hentschel, C. (2009). Scienstein: A research paper recommender system. *Proceedings of the international conference on Emerging trends in computing (ICETiC'09).*

Gipp, B., Beel, J., & Hentschel, C. (2009, January). Scienstein: A research paper recommender system. *Proceedings of the international conference on Emerging trends in computing (ICETiC'09), 309-315.*

Glusker, A., & Hoelscher, E. (2018). Transitioning from Print to Online-Only Resources. In Library Science and Administration (pp. 175–187). Hershey, PA: IGI Global. doi:10.4018/978-1-5225-3914-8.ch009

GO FAIR International Support and Coordination Office. (2018). *FAIR Principles - GO FAIR.* Available at: https://www.go-fair.org/fair-principles/

Goben, A., & Nelson, M. S. (2018). Teaching librarians about data: The ACRL Research Data Management RoadShow. *College & Research Libraries News*, *79*(7), 354. doi:10.5860/crln.79.7.354

Gold, A. K. (2007). Cyber infrastructure, data, and libraries, Part 1: A cyber infrastructure primer for librarians. *D-Lib Magazine*, *13*(9/10). Retrieved from http://digitalcommons.calpoly.edu/cgi/viewcontent.cgi?article=1015&context=lib_dean

Gooding, P., Terras, M., & Berube, L. (2018). Legal Deposit Web Archives and the Digital Humanities: a Universe of Lost Opportunity? In Digital Humanities 2018 (pp. 590-592). Academic Press.

Gori, M., & Pucci, A. (2006). *Research paper recommender systems: A random-walk based approach.* Paper presented at the 2006 IEEE/WIC/ACM International Conference on Web Intelligence, Hong Kong, China.

Gori, M., & Pucci, A. (2006). *Research paper recommender systems: A random-walk based approach.* Paper presented at the IEEE/WIC/ACM International Conference on Web Intelligence.

Gramstadt, M.-T. (2018). Kultivating Kultur: Increasing arts research deposit. *Ariadne.*

Gregory, S. (2005). *NCIP Basic Patron Authentication Profile.* Colorado State Library. Retrieved from http://www.ncip.info/uploads/7/1/4/6/7146749/ncip_basicauthenticationprofile_20050317.pdf

Gregory, V. L., & Hanson, A. (2006). *Selecting and managing electronic resources: A how-to-do- it manual for librarians* (Rev. ed). New York, NY: Neal-Schuman Publishers.

Guan, Z., Wang, C., Bu, J., Chen, C., Yang, K., Cai, D., & He, X. (2010). Document recommendation in social tagging services. *Proceedings of the 19th international conference on World wide web.* 10.1145/1772690.1772731

Guise, J. M., Savitz, L. A., & Friedman, C. P. (2018). Mind the gap: Putting evidence into practice in the era of learning health systems. *Journal of General Internal Medicine*, 1–3. PMID:30155611

Gupta, S., & Varma, V. (2017). Scientific Article Recommendation by using Distributed Representations of Text and Graph. *Proceedings of the 26th International Conference on World Wide Web Companion*. 10.1145/3041021.3053062

Guru Nanak Dev University Amritsar. (n.d.). Retrieved from http://www.gndu.ac.in/gndu2014/aboutus.html

Hadro, J. (2008). OCLC acquires EZproxy. *Library Journal, 133*(3), 23. Retrieved from https://search.proquest.com/docview/196880015

Hajjem, C., Harnad, S., & Gingras, Y. (2006). *Ten-year cross-disciplinary comparison of the growth of open access and how it increases research citation impact*. Retrieved from https://arxiv.org/pdf/cs/0606079

Hamel, G. (2006). The why what, and how of management innovation. *Harvard Business Review, 84*(2), 72. PMID:16485806

Han, J., Pei, J., & Kamber, M. (2011). Data mining: concepts and techniques. Amsterdam, The Netherlands: Elsevier.

Hanyurwimfura, D., Bo, L., Havyarimana, V., Njagi, D., & Kagorora, F. (2015). An effective academic research papers recommendation for non-profiled users. *International Journal of Hybrid Information Technology*, *8*(3), 255–272. doi:10.14257/ijhit.2015.8.3.23

Harnad, S., Brody, T., Valliares, F. O., Carr, L., Hitchcock, S., Gingras, Y., & Hilf, E. R. (2004). The access/impact problem and the green and gold roads to open access. *Serials Review, 30*(4), 310-314. Retrieved from https://eprints.soton.ac.uk/259940/6/34.html

Harnard, S., Brody, T., Vallieres, F., Carr, L., Hitchcock, S., Gingras, Y., & Hilf, E. (2008). The access/impact problem and the green and gold roads to Open Access: An update. *Serials Review, 34*(1), 36–40. doi:10.1080/00987913.2008.10765150

Hawks, J. (2015). Research Information Management: making sense of it all. London, UK: Digital Science.

He, J., Nie, J.-Y., Lu, Y., & Zhao, W. X. (2012). *Position-aligned translation model for citation recommendation*. Paper presented at the International Symposium on String Processing and Information Retrieval. 10.1007/978-3-642-34109-0_27

Hedberg, R., Gulliksson, S., Jones, M., & Bradley, J. (2018). *OpenID Connect Federation 1.0 - draft 04*. Retrieved from http://openid.net/specs/openid-connect-federation-1_0.html

Henderson, M. E. (2017). *Data Management: A Practical Guide for Librarians*. Lanham, MD: Rowman & Littlefield Publishers.

Henderson, M. E., & Knott, T. L. (2015). Starting a Research Data Management program based in a University Library. *Medical Reference Services Quarterly*, *34*(1), 47–59. doi:10.1080/02763869.2015.986783

Henty, M. (2007). Ten major issues in providing a repository service in Australian Universities. *D-Lib Magazine, 13*(5/6). doi:10.1045/may2007-henty

He, Q., Kifer, D., Pei, J., Mitra, P., & Giles, C. L. (2011). Citation recommendation without author supervision. *Proceedings of the fourth ACM international conference on Web search and data mining*. 10.1145/1935826.1935926

He, Q., Pei, J., Kifer, D., Mitra, P., & Giles, L. (2010). Context-aware citation recommendation. *Proceedings of the 19th international conference on World wide web*. 10.1145/1772690.1772734

Herring, S. D. (2002). Use of electronic resources in scholarly electronic journals: A citation analysis. *College & Research Libraries, 63*(4), 334–340. doi:10.5860/crl.63.4.334

Hey, T., & Hey, J. (2006). E-science and its implications for the library community. *Library Hi Tech, 24*(4), 515–528. doi:10.1108/07378830610715383

Himmelstein, D. S., Romero, A. R., Levernier, J. G., Munro, T. A., McLaughlin, S. R., Tzovaras, B. G., & Greene, C. S. (2018). Sci-Hub provides access to nearly all scholarly literature. *eLife, 7*, e32822. doi:10.7554/eLife.32822 PMID:29424689

Hindawi. (2018). Open Research, Publishing with Hindawi. *Hindawi*. Retrieved from https://about.hindawi.com/

Hole, B., Lin, L., McCann, P., & Wheatley, P. (2010). LIFE3: A Predictive costing tool for digital collections. *New Review of Information Networking, 15*(2), 81–93. doi:10.1080/13614576.2010.526014

Hong, K., Jeon, H., & Jeon, C. (2012). *UserProfile-based personalized research paper recommendation system*. Paper presented at the 2012 8th International Conference on Computing and Networking Technology (ICCNT).

Hong, K., Jeon, H., & Jeon, C. (2013). Advanced personalized research paper recommendation system based on expanded userprofile through semantic analysis. *International Journal of Digital Content Technology and its Applications, 7*(15), 67.

Huang, Y.-C. (2007). *Combining Social Networks and Content for Recommendation in a Literature Digital Library*. Taiwan: National Sun Yat-Sen University.

Huang, Z., Chung, W., Ong, T.-H., & Chen, H. (2002). A graph-based recommender system for digital library. *Proceedings of the 2nd ACM/IEEE-CS joint conference on Digital libraries*. 10.1145/544220.544231

Huston, G. (2018). *IPv4 Address Report*. Retrieved from http://www.potaroo.net/tools/ipv4/

Hwang, S.-Y., Hsiung, W.-C., & Yang, W.-S. (2003). A prototype WWW literature recommendation system for digital libraries. *Online Information Review, 27*(3), 169–182. doi:10.1108/14684520310481436

Ibberson, P. (2010). Symplectic Elements research information software. In *UAS Conference 2010*. The University of Oxford, Oxford, UK.

Idiegbeyan-Ose, J., Idahosa, M., & Adewole-Odeshi, E. (2014). Adoption and Use of Information and Communication Technologies (ICTs) in Library and Information Centres: Implications on Teaching and Learning Process. In B. F. Adeoye (Ed.), *Effects of Information Capitalism and Globalization on Teaching and Learning*. Hershey, PA: IGI Global. Available at https://www.igi- global.com/chapter/adoption-and- use-of-information-and -communication- technologies-icts-in-library-and- information-centres/1132422

Idiegbeyan-ose, J., Ilo, P., & Isiakpona, C. (2015). The 21st Century Library and Information Services for the Enhancement of Teacher Education. In P. O. Nwachukwu (Ed.), *Handbook of Research on Enhancing Teacher Education with Advanced Instructional Technologies*. Hershey, PA: IGI Global. Available at https://www.igi-global.com/chapter/the- 21st-century-library-and-information-services-for-the-enhancement-of-teacher- education/133804

Idiegbeyan-ose, J., Nduka, S., Adekunjo, O. A., & Okoedion, I. (2015). An Assessment of Digital Library Functions and Services in Nigerian Academic Libraries. In S. Thanuskodi (Ed.), *Handbook of Research on Inventive Digital Tools for Collection Management and Development in Modern Libraries*. Hershey, PA: IGI Global. Available at https://www.igi-global.com/chapter/an-assessment-of-digital-library-functions-and-services-in-nigerian- academic-libraries/133967

Idiegbeyan-Ose, J., Nkiko, C., Idahosa, M., & Nwokocha, N. (2016). Digital Divide: Issues and Strategies for Intervention in Nigerian Libraries. *Journal of Cases on Information Technology, 18*(3), 29-39. Available at https://www.igi-global.com/article/digital- divide/172153

Idiegbeyan-Ose, J., Okosun, H., Eruanca, C., & Ojo-Igbinoba, M. E. (2005, June). Benson ldahosa University Virtual Library: A case study. *A Compendium of Papers Presented at the 43rd National Annual Conference & AGM of the Nigerian Library Association at Cultural Centre*. Available at http://eprints.covenantuniversity.edu.ng/4914/1/Mr%20Jerome.pdf

Idiegbeyan-ose, J., & Akpoghome, T. U. (2009). Distance Learning in Nigeria and the Role of Virtual Library. Gateway. *Library Journal, 12*(2), 75–85.

Idowu, B. (2012). Open and Distance Learning: Achievements and challenges in a developing sub-educational sector in Africa. In O. M. Modise (Ed.), Cases on Leadership in Adult Education (pp. 27-62). Hershey, PA: IGI Global.

Ifidon, S. E., & Okoli, G. N. (2002, June). *40 Years of academic and research library services in Nigeria: Past, present, and future*. A paper presented at the 40th anniversary National Conference and Annual General Meeting of the NLA held at the Administrative Staff College of Nigeria, Togo-Badagry.

Ifijeh, G., Idiegbeyan-ose, J., Ilogho, J., & Isiakpona, C. (2015). Disaster and Digital Libraries in Developing Countries: Issues and Challenges. In E. N. Decker (Ed.), *Handbook of Research on Disaster Management and Contingency Planning in Modern Libraries*. Hershey, PA: IGI Global. Available at https://www.igi-global.com/chapter/disaster-and-digital- libraries-in-developing-countries/135207

IFLA. (2012). *Key Issues for e-resources Collection Development: A Guide for Libraries.* IFLA.

Igun, I. E. (2006). Human Capital for Nigerians Libraries in the 21st century. *Library Philosophy and Practice, 8*(2).

Implementing FAIR Data Principles: The Role of Libraries. Retrieved from the Association of European Research Libraries: https://libereurope.eu/wp-content/uploads/2017/12/LIBER-FAIR-Data.pdf

Ingram, C. (2016). *How and why you should manage your research data: a guide for researchers.* Retrieved from https://www.jisc.ac.uk/guides/how-and-why-you-should-manage-your-research-data

Institute for the Future. (2001). *E-Journal Usage and Scholarly Practice: An Ethnographic Perspective on the Role and Impact of E-Journal Usage among Users of Biomedical Literature.* Palo Alto, CA: Stanford University, Institute for the Future.

Interfaces, I. (2018). *Proxy Rewrite Method.* Retrieved from https://csdirect.iii.com/tutorials/wam/setup2_2_2.html

Ivwighreghweta, O. (2012). An Investigation to the Challenges of Institutional Repositories development in six Academic Institutions in Nigeria. *International Journal of Digital Library Services, 2*(4), 1–16.

Jack, K. (2012). *Mendeley: recommendation systems for academic literature. Presentation at Technical University of Graz, Graz, Austria.*

Jain, P., Bentley, G., & Oladiran, M. T. (2008). *The Role of Institutional Repository in Digital Scholarly Communications.* Retrieved from www.library.up.ac.za/digi/docs/jain_paper.pdf

Jammu University Tawi. (2009). Retrieved from http://www.jammuuniversity.in/uni_profile.asp

Jantz, R. C. (2013). *Incremental and radical innovations in research libraries: An exploratory examination regarding the effects of ambidexterity, organizational structure, leadership and contextual factors* (Doctoral dissertation). Retrieved from ProQuest Dissertations and Theses. (3597757)

Jantz, R. C. (2012). Innovation in academic libraries: An analysis of university librarians' perspectives. *Library & Information Science Research, 34*(1), 3–12. doi:10.1016/j.lisr.2011.07.008

Jantz, R. C., & Wilson, M. C. (2008). Institutional repositories: Faculty deposits, marketing, and the reform of scholarly communication. *Journal of Academic Librarianship, 34*(3), 186–195. doi:10.1016/j.acalib.2008.03.014

Jeffery, K. G. (2006). Open Access: an introduction. *Ercim News, 64*(3). Retrieved from https://www.researchgate.net/profile/Keith_Jeffery/publication/228635875_Open_Access_an_introduction/links/00b7d527a52273637a000000.pdf

Jiang, Y., Jia, A., Feng, Y., & Zhao, D. (2012). Recommending academic papers via users' reading purposes. *Proceedings of the sixth ACM conference on Recommender systems.* 10.1145/2365952.2366004

Jindal, S., & Pant, A. (2013). Availability of E-books in Science: Case study of University of Delhi. *The Electronic Library, 31*(3), 313–328. doi:10.1108/EL-12-2010-0159

JISC. (2010). *Research information management: Developing tools to inform the management of research and translating existing good practice*. Imperial College London.

John-Okeke, R. (2008). Developing Institutional Repositories: Considering Copyright Issues. *Journal of Applied Information Science and Technology, 2*, 11–18.

Johnson, K., & Magusin, E. (2005). *Digital libraries: a cultural understanding*. Academic Press.

Jomsri, P., Sanguansintukul, S., & Choochaiwattana, W. (2009). *A comparison of search engine using "tag title and abstract" with CiteULike—An initial evaluation.* Paper presented at the International Conference for Internet Technology and Secured Transactions (ICITST 2009), London, UK.

Jomsri, P., Sanguansintukul, S., & Choochaiwattana, W. (2009). *A comparison of search engine using "tag title and abstract" with CiteULike—An initial evaluation.* Paper presented at the International Conference for Internet Technology and Secured Transactions, 2009. ICITST 2009.

Jomsri, P., Sanguansintukul, S., & Choochaiwattana, W. (2009). *Improving research paper searching with social tagging—A preliminary investigation.* Paper presented at the Eighth International Symposium on Natural Language Processing (SNLP'09), Bangkok, Thailand.

Jones, R., Andrew, T., & McColl, J. (2006). *The Institutional Repository.* Oxford, UK: Chandos Publishing. doi:10.1533/9781780630830

Jones, S., Pryor, G., & Whyte, A. (2013). *'How to Develop Research Data Management Services - a guide for HEIs'. DCC How-to Guides*. Edinburgh, UK: Digital Curation Centre. Retrieved from http://www.dcc.ac.uk/resources/how-guides

Joseph, A. S. (2013). Conceptual, impact-based publications recommendations. Fayetteville, AR: University of Arkansas.

Joseph, A. S. (2013). *Conceptual, impact-based publications recommendations*. University of Arkansas.

Joshipura, S. (2008). Selecting, Acquiring And Renewing Electronic Resources. In H. Yu, & S. Breivod (Eds.), Electronic Resource Management in Libraries: Research and Practice. New York, NY: Information Science Reference. doi:10.4018/978-1-59904-891-8.ch004

Kapoor, N., Chen, J., Butler, J. T., Fouty, G. C., Stemper, J. A., Riedl, J., & Konstan, J. A. (2007). Techlens: a researcher's desktop. In *Proceedings of the 2007 ACM conference on Recommender systems (pp. 183-184)*. ACM. 10.1145/1297231.1297268

Katerbow, M., & Feulner, G. (2018). *Recommendations on the Development, Use and Provision of Research Software [Handreichung zum Umgang mit Forschungssoftware]*. Research Software Working Group, Digital Information of the Alliance of German Science Organisations.

Kaur, S., & Satija, M. P. (2007). Collection Development in Digital Environment: Trends and Problems. *SRELS Journal of Information Management*, *44*(2), 139–15.

Keil, D. E. (2014). Research data needs from academic libraries: The perspective of a faculty researcher. *Journal of Library Administration*, *54*(3), 233–240. doi:10.1080/01930826.2014.915168

Kennan, M. A. (2011). Learning to share: Mandates and open access. *Library Management*, *32*(4/5), 302–318. doi:10.1108/01435121111132301

Kennan, M. A., & Markauskaite, L. (2015). Research data management practices: A snapshot in time. *International Journal of Digital Curation*, *10*(2), 69–95. doi:10.2218/ijdc.v10i2.329

Kennedy, M. R. (2004). Dreams of perfect programs: Managing the acquisition of electronic resources. *Library Collections, Acquisitions & Technical Services*, *28*(4), 449–458.

Khatri, N. K. (2008). Funding Opportunities for Mathematics Resources: A case study at I.S.I. Delhi Centre Library. In *Proceedings of the International Conference on Shaping the Future of Special Libraries: Beyond Boundaries*. Special Library Association.

Khatri, N. K. (2010, April). Enhancing Usage of E-Resources at Indian Statistical Institute Delhi Centre Library Through Consortia Based Subscription. In *Proceedings of the National Conference on Knowledge Management in the Globalization Era*. IASRI.

Kissling, A. D., & Ballinger, K. D. (2018). Implementation of a Research Information Management System in a Pediatric Hospital. *Medical Reference Services Quarterly*, *37*(2), 184–197. doi:10.1080/02763869.2018.1439224 PMID:29558332

Kitchin, R., Collins, S., & Frost, D. (2015). Funding models for Open Access digital data repositories. *Online Information Review*, *39*(50), 664–681. doi:10.1108/OIR-01-2015-0031

Klein, K. J., Conn, A. B., & Sorra, J. S. (2001). Implementing computerized technology: An organizational analysis. *The Journal of Applied Psychology*, *86*(5), 811–824. doi:10.1037/0021-9010.86.5.811 PMID:11596799

Kodakateri Pudhiyaveetil, A., Gauch, S., Luong, H., & Eno, J. (2009). Conceptual recommender system for CiteSeerX. In *Proceedings of the third ACM conference on Recommender systems, (pp. 241-244)*. ACM.

Kodakateri Pudhiyaveetil, A., Gauch, S., Luong, H., & Eno, J. (2009). Conceptual recommender system for CiteSeerX. *Proceedings of the third ACM conference on Recommender systems.*

Koler-Povh, T., Južnič, P., & Turk, G. (2014). Impact of open access on citation of scholarly publications in the field of civil engineering. *Scientometrics*, *98*(2), 1033–1045. doi:10.100711192-013-1101-x

Konstan, J. A., McNee, S. M., Ziegler, C.-N., Torres, R., Kapoor, N., & Riedl, J. (2006). Lessons on applying automated recommender systems to information-seeking tasks. In *AAAI* (Vol. 6, pp. 1630-1633). Academic Press.

Koulouris, A., Kyriaki-Mamessi, D., Giannakopoulos, G., & Zervos, S. (2013). Institutional Repository Policies: Best Practices for Encouraging Self-Archiving. *Procedia: Social and Behavioral Sciences*, *73*, 769–779. doi:10.1016/j.sbspro.2013.02.117

Kraft, A., Dreyer, B., Löwe, P., & Ziedorn, F. (2017). 14 Years of PID services at the German National Library of Science and Technology (TIB): Connected frameworks, research data and lessons learned from a national research library perspective. *Data Science Journal*, *16*(36), 1–10.

Krallinger, M., Erhardt, R. A.-A., & Valencia, A. (2005). Text-mining approaches in molecular biology and biomedicine. *Drug Discovery Today*, *10*(6), 439–445. doi:10.1016/S1359-6446(05)03376-3 PMID:15808823

Kruse, F. & Thestrup, J.B. (2017). Research Data Management - A European perspective. Munich, Germany: De Gruyter Saur. doi:10.1515/9783110365634

Kuberek, M., & Mönnich, M. (2012). *Einsatz von Recommender systemen in Bibliotheken.* Recommender systems in libraries: Presentation.

Küçüktunç, O., Kaya, K., Saule, E., & Çatalyürek, Ü. V. (2012, August). Fast recommendation on bibliographic networks. In *2012 IEEE/ACM International Conference on Advances in Social Networks Analysis and Mining* (pp. 480-487). IEEE. 10.1109/ASONAM.2012.82

Küçüktunç, O., Saule, E., Kaya, K., & Çatalyürek, Ü. V. (2012). *Direction awareness in citation recommendation.* Academic Press.

Küçüktunç, O., Saule, E., Kaya, K., & Çatalyürek, Ü. V. (2013). Result diversification in automatic citation recommendation. *Proceedings of the iConference workshop on Computational scientometrics: theory and applications,* 1-4.

Kumbar, B. D., & Hadagali, G. S. (2007). Collection Development Policy in Academic Libraries in a changing Environment: Problems and Prospects. *PEARL: Journal of Library and Information Science*, *1*(1), 33–43.

Kurukshetra University Kurukshetra. (2010). Retrieved from http://www.kuk.ac.in/

Kwon, N. (2017). How work positions affect the research activity and information behaviour of laboratory scientists in the research lifecycle: applying activity theory. *Information Research: An International Electronic Journal, 22*(1).

Laakso, M., & Björk, B. C. (2012). Anatomy of open access publishing: A study of longitudinal development and internal structure. *BMC Medicine*, *10*(1), 124. doi:10.1186/1741-7015-10-124 PMID:23088823

Lao, N., & Cohen, W. W. (2010). Relational retrieval using a combination of path-constrained random walks. *Machine Learning*, *81*(1), 53–67. doi:10.100710994-010-5205-8

Latham, B. (2017). Research Data Management: Defining roles, prioritizing services, and enumerating challenges. *Journal of Academic Librarianship*, *43*(3), 263–265. doi:10.1016/j.acalib.2017.04.004

Lavoie, B., Henry, G., & Dempsey, L. (2006). A service framework for libraries. *D-Lib Magazine*, *12*(7/8), 1082–9873. doi:10.1045/july2006-lavoie

Lawrence, S. (2001). Free online availability substantially increases a paper's impact. *Nature*, *411*(6837), 521. doi:10.1038/35079151 PMID:11385534

Lawrence, S., Giles, C. L., & Bollacker, K. (1999). Digital libraries and autonomous citation indexing. *Computer*, *32*(6), 67–71. doi:10.1109/2.769447

Le Anh, V., Hai, V. H., Tran, H. N., & Jung, J. J. (2014). Scirecsys: A recommendation system for scientific publication by discovering keyword relationships. In *International Conference on Computational Collective Intelligence* (pp. 72-82). Cham, Switzerland: Springer. 10.1007/978-3-319-11289-3_8

Learning Tools Interoperability. (2018). Retrieved from http://www.imsglobal.org/activity/learning-tools-interoperability#LTIpublic

Leary, J. & Berge, Z. (2007). Successful distance education programs in sub-Saharan Africa. *Turkish Online Journal of Distance Education, 8*(2), 136-145.

Lee, J., Lee, K., Kim, J. G., & Kim, S. (2015). *Personalized Academic Paper Recommendation System*. Academic Press.

Lee, L. Z. (2001). Growing a national learning environments and resources network for science, mathematics, engineering, and technology education. *First Monday*, *6*(4).

Lémdani, R., Polaillon, G., Bennacer, N., & Bourda, Y. (2011). A semantic similarity measure for recommender systems. *Proceedings of the 7th International Conference on Semantic Systems*. 10.1145/2063518.2063545

Lerra, M. D. (2014). The Dynamics and challenges of distance education at private higher institutions in South Ethiopia. *Asian Business Consortium*, *1*(3), 137–150.

Letha, M. M. (2006). Library portal: A tool for web-enabled information services. *DESIDOC Journal of Library and Information Technology*, *26*(5).

Lewis, D. W. (2007). *A strategy for academic libraries in the first quarter of the 21st century.* Academic Press.

Lewis, D. W. (2007). A strategy for academic libraries in the first quarter of the 21st century. *College & Research Libraries*, *68*(5), 418–434. doi:10.5860/crl.68.5.418

Liang, Y., Li, Q., & Qian, T. (2011). *Finding relevant papers based on citation relations.* Paper presented at the International Conference on Web-Age Information Management. 10.1007/978-3-642-23535-1_35

Liang, T.-P., Yang, Y.-F., Chen, D.-N., & Ku, Y.-C. (2008). A semantic-expansion approach to personalized knowledge recommendation. *Decision Support Systems*, *45*(3), 401–412. doi:10.1016/j.dss.2007.05.004

Library of Congress. (2015). Selected Internet Resources Eprints: Quick Guide to Open-Access Archives in Science, Technology & Medicine. *The Library of Congress.* Retrieved from https://www.loc.gov/rr/scitech/selected-internet/eprints.html

Library of Congress. (2017a). *Collecting digital content at the Library of Congress.* Library Services Collection Development Office.

Library of Congress. (2017b). *Data Sets-Interim Guidance-Library of Congress.* Author.

Lietzau, Z. (2009). US Public Libraries and Web 2.0: What's Really Happening? *Computers in Libraries*, *29*(9), 6–10.

Lin, S. K. (2006). *Delayed open access or permanent non-open access.* Retrieved from http://www.mdpi.com/1420-3049/11/7/496/pdf

Lindstädt, B. (2016). Management und Publikation von Forschungsdaten – Serviceleistungen einer wissenschaftlichen Bibliothek. *Bibliotheksdienst*, *50*(7), 636–648. doi:10.1515/bd-2016-0078

Liu, X., Zhang, J., & Guo, C. (2016). Citation recommendation via proximity full-text citation analysis and supervised topical prior. *Proceedings of IConference 2016.*

Livingston, H., & Nastasie, D. (2009). The Role of Academic Libraries in the Sustainability, Preservation and Access control of Digital Repositories. *Proceedings of 60 DCC State of the Art Report EDUCAUSE Australasia '09.* Retrieved from http://www.caudit.edu.au/educauseaustralasia09/authorspapers/Livingston.pdf

Livingston, S. (2018). *Exploring new technologies to better serve users.* Presentation, ALA Annual Conference and Exhibition 2018.

Li, Y., & Banach, M. (2011). Institutional Repositories and Digital Preservation: Assessing Current Practices at Research Libraries. *D-Lib Magazine*, *17*(5&6). doi:10.1045/may2011-yuanli

Lodwick, D. (2015). Access and Identity Management for Libraries: Controlling Access to Online Information. *Technical Services Quarterly*, *32*(1), 112–113. doi:10.1080/07317131.2015.972909

Lopes, G. R., Souto, M. A. M., Wives, L. K., & de Oliveira, J. P. M. (2008). A personalized recommender system for digital libraries. *Proceedings of the 14th Brazilian Symposium on Multimedia and the Web*. 10.1145/1666091.1666103

Lopez-Cozar, E. D., Robinson-Garcia, N., & Torres-Salinas, D. (2012). *Manipulating Google Scholar citations and Google Scholar metrics: Simple, easy and tempting*. arXiv preprint arXiv:1212.0638

Lougee, W. P. (2003, May). Diffuse libraries. *The 142nd Association of Research Libraries Membership Meeting, Program Session II*. Available at http://www.arl.org/arl/proceedings/142/lougee.html

Lovins, J. B. (1968). *Development of a stemming algorithm*. Academic Press.

Lukasiewicz, A. (2007). Exploring the role of digital academic libraries: Changing student needs demand innovative service approach. *Library Review*, *56*(9), 821–827. doi:10.1108/00242530710831275

Lwoga, E. T. (2011). Making Web 2.0 technologies work for higher learning institutions in Africa. *Campus-Wide Information Systems*, *29*(2), 90–107. doi:10.1108/10650741211212359

Lynch, C. (2003). Institutional Repositories: Essential infrastructure for Scholarship in the Digital Age Portal. *Libraries and the Academy*, *3*(2). Retrieved from http://muse.jhu.edu/journals/portal_libraries_and_the_academy/v003/3.2lynch.html

Lynch, C. A. (2003). Institutional repositories: Essential infrastructure for scholarship in the digital age. *Portal (Baltimore, MD)*, *3*, 327.

Ma, L., Zhang, Y., Sunderraman, R., Fox, P. T., Laird, A. R., Turner, J. A., & Turner, M. D. (2015). Hybrid feature selection methods for online biomedical publication classification. In *2015 IEEE Conference on Computational Intelligence in Bioinformatics and Computational Biology (CIBCB)* (pp. 1-8). IEEE. 10.1109/CIBCB.2015.7300320

Maake, B. M., Ojo, S. O., & Zuva, T. (2019). A Serendipitous Research Paper Recommender System. *International Journal of Business and Management Studies*, *11*(1), 38–53.

Macalester College. (2018). *Defining Research Data - Data Module #1: What is Research Data?* Retrieved from http://libguides.macalester.edu/data1

Mackey, T. P., Forte, M., Allain, N., Jacobson, T. E., & Pitera, J. (2015). MOOC talk: A connectivist dialogue about our metaliteracy MOOC experience. *All About Mentoring*, *46*, 34–40. Retrieved from https://www.esc.edu/news/magazines-journal/all-about-mentoring

Mackey, T. P., & Jacobson, T. E. (2011). Reframing information literacy as a metaliteracy. *College & Research Libraries*, *72*(1), 62–78. doi:10.5860/crl-76r1

Mackey, T. P., & Jacobson, T. E. (2014). *Metaliteracy: Reinventing information literacy to empower learners*. Chicago, IL: ALA Neal-Schuman.

Magara, M. B., Ojo, S. O., & Zuva, T. (2018). Towards a Serendipitous Research Paper Recommender System Using Bisociative Information Networks (BisoNets). In *2018 International Conference on Advances in Big Data, Computing and Data Communication Systems (icABCD)* (pp. 1-6). IEEE.

Magara, M. B., Ojo, S. O., & Zuva, T. (2018, August). *Towards a Serendipitous Research Paper Recommender System Using Bisociative Information Networks (BisoNets)*. Paper presented at the 2018 International Conference on Advances in Big Data, Computing and Data Communication Systems (icABCD).

Maharshi Dayanand University Rohtak. (2011). Retrieved from http://www.mdurohtak.ac.in/

Maness, J. M. (2006). Library 2.0 theory: Web 2.0 and its implications for libraries. *Webology*, *3*(2), 2006.

Mann, F., von Walter, B., Hess, T., & Wigand, R. T. (2009). Open access publishing in science. *Communications of the ACM*, *52*(3), 135–139. doi:10.1145/1467247.1467279

Marchionini, G., & Maurer, H. (1995). The roles of digital libraries in teaching and learning. *Communications of the ACM*, *38*(4), 67–75. doi:10.1145/205323.205345

Martín Hernández, P., Salanova, M., & Peiró, J. M. (2007). Job demands, job resources and individual innovation at work: Going beyond Karasek's model? *Psicothema*, *19*(4). PMID:17959117

Martín, G. H., Schockaert, S., Cornelis, C., & Naessens, H. (2010). *Metadata impact on research paper similarity.* Paper presented at the International Conference on Theory and Practice of Digital Libraries, Glasgow, UK.

Martín, G. H., Schockaert, S., Cornelis, C., & Naessens, H. (2010). *Metadata impact on research paper similarity.* Paper presented at the International Conference on Theory and Practice of Digital Libraries.

Martins, E. C., & Terblanche, F. (2003). Building an organisational culture that stimulates creativity and innovation. *European Journal of Innovation Management*, *6*(1), 64–74. doi:10.1108/14601060310456337

Max-Planck-Gesellschaft München. (2018). Berlin Declaration on Open Access to Knowledge in the Sciences and Humanities. *Open Access*. Retrieved from https://openaccess.mpg.de/Berlin-Declaration

Maxwell, C. C. (2015). Challenges for open and distance learning (ODL) students: Experiences from students of the Zimbabwe Open University. *Journal of Education and Practice*, *6*(18), 55–69.

McCord, A. (2003). Institutional Repositories: Enhancing Teaching, Learning and Research. *EDUCAUSE National Conference.*

McLaughlin, L. K. (2018). Forever agile: Hospital librarians and the NLM's Strategic Plan. *Journal of Hospital Librarianship, 18*(3), 259–265. doi:10.1080/15323269.2018.1472004

McNee, S. M., Albert, I., Cosley, D., Gopalkrishnan, P., Lam, S. K., Rashid, A. M., ... Riedl, J. (2002). On the recommending of citations for research papers. *Proceedings of the 2002 ACM conference on Computer supported cooperative work.* 10.1145/587078.587096

McNee, S. M., Kapoor, N., & Konstan, J. A. (2006). Don't look stupid: avoiding pitfalls when recommending research papers. *Proceedings of the 2006 20th anniversary conference on Computer supported cooperative work.* 10.1145/1180875.1180903

McVeigh, M. E. (2004). *Open access journals in the ISI citation databases: analysis of impact factors and citation patterns: a citation study from Thomson Scientific.* Philadelphia, PA: Thomson Scientific. Retrieved from http://www.academia.edu/download/39476484/openaccesscitations2.pdf

Mears, J., Potter, A., & Zwaard, K. (2017). Collections as data: preservation to access to use to impact. In *14th International Conference on Digital Preservation*, Kyoto, Japan.

Mestri, D. D. (2008). Doctoral Theses in Library and Information Science Completed in Indian Universities, 2001–2007. *Education for Information, 26*(3), 213–234. doi:10.3233/EFI-2008-263-405

Metaliteracy Learning Collaborative. (2014, Sept. 11). Goals and learning objectives: Developing meta-literate learners [Web log post]. Retrieved from https://metaliteracy.org/learning-objectives

Meyer, D. (2015). *Transforming DSpace into a Research Information Management System: Ingestion Manager and Report Writer Components.* Computer Science Honours Final Paper, University of Cape Town.

Mishra, G. (2012). Optimised research paper recommender system using social tagging. *International Journal of Engineering Research and Applications, 2*(2), 1503–1507.

Mohanachandran, D. K., & Ramalu, S. S. (2013). Work and schooling challenges of open distance learning: Case study. *Research Journal of Social Sciences and Management, 2*(10), 198–207.

Mönnich, M., & Spiering, M. (2008). Adding value to the library catalog by implementing a recommendation system. *D-Lib Magazine, 14*(5/6), 1082–9873. doi:10.1045/may2008-monnich

Mönnich, M., & Spiering, M. (2008). Erschließung. Einsatz von BibTip als Recommender system im Bibliothekskatalog. *Bibliotheksdienst, 42*(1), 54–59. doi:10.1515/bd.2008.42.1.54

Morton, J., Rasins, R., & Bubalo, V. (2016). *Implementing Symplectic elements at Macquarie University as a hosted publication sourcing solution.* Prezi.

Moxley, J. M. (2001). American Universities Should Require Electronic Theses and Dissertations. *EDUCAUSE Quarterly*, *61*(3). Retrieved from http://scholarcommons.usf.edu/cgi/viewcontent.cgi?article=1112&context=eng_facpub

Mpofu, S. (2016). The Challenges facing distance education in Southern Africa. In S. J. Levine (Ed.), Making distance education work: Understanding learning and learners at a distance (pp. 221-229). LearnersAssociates.net.

Mueller-Langer, F., & Watt, R. (2014). *The Hybrid Open Access Citation Advantage: How Many More Cites is a $3,000 Fee Buying You?* Retrieved from https://mpra.ub.uni-muenchen.de/61801/1/MPRA_paper_61801.pdf

Murray, P. E. (2001). Library web proxy use survey results. *Information Technology and Libraries*, *20*(4), 172–178. Retrieved from https://search.proquest.com/docview/215832929

Musmann, K. (1993). *Technological innovations in libraries, 1860 – 1960: An anecdotal history*. Westport, CT: Greenwood Press.

Naak, A. (2009). *Papyres: un système de gestion et de recommandation d'articles de recherche*. Academic Press.

Naak, A., Hage, H., & Aïmeur, E. (2008). *Papyres: A research paper management system.* Paper presented at the 2008 10th IEEE Conference on E-Commerce Technology and the Fifth IEEE Conference on Enterprise Computing, E-Commerce and E-Services. 10.1109/CECandEEE.2008.132

Namaganda, A. (2012). *Institutional Repositories and Higher Education in Uganda: The Role of the Consortium of Uganda University Libraries.* Retrieved from https://www.academia.edu/3617835/Institutional_Repositories_and_Higher_Education_in-Uganda_The_Role_of_the_Consortium_of_Uganda_University_Libraries

Nanba, H., & Okumura, M. (2005). *Automatic detection of survey articles.* Paper presented at the International Conference on Theory and Practice of Digital Libraries, Vienna, Austria.

Nanba, H., & Okumura, M. (2005). *Automatic detection of survey articles.* Paper presented at the International Conference on Theory and Practice of Digital Libraries.

Nascimento, C., Laender, A. H., da Silva, A. S., & Gonçalves, M. A. (2011). A source independent framework for research paper recommendation. *Proceedings of the 11th annual international ACM/IEEE joint conference on Digital libraries.* 10.1145/1998076.1998132

National Library of Medicine. (2017). *A Platform for Biomedical Discovery and Data-Powered Health: the National Library of Medicine Strategic Plan 2017–2027.* US Department of Health and Human Services National Institute of Health.

Ndayambaje, I., & … . (2012). A study on the practices and challenges of Distance Training Programme (DTP) under Kigali Institute of Education (KIE). *Rwandan Journal of Education*, *1*(2), 69–76.

Needleman, M., Bodfish, J., O'Brien, T., Rush, J., & Stevens, P. (2001). The NISO circulation interchange protocol (NCIP) – an XML based standard. *Library Hi Tech, 19*(3), 223–230. doi:10.1108/07378830110405526

Nelson, D.-B. (1991). Conditional Heteroscedasticity In Asset Returns, A New Approach. *Econometrica, 59*(2), 347–370. doi:10.2307/2938260

Nitecki, D. A., & Davis, M. E. (2017). *Expanding Librarians' roles in the research life cycle.* IFLAWLIC Satellite Meeting. Retrieved from http://library.ifla.org/1798/1/S06-2017-nitecki-en.pdf

Nkiko, C., Bolu, C. & Micahel-Onuoha, H. (2014). *Managing a Sustainable Institutional Repository: The Covenant University Experience.* Academic Press.

Nkosi, D. S. (2008). *Establishing an Institutional Repository: A UNISA Case Study.* Retrieved from http://uir.unisa.ac.za/bitstream/handle/10500/4297/22_D-S-_Nkosi-2.pdf?sequence=1&isAllowed=y

Nnadi, E. J. (2014). Challenges and strategies for improvement in distance education of students in Abagana Study Centre, Anambra state, Nigeria. *Ind. J. Sci. Res. and Tech, 3*(2), 34–37.

Nwalo, K. I. N. (2003). *Fundamentals of library practice: A manual on library routines.* Ibadan, Nigeria: Sterling-Horden Publishers

Nyirenda, M. (2017). *Issues and challenges of research information management in higher education institutions – and possible solutions.* The Association of Commonwealth Universities.

OCLC: Lorcan Dempsey's Weblog. (2014, October 14). *Research Information Management Systems – A New Service Category?* Retrieved from http://orweblog.oclc.org/research-information-management-systems-a-new-service-category/

Ofoegbu, F. I., & Alonge, H. O. (2016). Internally generated revenue and effectiveness of University Administration in Nigeria. *Journal of Education and Learning*, *5*(2), 1–8.

Ogbomo, E. F., & Muokebe, B. O. (2015). Institutional Repositories as Emerging Initiative in Nigerian University Libraries. *Information and Knowledge Management, 5*(1). Retrieved from http://www.iiste.org/Journals/index.php/IKM/article/view/19418/19409

Ogundipe, O. O. (2005). *The Librarianship of Developing Countries: the librarianship of diminished resources.* Lagos, Nigeria: Ikofa Press Limited.

Ohta, M., Hachiki, T., & Takasu, A. (2011). *Related paper recommendation to support online-browsing of research papers.* Paper presented at the 2011 Fourth International Conference on the Applications of Digital Information and Web Technologies (ICADIWT).

Ohta, M., Hachiki, T., & Takasu, A. (2011). *Related paper recommendation to support online-browsing of research papers.* Paper presented at the 2011 Fourth International Conference on the Applications of Digital Information and Web Technologies, University of Wisconsin, Madison, WI.

Okoye, M. O., & Ejikeme, A. N. (2011). Open access, institutional repositories, and scholarly publishing: the role of librarians in South Eastern Nigeria. *Library Philosophy and Practice.*

Omekwu, C. O., & Echezona, R. I. (2008). *Emerging challenges and opportunities for Nigerian libraries in global information environment.* Paper presented at the 46th annual NLA conference in Kaduna, Nigeria.

Open, O. (2005). *SAML Executive Overview.* Retrieved from https://www.oasis-open.org/committees/download.php/11785/sstc-saml-exec-overview-2.0-draft-06.pdf

Pampel, H., Vierkant, P., Scholze, F., Bertelmann, R., Kindling, M., Klump, J., ... Dierolf, U. (2013). Making Research data repositories visible: The re3data.org Registry. *PLoS One*, *8*(11), 78080. doi:10.1371/journal.pone.0078080 PMID:24223762

Pan, C., & Li, W. (2010). *Research paper recommendation with topic analysis.* Paper presented at the 2010 International Conference on Computer Design and Applications (ICCDA).

Panjab University Chandigarh. (2016). Retrieved from http://puchd.ac.in/

Pant, A. (2014). Distance Learning: History, Problems and Solutions. *Advances in Computer Science and Information Technology*, *1*(2), 65–70.

Paraschiv, I. C., Dascalu, M., Dessus, P., Trausan-Matu, S., & McNamara, D. S. (2016). *A Paper Recommendation System with ReaderBench: The Graphical Visualization of Semantically Related Papers and Concepts. In State-of-the-Art and Future Directions of Smart Learning* (pp. 445–451). Springer.

Parker, S. K., Williams, H. M., & Turner, N. (2006). Modelling the antecedents of proactive behavior at work. *The Journal of Applied Psychology*, *91*(3), 636–652. doi:10.1037/0021-9010.91.3.636 PMID:16737360

Parra, D., & Brusilovsky, P. (2009). Collaborative filtering for social tagging systems: an experiment with CiteULike. *Proceedings of the third ACM conference on Recommender systems.* 10.1145/1639714.1639757

Peacock, J. (2005). Information literacy education in practice. In P. Levy & S. Roberts (Eds.), *Developing the New Learning Environment: The Changing Role of the Academic Librarian* (pp. 153–180). London, UK: Facet Publishing. Available at http://eprints.qut.edu.au/archive/00000706/01/Peacock_Levy2.PDF

Peters, D., & Hahnel, M. (2017). *A National Research Data Management strategy for South African Universities.* Retrieved from https://conference.eresearch.edu.au/2017/08/a-national-research-data-management-strategy-for-south-african-universities/

Peters, C., & Dryden, A. R. (2011). Assessing the academic library's role in campus-wide research data management: A first step at the University of Houston. *Science & Technology Libraries*, *30*(4), 387–403. doi:10.1080/0194262X.2011.626340

Pickton, M., & Barwick, J. (2006). *A Librarian's guide to Institutional Repositories*. Loughborough, UK: Loughborough University. Retrieved from http://magpie.lboro.ac.uk/dspace/handle/2134/1122

Pinfield, S., Gardner, M., & MacColl, J. (2002). Setting up an institutional e-print archive. *Ariadne*, (31). Retrieved from http://www.ariadne.ac.uk/issue31/eprint-archives/intro.html

Pinfield, S., Cox, A. M., & Smith, J. (2014). Research Data Management and libraries: Relationships, activities, drivers and influences. *PLoS One*, *9*(12), e114734. doi:10.1371/journal.pone.0114734 PMID:25485539

PLOS. (2018). About PLOS: who we are, our history, core principles. *Public Library of Science (PLOS)*. Retrieved from https://www.plos.org/history

Pohl, S., Radlinski, F., & Joachims, T. (2007). Recommending related papers based on digital library access records. *Proceedings of the 7th ACM/IEEE-CS joint conference on Digital libraries*. 10.1145/1255175.1255260

Pringle, J. (2005). Partnering helps Institutional Repositories thrive. *Knowledge Link Newsletter*. Retrieved from http://scientific.thomson.com/news/newsletter/2005-02/8264025/

Prinsloo, P. (2016). Metaliteracy, networks, agency, and praxis. In T. E. Jacobson & T. P. Mackey (Eds.), *Metaliteracy in practice* (pp. 183–201). Chicago, IL: ALA Neal-Schuman.

Procter, R., Halfpenny, P., & Voss, A. (2012). Research data management: opportunities and challenges for HEIs. In G. Pryor (Ed.), *Managing Research Data* (pp. 135–150). London, UK: Facet Publishing. doi:10.29085/9781856048910.008

Publications, C. (2018). Welcome to Copernicus.org! *Copernicus Publications, Meetings and Open Access Publishing*. Retrieved from https://publications.copernicus.org/open-access_journals/open_access_journals_a_z.html

Radford, W. (2011). Learning at a Distance: Undergraduate Enrollment in Distance Education Professional approach. *INFOLIB*, *7*(1-4), 19–23.

Ranganathan, S. R. (1963). *The five laws of library science*. Bombay, India: Asia Publishing House.

Rao, N. K., Tripathi, M., & Kumar, S. (2016). Cost of Print and Digital Books: A Comparative Study. *Journal of Academic Librarianship*, *42*(4), 445–452. doi:10.1016/j.acalib.2016.04.003

Rashid, N., & Rashid, M. (2012). Issues and problems in distance education. *Turkish Online Journal of Distance Education*, *13*(1), 20–26.

Rau, H., Goggins, G., & Fahy, F. (2018). From invisibility to impact: Recognising the scientific and societal relevance of interdisciplinary sustainability research. *Research Policy*, *47*(1), 266–276. doi:10.1016/j.respol.2017.11.005

Ray, J. M. (Ed.). (2014). *Research Data Management: Practical Strategies for Information Professionals*. West Lafayette, IN: Purdue University Press.

Reaching across Illinois library system (RAILS) selects auto-graphics SHAREit® for resource sharing. (2018, April 5). *PR Newswire*. Retrieved from https://search.proquest.com/docview/2021790309

Register | Project Counter. (2018). Retrieved from https://www.projectcounter.org/about/register/

Reimer, T. (2018). The once and future library: the role of the (national) library in supporting research. *Insights*, 31.

Rena, R. (2007). Challenges in introducing distance education programme in Eritrea: Some observations and implications. *Turkish Online Journal of Distance Education*, *8*(1), 191–205.

Rens, A., & Kahn, R. (Eds.). (2009). *Access to knowledge in South Africa: part of the access to knowledge research series*. Cape Town, South Africa: University of Cape Town. Retrieved from http://www.academia.edu/download/30876140/A2K-in-SA.pdf

Ricci, F., Rokach, L., & Shapira, B. (2011). Introduction to recommender systems handbook. Boston, MA: Springer. doi:10.1007/978-0-387-85820-3

Rice, R. (2009). *DISC-UK DataShare project: Final report*. Available at http://ie-repository.jisc.ac.uk/336/1/DataSharefinalreport.pdf

Rieh, S. Y., Markey, K., Jean, B., Yakel, E., & Kim, J. (2007). Census of institutional repositories in the U.S.: a comparison across institutions at different stages of IR development. *D-Lib Magazine*, *13*(11/12). Retrieved from http://www.dlib.org/dlib/november07/rieh/11rieh.html

Rodriguez, M. (2017). Upgrading EZproxy from Local to Hosted Solution. In *Reframing Librarianship in the 21st Century*. Burlington, VT: University of Massachusetts Amherst Libraries. Retrieved from https://scholarworks.umass.edu/acrl_nec_conf/2017/posters/20/

Rogers, E. (2003). *Diffusion of innovations*. New York, NY: Free Press.

Rosenberg, D. (2005). *Towards the digital library: Findings of an investigation to establish the current status of university libraries in Africa*. Oxford, UK: INASP.

Rothblatt, S. (1988). Supply and demand: The "two histories" of English education. *History Education Quarterly*, *28*(4), 627-644.

Rothblatt, S., Muller, D. K., Ringer, F., Simon, B., Bryant, M., Roach, J., ... Simmons, D. E. (2002). The forum report: e-learning adoption rates and barriers. In A. Rossett (Ed.), *The ASTD E-Learning Handbook* (pp. 19–23). New York, NY: McGraw-Hill.

Scammell, A. (Ed.). (2001). *Handbook of information management* (8th ed.). London, UK: Aslib-imi. doi:10.4324/9780203403914

Schafer, J., Frankowski, D., Herlocker, J., & Sen, S. (2007). Collaborative filtering recommender systems. In *The adaptive web* (pp. 291-324). Berlin, Germany: Springer.

SCONUL. (2011). The SCONUL Seven Pillars of Information Literacy. Core Model for Higher Education. London, UK: Society of College, National and University Libraries; Working Group on Information Literacy.

Scopus. (2018). What is Scopus about? *Elsevier/Scopus: Access and use Support Center.* Retrieved from https://service.elsevier.com/app/answers/detail/a_id/15100/supporthub/scopus/

SecureThoughts. (2018). *Best VPN | List of The TOP VPN services with full VPN reviews.* Retrieved from https://securethoughts.com/best-vpn/

Sharma, J., & Chakravarty, R. (2017). Usage of Multi-Parameters on Research Output of Library and Information Science Faculty for Ranking of Select North Indian Universities. *Diviner: A Research Journal of the Humanities and Social Sciences, 14*(1), 239–244.

Shawish, A., & Salama, M. (2018). Cloud-Based Digital Library Era. In Library Science and Administration (pp. 1276–1293). Hershey, PA: IGI Global. doi:10.4018/978-1-5225-3914-8.ch061

Sheehan, J., Hirschfeld, S., Foster, E., Ghitza, U., Goetz, K., Karpinski, J., & Huerta, M. (2016). Improving the value of clinical research through the use of Common Data Elements (CDEs). *Clinical Trials, 13*(6), 671–676. doi:10.1177/1740774516653238 PMID:27311638

Shen, Y., & Varvel, V. E. Jr. (2013). Developing data management services at the Johns Hopkins University. *Journal of Academic Librarianship, 39*(6), 552–557. doi:10.1016/j.acalib.2013.06.002

Shimbo, M., Ito, T., & Matsumoto, Y. (2007). Evaluation of kernel-based link analysis measures on research paper recommendation. *Proceedings of the 7th ACM/IEEE-CS joint conference on Digital libraries.* 10.1145/1255175.1255245

Shinde, S. B., & Potey, M. M. (2016). Research Paper Recommender System Evaluation Using Coverage. *International Research Journal of Engineering and Technology, 3*(6).

Shipman, J., Martin, E., Kaplan, R., & Albright, E. (2018). *Exploring the need for a research data management librarian academy.* Retrieved from https://libraryconnect.elsevier.com/articles/exploring-need-research-data-management-librarian-academy

Siemens, G. (2012, June 3). *What is the theory that underpins our MOOCs?* Retrieved from http://www.elearnspace.org/blog/2012/06/03/what-is-the-theory-that-underpins-our-moocs/

Sivakumaren, K. S. (2015). Electronic thesis and dissertations (ETDs) by Indian universities in Shodhganga project: a study. *Journal of Advances in Library and Information Science, 4*(1), 62-66. Retrieved from http://jalis.in/pdf/4-1/Sivamit.pdf

Smeaton, A. F., & Callan, J. (2005). Personalisation and recommender systems in digital libraries. *International Journal on Digital Libraries, 5*(4), 299–308. doi:10.100700799-004-0100-1

Smith, I., & Veldsman, S. (2018). Data driving sustainability: the African Open Science Platform Project. *ELPUB 2018.* Retrieved from https://elpub.episciences.org/4610/pdf

Sommers, P. C. (2005). The role of the library in a wired society–compete or withdraw: A business perspective. *The Electronic Library*, *23*(2), 157–167. doi:10.1108/02640470510592915

Sompel, H. V. D., Payette, S., Erickson, J., Lagoze, C., & Warner, S. (2004). Rethinking scholarly communication: Building the system that scholars deserve. *D-Lib Magazine*, *10*(9). Retrieved from http://dlib.org/dlib/september04/vandesompel/09vandesompel.html

Sottong, S. (2001). E-Book Technology: Waiting for the "False Pretender". *Information Technology and Libraries*, *20*(2), 72–80.

SPARC. (2018). Open Access. *SPARC*. Retrieved from https://sparcopen.org/open-access/

Spiller, D. (2001). *Book Selection: Principles and Practice*. London, UK: Clive Bingley.

Springer. (2018). *What is Open Access?* Berlin, Germany: Springer. Retrieved from https://www.springer.com/gp/authors-editors/authorandreviewertutorials/open-access/what-is-open-access/10286522

Standing Conference of Eastern, Central, and South Africa Library and Information Association (SCECSAL) in Nairobi, Kenya. (2012). *Challenges to Open Access and Institutional Repositories in Africa*. Author.

Steeves, V. (2017). Reproducibility librarianship. *Collaborative Librarianship, 9*.

Stocker, M., Paasonen, P., Fiebig, M., Zaidan, M. A., & Hardisty, A. (2018). Curating scientific information in knowledge infrastructures. *Data Science Journal*, *17*(21), 1–16.

Stoffle, C. J., Renaud, R., & Veldof, J. R. (1996). Choosing our futures. *College & Research Libraries*, *57*(3), 213–225. doi:10.5860/crl_57_03_213

Strasser, C. A. (2014). *Data Management for Libraries: A LITA guide*. Chicago, IL: ALA TechSource.

Strohman, T., Croft, W. B., & Jensen, D. (2007). Recommending citations for academic papers. *Proceedings of the 30th annual international ACM SIGIR conference on Research and development in information retrieval*.

Strohman, T., Croft, W. B., & Jensen, D. (2007, July). Recommending citations for academic papers. In *SIGIR (Vol. 7, pp. 705-706)*. ACM.

Stvilia, B., Wu, S., & Lee, D. J. (2018). Researchers' participation in and motivations for engaging with research information management systems. *PLoS ONE, 13*(2), e0193459.

Suber, P. (2007). *Open access overview*. Retrieved from https://www.researchgate.net/profile/Arunachalam_Subbiah/publication/48547497_Open_access_to_science_in_the_developing_world/links/09e415058b88dbf15c000000/Open-access-to-science-in-the-developing-world.pdf#page=8

Sugiyama, K., & Kan, M.-Y. (2010). Scholarly paper recommendation via user's recent research interests. *Proceedings of the 10th annual joint conference on Digital libraries*. 10.1145/1816123.1816129

Sugiyama, K., & Kan, M.-Y. (2015). A comprehensive evaluation of scholarly paper recommendation using potential citation papers. *International Journal on Digital Libraries*, *16*(2), 91–109. doi:10.100700799-014-0122-2

Suryani, I., Yaacob, A., Hashima, N., Rashid, S. A., & Desa, H. (2013). Research publication output by academicians in public and private universities in Malaysia. *International Journal of Higher Education*, *2*(1), 84–90. doi:10.5430/ijhe.v2n1p84

Swan, A. (2007). *Open Access Self-archiving: An Author Study.* Cornwall, UK: Key Perspective. Available on www.keyperspectives.co.uk

Swan, A. (2010). *The Open Access citation advantage: Studies and results to date.* Retrieved from https://eprints.soton.ac.uk/268516/2/Citation_advantage_paper.pdf

Swan, A., & Brown, S. (2008). *The Skills, Role and Career Structure of Data Scientists and Curators: An Assessment of Current Practice and Future Needs.* Truro: Key Perspectives. Retrieved from http://www.jisc.ac.uk/publications/documents/dataskillscareersfinalreport.aspx

Symplectic. (2016). *The Wealth of Institutions: understanding research information.* Symplectic. Retrieved from https://symplectic.co.uk/wp-content/uploads/The_Wealth_Of_Institutions_White_Paper.pdf

Takano, K., & Li, K. F. (2009). *An adaptive personalized recommender based on web-browsing behavior learning*. Paper presented at the 2009 International Conference on Advanced Information Networking and Applications Workshops. 10.1109/WAINA.2009.160

Tang, T. Y., & McCalla, G. (2003). *Smart recommendation for an evolving e-learning system.* Paper presented at the Workshop on Technologies for Electronic Documents for Supporting Learning, AIED.

Tang, X., & Zeng, Q. (2012). Keyword clustering for user interest profiling refinement within paper recommender systems. *Journal of Systems and Software*, *85*(1), 87–101. doi:10.1016/j.jss.2011.07.029

Tanner, S., & Deegan, M. (2011). Inspiring research, inspiring scholarship. In *The Value and Benefits of Digitised Resources for Learning, Teaching, Research and Enjoyment.* London, UK: JISC. Retrieved from http://www.kdcs.kcl.ac.uk/fileadmin/documents/Inspiring_Research_Inspiring_Scholarsh ip_2011_SimonTanner.pdf

Taylor, S.-J. (1986). *Modelling Financial Time Series*. Chichester, UK: John Wiley & Sons.

Teets, M. (2009). What is Web-Scale? *Designing the future blog, 7.*

Tenopier, C., Sandusky, R. J., Allard, S., & Birch, B. (2014). Research Data Management services in academic research libraries and perceptions of librarians. *Library & Information Science Research, 36*(2), 84–90. doi:10.1016/j.lisr.2013.11.003

Tenopir, C., Birch, B., & Allard, S. (2012). Academic libraries and research data services: current practices and plans for the future. *Association of College and Research Libraries.* Retrieved from http://www.ala.org/acrl/sites/ala.org.acrl/files/content/publications/whitepapers/Tenopir_Birch_Allard.pdf

Tenopir, C., Sandusky, R. J., Allard, S., & Birch, B. (2013). Academic librarians and research data services: Preparation and attitudes. *IFLA Journal, 39*(1), 70–78. doi:10.1177/0340035212473089

Terras, M. (2015). Opening Access to collections: The making and using of open digitised cultural content. *Online Information Review*, *39*(5), 733–752. doi:10.1108/OIR-06-2015-0193

Terras, M., & Ramsay, J. (2015). Massive open online courses (MOOCs): Insights and challenges from a psychological perspective. *British Journal of Educational Technology*, *46*(3), 472–487. doi:10.1111/bjet.12274

Thata, M. B. (2007). *Building a Digital Library at the University of Zimbabwe: A Celebration of teamwork and collaboration.* Retrieved from http://r4d.dfif.gov.uk/PDF/Outputs/Peri/Zimbabwe

The Need for Next Generation Research Repository. (n.d.). Retrieved from https://www.exlibrisgroup.com/wp-content/uploads/The-Need-for-a-Next-Gen-Research-Repository-Ex-Libris-Paper.pdf

The Spotify of the textbook world takes off as Bibliotech is go. (2018). Retrieved from https://www.jisc.ac.uk/news/the-spotify-of-the-textbook-world-takes-off-as-bibliotech-is-go-01-aug-2017

Thomas, S., & Mitchell, H. (2005). *GARCH Modeling of High-Frequency Volatility in Australia's National Electricity Market* (Discussion Paper). Melbourne Centre for Financial Studies.

Thomas, S. (2013). *Technobiophilia: Nature and cyberspace*. London, UK: Bloomsbury Academic.

Torres, R., McNee, S. M., Abel, M., Konstan, J. A., & Riedl, J. (2004). Enhancing digital libraries with TechLens+. In *Proceedings of the 4th ACM/IEEE-CS joint conference on Digital libraries (pp. 228-236). ACM.*

Torres, R., McNee, S. M., Abel, M., Konstan, J. A., & Riedl, J. (2004). Enhancing digital libraries with TechLens+. *Proceedings of the 4th ACM/IEEE-CS joint conference on Digital libraries.*

Tran, H. N., Huynh, T., & Hoang, K. (2015). *A Potential Approach to Overcome Data Limitation in Scientific Publication Recommendation.* Paper presented at the 2015 Seventh International Conference on Knowledge and Systems Engineering (KSE). 10.1109/KSE.2015.76

Traxler, J. (2018). Distance Learning—Predictions and Possibilities. *Turkish Online Journal of Distance Education, 8*(2), 136-145.

Tsang, D. C. (2014). *Research Data Management: Challenges and Opportunities.* Presentation at Singapore Management University, Li Ka Shing Library, Singapore. Available at: https://ink.library.smu.edu.sg/lib_events/2/

Uchiyama, K., Nanba, H., Aizawa, A., & Sagara, T. (2011). OSUSUME: cross-lingual recommender system for research papers. *Proceedings of the 2011 Workshop on Context-awareness in Retrieval and Recommendation.* 10.1145/1961634.1961642

Uğurlu E. (2014). Modelling Volatility: Evidence from The Bucharest Stock Exchange. Journal of Applied Economic Sciences, 9(4-30), 718-727.

Ugurlu, E. (2009). Real exchange rate and economic growth: Turkey. *Manas University Journal of Social Sciences*, *22*, 191–212.

Ugwuanyi, C. F. (2011). Influence of ICT literacy skills on its application for library use among academic librarians in south east Nigeria. *Journal of Education and Learning, 5*(2).

UK Data Archive. (2015). *Create and manage data: research data lifecycle.* Retrieved from http://www.data-archive.ac.uk/create-manage/life-cycle

University of Bradford. (2018). *What are Open Access repositories?* Bradford, UK: University of Bradford. Retrieved from https://www.bradford.ac.uk/library/resources/open-access-publishing/what-are-open-access-repositories/

University of Lucknow. (2016). Retrieved from http://www.lkouniv.ac.in/history.html

University of Warwick Library. (2018). *Accessing Research Data.* Available at: https://warwick.ac.uk/services/library/staff/research-data/accessing-research-data/

Uzwyshyn, R. (2016). Research data repositories: The what, when, why, and how. *Computers in libraries*, *36*(3). Retrieved from http://www.infotoday.com/cilmag/apr16/Uzwyshyn--Research-Data-Repositories.shtml

van Deventer, M., & Pienaar, H. (2008). *South African Repositories: Bridging Knowledge Divides.* Retrieved from http://repository.up.ac.za/bitstream/handle/2263/8615/VanDeventer_South(2008).pdf?sequence=1

van Myk, B., & Mostert, J. (2012). *African Institutional Repositories as contributors to Global Information: A South African Case Study.* Retrieved from http://etd2012. unmsm.edu.pe/pdf/presentation/VWyKETD2012FT.pdf

Vashishth, C. P. (2011). Building Library Collection in e-environment: Challenges & Opportunities. *Library Herald*, *49*(1), 15–33. doi:10.5958/0976-2469.2015.00003.2

Vaughan, D. S. (2007). *Planning for information technology: A comparative case study of the factors affecting the alignment of institutional strategic plans and information technology plans* (Doctoral dissertation). University of Michigan.

Vellino, A. (2009). Recommending journal articles with pagerank ratings. *Recommender Systems, 2009*.

Vellino, A., & Zeber, D. (2007). A hybrid, multi-dimensional recommender for journal articles in a scientific digital library. *Proceedings of the 2007 IEEE/WIC/ACM international conference on web intelligence and international conference on intelligent agent technology*. 10.1109/WI-IATW.2007.29

Vellino, A. (2010). A comparison between usage-based and citation-based methods for recommending scholarly research articles. *Proceedings of the American Society for Information Science and Technology*, *47*(1), 1–2. doi:10.1002/meet.14504701330

Verma, M. K., & Verma, N. K. (2014). Concept of hybrid, digital and virtual library: A professional approach. *InfoLib*, *7*(14), 19–23.

Vijayakumar, J. K., & Murthy, T. A. V. (2001). *Need of a Digital Library for Indian Theses and Dissertations: a model on par with the ETD initiatives at International Level*. Retrieved from http://eprints.rclis.org/7217/1/vijayakumarjk_06.pdf

Virtual Private Network (VPN). (2013). In D. Downing (Ed.), *Barron's business guides: Dictionary of computer and internet terms* (11th ed.). Hauppauge, NY: Barron's Educational Series. Retrieved from https://search.credoreference.com/content/entry/barronscai/virtual_private_network_vpn/0?institutionId=292

Vrana, R. (2017). The perspective of use of digital libraries in era of e-learning. In 40th jubilee international convention-MIPRO 2017. Croatian Society for Information and Communication Technology, Electronics and Microelectronics-MIPRO. doi:10.23919/MIPRO.2017.7973555

Wang, C., & Blei, D. M. (2011). Collaborative topic modeling for recommending scientific articles. *Proceedings of the 17th ACM SIGKDD international conference on Knowledge discovery and data mining*. 10.1145/2020408.2020480

Ware, M. (2004). *Pathfinder Research on Web-based Repositories*, Publisher and Library/Learning Solutions. Retrieved from http://www.palsgroup.org.uk/palsweb.nsf/0/8c43ce800a9c67cd80256e370051e8

Watanabe, S., Ito, T., Ozono, T., & Shintani, T. (2005). A paper recommendation mechanism for the research support system papits. *Proceedings of the 2005 International Workshop on Data Engineering Issues in E-Commerce*. 10.1109/DEEC.2005.3

Way, D. (2010). The impact of web-scale discovery on the use of a library collection. *Serials Review*, *36*(4), 214–220. doi:10.1080/00987913.2010.10765320

Weber, R. (1990). The Clouded Future of Electronic Publishing. *Publishers Weekly*, *237*(26), 76–80.

Wei, Q., Chang, Z., & Cheng, Q. (2015). Usability study of the mobile library App: An example from Chongqing University. *Library Hi Tech*, *33*(3), 340–355. doi:10.1108/LHT-05-2015-0047

Welch, J. M. (2002). Hey! what about us?! Changing roles of subject specialists and reference librarians in the age of electronic resources. *Serials Review*, *28*(4), 283–286. doi:10.1080/00987913.2002.10764760

Wesley-Smith, I., & West, J. D. (2016). Babel: a platform for facilitating research in scholarly article discovery. *Proceedings of the 25th international conference companion on world wide web*. 10.1145/2872518.2890517

Westbrook, L. (1994). Qualitative research methods: A review of major stages, data analysis techniques, and quality controls. *Library & Information Science Research*, *16*(3), 241–254.

Westervelt, T. (2015). Acquisition and management of digital content at the Library of Congress. *The Serials Librarian*, *68*(1-4), 269–273. doi:10.1080/0361526X.2015.1026299

West, J. D., Wesley-Smith, I., & Bergstrom, C. T. (2016). A recommendation system based on hierarchical clustering of an article-level citation network. *IEEE Transactions on Big Data*, *2*(2), 113–123. doi:10.1109/TBDATA.2016.2541167

What is publication? definition and meaning. (n.d.). Retrieved from http://www.businessdictionary.com/definition/publication.html

What is RA21 – RA21: Resource Access for the 21st Century. (2018). Retrieved from https://ra21.org/index.php/what-is-ra21/

Whyte, A., Jones, S., & Pryor, G. (2014). *Delivering Research Data Management Services: Fundamentals of Good Practice*. London, UK: Facet Publishing.

Whyte, A., & Tedds, J. (2011). *Making the case for Research Data Management. DCC Briefing Papers*. Edinburgh, UK: Digital Curation Centre. Retrieved from http://www.dcc.ac.uk/resources/briefing-papers

Whyte, A., & Tedds, J. (2011). *Making the Case for Research Data Management. In DCC Briefing Papers*. Edinburgh, UK: Digital Curation Centre. Available at http://www.dcc.ac.uk/resources/briefing-papers

Whyte, A., & Wilson, A. (2010). *How to appraise and select research data for curation. DCC How-to Guides*. Edinburgh, UK: Digital Curation Centre. Retrieved from http://www.dcc.ac.uk/resources/how-guides

Wiley, C. A., & Kerby, E. E. (2018). Managing Research Data: Graduate Student and Postdoctoral Researcher Perspectives. *Issues in Science and Technology Librarianship*. Available at http://www.istl.org/18-spring/refereed1.html

Wilkinson, F. C., & Lewis, L. K. (2003). *The complete guide to acquisitions management*. London, UK: Libraries Unlimited.

Wilson, J. A., Fraser, M. A., Martinez-Uribe, L., Jeffreys, P., Patrick, M., Akram, A., & Mansoori, T. (2010). *Developing infrastructure for Research Data Management at the University of Oxford*. Retrieved from http://www.ariadne.ac.uk/issue65/wilson-et-al

Witt, M. (2008). Institutional repositories and research data curation in a distributed environment. *Library Trends*, *57*(2), 191–201. doi:10.1353/lib.0.0029

Woodruff, A., Gossweiler, R., Pitkow, J., Chi, E. H., & Card, S. K. (2000). Enhancing a digital book with a reading recommender. *Proceedings of the SIGCHI conference on Human factors in computing systems*. 10.1145/332040.332419

Wu, H., Hua, Y., Li, B., & Pei, Y. (2012). *Enhancing citation recommendation with various evidences*. Paper presented at the 2012 9th International Conference on Fuzzy Systems and Knowledge Discovery. 10.1109/FSKD.2012.6234002

Xia, F., Asabere, N. Y., Liu, H., Deonauth, N., & Li, F. (2014, April). Folksonomy based socially-aware recommendation of scholarly papers for conference participants. In *Proceedings of the 23rd International Conference on World Wide Web* (pp. 781-786). ACM.

Xia, F., Liu, H., Lee, I., & Cao, L. (2016). Scientific article recommendation: Exploiting common author relations and historical preferences. *IEEE Transactions on Big Data*, *2*(2), 101–112. doi:10.1109/TBDATA.2016.2555318

Xia, J., & Sun, L. (2007). Factors to assess self-archiving in institutional repositories. *Serials Review*, *33*(2), 73–80. doi:10.1080/00987913.2007.10765100

Xue, H., Guo, J., Lan, Y., & Cao, L. (2014). *Personalized paper recommendation in online social scholar system*. Paper presented at the 2014 IEEE/ACM International Conference on Advances in Social Networks Analysis and Mining. 10.1109/ASONAM.2014.6921649

Yeager, A. (2018). *Sweden Cancels Agreement With Elsevier Over Open Access*. Retrieved from https://www.the-scientist.com/?articles.view/articleNo/54593/title/Sweden-Cancels-Agreement-With-Elsevier-Over-Open-Access/

Yeager, H. J. (2017). Using EZproxy and Google Analytics to Evaluate Electronic Serials Usage. *Serials Review*, *43*(3-4), 208–215. doi:10.1080/00987913.2017.1350312

Yin, P., Zhang, M., & Li, X. (2007). *Recommending scientific literatures in a collaborative tagging environment*. Paper presented at the International Conference on Asian Digital Libraries. 10.1007/978-3-540-77094-7_60

Youngman, P. (2009). Procyclicality and value at risk. *Bank of Canada Financial System Review*.

Young, P. (2017). Research Access and Discovery in University News Releases: A Case Study. *Journal of Librarianship and Scholarly Communication*, *5*(1). doi:10.7710/2162-3309.2155

Yusuf, M. O. (2006). Problems and prospects of open and distance education in Nigeria. *Turkish Online Journal of Distance Education*, *7*(1), 22–29.

Zare Mehrjerdi, Y. (2009). RFID-enabled supply chain systems with computer simulation. *Assembly Automation*, *29*(2), 174–183. doi:10.1108/01445150910945624

Zarrinkalam, F., & Kahani, M. (2012). *A multi-criteria hybrid citation recommendation system based on linked data.* Paper presented at the 2012 2nd International eConference on Computer and Knowledge Engineering. 10.1109/ICCKE.2012.6395393

Zarrinkalam, F., & Kahani, M. (2013). SemCiR: A citation recommendation system based on a novel semantic distance measure. *Program*, *47*(1), 92–112. doi:10.1108/00330331311296320

Zhang, H., Ni, W., Zhao, M., Liu, Y., & Yang, Y. (2014). *A hybrid recommendation approach for network teaching resources based on knowledge-tree.* Paper presented at the 2014 33rd Chinese Control Conference. 10.1109/ChiCC.2014.6895511

Zhang, Z., & Li, L. (2010). *A research paper recommender system based on spreading activation model.* Paper presented at the 2010 2nd International Conference on Information Science and Engineering. 10.1109/ICISE.2010.5689417

Zhang, M., Wang, W., & Li, X. (2008, December). *A paper recommender for scientific literatures based on semantic concept similarity. In 2008 11th International Conference on Asian Digital libraries (pp. 359-362). Berlin, Germany:* Springer. doi:10.1007/978-3-540-89533-6_44

Zhang, Y., Callan, J., & Minka, T. (2002). Novelty and redundancy detection in adaptive filtering. *Proceedings of the 25th annual international ACM SIGIR conference on Research and development in information retrieval.* 10.1145/564376.564393

Zhao, F. (2005). Technological and organizational innovations: A Case study of Siemens (Australia). *International Journal of Innovation and Learning*, *3*(1), 95-109.

Zhao, W., Wu, R., Dai, W., & Dai, Y. (2015). *Research Paper Recommendation Based on the Knowledge Gap.* Paper presented at the 2015 IEEE International Conference on Data Mining Workshop (ICDMW).

Zhao, W., Wu, R., Dai, W., & Dai, Y. (2015, November). Research Paper Recommendation Based on the Knowledge Gap. In *2015 IEEE International Conference on Data Mining Workshop* (pp. 373-380). IEEE.

Zhou, D., Zhu, S., Yu, K., Song, X., Tseng, B. L., Zha, H., & Giles, C. L. (2008). Learning multiple graphs for document recommendations. *Proceedings of the 17th international conference on World Wide Web.* 10.1145/1367497.1367517

Zhu, Z., Zong, J., & He, N. (2012, June). Discussion on application of VPN technology in library management system. In *Proceedings of 2012 IEEE Symposium on Robotics and Applications (ISRA)* (pp. 809–812). IEEE. 10.1109/ISRA.2012.6219314

Zimmer, M. (2015). The Twitter archive at the Library of Congress: Challenges for information practice and information policy. *First Monday*, *20*(7), 7. doi:10.5210/fm.v20i7.5619

About the Contributors

Raj Kumar Bhardwaj is a Librarian at St. Stephen's College, University of Delhi (India). Prior to his current position, he served as Deputy Librarian at Nalanda University and Judges Library, High Court of Punjab and Haryana, Chandigarh. He holds MCA, MLIS and M.Phil, PhD from University of Delhi. He has also qualified UGC-NET. He has published four books, 40 research papers in various reputed journals published by Emerald Publishing, Taylor & Francis, Cambridge University Press, Phcog.Net, DRDO, and three conference papers, and has delivered several invited talks at various international conferences and seminars. He has completed two major research projects. He is the reviewer for five international LIS journals of repute. He is the recipient of UNESCO fellowship for Information Management and prestigious Commonwealth Professional Fellowship, United Kingdom. He is also the elected member of IFLA Standing Committee on Indigenous Matters for 2019-23 and corresponding member of IFLA -Law Libraries Section. He has developed an online legal information system, accessible at: http://www.olisindia.in. His areas of specializations are institutional repositories, evaluation of information systems, legal information system, open access, legal and legislative metadata, e-learning, social media analytics, text mining, scientometrics, semantic web and digital library development.

Paul Banks is currently working at The Royal Society of Medicine, UK. Prior to this, he was Head of Library Planning at London School of Business, UK and Head of Law Library Services at City Law School. He holds an MA from the University of London. He contributes 10 chapters to a biennial professional law manual published by OUP and serves on the editorial board of Legal Information Management, a journal published by CUP. He oversaw the introduction of an institutional repository and open access workflows at London Business School and is involved in implementing Research Data Management practices at the School. His specialist interests include open access, institutional repositories, library support for academic research, legal research training, resource allocation in libraries and staff development.

* * *

Adi Alter is Director of Product Management – Research Solutions at Ex Libris. Adi has over 20 years of technology and managerial experience in a variety of roles including product management and software development. In his current role, Adi is in charge of the product management of Ex Libris Esploro Research Services Platform. Prior to this role, Adi served as the product manager of Ex Libris Rosetta Digital Asset Management and Preservation solution. Adi holds a BSc in Computer Science and an MA in Jewish History, both from the Hebrew University of Jerusalem, and an MBA from the Interdisciplinary Center Herzliya.

Viral Asjola holds Masters and Doctoral degree in Library and Information Science from Hemchandracharya North Gujarat University, Patan. Currently working at Indian Institute of Technology Gandhinagar. Prior to joining IITGn, he worked at Augure India, DDB Mudra Group and Unimark Remedies.

Aregbesola Ayooluwa is an Information Scientist and the Collection Development Librarian of Centre for Learning Resources, Landmark University. He holds Master's Degree in Information Science from the University of Ibadan. He has a considerable number of publications in reputable local and international journals. He is a Member of the Nigerian Library Association (NLA), Member Information Technology Section of the Nigerian Library Association and a Certified Librarian of Nigeria (CLN). His research interest spans the field of Information Systems Adoption and Use, Collaborative and Social Computing, Information Security and Library Automation.

Josiline Phiri Chigwada is the Sub Librarian for Information services at Bindura University of Science Education Library in Zimbabwe. She holds a Doctor of Literature and Philosophy in Information Science from the University of South Africa (UNISA), Master of Science Degree and Bachelor of Science Honours Degree in Library and Information Science from the National University of Science and Technology (NUST), Bulawayo, Zimbabwe. Her research interests are research data management, value addition, open science, information literacy, indigenous knowledge, advocacy, marketing library products and services, and the changing role of librarians. She has vast experience in academic librarianship and her career is centered on academic and special libraries. She has authored a number of peer reviewed chapters and journals articles.

Blessing Chiparausha is Deputy Librarian at Bindura University of Science Education, Zimbabwe. He holds a BSc (Hons) Library and Information Science degree and MSc Library and Information Science degree from the National University of Science and Technology, Zimbabwe. He has keen interest in the use of information and communication technologies in libraries.

Toluwani A. Eyiolorunshe is a Librarian/Faculty in the Centre for Learning Resources, Landmark University, Omu-Aran, Kwara State, Nigeria. Her research interests are: Information literacy, Scholarly Communication, and Library Services. She has written some articles in local and international journals.

Okocha Foluke is an Information Professional with research interests in Ubiquitous learning and Social and Collaborative computing. She holds a bachelor's degree in Management Information Systems and a master's degree in Information Science. She currently works as the Serials Librarian, Landmark University, and has written several articles in local and international journals.

Dani Guzman, is the Product Marketing Director at Ex Libris.

Thembelihle Hwalima is a Faculty Librarian for Commerce and Institutional Repository (IR) Manager at Lupane State University Library in Zimbabwe. She is a co-developer of a framework for librarians on research data management for developing countries in the AOSP Project. Thembelihle is a qualified librarian with seven years of work experience in an academic and research library setting and is an expert in faculty liaison work, Information Literacy training, Institutional Repository management, and research support. She holds a masters in Library and Information Science from NUST (Zim), Honours degree in Library and Information science from UKZN, and Bachelor's degree in Library & Information Science from UFH. Thembelihle has presented papers at CARLIGH 2018 and IDW 2018 and facilitated workshops on Research Data Management.

Jerome Idiegbeyan-ose holds BLIS, MLS and Ph.D in Library and Information Science. He has written several articles in local and international journals including chapters in books. He is a reviewer of some journals indexed in SCOPUS, a certified Librarian of Nigeria (CLN) by the Librarian Registration Council of Nigeria (LRCN). Member Nigerian Library Association, Member Cataloguing and Classification Section of the Nigerian Library Association, Member Research and Development Network (International Research and Development Institute). He was the immediate past University Librarian of Covenant University, Ota, Ogun State, and currently the University Librarian, Landmark University, Omu-Aran, Kwara State, Nigeria.

N. K. Khatri is a highly-motivated, skilled, experienced (36 years) library professional who served as Associate Scientist, Indian Statistical Institute, Delhi Centre Library (India). Dr. Khatri is a leading force behind success of Ranganathan Research Circle, a well-known leading library association in Delhi, India. He has presented and published locally, nationally and internationally. Dr. Khatri organized 'National Workshop on 'Using Different Metrics for Assessing Research Productivity'. He edited the Workshop Proceedings "Metrics Based Research Assessment and Evaluation" and compiled the book "Twenty Years of Library Herald: A Cumulative Index", published by Delhi Library Association in 1983. He had served on the editorial board of "Gyankosh: The Journal of Library and Information Management". His areas of interest include: E-resources, resource sharing, consortium based subscription, scientometrics, readers assistance, arranging lectures and seminars. He is Convener, Ranganathan Research Circle (RRC) and Assistant Secretary, Ranganathan Research Trust (RRT), New Delhi (India), life member of Delhi Library Association (DLA), Indian Library Association (ILA) and Indian Association of Special Libraries and Information Centres (IASLIC).

Nancy Kwangwa is an Assistant Librarian at the University of Zimbabwe. She holds Master's and Bachelor's Degrees in Library and Information Science from the National University of Science and Technology. She is the 2018/2019 United States Department of State Community Solutions Programme Fellow. Research Interests include knowledge management, research data management, GIS and spatial planning librarianship, contemporary issues in academic librarianship, information literacy, electronic resources management, access to information and community development.

Benard Magara Maake is a doctorate student in the department of Computer Systems Engineering at the Tshwane University of Technology, South Africa. He holds a Master of Science in Computer Science and a Bachelor of Computer Application from Periyar University, India. His research interests are; Information Retrieval, Recommender Systems, Data Mining, Machine Learning and Artificial Intelligence. He has authored and co-authored journals and conference papers in the above-mentioned disciplines. He is a member of the International Association of Engineers (IAENG).

Amitabh Kumar Manglam is presently working as Assistant Librarian at Tripura University (A Central University), Agartala, Tripura. He obtained his M.Sc. from Vinoba Bhave University, MLISc. from Banaras Hindu University and AIS from NISCAIR, New Delhi. He has qualified UGC-NET. He is presently working as Assistant, Tripura University, (A Central University), India. Prior to this, he has served as Library & Information Assistant at Birla Institute of Technology. He has published more than five papers in reputed journals and he has attended many seminars, conferences, and workshops in the field of Library and Information Science. His research interests include Bibliometric, Scientometrics, Knowledge Organization, Digital Library, Library automation and digitization, Open Source Software, etc.

T. R. Manu is pursuing doctoral research at School of Library and Information Science, Central University of Gujarat, Gandhinagar and working at Adani Institute of Infrastructure Management, Ahmedabad. He also has library professional experience from Indian Institute of Technology Gandhinagar (IITGn). Manu holds Masters in Library and Information Science from University of Mysore, Mysore. He is a member of ASIS&T, Indian Library Association (ILA) and Mysore University Library and Information Science Alumni Network (MILAN) and he has been actively participating in the professional activities. Manu has published several research papers including journal articles, conference papers and poster presentation.

Champeswar Mishra is working as Deputy Librarian, Tripura University, (A Central University), Agartala, Tripura. He has over 11 years of experience in Library and Information Science with expertise in setting up state-of-the-art libraries. He completed his Post-Graduate and M.Phil in Library and Information Science from Sambalpur University, Odisha; and Post Graduate Diploma in Library and Information Management (PGDLIM) from Tata Institute of Social Sciences, Mumbai. He has qualified UGC-NET, University Grant Commission, Government of India, and Andra Pradesh State Eligibility Test (APSET), Government of Andra Pradesh. He was credited with 20 research papers published in national and international levels. He has attended more than 30 National and International conferences including visits to the University of Malaysia. He has awarded the Course Grant Fellowship for developing country from ALCTS, a division of American Library Association. His research interest areas are Digital Library, Knowledge Management, Library Leadership and Strategic Management, Capacity Building, Information Literacy, Research Methodology, Innovation, and Creativity, etc.

Sunday Oguntayo holds Bachelor of Library Science (BLS) Degree from Ahmadu Bello University, Zaria and Masters in Library and Information Science MLIS from Delta State University, Abraka. He is a member of the Nigerian Library Association (NLA) and a registered member of the Librarian Registration Council of Nigeria (LRCN). He is currently the head of the Technical Services Section of the Centre for Learning Resources, Landmark University. He has published extensively in peer-reviewed journals in local and international journals.

Sunday O. Ojo holds BSc Honours and PhD degrees in Computer Science from the Universities of Ibadan and Glasgow, respectively. His academic career in a number of Universities spans more than 35 years, in the field of Computing Science and Technology. He currently holds a position as a Research Professor in the Faculty of ICT, at the Tshwane University of Technology in Pretoria, South Africa. He previously served as the Executive Dean in the same faculty for a five-year period. Prior to this, he was a member of the pioneering team that established the Department of Computer Science at the University of Botswana and later rose to become the Head of the Department for a six-year period. He also held the position as Coordinator of Computer Science Department at the University of Ibadan. He has a wealth of experience in the teaching of under- and post-graduate courses in the field of Computing Science and Technology, and in promoting several honours, masters and doctoral students' dissertations and theses. He is also well published with extensive experience in sustained research and publications, in peer reviewed journals and conference proceedings, as well as books and chapters in books. He is presently the leader of the ICT for Development niche area in his University. He also leads the Data Scientia Research project in collaboration with a counterpart at the University of Trento, Italy, aimed at the digital preservation of African languages and cultural heritage. His national and international professional services experience include serving as a consultant and resource person for several national and international bodies on ICT related projects, including. Botswana National Innovation Capability Database System, USAID Botswana Confederation of Commerce, Industry and Manpower Economic Research database system, Botswana National ICT Policy development, Commonwealth Network for Information Technology (COMNET-IT) ICT capacity building project for Commonwealth countries. Others are the Eurafrica-ICT Reference panel work on producing a manifesto for strategic EU-Africa partnership on ICT Research, and European Commission Scenarios for Research and Technology Development Cooperation with Europe project.

Sola Owolabi is a bibliophile and a bibliotherapist. As a librarian, his contribution to knowledge nationally and internationally focuses on Soft Skills, User/Knowledge Management, Metadata, Digital Libraries/ICT and Bibliotherapy. He is currently on a doctoral study with focus on reading problems among Nigerian students. He heads the Readers' Services Section of the Centre for Learning Resources, Landmark University and holds first degree in Library Science/Communication Language Arts and a Master degree in Library and Information Science from the University of Ibadan. Sola Owolabi, certified by the Librarians Registration Council of Nigeria (LRCN) is the current Publicity Secretary of Nigeria Library Association, Kwara State Chapter.

Surendra Kumar Pal is working as Assistant Librarian at Tripura University (A Central University), Agartala, Tripura. He did his Bachelor in Chemistry and Botany from the University of Lucknow and Master Degree in Library & Information Science from Babasaheb Bhimrao Ambedkar Central University, Lucknow. Besides this, he has acquired Post Graduate Diploma in Computer Application form Annamalai University in 2012. Prior to this, he was working with NKRC-Consortium, National Science Library, NISCAIR-New Delhi. He earlier worked with the Indian Institute of Science Education & Research (IISER), Trivandrum, Kerala. He has published 24 articles/research papers in national & international journals, conference proceedings, and edited books. He has also edited one Book. His areas of interest are Librarianship, Academic Library System, ICT Application in Libraries, Knowledge Management, Library Automation and Networking, Digital Library, e-learning, Cloud Computing, Web Discovery System, Bibliometric, etc. He is a life member of ILA, IATLIS, IASLIC, MANLIBNET, SALIS, SAL-New Delhi etc. He has been associated with a few journals as a Member of Editorial Board. He served as a reviewer for a few Indian and foreign journals.

Minaxi Parmar is working as Assistant Professor at Central University of Gujarat, Gandhinagar. She holds a PhD degree from Hemchandracharya North Gujarat University, Patan and MLIS degree from Gujarat Vidyapith. Dr. Parmar has teaching experience from Library and Information Science Department, C U Shah University, Wadhavan, Surendranagar and seven years of experience as librarian in various institutions including Ahmedabad Institute of Medical Science, Ahmedabad Institute of Nursing Science, City Commerce College, M N Law College & I M Nanavati Law College.

Jyoti Sharma is working in Department cum Centre for Women Studies and Development, Panjab University, Chandigarh. She has more than 10 years of work experience. Academic qualifications are: M.Com. M.Lib., UGC-NET, PGDLAN (Gold Medal) and Ph.D. Published two books, more than 20 publications in many peer-reviewed National and International Journals and more than 15 publications in National and International Seminars/Conferences. She also participated in more than 25 National and International Seminars/Conferences/Workshops/Training Programmes including International Conference on "Books, Publishing, and Libraries" held on November 2014 at Simmons College, Boston, USA. Areas of Interest: Bibliometric, Open Access, etc.

A. A. Shashikumara is working as Assistant Librarian at Dhirubhai Ambani Institute of Information and Communication Technology (DA-IICT), Gandhinagar. He also has professional experience from British Council, Augure India, TechUnique and HGCE Ahmedabad. Shashikumara has earned the Masters in Library and Information Science from University of Mysore, Mysore, and is pursuing PhD at Central University of Gujarat, Gandhinagar. He is a member of ASIS&T, ILA, ADINET, SALIS & Computer Society of India, and has been actively contributing in professional activities. Shashikumara has authored more than 25 research papers; he has interests in data visualization, digital assets management, open source software, website planning/design, information curation, etc.

Shiva Sukula is Deputy Librarian at the Central Library, Jawaharlal Nehru University, and New Delhi. Dr. Sukula has authored 10 books and published several technical papers in renowned national and international journals and conferences. Dr. Sukula is currently involved in Digital Library Development and creating Institutional Repositories. She has successfully completed two major projects on the same. Her professional competencies involve integration of new technologies towards development of networked information services and implementation of active information literacy programs for enhancing library services for providing high-quality services to end-users.

Kristina Symes is the Technical Solutions Lead at OpenAthens and author of 'Access to online resources: A guide for the modern librarian'. Determined to make the librarian's job easier, Kristina frequently speaks in conferences and educational events around the world. She is keenly interested in ways technology can help digital libraries deliver more value to communities they serve.

Erginbay Uğurlu is an Associate Professor in the Department of Economics and Finance at Istanbul Aydın University. He received a B.A. in Econometrics from Marmara University, and an M.Sc. in Economics from the Istanbul Technical University. He received his Ph.D. in Econometrics from Gazi University in 2011. In 2013, he was a Visiting Scholar in the Department of Economics at Columbia University and at the same time Post Doctoral Academic Researcher at the Columbia Consortium for Risk Management. Uğurlu's research interests include econometrics, time series econometrics, panel data econometrics and limited dependent variables on economics and finance.

Showkat Ahmad Wani is working as Senior Library Assistant at SKUAST-K Central Library, Shalimar J&K (190025). The author was also working as Research Fellow in DLIS-University of Kashmir (190006) in UGC approved Mega Research Project (MRP) - "towards designing an information portal for arts and crafts in J&K state". He did his master's degree in Library & Information Science from the same Department and University and also qualified J&KSET-exam (Eligibility for Assistant Professor Post). He has authored a number of journal publications & book chapters in reputed journals and books published by renowned publishers (e.g. Emerald, IGI-Global, etc.). He has also attended several national & international conferences, seminars and workshops on different themes.

Zahid Ashraf Wani is the Senior Assistant Professor in Department of Library and Information Science at Kashmir University. He has authored a number of journal publications, book chapters and attended a number of seminars/conferences. He bagged first position in Best Paper Award category for papers titled "Disaster Management and Preparedness of Prominent Libraries in Kashmir" in International Conference on The Convergence of Libraries, Archives and Museums (2014) and "Citation Analysis in Open Access World: A Case Study of Health Science Open Access Repositories" in Fourth International Conference on Digital Libraries (ICDL-2013). He is working on a research project titled "Towards Designing an Information Portal for Arts and Crafts of Jammu & Kashmir" under Major Research Project (MRP) funded by University Grants Commission (UGC).

Enrique Wulff has a MS in Biomedicine from University of Cádiz (UCA School of Medicine in Spain) and a licentiate degree in documentation. He is a Research Librarian with Spanish National Research Council (CSIC) at the Marine Science Institute of Andalusia, and was selected by competitive examination for the post of librarian at the Spanish National Library (BNE) in Madrid. Publications at international level: *Clinical and Translational Oncology* (ISSN 1699-048X), *Data Science Journal* (ISSN 1683-1470), *Publications* (ISSN 2304-6775), *Scientometrics* (0138-9130). Conferences/Workshops: CODATA '99 DSAO Workshop, July 1999 (Tsukuba, Japan), CODATA/DSAO Workshop database, June 2000 (Taipei, Taiwan), COMMUNIA conference on Public Domain in the Digital Age, July 2008 (Louvain-la-Neuve, Belgium), 21st International CODATA Conference, October 2008 (Kyiv, Ukraine), IMDIS International Conference on Marine Data and Information Systems, November 2018 (Barcelona, Spain).

Tranos Zuva is an Associate Professor in the Department of ICT at Vaal University of Technology, South Africa. His research areas include recommender systems, networking, Data mining, Business Intelligence and image processing. He is an IEEE member.

Index

P

R

S

T

U

V

W

Z

www.ingramcontent.com/pod-product-compliance
Lightning Source LLC
LaVergne TN
LVHW080345011026
849161LV00009B/2199
* 9 7 8 1 5 2 2 5 8 4 3 7 7 *